W9-AFM-612

BUDDHISM AND POLITICS IN TWENTIETH-CENTURY ASIA

BUDDHISM AND POLITICS IN TWENTIETH-CENTURY ASIA

EDITED BY
IAN HARRIS

PINTER

London and New York

PINTER
A Cassell imprint
Wellington House, 125 Strand, London WC2R 0BB
370 Lexington Avenue, New York, NY 10017–6550

First published 1999
© 1999 Ian Harris and the contributors

British Library Cataloguing in Publication Data
A catalogue record for this book is available from the British Library.
ISBN 1 85567 598 6

Library of Congress Cataloging-in-Publication Data
Buddhism and politics in twentieth-century Asia / edited by Ian
   Harris.
      p.   cm.
   Includes bibliographical references and index.
   ISBN 1–85567–598–6
      1. Buddhism and politics—Asia—History—20th century. 2. Asia—Politics and
   government—20th century. I. Harris, Ian Charles.
BQ270.B83   1999
294.3'377' 0950904—dc21   98–43860
                                                                            CIP

Typeset by York House Typographic Ltd, London
Printed and bound in Great Britain by Cromwell Press Ltd, Trowbridge, Wiltshire

CONTENTS

LIST OF CONTRIBUTORS

TESSA BARTHOLOMEUSZ Associate Professor of Religion at Florida State University.

TIMOTHY FITZGERALD Associate Professor at Aichi Gakuin University, Japan.

IAN HARRIS Reader in Religious Studies at the University College of St Martin, Lancaster.

HIROKO KAWANAMI Lecturer in Buddhist Studies at the Department of Religious Studies, Lancaster University.

BRUCE MATTHEWS C.B. Lumsden Professor of Comparative Religion at Acadia University, Nova Scotia.

RONALD D. SCHWARTZ Professor of Sociology at Memorial University of Newfoundland, Canada.

HENRIK H. SØRENSEN Senior Researcher in the Ethnographical Collection at the National Museum in Copenhagen.

DONALD K. SWEARER Charles and Harriet Cox McDowell Professor of Religion at Swarthmore College, Pennsylvania.

MARTIN STUART-FOX Professor and Head of History at the University of Queensland.

THIÊN DÔ Member of staff of the SEA Studies Programme at the National University of Singapore.

PREFACE

The idea that religion and politics are mutually exclusive categories, the one oriented in an other-worldly direction and the other concerned with practical matters of social organization, has become commonplace. This separation is assumed by many Buddhists today, some claiming that the mixing of the *dharma* with politics is a corruption of the Buddha's original message. However, the Buddha's teaching clearly possesses a political dimension for, without adequate political support, the monastic order would not have flourished and Buddhism would never have emerged as a historical phenomenon influenced by, and on occasions influencing, patterns of political power in the societies in which it was located. Any presentation of Buddhism as a tradition that focuses on its quietistic, meditation-oriented dimension alone will necessarily be one-sided. The uproar in Sri Lanka around November 1993 surrounding the publication of *Buddhism Betrayed?* by the Harvard-based Tamil scholar Stanley Tambiah is a case in point. The book, issued by the University of Chicago Press, a highly regarded academic publishing house not given to the dissemination of tendentious tracts, investigates the Buddhist contribution to the rise of militant Sinhalese nationalism in the modern period. Since publication it has become the focus of a high-profile campaign, led by prominent monks and Buddhist laypersons, to have it banned on the grounds that it is an insult to Buddhism and to the monastic order, even though most of the issues raised in the work have been generally accepted by the academic community for a considerable period. Indeed, in a partial parallel to the Rushdie affair, the book has become difficult to obtain in Sri Lanka and many of its critics have never properly examined its contents. Here, then, is a recent and eloquent demonstration of the fact that Buddhism and politics may never be entirely separated.

This volume began life as an attempt to update Jerrold Schecter's *The New Face of Buddha: The Fusion of Religion and Politics in Contemporary Buddhism* (1967). This pioneering work on the interaction between Buddhism and politics in selected countries of Asia is still of great interest. However, it had begun to look era-bound, particularly given its strong focus on the situation in Vietnam in the 1960s and its thesis that Buddhist political engagement was an entirely novel response to the recent historical situation. It is also the work of a journalist rather than a scholar with a sound grounding in the study of both Buddhism and the history of Asian cultures. In this light it became clear that it would be better to write an entirely new book taking a rather different approach. However, one problem today is that scholarship on Asian Buddhist culture has developed a good deal since Schecter's time, making it difficult for one author to do justice to the entire Asian Buddhist region. The approach here has been to assign individual countries to authors with a specific expertise in the field, with myself acting as overall editor. All the countries of Asia in which Buddhism is a significant presence are covered, with the exception of China and Mongolia. This omission is explained in two ways. In the first place, the prevailing political culture in both countries has prevented Buddhism from flourishing to any great extent in the period to which this study is dedicated. Secondly, and as a partial consequence of this, it has proved difficult to find suitably qualified scholars to write with authority on Buddhism under communism. To make good these inadequacies I have included a general discussion of the modern history of Buddhism in communist Mongolia and China in the introductory chapter, 'Buddhism and Politics in Asia: The Textual and Historical Roots', which begins by examining the evidence for political thinking in the early Buddhist textual tradition, particularly the way in which pre-existing Indian notions of kingship were remodelled to bring them into line with Buddhist ethical norms. The paradigmatic rule of Asoka Maurya (third century BCE) and his modification of the canonical position on the respective relations of the Buddhist order (*sangha*) and the state are also considered, as are the various attempts to reproduce this political arrangement throughout Buddhist Asia. Alternative models of socio-political organisation are also justified by the Buddhist tradition, and these are explored in theory and in practice. The chapter concludes by providing a historical introduction to the transformation of canonical and classical Buddhist political norms in the period immediately prior to the emergence of the modern epoch. As such, it sets the scene for the following chapters.

In the first country-specific contribution, 'The Legacy of Tradition and Authority: Buddhism and the Nation in Myanmar', Bruce Matthews considers the history of Buddhist *sangha* organizations and activism in Burmese colonial and post-colonial history. Particular emphasis is placed on the U Nu *khit* (era) and efforts to make Buddhism the state religion, which became one of the factors behind the Ne Win takeover thirty-five years ago. Since then, however, the military regime has often resorted to Buddhism in defence of its ideology, and has regularly sought religious legitimation of its rule. The monastic order has been clearly divided over the matter of support for the regime and many monks have been compromised by allowing themselves to be bought off with gifts and privileges. Others have fled to Thailand while many soldier on quietly in Burma, waiting for an opportunity to become involved in the inevitable political upheaval and sea change in the nation's spiritual and moral destiny. To this end, monastic organizations with an activist agenda have been quietly re-established although, since many have their own traditionalist agenda and claims for a role in the nation's future, they do not all support the National League for Democracy (NLD) of Aung San Suu Kyi.

My 'Buddhism *in Extremis*: The Case of Cambodia' examines the manner in which Khmer Buddhism has been forced to adapt itself to a wide range of external influences throughout the modern period. Just as Cambodia was breaking free from oscillating Thai and Vietnamese overlordships in the middle of the nineteenth century the French arrived on the scene and effectively isolated the Khmer *sangha* from the rest of the Theravāda Buddhist world. The

French were particularly hostile to a new Thai-inspired monastic grouping. However, despite considerable initial reluctance, the colonial authorities did promote the expansion and modernization of Buddhist education and scholarship. However, in the wake of an unsuccessful attempt to modernize many aspects of Khmer life, Buddhist monks led the first large-scale protest against French rule, and after the country gained independence King Sihanouk experimented with a version of Buddhist socialism. These experiments failed and, in their aftermath, a set of tragic, short-lived and futile regimes tore the country apart. Buddhism reached its nadir during the Khmer Rouge period. Since the Vietnamese invasion of 1979 the *sangha* has very gradually reasserted itself as the only trustworthy nationwide organization capable of healing the populace after the traumas of the recent past. Restrictions on Buddhist practice have slowly lifted and exposure to external influences is accelerating. The impact of some foreign NGOs, who regard Buddhism as the only effective non-government national network, has led to a recent rise in Buddhist social and environmental activism and certain high-profile Buddhist peace activists are now tolerated by the authorities.

India is the land of Buddhism's origin, yet the religion had virtually disappeared from the subcontinent by the end of the fourteenth century. There has been some resurgence in modern times, and active Buddhist communities may be identified in Ladakh, Bengal, Maharashtra and among Tibetan refugee groups. Timothy Fitzgerald's 'Politics and Ambedkar Buddhism in Maharashtra' addresses the third area in this list. Most Ambedkar Buddhists belong to one large and politically important untouchable caste who were previously called Mahar and who have 'converted' to Buddhism from Hinduism since 1956. Members of this caste are located in both urban and rural areas and the author's analysis of the movement is based on the ethnography of three representative groups within the larger configuration: urban intellectuals, village peasants and temple-based monks or 'dhammacharis'. The chapter also includes a brief biography of Dr. B.R. Ambedkar (himself an untouchable, first Law Minister of independent India and the founder of the movement), along with a summary of his political and soteriological goals and his interpretation of Buddhist values and concepts.

In 'Japanese Nationalism and the Universal *Dharma*' Hiroko Kawanami shows how Buddhism has been patronized by the Japanese state and has played a major role as a legitimator of political power throughout much of its history. Buddhism was replaced as the effective state religion by State Shintō in 1872, when an ideologically constructed myth of the Emperor as direct descendant of the Sun Goddess was elaborated. However, the feudal legacy of Japanese Buddhism continued to express itself in the conservative and authoritarian nature of the Buddhist priestly class, and in the hierarchical structure of temple organizations and their support for political power well into the present century. Moreover, Buddhist organizations actively supported and served the military regime during the 1930s when right-wing fascists held power. There were meagre attempts in the same period by liberal Buddhists to initiate a

Buddhist revolutionary movement by joining forces with Marxist and socialist groups, but this alliance was brutally crushed as the country expanded militarily into China and the Asian continent. Religion and politics were only formally separated after defeat in the Second World War and the freedom of religion guaranteed by the 1947 Constitution brought about radical change in the religious arena. Disenchantment with established religion became widespread, leading to a growth of 'new religions', many of a social activist and explicitly political character. The Buddhist establishment also sought new modes of engagement, leading to active participation in peace movements, co-operation with other religious organizations, and a closer relationship with other Asian Buddhist nations.

Henrik Sørensen's 'Buddhism and Secular Power in Twentieth-Century Korea' starts with the opening up of the 'Hermit Kingdom' to outside influences towards the end of the last century. The impact of Japanese colonization and the role of the Japanese missionaries in the regeneration of Korean Buddhism is considered as are the internal struggles between anti- and pro-Japanese factions within the *saṅgha*. The importance of a publishing boom in Buddhist periodical literature in defining the respective positions of these factions is an important issue here. With the establishment of the First Republic in 1945 Buddhist power struggles and sectarian infighting continued, particularly over the issue of married clergy – itself a consequence of Japanese influence. As a result new schools and sects emerged. Since independence the relationship between *saṅgha* and state has oscillated, depending on the political and religious affiliations of the President and his circle. However, during the period of Park Chunghee Buddhism was manipulated in an explicitly nationalistic direction, in part as a reaction to the outcome of the Korean conflict of the early 1950s. Some important disputes broke out between the government and the Chogye order in the mid 1980s but, as with so many other countries of Buddhist Asia, lay-oriented, social activist forms of religion have increasingly threatened the vigour of the monastic sector in recent times.

By the end of the nineteenth century France had gained control of those Lao territories now making up the modern state of Laos. In 'Laos: From Buddhist Kingdom to Marxist State' Martin Stuart-Fox shows how the resurgence of Buddhism during the French period had much to do with the colonial power's desire to differentiate Lao from Thai identity. By the 1940s Lao Buddhism was closely bound up with Lao nationalism, a relationship which continued under the independent Royal Lao regime after 1946. During the long-drawn-out civil war from 1946 to 1975, Buddhism was used by both sides in support of their own political agendas: by the Royal Lao government to commend its development programme to ethnic Lao; and by the Pathet Lao insurgents to criticize the impact of the American presence on traditional Lao culture and values. Within their own jurisdictions, however, both sides moved to reduce the independence of the *saṅgha* and to make it an agent of government policy, a process for which each criticized the other and which engendered some opposition from within the monastic order. This process of enforced political control was taken much further after the declaration of the Lao People's Democratic Republic in 1975. Sectarian divisions were eliminated, while the Party-controlled Lao Buddhist Association became just one of the member organizations of the Lao Patriotic Front. By 1980, however, repression of the Buddhist order began to decline and members of the Politburo started to attend Buddhist ceremonies. As a result Buddhism in Laos experienced something of a revival, a process that continues as Marxism loses its ideological appeal, and the Party resorts to nationalism as a basis for its own legitimation.

Tessa Bartholomeusz's 'First Among Equals: Buddhism and the Sri Lankan State' explores the extent to which Buddhism has shaped politics in Sri Lanka since the 1890s, the decade that gave rise to a Sinhala-Buddhist nationalism that has continued to inform politics and religion to the present. The chapter pays careful attention to the relationship between ethnicity, nationalism and religion in mainstream political discourse since independence and considers the embodiment of ideas about the appropriate relationship between politics and Buddhism in the constitutions of pre- and post-independence Sri Lanka. It also indicates the influence of organized Buddhist groupings, both monastic and lay, in the creation of Buddhist responses to the 'Tamil question' and considers the ethnic and religious minority views that continuously contest the hegemony of Buddhism in an allegedly secular state. Sri Lanka regards itself as a secular country, which nevertheless gives Buddhism the 'foremost place' in its constitution. Detailed consideration of this tension provides a window into the paradoxical nature of the factors that have shaped, and have continued to shape, the relationship between Buddhism and the state in the modern world.

In 'Centre and Periphery: Buddhism and Politics in Modern Thailand' Donald Swearer examines two specific periods in recent Thai history. During the reigns of Rama IV–VI, from the mid nineteenth century up until World War II, the *sangha* was reformed and a common national religion created. Additionally, a distinctive civil religion was conjoined with Buddhism yet distinguished from it, as expressed in the formula 'Buddhism, King, Nation'. Since the 1960s, government-sponsored programmes involving the *sangha* have proliferated. One of the aims of these programmes has been to foster national unity, for example to integrate hill tribe minorities in northern Thailand into the nation-state, or to counter communist influence in the north-east of the country. Yet tensions in Thai Buddhism which focus on liberal lay and monastic reformers (e.g. Buddhadāsa and Sulak Sivaraksa on the one hand, and sectarian movements like Thammakāi and Santi Asok on the other) have emerged. All, to a greater or lesser extent, may be read as a challenge to the religious settlement of the former period. The chapter also explores anomalies associated with the political potency of charismatic monks within the modern Theravāda forest tradition.

The twentieth-century history of Tibetan Buddhism is without precedent. Following the Chinese communist invasion in 1950 and the suppression of religion following the 1959 uprising, a significant proportion of Tibetans, including the Dalai Lama himself, fled their homeland to follow the religious life in the security of exile in India, or even further afield. In 'Renewal and

Resistance: Tibetan Buddhism in the Modern Era', Ronald Schwartz investigates the relations between Buddhism and the state in pre-1950 Tibet, with particular emphasis on the influence of the large monastic segment in Tibetan society. The chapter also assesses the role of Buddhism in the politics of diaspora and the Dalai Lama's symbolic importance in resolving regional and sectarian issues among the exile community. Another important issue is the politicization of Buddhism in Tibet itself and the relationship of religious ritual to political protest in the demonstrations of young monks and nuns since 1987. Schwartz concludes by considering Chinese strategies for controlling religion in Tibet, their campaigns against the Dalai Lama, and the ongoing controversy over the selection of the Panchen Lama.

In the final contribution to this volume, 'The Quest for Enlightenment and Cultural Identity: Buddhism in Contemporary Vietnam', Thiên Dô examines the evidence for Buddhist decline in Vietnam in the nineteenth century and before. He concludes that the 'theory of decline' owes more to the prejudices of the court-based Confucian literati and state-sponsored Zen fundamentalism than to any hard evidence. Against a background of French colonial involvement, popular Buddhist millenial movements of resistance are attested from the 1860s. However, the 1930s were a particular period of revitalization as Buddhists began to occupy the vacuum created by the court literati's lack of nerve in the continuing anti-colonial agitation. To this period we can also assign the first modern attempts to organize Buddhism on a national basis. Mass publishing and a variety of periodicals advanced the Buddhist cause. Despite growing criticism of Buddhism from Marxist intellectuals a more engaged version of Buddhism emerged, culminating in the famous events of 1963 which ultimately led to the downfall of Diem and his government. Since that highwater mark a variety of schisms relating to the fundamental tension between quietism and social activism have adversely affected Vietnamese Buddhism. Since the unification of the country in 1975 the *sangha* has suffered from differing levels of state repression, although lay-based movements seem to have fared more favourably.

Let me conclude by thanking a number of people, not forgetting the contributors themselves, who have helped make this project possible. Brian Gates, Head of the Department of Religious Studies and Social Ethics, University College of St Martin, Lancaster, aided by the Departmental Research Committee, ensured that I had sufficient sabbatical leave and funding to plan, organize and complete this undertaking. The Trustees of the Spalding Trust also provided financial support relating to my research visit to Cambodia, for which I am exceedingly grateful. On a more personal note, and in this specific connection, I would like to thank David Channer for his help and encouragement in the initial stages of my work. Finally, I would like to thank my wife Gwen, who has acted as a critic, proofreader and support mechanism throughout.

Ian Harris
Lancaster
March 1998

1

BUDDHISM AND POLITICS IN ASIA: THE TEXTUAL AND HISTORICAL ROOTS

IAN HARRIS

Buddhism has often been characterized as an entirely other-worldly religion with a gnostic distaste for the worldly order. Furthermore, the intensely individualistic flavour of the Buddha's spiritual message has led some to suppose that its attitude towards the political order should be lukewarm, to say the very least. Such views are well-attested in the scholarly community, as well as among Buddhists themselves. From this perspective, Buddhism presents a passive and detached face to worldly affairs in stark contrast to the Semitic religions, such as Christianity and Islam, which are both 'strongly oriented to the reconstruction of the world and very militant in this pursuit' (Eisenstadt 1993, 23). However, this stereotyped picture could not be further from the truth. Of course there are, and always have been, Buddhist ascetics who shun the settled world, opting instead for a life of meditation and seclusion in remote forest or mountain. But most members of the monastic order have chosen to reside close to regions of permanent settlement. Indeed, for a variety of reasons, the great cultural and political centres of Asia have tended to act as a magnet for organized Buddhism. Under such conditions, the temptation to influence the political process in a direction conducive to the continued well-being of the Buddha's teaching and the maintenance of stable Buddhist institutions has always seemed attractive to some.

In modern western intellectual discourse it is a commonplace to treat politics – understood as the accumulation, organization and marshalling of the power to govern and control the principal institutions of a society – as entirely separate from religion. Yet this was not always so, and some have argued that the fuzzy relationship between the two categories in pre-modern Europe also best fits the traditional Asian situation (Panikkar 1983, 51). Certainly, the concept of political authority in ancient India, for instance, would be incomprehensible without a consideration of the religious background to the acceptable forms of rationality that operated during the period. No doubt the same principle applies elsewhere, whether it be Tang China, Korea during the Koryŏ era, or late nineteenth-century Bangkok. However, we should be careful not to conflate the disparate and historically distinct cultures and political systems of Asia, particularly when their only common feature may be shared commitment to Buddhism, and glib generalizations about the precise relation between religious and political spheres in Buddhist cultures are best avoided. The purpose of this introductory chapter, then, is to examine the major elements of political thought contained in the early textual traditions of Buddhism. The practical consequences of such ideas are traced as they work their way out in the historical record, and deviations from canonical norms, particularly as Buddhism moves from its place of origin to other regions of Asia, are documented. Finally, the chapter sets the scene for the rest of the book in which individual experts examine, on a chapter by chapter basis, the modern interactions of religion and politics in specific countries of Buddhist Asia.

THE *SANGHA* AND POLITICAL AUTHORITY: TEXTUAL EVIDENCE

Insofar as we can know anything with certainty about the Buddha and his time, it looks likely that he belonged to a tribe of people, the Sākyans, who ordered their affairs on republican lines. The Sākyans were vassals of Pasenadi, king of Kosala, but this clash of political systems does not seem to have prevented the Buddha from enjoying good relations with a number of contemporary kings in the north-east of India. Despite the fact that one of the Buddha's epithets was 'all-conqueror' (*sabbābhibhū*) (Vin.i.8) he was practically unable to make kings submit to his will.[1] Indeed, evidence exists that he did much to accommodate the authority of the state to the monastic rule. Thus monks may postpone the rains retreat (*vassa*) if a king so wishes and the *sangha* has no right of asylum. The monastic ordination ceremony itself was constructed so that enemies of the state and those guilty of various offences were precluded from entry.

Motivation for joining the *sangha* has always been a complex matter. Although the desire to find a way out of suffering must always have been highly significant, the monastic order also acted as a refuge for those disgruntled with the prevailing socio-political order.[2] This in turn could provide a major cause of tension between the Buddhist order and the secular power. The early *Brahmajāla Sutta*, for instance, takes a rather dim view of the 'Kshatriya science' (*khattavijjā*) (D.i.9). This is a reference to the dominant political theory of the third century BCE *Arthaśāstra*, which justified violence and coercion as central features of the ruler's power. Early Buddhist texts deemed such a polity to be contrary to morality. Since it is based on a 'creed of unbridled selfishness' its proponents are destined for rebirth in hell (J.v.490). Such unrighteous kings even delight in eating human flesh (J.v.456–511). Perhaps unsurprisingly, kings are more generally defined as 'those who do filthy things'.[3] The negative aspects of this kind of kingship are well-illustrated by the story of Bhaddiya. On attaining nirvana he was prone to exclaim 'Ah, happiness, Ah happiness' (Thag. 842–65). On being questioned by the Buddha about this he revealed that, as a ruler, prior to renouncing the world he had been permanently terrified of assasination and the like. Now those fears had vanished. The distaste for the 'Kshatriya science' is also attested in Māhāyana writings. The *Lotus Sūtra*, for instance, advises *bodhisattvas* not to attach themselves to the courts of king or political officials,[4] and Āryadeva argues that kings must not hide behind the sayings of ancient sages such as Kauṭilya, the author of the *Arthaśāstra* to justify their immoral deeds.[5] On the contrary, they should act according to the universal law of righteousness, and not be swayed by subsidiary factors, such as caste duty and the like.

A text of the Pāli canon, the *Aggaññasutta* tells of the emergence and gradual degradation of human society. At the lowest point in the process, humans are obliged to elect a Great Chosen One (Mahāsammata) who will protect the people and their property and administer an equitable justice in return for food. The contract between the two parties, then, is symbolized by a form of taxation, and this has been seen by some as the first ever reference to the idea of a social contract in which a king is chosen by his peers. However, this theory is unlikely ever to have been used as 'a political argument' by 'actual historical agents' (Collins 1993, 387).

The *Aggaññasutta* insists that Mahāsammata should be the most handsome of men, and this prejudice is reinforced by other texts, which prohibit those of low socio-ritual status such as the disabled and women from ascending to the throne. His election is said to represent the origin of the aristocratic (*khattiya*) estate. During his reign torture, fines and exile are unknown. A variety of historical Buddhist kings, particularly in Burma and Sri Lanka, trace their descent from Mahāsammata. Mahāsammata is alive in modern Asian political discourse, 'albeit in civilian clothes, as the First Statesman or First Democrat . . . of Buddhist politicians and Theravāda newspaper editors' (Collins and Huxley 1996, 644). Purely on the level of theory, there are some weaknesses in the notion of election, for Mahāsammata is dissociated from the practice of making law. As Lingat (1950, 18) has observed, he administers justice but does not proclaim the law.

However, not all early Buddhist texts support the notion of a social contract. The practice of kingly primogeniture is also well-attested (Spellman 1964, 57). One canonical example is Ajātasattu, who came to the throne of Magadha after killing his father, Bimbisāra. Although he is said to have plotted the Buddha's death on more than one occasion he repented after hearing the *Sāmaññaphala Sutta*. In that text the Buddha explains how a king should rise from his seat and greet an ordained monk with deference (D.i.61), thus underlining the status difference between secular authority and the person who renounces the household life and becomes a *bhikkhu*.[6] On another occasion the Buddha extolled the virtues of the aristocratic clan-republic of the Vajjians to Ajātasattu. The happiness and prosperity of the Vajjians sprang from the fact that they held to seven practices conducive to welfare: they held frequent meetings attended by all, made decisions and carried them out in concord, protected their traditions and honoured their pledges, respected elders, did not abduct or coerce women and girls, maintained and respected all shrines, and supported and defended holy persons (D.ii.73f). This example of public spirit, wise conservatism, moral rectitude and piety (Ghosal 1959, 77) seems to have led Ajātasattu to distinguish between his sphere (or wheel) of authority (*āṇācakka*) and that of the *saṅgha* (*dhammacakka*),[7] an early expression of the theory of 'two wheels of *dhamma*' (Reynolds 1972). Certainly, some kind of distinction between the temporal (*diṭṭhadhamma*) and the spiritual (*samparāya*) spheres can be traced back to the earliest period of Buddhism (Gokhale 1969, 732).

IDEAL KINGSHIP: THE *CAKKAVATTI*

The ideal Buddhist king, then, must rule according to the norms of *dhamma*, norms that are held to have motivated the rule of ancient kings. When *dhamma* flourishes, the king's reign will be long, the fruits of the earth will be uncommonly sweet and flavourful and rain and the fertility of the soil will be assured. Such a king possesses ten royal virtues (*dasarājadhamma*), namely alms-giving, morality, charity, justice, penitence, peace, mildness, mercy, meekness and patience (J.iv.200).

Gunawardana (1979, 344) has suggested that the early Buddhist attitude to kingship is one of 'antagonistic symbiosis'. On the one hand, the *sangha* maintains advantageous status boundaries between itself and the secular power. From this perspective the king's use of coercive power means that he necessarily offends against the Buddha's teaching and must be condemned. However, monks, in order to flourish, are themselves in need of powerful protection and patronage. From this angle the king may receive legitimation of his rule when he acts in accordance with a monastically created and restraining *dhamma*, as defined by the *dasarājadhamma*, etc. The concept of the 'wheel-turning' king (*cakkavatti*; Skt. *cakravartin*) derives from such considerations and, it could be argued, represents a second stage in the political thinking of Buddhism at the point where it was realized that the king could effectively advance the cause of Buddhism. Here the original notion of a contract between the people and Mahāsammata is replaced by the idea of *dhamma* itself as the basis of the state and the ideal ruler is elevated as the secular equivalent of the Buddha. Gokhale (1969, 736–7) argues that this second phase in the Buddhist theory of kingship may have been associated with the actual growth and extension of the powers of actual Indian states.

In the textual tradition, the mythical Mahāsudassana (D.ii.169f) may be taken as the prototypical *cakkavatti*. Like the Buddha, he possesses all the major and minor marks of a superman (*mahāpurisa*) and his early life is spent in much the same way as Gotama's. As was the case with Mahāsammata, he is physically beautiful, lives much longer than the average life span, remains in good health, and is popular with all classes of his subjects. These qualities are a consequence of the fact that he is held to have accumulated a vast store of merit in previous existences.[8] He possesses the five strengths, that is, physical and mental strength, strength of officials, strength of nobility and strength of wisdom (J.iv.120), and always acts judiciously, having eschewed favouritism, hatred, delusion and fear. He rules without violent coercion since his power is based on the *dhamma*, not the sword. Since he is proficient in the four meditational stages (*jhāna*) he suffuses his realm with love, compassion, sympathetic joy and equanimity (i.e. the four *brahmavihāras*) and he engages in conspicuous and frequent acts of generosity.

The *Cakkavatisīhanāda Sutta*, the *locus classicus* of the doctrine, maintains that, at the end of his reign, the *cakkavatti* should withdraw from the throne and take up the homeless life as a wandering ascetic, handing the kingdom over to his eldest son (D.iii.60).[9] In this way the superiority of the *bhikkhu* and the principle of primogeniture are both conserved. For related reasons, a woman may not rule as a *cakkavatti*.[10] Territorial conquest is achieved without recourse to violence. The willing submission of his fellow rulers is simply accomplished by a visitation of the *cakkavatti* accompanied by his 'non-threatening' fourfold army of elephants, cavalry, chariots and infantry. This construction of a 'fantasy world in which royal rule is possible without violence' (Collins 1996, 442) provides a good indication of the difficulties that might be faced by any actual ruler engaged in the establishment of an authentic Buddhist polity. Fortunately, the early tradition does not speak with one voice on the subject, no doubt because of the previously mentioned 'antagonistic symbiosis' between monks and rulers. Certainly one consequence of the 'two wheels of *dhamma*' doctrine is that war is placed within the king's own sphere of authority. As such, many sources maintain a relatively neutral attitude towards the prosecution of warfare. 'The horrors of war are duly recognised but no decisive or overt effort seems to be made to insist on outlawing war itself ... the Buddha [never] advised his contemporary kings to disband their armies and beat their swords into ploughshares' (Gokhale 1969, 734).

Although the historical record relating to actual Buddhist kingship is far from complete, the tradition seems to possess a sort of 'just-war' doctrine. Thus, the Sinhalese King Duṭṭhagāmaṇī (101–77 BCE) is supposed to have ridden into battle against the Tamils with a Buddha relic on his spear accompanied by many monks who left the *sangha* specifically for this purpose. His monastic advisors absolved him of any great demerit by characterizing the enemy as 'wicked men of wrong views' (Mhv.xxv.1 and 108–11) hardly distinguishable from beasts. This demonization of the 'opponents' of the Buddha's teaching is the usual method through which violence in Buddhism has been justified. Subduing them, be they heretics, landlords, bandits, imperialists or counter-revolutionaries can then be rendered as a compassionate act. Demièville (1973, 353) notes that, while the Pāli texts generally 'remained strict in the prohibition of killing ... the Mahayana ... ended up finding excuses for murder and even for its glorification'. In the *Upāyakauśalya Sūtra*,[11] for instance, the Buddha tells of how, in a previous existence, he speared a wicked man to death so that a greater number of innocent folk could be saved. Indeed, since the act was committed out of compassion the future Buddha experienced no demerit.

While Mahāsudassana may be the mythical prototype of the *cakkavatti*, the Buddhist tradition actually looks to Asoka Maurya (268–39 BCE) as the pre-eminent historical model of the ideal ruler. As a member of the powerful north Indian Mauryan dynasty founded by his grandfather Candragupta, Asoka never claimed to be an elected king. It is difficult to separate historical fact from mythological accretion, but Asoka speaks most clearly to us through his inscriptions. One of Asoka's epithets is 'beloved of the gods' (*devānāmpriya*), perhaps indicating a halfway house towards the full-blown divine titles enjoyed by later Indian kings. He also regarded himself as 'father of the people'. Although never a monk, Asoka seems to have become a lay Buddhist after experiencing remorse for the death and destruction caused by his conquest of Kaliṅga around 260 BC. In consequence, he dedicated the remainder of his reign to the *dhamma*.

The essence of Asoka's message from this point on was 'To avoid sin, practice virtue and perform the duties of human solidarity ... [and] general rules of moral life under the aegis of the Buddha' (Lamotte 1988, 228). He appointed officials to care for and have oversight of the Buddhist *saṅgha* and the various other sects that flourished at the time, and performed many traditional merit-making activities such as bridge-building, tree-planting, etc. He also seems to have discouraged excessive ritualism. In the *Bhābrā Edict*, promulgated in the thirteenth year of his reign, he specifically addresses the Buddhist order, expressing respect and faith in the triple jewel of Buddha, *dhamma* and *saṅgha*. Additionally, he praises the Buddha's teachings and singles out seven sermons for the special attention of his audience. This could be interpreted as going beyond the role of subservience to the *saṅgha* laid down for a king in texts such as the *Sāmaññaphala Sutta*. The *Kauśāmbī Edict* certainly does step over this line in that Asoka formulates a number of restrictions for *saṅgha* entry and condemns disunity in the order, laying down the return to lay life for anyone found guilty of such an act. The Theravāda also preserves a tradition, unsupported by any hard historical evidence, that Asoka sponsored a general Buddhist council (the so-called Third Council) at his capital Pāṭaliputra (present-day Patna) around 250 BC. According to this account, which incidentally forms a part of the Theravāda foundation myth, the council concluded with the expulsion of 60,000 heretics and a full purification of the monastic order. Such purifications, often accompanied by the promulgation of a royal edict on monastic discipline (*katikāvata*),[12] have been reasonably commonplace throughout the history of the Theravāda. Their authority has been generally premised on the example of Asoka. Indeed, the modern Sri Lankan reformer Anagārika Dharmapāla was so impressed by this ancient prototype of Buddhist sovereignty that he allowed himself the rather dubious luxury of characterizing Asoka's state as 'the greatest democratic empire in history' (Bechert 1966, 128).

Of course, the 'top-down purification' (Huxley 1996, 152) associated with classical Buddhist kingship is not the only way to reintroduce order into the *saṅgha* and we should remember that, in any Buddhist culture, the support of monks by the laity is not a foregone conclusion. The laity may, like the ancient inhabitants of Kosambī (Vin.i.352), decide that the quarrelsome behaviour of the *saṅgha* is unworthy of respect. Under such conditions monks will not be fed nor greeted reverently with joined palms, a situation that can occasionally happen even in the modern period. A good example of the turning away of monastic privileges as a response to undecorous behaviour in nineteenth-century Burma is discussed by Hall (1908, 134). We may regard this as a 'bottom-up purification'.

Texts on Buddhist statecraft are not confined to the canonical period. The Mahayanist *Sūtra of Golden Light* (*Suvarnabhāsottama Sūtra*) contains a chapter entitled 'Instruction Concerning Divine Kings' in which a (probably mythical) textbook on the polity of the righteous king is mentioned.[13] More concretely, a variety of Pāli law codes, beginning with the thirteenth-century Burmese monk Dhammavilāsa's *Dhammathat* and continuing up to the beginning of the modern period with Rājabala-kyaw-din's influential *Mohavicchedanī*, written in 1832, are extant (Bode 1909, 33, 84–9).[14] Although originally based on the model of the Hindu *Dharmaśāstras*, these texts eliminate elements associated with the sacrificial cult of the Vedas and continue to crystallize the doctrine of the righteous Buddhist king in the post-canonical period. They seem to have been instrumental in the development of Burmese and Thai kinghip, particularly in the Ayutthaya period (1351–1767). We certainly hear of the kings of Ayutthaya studying these codes and upholding 'the four principles of justice, namely: to assess the right or wrong of all service or disservice rendered to him, to uphold the righteous and truthful, and to maintain the prosperity of his state through none but just means' (Nivat 1947, 163). It is a great pity that the study of such important sources has been largely overlooked by western scholars, one exception being the fifteenth-century *Lokaneyyappakaranam*, 'a virtual textbook on polity unlike anything found elsewhere in Pāli literature' (Jaini 1986, xl).

THE JUSTIFICATION OF REBELLION

The correct means of overthrowing an unrighteous king is a very difficult issue for the Buddhist. Very occasionally we hear of monks attempting to gain the throne. Thus, Chao Phitsanulok of Fang (1767–8), along with other monastics, managed to establish a short-lived independent state around Pitsnulok in the north of Thailand (Lingat 1958). Their opposition towards Taksin (1767–82). King of Thonburi,[15] seems to have been based on his claim, disputed by the *sangha*, to have reached the spiritual status of a stream-enterer (*sotāpanna*). However, such examples are isolated cases.

As we have already seen, some scriptural justification for ignoring the first ethical precept on non-killing may be gleaned, particularly from Mahāyāna sources. However, to 'threaten the bad king with rebellion, and thus, in effect, to treat his oath as part of constitutional law may be counted as *lèse majesté*; to threaten him with the supernatural is acceptable piety' (Collins and Huxley 1996, 635). The better part of valour, then, is discretion, and with this in mind, it is hardly surprising that Buddhists have turned to mythology as a support for revolutionary ideals. Ancient works of political prophecy, such as *The Prophecy of Gośṛnga* discovered at Dun-huang, are well-attested and Tibetan, Mongolian and Chinese Buddhist literature is sprinkled with material of a similar kind (Sárkōzi 1992, 11). Such literature is generally premised on the idea of the inevitable decline of humanity and a falling away from the Buddha's teaching.

Maitreya is probably the figure who most regularly crops up in this connection since the expectation is that he will renew the *dhamma* at the end of this period of decline. Since tradition regards him as the future Buddha who will be reborn as a great king before revealing his full identity, he represents a fusion of the ideals of the *tathāgata* and *cakkavatti*. This is well symbolized by the Sri Lankan king Dhātusena (460–78 CE), who seems to have worshipped an image of Maitreya in full kingly regalia in a specially constructed temple (Cv.xxxviii.68). In unstable phases of Buddhist history, particularly in central, east and south-east Asia, the cult of Maitreya has developed in a strongly chiliastic direction. We know, for instance, of apocalyptic Buddhist *Sūtras* circulating in sixth-century China that predicted the imminent arrival of Maitreya and a subsequent battle in which the forces of evil would be routed. Three separate figures claiming to be Maitreya reborn are recorded as having led insurrections in the period 610 to 613, only to have their aspirations cut short by the Sui authorities (Nattier 1988, 31). Although they were precluded from occupying the role of *cakravartin*, it seems to have been acceptable for them to assume Maitreya's identity. Thus, in 683, the Duke of Liang provided a Buddhist justification for the Empress Wu Ze-tian's assumption of the Chinese throne by claiming that she was the final manifestation of the coming Buddha. It was also quite common for Asian rulers, for example the kings of Khotan (Emmerick 1967, 25, 29), to bolster their own authority by claiming to be incarnations of Maitreya and, as late as 1813, around 80,000 followers of Lin Qing, the leader of the Eight Trigrams rebellion who also claimed to be an incarnation of Maitreya, lost their lives in a challenge to the Manchu (Qing) dynasty (Naquin 1976, 65f). Intriguingly, Chinese devotees who awaited the appearance of Maitreya in the years immediately preceding 1813 believed that he would be identified by the characters for the 'sun' and 'moon' (which together make up the word Ming, i.e. the title of the previous Chinese dynasty) on his hands. Similarly messianic figures are to be found in connection with the protest movements of early modern Southeast Asia, as the chapters on Burma (Myanmar) and Cambodia in this volume make clear.

It has been suggested that the other-worldly orientation of early Indian Buddhism did not predispose it towards the construction of city-based political centres (Eisenstadt 1993, 19). Others argue that, even in the modern period, the basic Buddhist civilizational unit is the village monastery rather than the 'dharma realm of the capital' (Silber 1995, 101). However, caution is necessary for, although this may hold good for some of the Theravāda societies of Southeast Asia, it is less applicable to the centralized Buddhist states of the Far East. In a variation of this theme, Tambiah proposes a model for the Buddhist polities of Theravāda Southeast Asia in which a central political entity is surrounded by several smaller replica polities, the whole structure in a continual process of 'fission and incorporation' (1976, 70). These galactic structures, or *maṇḍalas*, such as that at Ayutthaya (1351–1767), wax and wane in 'concertina-like fashion' (Wolters 1982, 12). When the centre is weak the *sangha* suffers from inadequate patronage and tends towards disintegration. When it is strong there is a danger of 'excessive regulation of the *sangha* ... and a search for legitimacy by involving monks in more and more rituals of state' (Tambiah 1976, 512–3), resulting in a potential erosion of the spiritual life of the monkhood. These shifts in the *sangha's* fortunes are readily seen in the history of the Chakri dynasty in Bangkok, as Swearer's essay in this volume illustrates.

Conflicts between monks and kings have often been brought to a head by a withdrawal of the monastic sector from the political centre. Thus, we hear of monks leaving the Sri Lankan capital of Udaya III (934–7) over a breach of their right of sanctuary. After protests by the army and laity, the king was forced into a humiliating climbdown before the monks could be persuaded to return and vouchsafe his reign by their presence (Gunawardana 1979, 208, 211). Evidence like this suggests that, by and large, kings have been more in need of the support of the *sangha* than vice versa (Silber 1995, 99–100).

BUDDHISM AND POWER IN CHINA

The bureaucratic control of the *sangha* in China can be traced back to the late fourth century. By appointing the cleric Fa gou as official administrator of the *sangha*, Emperor Tai zu, first ruler of the Northern Wei, established his authority over the monastic order. In order to extract himself from his delicate position of subservience, symbolized by the need to bow before the ruler, Fa gou argued that the Emperor and the Tathāgata were one and the same and by bowing to the former he was actually paying his respects to the Buddha (Ch'en 1973, 82). Even though the matter had been debated before, Hui-yuan (early fifth century) crystallized the major arguments against this state of affairs in his *Treatise on the Monk not Paying Homage to the Ruler*.[16] In a nutshell, the monk is trying to emancipate himself from the world. In order to do this he must be virtuous and this virtue has a beneficial effect on the rest of society. However, he should not be constrained by secular restrictions and although he respects the emperor he should not be expected to pay the formal homage to him expected of the laity. The argument seems to have been accepted by Huan-xuan when he came to the throne in 404. However, this was not the end of the matter, for in 662 supporters of the Tang emperor appealed to the *Vimalakīrtinirdeśa Sūtra*, in which monks make obeisance to the householder-*bodhisattva* Vimalakīrti, as authority for monastic homage to the Emperor (Ch'en 1973, 79–80). Indeed, it seems that Indian Buddhist texts, with their 'subaltern point of view on monarchical government', failed to find influential patrons in China and were rather sidelined. One unexpected consequence of the need to flatter the higher reaches of the Imperial administration, however, was that criticism was deflected towards less significant functionaries, (for example local magistrates (*xian guan*)), who were often characterized in a highly unflattering light by Chinese Buddhist writers (Barrett 1996, 1).

Once the precedent of subordination had been set it was not long before admission to the Chinese *sangha* itself was controlled by a government bureau and ordination quotas were set. Monks and nuns were also required to register their particulars both locally and with the central Bureau of National Sacrifice (Ci pu – it was given jurisdiction over the Buddhist order in 694), even though such registration is specifically denounced in the *Renwang-jing*[17] as an unjustified means of keeping the *sangha* in bondage. The state also ensured that foreign monks, particularly those from Japan,[18] were kept under very close supervision. Indeed, all monks were obliged to obtain travel permits before leaving their home monasteries. The official certification of ordinands allowed plenty of scope for fraud and we know of certificates being available, around 755, to anyone prepared to offer 100 strings of cash (Ch'en 1973, 90). Clearly, this meant that those seeking to evade the grosser forms of official surveillance, and with sufficient funds, could enter the *sangha* for a variety of unorthodox reasons.

Also in the Tang period, the secular *Dao-sengge* (Rules Concerning Buddhist and Taoist Clergy) was employed side by side with the *vinaya* as a means of regulating the *sangha*. Although no longer extant, a Japanese work, the *Sōniryō*,[19] is based on it and gives a good flavour of its harsh approach, an approach far more severe than that contained in any Indian-derived *vinaya* tradition. Thus the *Sōniryō* prescribes thirty days' hard labour for drinking alcohol, while the Pāli *vinaya* classes the offence as one requiring mere confession before the assembled order alone. Many less serious offences require a series of lashes graded in categories of between 10 and 100 strokes, while the most serious crimes, such as murder, which in the Pāli result in permanent exclusion from the *sangha*, are punished by beheading in the Chinese code.

The high water mark of Chinese state interference in monastic affairs was during the suppression of Buddhism from 842 to 845 when all monks and nuns were ordered to return to the lay life and monastic lands were confiscated. While the causes underlying this event are complex, and certainly as convoluted as those behind Henry VIII's dissolution of the English monasteries in the late 1530s, two factors are undeniable, namely, the wealth and consequent power of the *sangha*, and its role, whether implicit or explicit, as refuge for political malcontents.

TIBET AND MONGOLIA

An interesting example of joint control of religion and state by a single family is attested in tenth- and eleventh-century Western Tibet. Both king and son jointly ruled the territory of sPu-hrang, until the king entered the religious life as the royal lama, Ye-shes-'od. The country was then ruled by the son, lHa-lde, while the father devoted himself to religious activities including the sponsorship of a mission to India for the study and translation of Buddhist texts. Acting in his dual capacity as retired monarch and spiritual father of his people, Ye-shes-'od also issued an ordinance aimed at purifying Buddhism of 'corrupt practices', namely tantric sexual rituals, harming animals and the use of impure substances (Karmay 1980). This family-based arrangement may be seen as a model for some subsequent Tibetan religio-political developments. Thus, the Sa-skya school of Buddhism gained political control of a large part of Tibet in 1246 when Chinggis Qaγan's grandson, Godan, made Sa-skya Paṇḍita (1182–51), the chief lama of Sa-skya monastery, his viceregent. Leadership of Sa-skya has traditionally passed through the male line of the 'Khon clan, and even after the eclipse of the clan in the mid fourteenth century Tibetans recognized Sa-skya as a 'virtually autonomous political entity' into the twentieth century even though its subjects 'never quite understood questions about the right of the Sa sKya government to rule its people' (Cassinelli and Ekvall 1969, 9, 72).[20]

Buddhism arrived in Mongolia during the reign of Qubilai Qaγan (1260–94). Although Qubilai was already familiar with the forms of Buddhism that flourished among various Turkic tribes at the time, it was 'Phags pa (1235–80), nephew of Sa-skya Paṇḍita and hierarch of the Sa-skya school, arriving at the court of the Qaγan around 1260, who stimulated this interest in the direction of actual practice by bestowing the Hevajra initiation on Qubilai and members of his court. By so doing he became the Qaγan's tantric master. The occasion seems to have given rise to some problems of protocol. In particular, Qubilai was concerned about the respective seating positions of himself and 'Phags pa. Basically, who was to have the higher throne during the ritual? A Mongolian chronicle tells us that the matter was resolved by 'Phags pa, who ruled that 'when preaching the doctrine or bestowing an *abhiṣeka*-consecration, the lama sits on a dais, and the king beneath, and when conducting the affairs of state the lama and the Khan sit equally on the dais' (quoted in Moses 1977, 81). The *White History (Chagan Teukel)* gives a rather different reading: '... the lama is the root of the high religion and the lord of the doctrine; the emperor ... the head of the empire and the master of the secular power. The laws of the true doctrine, like the sacred cord, cannot be weakened; the laws of the great emperor, like the golden yoke, are indestructible' (Loewenthal 1955, 51).

Here is the basis of the 'so-called' Patron–Priest (Tib. *yon mchod*) relationship, in which in a princely or royal donor (*yon bdag*) is supposed to sponsor, and hence subordinate, along Erastian lines, a lama acting as donee (*mchod gnas*). However, the boundary between the two parties in this arrangement is not always easy to establish with any degree of certainty and it could be unwise to import western concepts, such as the separation of church and state, as a simplistic interpretative tool. For instance, the donee seems to play hardly any priestly role at all, and 'Phags pa, in any case, seems to have combined the two functions of donee and donor in his role as tantric *guru*. Ruegg (1995, 80f) argues that the relationship is essentially 'religious and personal rather than official and institutional'. Whatever the precise nature of the relationship it is clear that the precedent of Asoka does not fit the picture very well. Nevertheless, considerable secular advantages flowed in 'Phags pa's direction as a result of the relationship. He was appointed viceregent of Tibet, thus ensuring the pre-eminence of Sa-skya as the sole political power in Tibet for the next century and a half. He was also given a number of administrative roles in the Yuan empire culminating in the post of Imperial Preceptor (Dishi) in 1270, which gave him direct rule over the great monasteries of China (Moses 1977, 78).[21] Additionally, 'Phags pa wrote a work, *Instructions for the Qaγan*, which embodies the above idea of the 'dual principle', a notion reinforced in Qubilai's *Pearl Charter* which became the basis of all subsequent relations between the Qaγans and the ecclesiastical hierarchy until the incorporation of Mongolia into the Qing empire in the late eighteenth century (Zhukovskaya 1991, 244).

Altan Qaγan (1507–82) is the first significant Mongol leader after the fall of the Yuan. By 1574 he had established himself as supreme ruler of Mongolia and parts of northern China. Four years later he came into contact with the Tibetan dGe-lugs-pa lama bSod-nams rGya-mtsho for the first time, although tradition holds that bSod-nams had already taken a phantasmal form and commanded the Qaγan to desist from killing men and plunging his foot into their opened intestines as a cure for gout (Bawden 1961, 35). At their meeting in June 1578, Altan conferred the title Dalai Lama[22] on bSod-nams. The Qaγan received the designation Chos-kyi rGyal-po (*dharmarāja*), a title implying *cakravartin* status, in return.[23] Since bSod-nams was regarded by the Mongolians as an incarnation of 'Phags pa, this swapping of titles invested a high degree of legitimacy to Altan's rule. Mongolian laws were revised in the light of Buddhist teachings and the Mongolian nobility and the Buddhist ecclesiastical hierarchy were put on an equivalent footing (Moses 1977, 97). The dGe-lugs-pa steadily gained ground in Mongolia itself from this time on. Indeed, the *Khalkha Djiram*, an early eighteeth-century law code, elevates the Jetsundamba Qutuγtu, the most senior Mongolian lama to be appointed by the fourth Dalai Lama, above both Qaγans and princes (Riasanovsky 1965, 191). As such, he bore the traditional title of Edzen Qaγan (i.e. sovereign of the Mongols), and was regarded as entirely beyond both crime and punishment. His monastery was given special legal protection as a place of sanctuary.

Altan's successors cleverly manipulated the succession after, bSod-nams's death by ensuring that his reincarnation, the Fourth Dalai Lama, was found within the Mongol ruling family itself. As a result, the political supremacy of the dGe-lugs-pa over Tibet was achieved and lasted until the power of the Mongols waned. However, the institution of the Dalai Lama as we know it today really begins with the fifth in the line. The policy of the fifth Dalai Lama (1617–1682) and his Regent (*sde-srid*) was to unify religion and politics (*chos srid gnyis ldan*) through the construction of an elaborate government bureaucracy. Monastic and related affairs were handled by an ecclesiastical wing headed by four Great Monk Secretaries (Goldstein 1989, 8), while the secular administration was controlled by the Regent and headed by a Cabinet with authority over various agencies, including the secular courts (French 1995,46). Both halves of the government apparatus reported to the Office of the Dalai Lama on all important issues. Buddhist monasteries, particularly the three great dGe-lugs-pa monasteries of the Lhasa Valley, Ganden (dGa-'ldan), Drepung ('Bras-spungs), and Sera (Se-rwa), proved ideal training grounds for the emerging religio-bureaucracy, the creation of which clearly reduced the influence of the traditional aristocracy in Tibetan affairs.

The first Manchu (Qing) emperor of China, Shun-zhi (1644–61), seems to have recognized the value of the Dalai Lamas and invested the fifth with title Vajradhāra in 1652, using him as an international policeman in a variety of disputes between different Mongol tribes and also in the Tibet/Nepal border areas between 1661 and 1679 (Rahul 1969, 15–16). However, the passing of patronage of the dGe-lugs-pa from the Mongols to the Manchus held consider-able disadvantages, as recent events have all too readily demonstrated. The seventh Dalai Lama came to office through the intervention of the Manchu army in 1720 and, from that date until the fall of the Qing in 1912, the Manchus maintained Governors (Amban)[24] and a large army in Tibet. Since no Dalai Lama between numbers five and thirteen lived for more than twenty-three years, Tibet was ruled by Regents under Manchu control for a considerable period.

Interestingly, the office of Dalai Lama is never inherited, nor is he elected. He must be 'discovered' for he is thought to be an incarnation of Avalokiteśvara, the *bodhisattva* of compassion.[25] In many ways this is a more successful stategy for the transfer of power than the rule by genetic inheritance found among the Sa-skya. Rule by incarnation has proved a useful means of stifling dissent since it is very difficult to challenge the authority of a high ranking lama who is con-sidered to be the embodiment of a celestial being. Additionally, it is effective in curbing nepotism and incompetence and it weakens the power of the aris-tocracy to boot, for Dalai Lamas are generally discovered among the peasantry. Although the family of the chosen boy is ennobled, no member may ever be appointed to a political office, thus ensuring that the family never becomes too powerful (Rahul 1969, 10). The disadvantage is that the arrangement can confer a great deal of influence on the Regent.

Even though the Dalai Lama's position as head of state ensured the privileges of the dGe-lugs-pa school, other religious groupings, both Buddhist and Bon, were left free to pursue their own religious activities in freedom 'so long as they showed no overweening political ambitions' (Snellgrove 1987, 515). Indeed, once the dGe-lugs-pa power centre of Lhasa had been established, a number of previously powerful groups in Tibetan religious history largely renounced political amibition and withdrew to geographically remote locations.

BUDDHIST POWER IN JAPAN

Historians of Japan have tended to neglect the power of Buddhist temples in the early and medieval periods, preferring to concentrate on doctrine and aes-thetics rather than the reality of institutional Buddhism. This is surprising as temples seem to have controlled significant portions of all available lands, and the lives of those working on them, from the tenth to the fourteenth centuries (McMullin 1984, 6). Buddhism was officially endorsed in the Seventeen Article

Constitution (*Jūshichijō Kenpō*) of Prince Regent Shōtoku (604) and the situation was further underlined in the Taihō and Yōrō Legal Codes of 701 and 718 respectively. From the mid-seventh century, the state encouraged the frequent recitation of the *Sūtra of Golden Light* (*Konkōmyōkyō*) as a means of guiding and protecting the state and by the Nara (early ninth century) period we witness a wide ranging amalgamation of 'Buddhist Law' (*buppō*) and 'Imperial Law' (*ōbō*), the status of each *vis-à-vis* the other oscillating throughout the period.

By the late Heian (twelfth century) the phenomenon of 'prince-priests' (*monzeki*) or 'temple aristocratization' (*jiin-kizokuka*) was well-established, with all senior temple posts occupied by members of the nobility. Some of the more powerful Buddhist temples maintained their own 'armies' made up of 'priest-warriors' (*sōhei*) and we know of about 250 incidents between 981 and 1549 in which such *sōhei* were engaged in major displays of force (McMullin 1984, 22).[26] It is estimated that the Enryakuji controlled some 4,000 *sōhei* in the sixteenth century and another powerful temple, the Negoroji, became, by the sixteenth century, a major producer of European-style firearms and allowed its *sōhei* to act as mercenaries. Sometimes conflict was sparked off by inter-temple rivalry. On other occasions *sōhei* were employed to 'forcefully petition' (*gōso*) the authorities to grant their temple special favours. Under these circumstances, it is hardly a surprise to discover that around 25 per cent of all Japanese lands were owned or controlled by the Buddhist temples in the Heian period.

In the Kamakura period (1192–1333) new schools of Buddhism such as Jōdo Shinshū (Pure Land) and Nichirenshū emerged. Some scholars suggest that this is the point at which religion and politics begin to separate in Japanese history. Of particular relevance here is the Honganji branch of Shinshū. The centralized organizational structure of the school, the creation of its 'chief priest' Rennyo Kenju (1415–99), enabled the control and marshalling of vast numbers of lay adherents (*monto*) over a geographically diverse range. Rennyo urged his followers to be obedient to the civil authorities by asking them to 'engrave the *ōbō* on their foreheads and to preserve the *buppō* deep in their hearts' (McMullin 1984, 38). However, in 1473 he seems to have modified his position after a dispute between lay supporters and their local authorities escalated into conflict. He told the former that they should defend Buddhism without fear of death, for ultimately they would be saved by the power of the Amitābha Buddha. From this time on we witness the emergence of an 'enemy-of-the-[Buddhist]-Law logic (*hōteki ronri*)' in Shinshū circles. Until the decline of Shinshū power in the sixteenth century, uprisings (*ikki*), particularly over tax and debt related issues, were not uncommon. The largest occurred in 1488 in Kaga province and involved some 150,000 lay persons. As McMullin (1984, 40) notes, 'by the end of the fifteenth century the Honganji branch of Shinshū had become ... a competing world order, an order welded together by powerful bonds of religious loyalty'.

Nichiren (1222–82) was not the only Buddhist of the Kamakura period to believe that the Japanese people were living through a degenerate time (*mappō*) which represented the final days of the Buddha's teaching. However, he is the best-known and the most extreme proponent of measures to counteract this. In his *Risshō-ankoku-ron* (*Establishment of the Legitimate Teaching for Protection of the Country*) of 1260, he petitions the authorities to acknowledge that the recent run of disasters, both natural and man-made, including the prospect of an imminent Mongol invasion, can only be averted by repudiating false doctrines and turning to the true teaching of the Buddha embodied in the *Lotus Sūtra*. Elsewhere, in the *Kaimoku Shō* (*Opening of the Eyes*) of 1272, he appeals for extremely vigorous action and refutation (*shakubuku*) of the doctrines of heretical Buddhists such as members of the Pure Land schools (Yampolsky 1990, 143f). It is unclear whether he meant the government to suppress these heretical schools by physical violence or simply by bureaucratic procedures aimed at discouraging lay support. Finally, in the *Shufu Onfurumai Gosho* (*The Letter on Various Actions [of the Priest Nichiren]*) of 1276, he reveals himself as a messianic saviour, 'the soul of the people of Japan' (Yampolsky 1990, 50). Despite Nichiren's lack of success in his own lifetime (he suffered severe persecution which obliged him to live in exile and retirement for much of the time), it is clear that much religio-political capital was made of his inheritance in subsequent centuries, particularly of the idea that a purified Japan would be the altar (*kaidan*) from which the truth of the *Lotus Sūtra* would spread over the world. The support of the Rinzai master Shaku Sōen (1859–1919) for his government in the Russo-Japanese war (1904–5) on the grounds that 'Japan has entered with great reluctance, she pursues no egotistical purpose, but seeks the subjugation of evils hostile to civilization, peace and enlightenment' may be read in this light.[27]

REFORM AND REVOLUTION IN THE MODERN PERIOD

In the modern period a majority of traditional Buddhist cultures have come under some form of foreign dominion. Indeed, the only country not to have experienced any substantial colonial presence is Thailand. Thus, Sri Lanka, Burma and India were dominated by Britain, Vietnam, Laos and Cambodia by France, and Korea by Japan. In the post-colonial period Vietnam, North Korea, Laos and Cambodia have all experienced communist rule and Tibet has been incorporated, as an autonomous region, into the People's Republic of China. Regrettably, in many parts of the contemporary Buddhist world, most notably in Tibet, Burma, China, Vietnam and, to a lesser extent, Cambodia and Laos 'official' sources of information can be misleading. The scholar must rely on alternative sources of information, such as those emanating from human rights organizations, and the testimony of dissidents, refugees, etc. Likewise, officially sponsored research may be difficult or impossible.

As the contributors to this volume amply demonstrate, colonialism had both positive and negative consequences so far as organized Buddhism was concerned. Let us take Sri Lanka as an example. Around 1850 the British Crown relinquished the right, which had been enjoyed by previous Buddhist and

Hindu kings of the island, to appoint senior monks to positions within the *sangha* hierarchy, arguing that it would be inappropriate for a Christian power to confirm the officials of a 'heathenish' religion. Although in many ways a commendable decision, its effect, though unintentional, was effectively to disestablish the Buddhist order. Deprived of its traditional mode of support, the ecclesiastical hierarchy lost its confidence through factionalization and the like, and Sri Lankan Buddhism went into a serious organizational and spiritual decline (Malalagoda 1976, 122f). On a more positive note, the impact of Christian missionary activity on the island, particularly after the Pānadura debate of 1873 in which a Buddhist monk first successfully defended Buddhism against the Christian challenge, can be seen as one of the factors that galvanized Buddhists, particularly the newly emerging urban laity, into modernizing reforms (Malalagoda, 1973). Even in Thailand a scientific and 'protestant' modernizing spirit is apparent in the Buddhist reforms introduced during the reign of Mongkut (r.1851–68). A western influence is clearly visible here, a point eloquently reinforced by the later insistence of King Wachirawut (r.1910–25) that Thailand was the last bulwark in the defence of Buddhism; Burma and Sri Lanka having already fallen to colonial powers.

Not surprisingly Buddhism has been a factor in the anti-colonialist liberation struggles of modern times. Thus the Cambodian *sangha*-inspired 'Umbrella War' of 1942 has been seen by many commentators as a decisive step in the liberation of the Khmer people from French rule. Similarly, a few weeks before National Independence Day on 2 September 1945, the Vietnam Buddhist Association journal, Đuốc Tuệ (Torch of Knowledge), which had previously confined itself to purely religious topics, called for support of the 'people's government' and reported the formation of a National Salvation Association of Buddhist Monks and Nuns which, among other things, would dedicate itself to the elimination of 'superstition' and establish 'suicide units' for the defence of the country (Marr 1995, 507). Finally, anti-American feeling during the Korean War seems to have encouraged some Chinese monks to enlist, while their lay counterparts financed the construction of an aeroplane called 'Chinese Buddhist' to fight the US 'demons' (Welch 1972, 278–9).

Probably the most widely known act of protest associated with Buddhism in modern times was the self-immolation of the Vietnamese monk Thích Quảng Đú'c in Saigon on 11 June 1963. This deed has virtually no precedent in the Buddhist tradition[28] and one cannot be entirely certain of the motivation of the monk concerned. Although not directly connected with the independence struggle, it does relate to one of the legacies of the French colonial presence. Buddhist monks had been banned from displaying religious banners during the Buddha's birthday celebrations in Hué on 8 May 1963. In fact there was already a government ordinance prohibiting the carrying of such objects in force but President Ngo Dinh Diem's brother, the archbishop of Hué, had celebrated his episcopal jubliee a few days before and large crowds of Catholics carried banners with impunity. Buddhists were already incensed at Diem's pro-Catholic and autocratic policies and this was the final straw. Ten thousand Buddhists clashed with the police and around eight persons were killed. After Thich Quang Duc's high profile death, three more monks and a nun also immolated themselves in Saigon and an anti-government demonstration was held at the Xa Loi pagoda on 18 August.[29] Diem was assassinated in a US-backed coup on 1 November, but his attitude towards Buddhism is far from clear. During his presidency, the Republic of Vietnam government made 9 million piastres [c.$1,600,000] available for the building of pagodas and he himself is said to have made a major donation towards the reconstruction of the Xa Loi pagoda (Gheddo 1970, 176). However, this was rather cast into the shade at the time by his powerful sister-in-law, Mme. Nhu, who aroused indignation across the world by her contemptuous references to bonzes barbecueing themselves with American gasoline.

BUDDHISM AND COMMUNISM

In Mongolia, towards the fag-end of Manchu overlordship, the eighth Jetsundamba Qutuγtu issued a number of prophetic works with a decidedly anti-Chinese flavour, despite the fact that he had been born of Chinese parents himself.[30] One of the works defends the violent behaviour of a group of monastic colleagues who became involved in anti-Chinese agitation in Urga in the latter part of the nineteenth century (Sárközi 1992, 97, 100–11). He also conferred the title 'Duke of Mongolia' on the rebel leader, Togtog Taiji in 1911. During the brief period of Mongol autonomy (1911–24) a number of high ranking lamas served in the cabinet and only the Jetsundamba Qutuγtu possessed the authority to pull the dissipated segments of the country together. As such, he led the country through the revolution of 1921 until his death in 1924 (Zhukovskaya 1991, 248). Interestingly, the Mongolian People's Republic, the second communist state in the world, was only declared some days after he died. A search for his incarnation (*qubilgan*) was first impeded and then forbidden by the 7th Party Congress in 1928 (Moses 1977, 179–80).

Despite a rapid rise in anti-clericalism in the 1920s, just under 10 per cent of the membership of the Mongolian People's Revolutionary Party [MPRP] were lamas in the early communist period. The separation of Church and State was first codified in the Constitution of 1924, the Jetsundamba's domains having been appropriated the year before,[31] and by 1933 local courts were empowered to adjudicate in monastic disputes, depriving the *saṅgha* of its last vestige of autonomy (Moses 1977, 232). Mongolian communists were also able to exploit the Tibeto-Mongolian legend-cycles of Gesar and messianic/millenial expectations connected with the return of a king of Shambala from the north by relating them to the Russian origins of Leninism (Sarkisyanz 1958). This was particularly easy as the missions of the Buriat lama Ngawang Dorjieff had already familiarized Tibetans and Mongolians with the idea that salvation from present miseries would come in the from of the Russian tsar. In 1927, before his own 'liquidation' in the Stalinist purges, Dorjieff had addressed the All-Union

Congress of Buddhists of the Soviet Republics with the message that capitalism and the primacy of property are afflictions of the illusion of a permanent self which Buddhism denies. Following the first democratic elections in July 1990, the *soyonbo* – an ancient Buddhist symbol – has been adopted as the emblem of Mongolian independence and now appears on the national flag (Zhukovskaya 1991, 251).

The 1954 Chinese Constitution states: 'Every citizen of the People's Republic of China (PRC) shall have freedom of religious belief.' However, this should be understood in the context of current Marxist thinking on religion. The starting point is that the majority should be free not to believe. Freedom of belief, then, is a minority right and minorities are not expected to interfere in the rights of the majority. In the PRC, the term 'religion' is interpreted in the strict sense of ritual, doctrine and belief. As such, its prophetic role is most definitely ruled out (Yu 1987, 373) and anything of this sort comes under the legal heading of 'counter-religious activity'.[32] The law of the PRC, then, makes a hard and fast distinction between religion on the one hand and politics on the other. This is particularly troublesome for some minorities, particularly the Tibetans, whose customs and traditions do not reflect this way of thinking.

Nevertheless, long-standing traditions rooted in Asian culture, such as Buddhism[33] and Daoism, have been slightly more favourably treated than religions related to foreign imperialism, such as Christianity. Indeed, the pan-Asian character of Buddhism has occasionally been promoted by the government as part of wider foreign policy considerations. In order to keep Buddhism under strict central control, the Chinese Buddhist Association 'Zhongguo Fojiao Xiehui' was founded in 1953 through the agency of the Bureau of Religious Affairs to 'assist the government in its policy of religious freedom, to promote Buddhist culture and education, and to restore and promote China's relations with other Asian Buddhist nations'.

The position of all religions dramatically deteriorated during the Cultural Revolution (1966–76) and we hear of Red Guards binding Buddha images with ropes, denouncing them on platforms and sentencing them to be shot by firing squad (Welch 1969, 133). Exactly the same kinds of reports came out of Cambodia during the Khmer Rouge period (1975–9). In fact, the 1970s seems to have been particularly difficult for most Buddhists under communist governance. During a Vietnamese crackdown on all religions, in which Buddhists seem to have suffered the most, many monks died through ill-treatment in 're-education' camps and twelve monks and nuns immolated themselves, in November 1975, in protest (Boyle and Sheen 1997, 252–5). In response a Vietnam Buddhist Church was created by the government in 1981, mainly to counteract the increasingly anti-government line adopted by leaders of the earlier Unified Buddhist Church of Vietnam (UBCV), who were harassed, arrested and had their monastic and related properties dismantled or confiscated.[34]

The religious situation in China has eased a good deal since the Cultural Revolution, with some evidence to suggest that, in the countryside in particular, monasteries are beginning to flourish, admittedly from an appallingly low level, once more. The Party's policy on religion has also undergone significant evolution over the years and today there is a recognition that 'some mistakes' have been committed, particularly during the 1966–76 period (Boyle and Sheen 1997, 180). Regrettably, some commentators[35] have noticed the emergence of a new, harder line in very recent times.

CONCLUSION

Much early Buddhist thinking on political matters may be regarded as a special variant on the ancient Indian conception of kingship in which the power of the ruler is restricted by the application of Buddhist ethical teachings. Such restrictions, at least in theory, place the monastic order outside the jurisdiction of secular power. In practice, however, they have led to an 'ambiguous symbiosis' between throne and altar and this relationship can be observed, in its various forms, in many of the historical states of Buddhist Asia. In this context the example of Asoka Maurya, while deviating in some ways from strict canonical orthodoxy, became normative and many actual 'Buddhist polities', particularly in South and Southeast Asia, were modelled on this basis. The same applies, to a somewhat lesser extent, in China and other regions of Central and East Asia, where vigorous and deep-rooted indigenous traditions prevented full 'indianization' of the culture as a consequence of the arrival of Buddhism. Nevertheless, it would be wrong to conclude that kingship is the only form of governance authorized by the textual tradition and Buddhists in many regions of Asia have been able to flourish without a kingly protector. Indeed, the Buddha's own utterances also seem to give support to the idea of republican or socialist systems of political organization, although it is only in fairly recent times, for instance in the Burmese experiments with Buddhist socialism of the 1960s, or in the thought of the Thai monk Buddhadāsa Bhikkhu, that these matters have been properly thought through.

In the modern period, many classical Buddhist polities have collapsed, or have at the very least been significantly eroded, through contact with foreign powers, both Asian and from further afield. It is difficult to point to any part of the contemporary Buddhist world that has not been massively transformed by at least one aspect of modernity, be it colonialism, industrialization, telecommunications, consumerism, ultra-individualism, or totalitarianism of the left or right. In this radically new situation Buddhists have been forced to adapt, or risk the possibility of substantial decline. There is plenty of evidence, as the essays in this collection jointly testify, of significant Buddhist involvement in anti-colonial movements of protest, particularly since the Second World War. Similarly, new or revamped Buddhist organizations with a strongly nationalist, reformist, social-activist, therapeutic or reactionary-fundamentalist character are much in evidence throughout the twentieth century. In some countries the modification and re-presentation of religio-political concerns has been easier to achieve than in others. In this light, let us end by casting our thoughts in the direction of China, Tibet, Vietnam, North Korea and Burma, where, even today, men and women attempt to practise the *Buddhadharma* under heavily repressive clouds.

NOTES

1. On the canonical evidence for the Buddha's association with various kings, see Bareau (1993).
2. Buswell (1992, 197) tells an intriguing story of a modern Korean Son monk who burned off three fingers of his right hand (a well-documented and authentic, if rather rare, ascetic practice) rendering him unable to fire a rifle and therefore ineligible for conscription into military service.
3. See Vaidya, P.L. (ed.) *Divyāvadāna* Darbhanga: Mithila Institute, 1959, 351.11. Elsewhere kings are classed alongside dangers such as thieves, fire, beasts of prey, etc.
4. *Saddharmapuṇḍarīka* (H. Kern and Bunyiu Nanjio, eds); Osnabrück: Biblio Verlag, 1970, 180.
5. *Catuhśataka* (Hari Prasad Shasti, ed.) 91–2, in *Memoirs of the Asiatic Society of Bengal*, III/8 (1914). This is the sort of argument advanced by Bhīṣma, in defence of his poor conduct, in the *Mahābhārata*.
6. Chinese tradition, for instance, holds that Harsha, king of Kanauj (606–47), bowed before and kissed the feet of Xuanzang, the famous Chinese pilgrim, in an act of obeisance. See Ch'en, Kenneth, *The Chinese Transformation of Buddhism*, Princeton, NJ: Princeton University Press, 1973, 65.
7. For this important distinction see Jayawickrama, N.A. (trans.), *The Inception of Discipline, and the Vinayanidāna; being a translation and edition of the Bāhiranidāna of Buddhaghosa's Samantapās ādikā*, London: Luzac, 1962, 8.
8. The powers of the eighteenth-century Burman ruler Alaungmīntayā were popularly ascribed to his store of merit, particularly that earned through ascetic practices in previous existences (Wolters 1982, 103).
9. We do find the occasional historical record of kings renouncing the throne, at least temporarily, to take up monastic life. For example, the first Thai to have done this seems to have been Lö Thai (1298–1347), king of Sukhothai. Temporary ordination before taking up the throne is a far more common procedure, particularly in Theravāda lands. However, the fact that the king has previously been a monk does not always affect his future conduct. Thus Dhātusena, king of Sri Lanka (460–78CE), immediately killed a rival claimant to the throne on his return to lay life.
10. See M. iii. 65, which mentions the impossibility of a woman becoming a *cakkavatti*, and the *Kaṇḍina Jātaka* (J.i.153–6), which castigates men who allow themselves to fall under the dominion of a woman ruler. The reasons a woman may not become a *cakkavatti* are given at AA. i. 254.
11. See Chang, Garma C.C. (ed.), *A Treasury of Mahāyāna Sutras: Selections from the Mahāratnakūta Sūtra*, University Park and London: Pennsylvania State University Press, 1983, 456–7. Similar positions are outlined in the *Mahāparinirvāna* and *Gandavyūha Sūtras*: see Williams, Paul, *Mahāyāna Buddhism: The Doctrinal Foundations*, London and New York: Routledge, 1989, 161.
12. A good example is the the the purification of the Sinhalese *saṅgha* under Parakkamabāhu

I (1153–86). For further discussion of this important topic see Ratnapala, Nandsena, *The Katikāvatas: Laws of the Buddhist Order of Ceylon from the 12th Century to the 18th Century*, Munich, Fotodducke Mikropie 1971.

13. Emmerick, R.E. (trans.) *The Sutra of Golden Light: Being a Translation of the Suvarṇabhā-sottamasūtra*, London: Luzac, 1970, 57.

14. For further information on this important but neglected topic see Jardine, J., *Notes on Buddhist Law*, Rangoon: Government Press, 1882. Also Forchhammer, Emanuel *The Jardine Prize: An Essay on the Sources and Development of Burmese Law from the Era of the First Introduction of the Indian Law to the Time of the British Occupation of Pegu*, Rangoon: Government Press, 1885.

15. Taksin did eventually fall from grace because many of his subjects regarded him as insane (Somboon 1993, 118–9).

16. *Shamen bujing wangzhe lun* [T. 52.29c–82b], translated into English by Hurvitz (1957).

17. T. 8.245 [Kumārajīva's translation; Jap. *Bussetsu ninnō hannya haramitsu kyō (The Benevolent Kings' Sutra)*]. This text is particularly interesting in that its fifth chapter, 'Section on the Protection of the State', was periodically recited when foreigners, such as the Tibetans in 765, threatened the integrity of China. It was recited for similar purposes in Japan (Bellah 1957, 67, 87).

18. The *Nittō guhō junrei gyōki*, a travel account of the Japanese monk Ennin (794–864), based in Ch'ang-an in the years leading up to and following the suppression of 845, is particularly important in this regard.

19. The text is part of Koremune Naomoto's *Ryō no shuge* (Kuroita Katsumi, ed.), Tokyo: Yoshikawakobukan, 1966.

20. Subjects of Sa-skya seem to have been quite able to distinguish between the religious and political aspects of their hereditary leader (*khri chen*; lit: great throne) When he was regarded as a religious personage the proper attitude was conceived of as 'reverence based on faith' while as a government figure his actions were viewed with 'a respect for authority in the strict sense that, after a careful evaluation of the official's ability, the subject accepts the official as one qualified to take care of him' (Cassinelli and Ekvall 1969, 72).

21. In due course Sa-skya leaders were obliged to spend long periods at the emperor's court in order to qualify for the title of Di shi. This inevitably compromised them a good deal.

22. The title 'Dalai Lama' is actually an abbreviation of the Mongolian *bilig-ün dalai lama* (ocean of wisdom teacher). bSod-nams posthumously conferred the title on his two predecessors and is therefore classed as the third Dalai Lama.

23. The sixteenth-century Mongolian *White History (Tsagaan Tuuh)* classes Chinggis, Qubilai and Altan as *cakravartins*, and Mongolian histories dating from this time trace their geneaology from Mahāsammata (Riasanovsky 1965, 92f).

24. The present Tibetan government in exile regards the Ambans as ambassadors appointed to look after Manchu interests, and with no power to interfere with or veto government decisions.

25. Rule by incarnation is not uncommon in Tibet. Indeed the Dalai Lama was not the first lama to be chosen in this manner. Over the centuries the religious establishment (*bla-brang*) of some reincarnate lamas have become very substantial indeed. As such, they act as important political power bases often outside the control of the central authorities in Lhasa.

26. The phenomenon is also attested in China at about the same period. Thus we hear of

the monk Xue Huai-yi being appointed as an army general in the Tang period (Ch'en 1973, 220). For further being on *sōhei* see Renondeau (1957).

27. See Soyen (1974, 201–2). Shaku Sōen refused Tolstoy's invitation to sign a peace appeal, declaring that, since he was a loyal subject of the Emperor, this was unthinkable. This attitude was shared by his important lay disciple D.T. Suzuki.

28. Chapter 23 of the *Lotus Sūtra* tells the story of the self-immolation (*ātmaparityāga*) of Bhaiṣyaguru *bodhisattva* as an offering to the '*dharma* of the *Tathāgatas*'. However, there is no sense of protest in the act.

29. For a full account of the Buddhist Crisis see FitzGerald (1972, 128–37, 276–91).

30. Manchu policy prevented the accession of a native Mongol to the post of Jet-sundamba Qutuɣtu.

31. According to the 1918 census, about 45 per cent of the male Mongolian population were monks and by 1924 the Buddhist order controlled 20 per cent of all the livestock in the country (Moses 1977, 155) – a staggering proportion.

32. The situation is not much different in the 1982 Constitution (Article 36) although there is some evidence that the local authorities, particularly in country districts, turn a blind eye to religious activities that are not strictly regulated and hence, by definition, 'unpatriotic' (Boyle and Sheen 1997, 181).

33. There are *c*.100 million religious believers in contemporary China, of whom Buddhists make up the largest grouping. Mahayanists in South and Southeast China and Tibet dominate, although there are Theravāda groupings in south-west Yunnan, particularly among the Dai, Pulang, Penglung, Achang and Va minorities (Boyle and Sheen 1997, 177).

34. Nowadays virtually the whole of the UBCV leadership is under arrest and monks experience great difficulties in obtaining their all-important residency permit. The government in Hanoi is particularly unyielding in its dispute with the UBCV over the funeral and succession of the Patriarch and many arrests have resulted.

35. See Schwartz's essay on Tibet in this volume.

Note the following abbreviations are used

Cv.	*Cūlavaṃsa*
D.	*Dīgha nikāya*
J.	*Jātaka*
M.	*Majjhima nikāya*
Mhv.	*Mahāvaṃsa*
T.	*Taishō Issaikyō Kankōkai*
Thag.	*Theragāthā*
Vin.	*Theravāda Vinaya*

BIBLIOGRAPHY

Bareau, André (1993) 'Le Bouddha et les rois', *Bulletin de l'École Française d'Extrême-Orient* 80(1), 15–39.

Barrett, T.H. (1996) 'The Fate of Buddhist Political Thought in China: The Rajah Dons a Disguise', in Skorupski, Tadeusz (ed.) *The Buddhist Forum Volume IV: Seminar Papers 1994–1996*. London: School of Oriental and African Studies 1–7.

Bawden, Charles R. (1961) *The Jetsundamba Khutukhtus of Urga: Text, Translation and Notes*. Wiesbaden: Otto Harrassowitz (Asiatische Forschungen, Band 9).

Bechert, Heinz (1966) *Buddhismus, Staat und Gesellschaft in den Ländern des Theravāda Buddhismus* Vol. 1. Frankfurt and Berlin: Alfred Metzner.

Bellah, Robert N. (1957) *Tokugawa Religion: The Values of Pre-Industrial Japan*. New York: Free Press.

Bode, Mabel Haynes (1909) *The Pali Literature of Burma*. London: Royal Asiatic Society of Great Britain and Ireland.

Boyle, Kevin and Juliet Sheen (eds.) (1997) *Freedom of Religion and Belief: A World Report*. London and New York: Routledge.

Buswell, Robert E. (1992) *The Zen Monastic Experience: Buddhist Practice in Contemporary Korea*. Princeton, NJ: Princeton University Press.

Cassinelli, C.W. and Ekvall Robert B. (1969) *A Tibetan Principality: The Political System of Sa sKya*. Ithaca, NY: Cornell University Press.

Ch'en, Kenneth (1973) *The Chinese Transformation of Buddhism*. Princeton, NJ: Princeton University Press.

Collins, Steven (1993) 'Discourse on What is Primary (Aggañña-Sutta)', *Journal of Indian Philosophy* 21(4), 301–93.

Collins, Steven (1996) 'The Lion's Roar on the Wheel-Turning King: A Response to Andrew Huxley's "The Buddha and the Social Contract"' *Journal of Indian Philosophy* 24, 421–46.

Collins, Steven and Andrew Huxley (1996) 'The Post Canonical Adventures of Mahā-sammata', *Journal of Indian Philosophy* 24(6), 623–48.

Demièville, Paul (1973) 'Le Bouddhisme et la Guerre', in *Choix d'Études Bouddhiques (1929–1970)*. Leiden: E.J.Brill.

Eisenstadt, S.N. (1993) 'Religion and the Civilizational Dimensions of Politics', in Arjomand, Said Amir (ed.) *The Political Dimensions of Religion*. Albany: New Jersey: State University of New York Press, 13–41.

Emmerick, R.E. (1967) *Tibetan Texts Concerning Khotan*. New York: Oxford University Press.

FitzGerald, Frances (1972) *Fire in the Lake: The Vietnamese and the Americans in Vietnam*. Boston and Toronto: Little, Brown and Co.

French, Rebecca Redwood (1995) *The Golden Yoke: The Legal Cosmology of Buddhist Tibet*. Ithaca and London: Cornell University Press.

Gheddo, Piero (1970) *The Cross and the Bo-Tree: Catholics and Buddhists in Vietnam*. New York: Sheed & Ward.

Ghosal, U.N. (1959) *A History of Indian Political Ideas: The Ancient Period and the Period of Transition to the Middle Ages*. Bombay: Oxford University Press.

Gokhale, Balkrishna Govind (1969) 'The Early Buddhist View of the State', *Journal of the American Oriental Society* 89, 731–8.

Goldstein, Melvyn C. (1989) *A History of Modern Tibet, 1913–1951: The Demise of the Lamaist State*. Berkeley, CA: University of California Press.

Gunawardana, R.A.L.H. (1979) *Robe and Plough: Monasticism and Economic Interest in Early Medieval Sri Lanka*. Tucson, Ariz.: University of Arizona Press.

Hall, H. Fielding (1908), *The Soul of a People*. London: Macmillan.

Hurvitz, Leon (1957) '"Render unto Caesar" in Early Chinese Buddhism', *Sino-Indian Studies* 5(3/4), 80–114.

Huxley, Andrew (1996) 'The Vinaya: Legal System or Performance-Enhancing Drug?', in Skorupski, Tadeusz (ed.) *The Buddhist Forum Volume IV: Seminar Papers 1994–1996*.

London: School of Oriental and African Studies, 141–63.

Jaini, P.S. (ed.) (1986) *Lokaneyyappakaranam*. London: Pali Text Society.

Karmay, Samten G. (1980) 'The Ordinance of IHa Bla-ma Ye-shes-'od', in Aris, Michael and Aung San Suu Kyi, (eds.) *Tibetan Studies in Honour of Hugh Richardson*. Warminster: Aris & Phillips, 150–62.

Lamotte, Étienne (1988) *History of Indian Buddhism: From the Origins to the Śaka Era* (trans. Sara Webb-Boin). Louvain-la-Neuve: Institut Orientaliste.

Lingat, Robert (1950) 'Evolution of the Conception of Law in Burma and Siam', *Journal of the Siam Society* 38, 9–31.

Lingat, Robert (1958) 'La double crise de l'église bouddhique au Siam (1767–1851)', *Cahiers d'Histoire Mondiale* 4, 402–10.

Lingat, Robert (1989) *Royautés bouddhiques, Aśoka et la fonction royale à Ceylan*, deux études éditées par G. Fussman et É. Meyer. Paris: EHESS.

Loewenthal, Rudolf (1955) *The Mongol Chronicles of the Seventeenth Century*. Wiesbaden: Otto Harrassowitz.

McMullin, Neil (1984) *Buddhism and the State in Sixteenth-Century Japan*. Princeton, NJ: Princeton University Press.

Malalagoda, Kitsiri (1973) 'The Buddhist-Christian Confrontation in Ceylon, 1800–1880', *Social Compass* 20(2), 171–99.

Malalagoda, Kitsiri (1976) *Buddhism in Sinhalese Society 1750–1900*. Berkeley, CA: University of California Press.

Marr, David G. (1995) *Vietnam 1945: The Quest for Power*. Berkeley, CA: University of California Press.

Moses, W.L. (1977) *The Political Role of Mongol Buddhism*. Bloomington, Ind: Indiana University Asian Studies Research Institute.

Naquin, Susan (1976) *Millenarian Rebellion in China: The Eight Trigrams Uprising of 1813*. New Haven and London: Yale University Press.

Nattier, Jan (1988) 'The Meanings of the Maitreya Myth: A Typological Analysis', in Sponberg, Alan and Helen Hardacre (eds) *Maitreya, the Future Buddha*. Cambridge: Cambridge University Press, 23–47.

Nivat, Prince Dhani (1947) 'The Old Siamese Conception of the Monarchy', *Journal of the Siam Society* 36, 91–106.

Panikkar, Raimundo (1983) 'Religion or Politics: The Western Dilemma', in Merkl, Peter H. and Ninian Smart (eds) *Religion and Politics in the Modern World*. New York and London: New York University Press, 44–60.

Rahul, Ram (1969) *The Government and Politics of Tibet*. Delhi: Vikas.

Renondeau, G. (1957) 'Histoire des moines guerriers du Japon', *Mélanges publiées par l'Institut des Hautes Études Chinoises*, Tome I, Paris, 159–346.

Reynolds, Frank (1972) 'The Two Wheels of Dhamma: A Study of Early Buddhism', in Smith, Bardwell L. (ed.) *The Two Wheels of Dhamma: Essays on the Theravada Tradition in India and Ceylon*. Chambersburg, PA: American Academy of Religions, 6–30.

Riasanovsky, Valentin A. (1965) *Fundamental Principles of Mongol Law*. Bloomington, Ind: Indiana University Publications [Uralic and Altaic Series Vol. 43].

Ruegg, David Seyfort (1995) 'Matériaux pour l'histoire des fonctions de l'officiant-précepteur donataire et du roi donateur et leur relation dite *yon mchod/ mchod yon*', in *Ordre spirituel et ordre temporel dans la pensée bouddhique de l'Inde et du Tibet: Quatre Conférences au Collège de France par David Seyfort Ruegg*. Paris: Collège de France, 15–92.

Sarkisyanz, Emanuel (1958) 'Communism and Lamaist Utopianism in Central Asia', *Review of Politics* 20(4), 623–33.

Sárközi, Alice (1992) *Political Prophecies in Mongolia in the 17th to 20th Centuries*. Weisbaden: Otto Harrassowitz.

Silber, Ilana Friedrich (1995) *Virtuosity, Charisma, and Social Order: A Comparative Sociological Study of Monasticism in Theravada Buddhism and Medieval Catholicism*. Cambridge: Cambridge University Press.

Snellgrove, David L. (1987) *Indo-Tibetan Buddhism: Indian Buddhists and Their Tibetan Successors*. London: Serindia.

Somboon, Suksamran (1993) 'Buddhism, Political Authority, and Legitimacy in Thailand and Cambodia', in Ling, Trevor (ed.) *Buddhist Trends in Southeast Asia*. Singapore: Institute of Southeast Asian Studies.

Soyen, Shaku (1974) *Zen for Americans*. La Salle: Open Court.

Spellman, John W. (1964) *Political Theory of Ancient India: A Study of Kingship from the Earliest Times to circa A.D. 300*. Oxford: Clarendon Press.

Tambiah, Stanley J. (1976) *World Conqueror and World Renouncer: A Study of Buddhism and Polity in Thailand against a Historical Background*. Cambridge: Cambridge University Press.

Welch, Holmes (1969) 'Buddhism Since the Cultural Revolution', *China Quarterly* 40.

Welch, Holmes (1972) *Buddhism Under Mao*. Cambridge, MA: Harvard University Press.

Wolters, O.W. (1982) *History, Culture, and Religion in Southeast Asian Perspectives*. Singapore: Institute of Southeast Asian Studies.

Yampolsky, Philip B.(ed.) (1990) *Selected Writings of Nichiren*. New York: Columbia University Press.

Yu, David (1987) 'Religion and Politics in Asian Communist Nations', in Fu, C. Wei-hsun and G.E. Spiegler (eds.) *Movements and Issues in World Religions: A Sourcebook and Analysis of Developments Since 1945*. New York and Westport, CT: Greenwood Press, 371–92.

Zhukovskaya, N.L. (1991) 'Buddhism in the History of Mongols and Buryats: Political and Cultural Aspects', in Seaman, G. and D. Marks (ed.) *Rulers from the Steppe: State Formation on the Eurasian Periphery*. Los Angeles, University of Southern California, 242–54 [Ethnographics Monograph Series Vol. 2].

2
THE LEGACY OF TRADITION AND AUTHORITY: BUDDHISM AND THE NATION IN MYANMAR

BRUCE MATTHEWS

INTRODUCTION

The twentieth century has been a time of great restlessness and change for those people whose cultures and political systems have been closely associated with Theravāda Buddhism. It could be argued that Burma, one of the largest of the Theravāda countries, has proportionately experienced far greater challenges and strains in this century than neighbouring Thailand and even Sri Lanka.[1] The vicissitudes of the twentieth century have seen to that. The century began with a disharmonious colonial experience and the virtual destruction of the economic and political infrastructure of Burma in World War Two. The second half of the century tells a dismal political story, mostly associated with military rule, isolationism and repression of political and human rights. All these features have had a serious effect on Buddhism. Since 1962, a Dark Age has descended upon Burma. However, when there has been protest against the suffocating political conditions so long endured, Buddhism – its clergy, its lay devotees, its very symbolism as the acme of Burmese culture and even national identity – has often had a role to play. As the millennium arrives, Buddhism is one of the key elements that might be counted on to enable Burma to achieve a democratic polity and renewed sense of destiny. It is an active participant, however obliquely, in a great struggle for power in Burma between the military and the supporters of democracy. The State Law and Order Restoration Council (SLORC), now known as the State Peace and Development Council or SPDC – a rogue government which refuses to give up after losing the 1990 election to Daw Aung San Suu Kyi's National League for Democracy – has its clerical allies and makes its own pretence of being the protector of the faith, to be sure. But despite an outwardly sturdy appearance, backed as it is by an enormous army, this government is in peril. It is the final contention of this chapter that political freedom and decency will come to Burma, and that Buddhist values and leadership will yet help shape the future of this nation.

This chapter examines the way in which Buddhism has interpenetrated political life in Burma during the twentieth century. Structurally, it aims to review certain key historical moments, personalities and issues that, taken together, make up the extraordinary saga of a religion and culture forced to adapt to political circumstances far beyond its previous experience. By way of method, I propose first to trace out some of the critical events of the colonial era, a period of intense accommodation for Buddhism, particularly for its monastic order (*sangha*). It was also a time when Buddhism met and struggled with modernization, however defined.[2] Second, the chapter reviews the brief fourteen-year period of democratic government, which ended abruptly on 2 March 1962. This was an especially turbulent time for the Buddhist faith as it was suddenly swept into the ideological ferment that precipitated General Ne Win's military coup and the long night of authoritarian rule. Third, I examine the impact of this crisis on Buddhism as it seeks an appropriate voice in a time when no criticism, however constructive, is permitted. There are some who argue that these present conditions are not all that different from what they were in the pre-colonial Burmese polity, and that the Burmese are quite comfortable with strong-arm rule.[3] The events of the last four decades, however, reveal several times when Buddhism has shown an independence of spirit and participated in the political aspirations of the masses. I conclude by reflecting on the present, which finds a *sangha*, in part compromised by the military but in general as restless as any other segment of society, wishing to see fruitful change and political freedom as the longed-for goal.

THE COLONIAL ERA

By 1900, British rule was firmly in place in Burma. The last of three nineteenth-century Anglo-Burman wars associated with the annexation of Burma had ended fifteen years before. There followed a period of 'pacification', as Britain imposed its sense of law and order on a culture that had its own understanding of what these notions might mean.[4] Further, for purposes of administration, Burma was made a province of India (a humiliation that provoked considerable protest – even Ceylon had its own governor and colonial status). What the British encountered was a Buddhist religion that more than anything else defined what it meant to be Burmese.[5] Nor was the religion confined only to the majority Burmese. Many of the ethnic minorities were Buddhist as well. Thus at the turn of the century, as D.E. Smith (1965, 231) has observed, 'Buddhism offered a set of primary values capable of bridging all social, cultural and ethnic differences'.[6]

It is worth noting a few other features concerning Buddhism at the dawn of the colonial era. First, although it may strike one as a somewhat romantic perspective, Emmanual Sarkizyanz gives food for thought when he writes that 'Burma was perhaps the happiest country in the world before the British went there ... no aristocracy, priesthood, state church, army, poverty, castes, nobles, great landowners, bankers' (1965, 123). This egalitarian and charitable society is also attested by Harold Fielding Hall, a British official at the turn of the century who wrote sympathetically of the dilemmas faced by Burmese society as it saw its cohesion threatened and slowly pulled apart.[7] Buddhism was the common factor that held this society together, providing it with a world-view, a cosmology (based on a traditional Indian model) and even a sense of identity as a people and a nation.[8] Second, the soteriology (*dhamma*) offered by the faith was no different from what would be found elsewhere in the Theravāda world, with an emphasis on self-effort and on merit-making (*kutho*). The latter has traditionally been seen as the key to attaining better karma (*kan*) and ultimately salvation (*nibban* or *neban*), and is the central incentive in religious life for Burmese Buddhism. Merit-making is associated with such activities as caring for the clergy (*dāna* or *hsoon*) and participating in the construction of religious buildings.[9] But as elsewhere in the Theravāda world, so too in Burma there has long been an apotropaic form of Buddhism associated with magical protection, amulets and *nat* worship. This may not be exactly what cultural anthropologists call the Little Tradition, because it has its own literature, which is probably as old as the Pāli Canon itself. It has easily coexisted with the *dhamma* for a thousand years.[10] *Nat* veneration in particular is something peculiarly Burman and has seldom been seriously challenged or criticized by even the most orthodox clergy.[11]

A third feature associated with Buddhism in the colonial era concerns the *sangha* itself, the highly visible symbol of religion and culture and one of the Three Great Refuges. The Burmese *sangha* was not a monolithic institution, having experienced fragmentation into about ten sects, branches or 'fraternities' (*gaings*), some as recently evolved as the mid-nineteenth century (these small so-called 'Mindon sects' are identified with the rule of this great monarch, 1853–78).[12] However, these divisions were not seriously divisive for the religion as a whole, and were largely spurred on by puritanical revivals (*paramat*, or 'highest good') of one kind or another. By the twentieth century, only three or four of these sects had much prominence – the Thudhamma (nearly 90 per cent of the *sangha*), the strict Shwei-jin at 5 per cent, and the even stricter (in terms of adherence to the rules of monastic life, and asceticism) but even smaller Hngettwin and Dwara, known for their anti-ritualism. (These percentages have not changed over the last century.[13]) Although the *sangha* professed to have no formal interest or involvement in the polity, it had in fact been closely linked with political life in Burma for centuries. A long tradition of kingly rule based on the Asokan ideal was ritually legitimized by the holy order. In return, royal protection for the *sangha* was provided, including periodic 'purifications' aimed at rooting out heresy and troublesome monks. A particularly crucial aspect of this arrangement was the appointment of the head of all the sects of the *sangha*, the *thathanabaing* or Primate. This was the most visible link between Buddhist 'church' (*sasana*) and state, an example of what Trevor Ling (1979, 133) calls 'royal' Buddhism, which one finds everywhere in the Theravāda world.[14]

There had been a tradition of a *thathanabaing* in Burma since 1368. The last one to be appointed by the royal court was the Taungdaw Sayadaw. He died in 1895, and, because the court had been abolished by the British in 1886, the question of his appointed successor became an extremely vexing political as well as religious issue. Although the *sangha* nominated their candidate, the tradition of royal assent and protection was so ingrained that the *sangha* seemed completely bewildered when the British refused to uphold the old tradition.

Colonial religious policy was in fact one of neutrality. It was not hostile to Buddhism and made no deliberate attempt to disrupt the practice of the religion but, at the same time, the Crown declined to take on any traditional role of protector. It refused to appoint, or for eight years even endorse, a new *thathanabaing*. This provoked a great crisis, partly because after the rebellion of 1886 (in which monks openly participated) the *sangha* had agreed to recognize British rule in the expectation of some reciprocal benefits, now seen to be not forthcoming.[15] Finally, in 1903 the lieutenant governor, Sir Hugh Barnes, reluctantly agreed to recognize (but not appoint) the Taunggwin Sayadaw as *thathanabaing*, but only in Upper Burma.[16] This was the high colonial period of *divide et impera*, when British attitudes towards the non-Christian religions of their subjugated peoples anywhere were not particularly sympathetic.[17] Christian missionary enthusiasm and activism had seen to that. Besides, there was a concern that a well-organized and disciplined *sangha* under a strong central leader might become politicized and dangerous for colonial rule. When the Taunggwin Sayadaw died in 1938, the office lapsed for half a century. Ironically for the British, it was not a *thathanabaing* who would be troublesome, but the independent, radicalized monks in the 1920s and, '30s like U Ottama, U Wisara and the one-time *pongyi* Saya San.

A fourth feature that marked Buddhist involvement in the early colonial period was its unpreparedness to come to grips with ideological and intellectual issues associated with modernization and foreign cultural presence. Aung San Suu Kyi focuses on this when she notes that although Buddhism rang 'the first alarm bells', it did not have an effective strategy to help Burmese culture adapt to the gathering onslaught of new political, social, economic and technological ideas (1991, 103). This is in part because Burmese Buddhism did not seem able to accommodate itself to the sudden changes colonialism introduced. In India, by way of interesting contrast, and despite the rigidity of caste and pollution customs, many Hindu thinkers had accepted new scientific theories and supported the cultural reforms proposed by the Ārya and Brahmo Samāj. Further, the Hindu intelligentsia generally accepted the English language. This in turn allowed Hindu culture to defend itself better against British cultural hegemony. In Burma, on the other hand, a crepuscular Buddhist metaphysics and social theory had become static, not open to much debate or speculation. Unable to reinterpret its cosmological and mythological world-view for a new age, Buddhism was limited in its scope and strategy and essentially devoid of a meaningful prospect for the contingent future.[18] Finally, with one or two exceptions (e.g. Thakin Kudaw Hmain), Burma did not share India's rich legacy of an educated clerisy (e.g. Rabrindanath Tagore, Rammohan Roy), or a vigorous sector of society well-informed about other cultures and the geopolitical realities of the time.[19]

Thus, despite the fact that an active Western presence in the form of Christian mission work had commenced in coastal Burma as early as the 1820s, when British rule was suddenly extended to upper Burma in the late nineteenth century, the heartland of Buddhism and Burmese culture had little time to adjust. Classical Buddhist rationalist philosophy and village-level pantheism were both uncongenial to Western science as well, thereby delaying acceptance of technology and modernization. Additionally, as Sarkisyanz has pointed out, an anachronistic 'Burma-centrism', supported by an entirely mythological cosmology, had given the Burmese a 'disproportionate overestimation of their own power in a world of Victorian imperialism'. The influence of Protestant Christianity inspired some attempts to separate the *dhamma* from the more frankly folk aspects of the Burmese Buddhist tradition, but, when Burma lost its 'cosmic prototype' under the British, Burmese society and culture were 'thoroughly shaken under the impact of Copernican modernity' (1965, 99, 107).

Notwithstanding the confusions provoked by colonialism, a few organizations were formed along religio-cultural and nationalist lines to defend Burmese culture and political identity (*wuthanu athin*, literally 'heritage preservation groups'). Foremost was the Young Men's Buddhist Association of 1906, described in current YMBA literature as 'the first organized body to strengthen the political consciousness of Myanmar's young men. It gave birth to Myanmar politics and became the nucleus of national independence' (YMBA, 1994, 1).[20] Because the 'promotion of Buddhist doctrine' along with 'national language' and 'national spirit' were central policy objectives, the YMBA was also the first religio-cultural organization to co-operate with politicized monks.[21]

For some time, religion was the only unifying factor available in the face of colonialism, the only way Burmese nationalism could become self-conscious. The Buddhist renaissance aroused by the colonial experience produced several different sorts of Burmese responses. Silvertein identifies two of these as particularly self-evident (1996, 216). On the one hand, there was the response of the Anglicized Western-educated urban élite, who experimented with the ideologies of Europe ('communism, fascism, nationalism, democracy and others'). As elsewhere in the Theravāda world at this time, so too in Burma there was a strong interest in Marxism.[22] However, by the mid-1930s, Burmese nationalists prevailed and, in due course, formulated their position in the Dobama Asiayon ('We Burmans Association'). With the political goal of preserving and encouraging Burmese Buddhist culture, this organization represented the nationalist ambitions of a largely young intellectual class (Silverstein 1996, 217). Its membership took the title *thakin* ('master'), an address that had up to now been customarily used when addressing British officials.

On the other hand, there were nationalist groups associated with the traditionalist masses. Politically active monks were frequent participants, especially after Burma was excluded from India's constitutional reforms in 1917. (Burma had a partially elected legislative council by 1923, but political maturity was very slow to appear.) Among the first clerical activists was U Ottama, who became a major political figure in 1921 after a sojourn in India, where he had been much impressed with the anti-colonial strategy of the Indian National Congress and the emerging Gandhian practice of *satyagraha* (non-violent confrontation). He linked Buddhism with freedom from colonial rule, even claiming that the ultimate liberation in *nibbāna* was to be reached by means of the independence struggle. There were several other prominent politicized monks active during this period (e.g. U Wissera), most of them preaching often seditious and inflammatory messages, some with preposterous claims of venal British intentions to exterminate Buddhism.[23] In fact, the colonial policy of ignoring Buddhism as much as possible had seriously curtailed the ability of the British to deal with maverick monks or with the well-organized monasteries where large congregations lived immune from outside interference. With no *thathanabaing*, the *sangha* was not accountable to any central authority. Colonial policy had long decreed that pagodas and monasteries were not to be entered, nor their activities monitored, by state authorities. These religious shrines and buildings became especially important as the only places where nationalists could safely assemble and organize their strategies.[24]

Coincidentally, as conditions in everyday village life became harder, Buddhist millenarian expectations also became heightened. Expressed chiefly in the image of the *set kya min* or 'Restorer of the Golden Age' (sometimes called Bo Min Gaung), this chiliastic reaction anticipated the imminent arrival of a future Buddha and the restoration of the perfect society.[25] The *set kya min* is prophetically attested to in the Pāli Canon (D. iii. 59), but the notion had become intimately intertwined with Burmese folklore. The result was the bizarre appeal of Saya San, a one-time monk who took on the identity of Bo Min Gaung in December 1938. He struck a powerful, albeit romantic and adventurous, image at a time when rural antipathy towards colonial indifference was high. There was serious resentment over the matter of massive Indian immigration and the opening up of vast tracts of land for exploitation.[26] Further, although in 1937 Burma was at last administratively separated from India, there was widespread suspicion about long-term British policy with regard to independence. Cady notes that Saya San's claim to be the 'Thupannaka Galon Raja' (a mythological fabulous bird-king who would devour the foreigner) was not racially xenophobic but a 'deliberately planned affair based on traditional Burmese politics and religious patterns: the revival of kingship as a way to challenge British rule'.[27] Saya San's uprising spread quickly from his Pegu Yoma jungle capital, mostly in the economically depressed Irrawaddy delta region (upper Burma was not much affected). It was never a rebellion on the scale of, say, 1886. Although a number of monks joined as organizers, the important religious characteristics of the rebellion were more associated with *nat* invocation, amulets, protective tatoos and magical incantations. The cadres were both poorly armed and utterly unprepared for combat with trained British, Karen and Indian battalions. Nonetheless it took two years and twelve thousand troops to quell the rebellion. Saya San was duly hanged in 1937. The whole incident pointed up the naïvety of rural Burma, armed with magical animism as it confronted rifles. But Saya San's spiritual and political influence endured, stimulating and inspiring other expressions of nationalism. The uprising also indicated that, as World War Two approached, colonial authority at the village level was rapidly deteriorating.

The war began in earnest in Burma with the retreat of the British army from the Sittang River in February 1942. The subsequent Japanese occupation essentially brought the colonial era to an end. Many Burmese patriots saw the war as 'retribution' for British defiance of 'moral and historical law' and a chance to 'give Buddhism back to the Burmese and greatness back to Buddhism' (Sarkisyanz 1965, 177). The Japanese appealed to the Burmese *sangha* as fellow Buddhists to co-operate in their Greater East Asia Co-Prosperity Scheme. Some maintain that the monastic order was largely indifferent to Japanese imperialist ambitions, although a few monks actively collaborated, to be sure (Mendelson, 1973, 239). During the war years, Dr Ba Maw succeeded in getting partial 'independence' for Burma, styling himself *adipadi* ('great leader' and, by extension, protector of Buddhism). He also accepted a Japanese-imposed constitution in 1943, similar to the 1885 Meiji constitution, where the Minister of War was always a serving military officer. As Taylor perceptively acknowledges, 'this was the constitutional basis for the position in the cabinet of General Aung San as the head of the Burma National Army (BNA) and the beginning of a pattern of political equality between the head of state and the head of the army' (1987, 225). It was Bogyoke ('major general') Aung San and his nationalist united front, the Anti-Fascist People's Freedom League [AFPFL], that took Burma to the verge of independence. He was, alas, assassinated at the age of 32 on 19 July 1947, along with six members of his Executive Council.[28] U Nu, the only senior cabinet official left, became Prime Minister at Independence on 4 January 1948.

Aung San is the greatest nationalist hero in modern Burmese history. His frank and honest overture to the British gained their confidence at a critical hour.[29] More importantly, he deftly and honourably dealt with Burma's large ethnic minority population at the famous Panglong Conference of February 1947.[30] During his brief but highly influential presence on Burma's otherwise chaotic scene, Buddhism was politically quiescent. An essentially pragmatic leader, Aung San made no particular appeal to the *sangha*, nor did it make political demands on him. Buddhist activism had merely gone silent. But when U Nu became premier and Burma achieved full independence, Buddhist issues once again quickly worked their way into the centre of Burmese political life.

By way of focus, up to this point four key features pertinent to the political role of Buddhism in colonial twentieth-century Burma can be identified. First, unlike Ceylon (where colonial rule began seventy years before it did in Burma and Buddhism was well-prepared to meet the challenges of British cultural and political hegemony) Burma had little time to prepare for its cultural defence in intellectual or in practical terms. Second, although through the General Council of Burmese Associations, lay Buddhists claimed to speak for Buddhism and identify its role in achieving independence, in fact the *sangha* had a much more dramatic and vital role in articulating these aims.[31] Third, the Burmese *sangha* was generally not racist. It had close and friendly contact with the *sangha* among the ethnic minorities. Although there were several serious anti-Indian riots (e.g. in 1934 and 1939), the *sangha* was not in the forefront. The one exception was the Yahanpyo Aphwe (Young Monks Association), which promoted anti-Indian sentiment.[32] In short, the spiritual links between the *sangha* of the various ethnic communities were (and continue to be) stronger than the divisive, communalistic elements. Fourth, despite Saya San's curious but tenuous links with Buddhism, to the majority of educated Burmans his 'quixotic effect' was 'sheer madness, worse than futile' (Cady 1958, 317). Buddhist activists in pre-World War Two Burma in truth rarely engaged in violent anti-government actions.

FROM INDEPENDENCE TO THE MILITARY TAKEOVER: FOURTEEN TROUBLED YEARS

The central Burmese Buddhist figure during this turbulent period was the Prime Minister, U Nu, a *thakin*, one-time close associate of Aung San, and founding member of the Dobama Asiayon. A devout, quiet man (though not without his own political charisma), in his first two years in office U Nu focused entirely on holding the frail Union of Burma together. Confronted as it was by mutinies, ethnic secessionist rebellions in all the border territories, and a robust communist party with strong links to China, it is considered remarkable that Burma did not come apart. By February 1949, little more than Rangoon remained to the Burmese government.[33] Although later in the year Mandalay was recaptured, ethnic armies would roam the countryside and control vast border areas for years to come. Remarkably, however, U Nu wasted no time in demonstrating that one of his chief political aims was the restoration of Buddhism and the *sangha* to their pre-colonial status. Apart from this genuinely pious aim, he perhaps hoped as well to curb the influence of increasingly politicized monks. The *sangha* was not easily restrained and sensed an opportunity to reassert its authority as the legitimating power behind the polity. In part to keep ahead of them, U Nu introduced policies and amended the constitution where necessary to enforce his strategy and show himself to be the Mahathammada or true leader of the Buddha *dhamma*. It would be remiss not to note that U Nu was a thoroughly observant Buddhist, entirely sincere and highminded in his convictions. He was not a cynical politician using Buddhism as an instrument of political domination.[34] Unsurprisingly, U Nu and his ministers blamed colonialism and lax Western morals for the decline of Buddhist piety, though in retrospect it is clear that the then unacknowledged effects of modernization were really what was at stake here.

U Nu's AFPFL based its platform on a number of features, including Asokan Buddhist ideals of society and a socialist welfare state programme remarkably similar to English Fabianism.[35] There being only a small middle class, socialism was not much of an economic or political threat to anyone. U Nu's openly pro-Buddhist agenda was more problematic. It was based first on the establishment of a Buddhist Sasana Council.[36] The aim of the council was frank: to spread the *dhamma* and see to its proper foundation throughout the country. Second, in 1951 U Nu announced that Burma would host the Sixth Great Buddhist Council, to be held at Mandalay on the occasion of the 1954 Jayanti or 2500th anniversary of the Buddha's *parinibbāna* ('passing away'). This was an opportunity for Burma to take spiritual leadership in the Theravāda world, as King Mindon had last done in 1871 at the Fifth Council. The Council would further link Buddhism with the state, reintroducing the partial control over the *saṅgha* that the royal court used to have. Some even identified U Nu as the ideal Buddhist ruler expected to make himself manifest at this time. U Nu's strong attachment to Buddhism and honourable attempt to harness it for state purposes was clearly acceptable to the majority of Burmans. He even elevated *nat* worship to near state-religion status (D.E. Smith 1965, 176). Yet even though Buddhist enthusiasm had reached a high pitch by the late 1950s, clearly there was significant opposition to U Nu's religious policies. Some criticized the prospect of Buddhism becoming the state religion and of ostentatious state-funded religious functions.[37] Others felt that U Nu had failed to go far enough in putting forward the fusion of Buddhism and national identity. Apart from opposition by the religious minorities (Christians comprise 5 per cent and Muslims 3 per cent of the population), there was resistance on three other fronts. Although most monks supported U Nu (notably the Presiding Monks Association or Kyaungtaik Sayadaw Aphwe), others were concerned that equal privileges would in due course be extended to other faiths.[38] The Young Monks Association (Yahanpyo Aphwe), numbering over 30,000, actively agitated for stronger legislation against anything perceived to represent a threat to Buddhism. They tried to act as a kind of cultural guardian of purity, setting standards of dress (anti-Western) and stringent rules for society. (Ironically, they even found an ally in the armed forces, although this was to be short-lived.) On the other hand, a break away faction, the Younger Monks Association (Yahan: nge Aphwe), with roots in a social service group that had been active in the 1920s (Sangha Parahita Aphwegyok), appeared to be more progressive and knowledgeable about the need to concentrate political effort on economic and social matters. Alongside other critics, they questioned whether U Nu's agenda was the right one when so many other issues, economic and communal, were in urgent need of attention (Spiro 1982, 387).

A second sector concerned about the politicization of religion was a major wing of the governing party, the AFPFL. In 1958, U Ba Swe and U Kyaw Nyein broke off from U Nu's so-called 'Clean' AFPFL to form the 'Stable' AFPFL, carrying with them the support of many of U Nu's opponents. So much political uncertainty was precipitated that U Nu invited the armed forces (*tatmadaw*) to stabilize the situation with a brief, eighteen-month period of military rule. This was an ominous event, giving a muscular officer corps a taste of more or less absolute power. The military would return in 1962, but not before U Nu had one more chance to give Burma the stability and sense of national identity the opposition (however defined) found wanting. In the national elections of 1960, U Nu's Clean AFPFL easily won on a pledge to make Buddhism the state religion. But U Nu went too far. Cattle slaughter was abolished, a Buddhist lunar calendar introduced, death sentences commuted and a conciliatory approach to the communists enjoined, all gestures of a 'Buddhist' government thoroughly resented by the final sector that resisted U Nu's religious zeal, the armed forces. During its tenure in government from 1958 to 1960, the army had tried to use Buddhism as part of its war of words against communism. But it also took pains to rein in the *sangha*, and even infuriated it by registering monks in the same way that civilians were registered.[39] Although General Ne Win returned political power without demur in 1960, he continued to see U Nu's policies as giving encouragement to *sangha* activism and also as promoting irrational superstitious religious practices and beliefs (ironically something Ne Win was himself to take up vigorously in his later years). U Nu's flirtation with federalism and the possibility (however remote) of ethnic secessionism was the final justification invoked for the military coup of 1962. Further, because the army had modest representation from most ethnic groups in its ranks, there were claims that it was 'an authentic expression of the discipline and unity of Burmese nationalism in the Aung San tradition'.[40]

BUDDHISM AND THE SECULARIZATION OF THE POLITY IN THE NE WIN ERA, 1962–1988

The Revolutionary Council that deposed U Nu and his new Union Party on 2 March 1962 justified its action as being the only way to prevent Burma from fragmenting. U Nu's decade-long struggle to revive a Buddhist sense of nationalism appeared completely to monopolize state energy and initiative. But his overture to the minorities, designed to allay their concerns about further 'Burmanization', was all the army needed to step in and introduce dictatorial rule under General Ne Win.[41] There was no protest in defence of democracy, possibly because the political party system had not had sufficient time to really take root in the countryside.[42] Some argue that a return to authoritarian rule was made easier because this had been what the political culture was used to for most of its history.[43] Others aver that Burmese *nat* worship helped reinforce a dependency on autocratic rule.[44] Remarkably, the only defiance encountered by the military regime came from university students four months after the takeover. The protest was an important one and, although monstrously crushed, it continued to remain a symbol of defiance in student culture.[45]

After fourteen years of being courted and consulted by the government, suddenly the powerful Buddhist *sangha* found itself totally cut off from political life. It was denied any involvement in public affairs or consultation with the military. Monks were just simply surgically removed from the body politic, like diseased flesh. At first, the *sangha* had no idea of what was in store for it. The high pitch of Buddhist enthusiasm generated by U Nu had given the *sangha* an understandable presumptuousness as it relished its role as co-architect of a future Burma. Now those ambitions were completely frustrated. All vestiges of state support for Buddhism were eliminated at once, including the Sasana Council and Buddhist sabbath (lunar) holidays.[46]

The story of how Buddhism both struggled with the military regime and learned how to accommodate itself to this new political reality is a complicated one. In retrospect, several defining moments can be identified. First, unable to find any political party interested in being associated with his Revolutionary Council, Ne Win established his own – the Burma Socialist Programme Party (BSSP, sometimes called Lanzin, although technically this is the youth wing of the party). In 1964, all other parties were outlawed. Within a few months, the BSPP produced an ideological charter, the *System of Correlation of Man and His Environment: The Philosophy of the Burma Socialist Programme Party*. This was based at least in part on a Buddhist interpretation of reality (with an overlay of Marxist-Leninist thought). Written by a former Buddhist monk (U Chit Hlaing), it used some Pāli terms but, because its aim was to 'keep religion out of political life', there is no reference to such key notions as *saṃsāra, karma* or the renunciant life of the monk (Smith 1965, 291). The BSPP manifesto received virtually no support from the Buddhist clergy.[47] It was a time when the military government was determining just how fast it dare proceed in marginalizing the *saṅgha* and religious life in general. Only a few Buddhist spokesmen dared openly challenge this new status quo.[48]

A second feature of Buddhist–state relationships during the Ne Win *khit* is marked by the regime's efforts to control the *saṅgha* through monastic conventions or councils. Both the infrastructure of the *saṅgha* and its ideological and political identity were targets for government interference.[49] This resulted in three 'reform' councils (1965, 1980, 1985). *Saṅgha* (or *sāsana*) reform was nothing new, of course. In pre-colonial Burma, it was expected that monarchs would make periodic efforts to curb monastic excesses of one kind or another, and to conduct the necessary ritual 'purification' of the *saṅgha*. Thus when Ne Win ordered the 1965 All-Sangha All-Sect Convention at Hmawbi, he did so as the head of state and as 'propagator of the faith' (Wiant 1981, 63).[50] Two thousand monks were obliged to attend. They largely disregarded an order to register their members. Not unexpectedly, many were also resentful of efforts by the regime to undermine their autonomy and authority (notably repeals of formerly pro-Buddhist legislation, the Ecclesiastical Courts Act of 1949, the Pali University and Dhammacariya Act of 1950 and the Pali Education Board Act of 1952).[51] A second council took place in 1980. This time, over 1200 hand-picked delegates were invited. The council once again tackled such issues as registration for the *saṅgha*, who would be recognized as a *bhikkhu*, standards for Vinaya examinations and procedures for settling monastic disputes and disciplinary matters. More importantly, it involved a complete overhaul of *saṅgha* hierarchy and a new *saṅgha* constitution (Aung Thwin 1985a, 210; Bechert 1989, 306). This formation of a unified *saṅgha* ignored previous sectarian differences and put in place a hierarchical structure aimed at supervising and directing the monks, undergirded by the power and authority of the state. The constitution enjoined upon the *saṅgha*, with committees of monks at various levels (village, ward, district, state or division), gave it a structural location more or less parallel to the secular administration. At the top was a 300-member Central Working Committee, which in turn elected a 47-member Sangha Maha Nayaka Committee (a kind of executive council) and a president *sayadaw*. The latter, though not called a *thathanabaing*, in effect became the chief prelate. At a ratification of this in May 1985, there were clear indications the regime had at last got the *sangha* under its control.

A third feature of this period is marked by the paradoxical and surprising need of Ne Win and many of his compatriots to find solace and support from Buddhism and *nat* veneration. This reflects the growing ambivalence of the Ne Win *khit* towards religious matters. On the one hand, the early years of military rule had given Buddhism some rough treatment, and the 1974 constitution made a clear distinction between church and state. But in the 1980s, Ne Win appeared to be much more interested in merit-making activities, as the construction of two great pagodas (the Maha Wizaya Zedis) in Mandalay and Rangoon demonstrate.[52] He also engaged in arcane magical and numerological practices, sometimes with an odd outcome, such as the capricious change of bank notes from the usual decimal sequence to strange numbers like forty-five and ninety.

Ne Win formally resigned as president in 1981, yet as chairman of the BSPP he effectively remained in power until his retirement from that office on 23 July 1988. This latter unexpected event raised widespread hope that some return to democracy might be in the wind. But when the military did not relinquish its control, a swift sequence of events unfolded which directly involved the once-quiescent *sangha*. On 8 August 1988 (an auspicious day), Burma experienced one of the greatest outpourings of mass discontent in the history of modern Southeast Asia.[53] Monks were prominent among the millions who surged on to the streets of all cities and towns. The army responded with the usual ferocity, firing into crowds of protestors, killing hundreds. This event was a fateful one: it precipitated a rapid turnover of BSPP leadership. It metamorphosed into the State Law and Order Restoration Council (*Naing Gan Daw Nyein Wut Pyi Pya Aye* or SLORC) on 18 September.[54] Once again a massacre of civilian and monastic protestors took place – yet at the same time SLORC promised national elections for May 1990, clumsily assuming it would receive popular endorsement.

By way of summary, it has been argued that during the Ne Win *khit*, Buddhism was forced to distance itself from political life. At the same time, the military regime laid claim to the traditional role of the pre-colonial state as the agent of the *sangha's* purification and introduced major structural changes in *sangha* hierarchy. This rooted out clerical adversaries from positions of authority and provided an opportunity for the state to infiltrate the monastic order and gain some control over its administration and policies. Second, because there were few public or individual protests between 1962 and 1988, the *sangha* appeared to have retreated from all political activities. Even the Yahanpyo Aphwe (Young Monks Association), traditionally identified as the *sangha's* social and political conscience, went largely underground. Third, the ideology of the military regime's BSPP, despite its paying lip-service to certain Buddhist philosophical notions, essentially ignored the religion. However, it was not long before the BSPP platform proved itself to be inadequate, prompting Taylor to remark that 'twenty years after the collapse of the colonial state, no new basis for the state had been developed' (1987, 290). During this period the regime was unsuccessful in undermining the sheer moral strength and wisdom of the faith, or its unspoken commitment to participate where possible in the fashioning of a democratic Burma. Not all monks supported the notion of democracy, to be sure, but enough – far and away the majority – did so, and their efforts have lent legitimacy to the democratic spirit, a subject to which we now turn.

BUDDHISM AND POLITICS IN CONTEMPORARY BURMA: EVENTS SINCE 1988

The years of SLORC rule have greatly challenged both the spiritual integrity of Buddhism as a whole and the independence of the *sangha* in particular. Although the early military government of the 1960s kept a calculated distance from religious life, with the unification of the *sangha* in 1980 the generals unexpectedly seemed to revive the traditional Buddhist theory that the *sangha* and the state should not be independent. Since then, Buddhism has been increasingly invoked by the government as a unifying national force, and much more effort has been made to bring the faith alongside the state's political aims. SLORC recognizes the power of Buddhism and its potential to be a destabilizing adversary. Indeed, if SLORC has any ideology, it is to balance *ah na se* (secular rule) with *dhamma se* (the authority of the Buddhism) and to keep these two together. As one reviews the ways in which the SLORC regime has reacted to Buddhist political involvement (mostly monks, though lay Buddhists too have invoked the *dhamma* in defence of their perceived human and civil rights), and the ways in which Buddhist activists have reacted to SLORC, certain specific events stand out. First, the extraordinary occurrences immediately following the resignation of Ne Win on 23 July 1988 involved a high level of monastic activity. An estimated 60 per cent of the *sangha* may have participated in the demonstrations and mass assemblies. They did not, however, directly participate in the violence that accompanied these protests, and even prevented some attempted summary executions of regime officials caught by the crowd. Further, as Bertil Lintner observes, monks never served as initiators or 'storm troopers', but only as supporters of the demonstrators.[55] Still, the *sangha* was perceived by many to be the last hope for the democratic opposition, and the appropriate instrument to achieve democratic aims without bloodshed.

Second, although the 8 August 1988 mass demonstration was crushed by the state, on 26 August, Daw Aung San Suu Kyi, the Bogyoke's daughter, gave her momentous speech at Rangoon's central Buddhist shrine, the Shwe Dagon, and set in motion the formation of the National League for Democracy (NLD). Reflecting on Suu Kyi's perception of events at this time, Silverstein writes, 'for her, the 1988 peaceful revolution was an attempt by the people to act as the Buddha had taught and take back the right to rule and reverse the process of decline' (1996, 224). Although Suu Kyi was arrested on 20 July 1989, the *sangha* actively supported the NLD and was again in the forefront of agitation. On 27 May 1990, in remarkably free and fair elections, the NLD won 392 of the 485 seats in the Pyithu Hluttaw (parliament).[56] This evoked a tremendous surge of public enthusiasm. Many even unwisely burned their state identification cards, assuming the oppressive regime would just vanish. The vast majority had complete confidence that this was democracy's moment of triumph. Having flushed out its opponents, however, in a disheartening turnabout the military government imprisoned or killed thousands and chose to ignore the extraordinary election results completely. In the two years that followed, the *sangha* in particular was reprimanded and punished. An attempt was made to implicate activist elements of the *sangha* with the CIA and communists. This provided a justification for raids on hundreds of monasteries, with the accompanying arrest and disappearances of monks and *sayadaws*.[57] The regime even attacked a gathering of 7,000 monks in Mandalay at an anniversary assembly for the democracy movement on 8 August 1990. Shocked by this, the *sangha* struck back on 27 August by the imposition of what was in effect an act of excommunication (*patta ni kauz za na kan*, or 'the power of overturning the begging bowl'). This rare act of symbolic defiance lasted for two months. In a society where merit-making is a central responsibility, not being able to give alms to the *sangha* or receive religious instruction and blessings (*dhamma sambawga*) is a serious matter.[58] Eventually the military government obliged the Mingon Sayadaw, the most respected patriarch, to lift the proscription. But the episode showed the political strength of a united *sangha* and its potential to engage in political struggle. Up to 20,000 monks are thought to have participated in the boycott and a sympathetic public even showed its support by avoiding business with or riding in the same bus as the *tatmadaw*.

Third, the events of 1988–90 precipitated such a severe reaction by the state that thousands of student and monastic activists had to flee to the relative safety of Burma's ethnic enclaves, mostly on the border of Thailand. In 1992, an estimated 6,000 monks lived close to the Thai border. From this emerged important exile organizations, notably the All Burma Students Democratic Front (ABSDF) and the All Burma Young Monks Association (ABYMU). The latter maintained that Buddhist monks have a 'historic duty' to participate in resistance against SLORC.[59] There are as well other Buddhist organizations from Burma associated with specific ethnic communities, now mostly in Thailand, but their long-term residency there is precarious.[60]

Fourth, in March 1997, elements of the Buddhist *sangha* were implicated in a strange incident of anti-Muslim activism. Although subsequent analysis has shown that SLORC cunningly manipulated the sequence of events, the fact is that for the first time since 1990, there were overt protests by the *sangha* aimed at the regime and its unyielding rule.[61] Importantly, the incident involving the *sangha* closely followed a demonstration by peasant farmers in Shwebo, ostensibly in protest over an increase in the amount of rice they had to sell the government at a reduced price. This in turn came on the heels of a crucial university student protest in early December 1996. It was so serious that the regime closed the universities in Rangoon and Mandalay indefinitely. This wide range of protest by students, by farmers and by monks, though not overtly against the SLORC regime, nonetheless in an oblique way reveals seething discontent and near despair on the part of three crucial elements of society.

Apart from these recent specific events, there are three other important features concerning Buddhism and political life in contemporary Burma that warrant review. The first of these is the control still carefully exercised by SPDC over *sangha* structure and Buddhist education. Since 1962, the state has monitored the activities of all religions through the Ministry of Religious Affairs (Tharthanar ye-Wungyi Htar-na) and its administrative directorate (Tharthanar-ye Oo Si Htar-na). A second relatively new directorate added in 1988 is concerned specifically with the propagation and promotion of Buddhism (Tharthanar-ye Htunkar pyantpwar ye Oo Si Htar-na).[62] Importantly, since 1994 there has once again been a *thathanabaing* (in 1997, the Mingyan Sayadaw BaDanTaThaw), but *sangha* authority is really in the hands of an All Nikāyas Council (Gaing Paung Sone), an executive comprised of forty-seven abbots representative of all the sects. The Council is the object of much calculated ritual attention and acknowledgement by the state. Structurally, beneath this is the State Central Committee of the Sangha (three hundred representatives from all of Burma's fourteen states and divisions). Among other perfunctory tasks, it elects the *thathanabaing* and new appointments to the All-Nikāyas Council. A third and final body is the Vinaya court (Baho Wininto), with over 200 ecclesiastical judges. The Ministry of Religious Affairs also administers the Dhammacariya or state Buddhist examinations for monks (the odd token lay person as well), and has some oversight over the two Buddhist universities.[63] A second current feature involving Buddhism and the state is the very public increase of devotion on the part of the military regime towards the *sangha*. This translates into an unseemly, even coarse cultivation of *sangha* support. It is now not uncommon to encounter air-conditioned monastic residences, televisions, videos and automobiles, especially in the big centres like Sagaing where large congregations of monks are found. It can be argued that much of this largesse is directed at older monks who do not feel as uncomfortable with SPDC as their younger colleagues and who do not mind being compromised by gifts, or naïvely appearing on television with military officials. Third and finally, there is presently an upsurge in astrology, numerology, *nat* veneration and magical animism in general, reflective of the old cult of the Wishing Trees (*Padeytha Pin*) so common in earlier Burmese history (Sarkisyanz 1965, 88). There are many ways in which this enigmatic spiritual world is contacted to obtain its energy, grace and blessing. For example, SPDC officials and their families make special journeys to sacred sites, looking for so-called 'Victory Sports' (*aung myay*) where spirit power is thought to be transmitted to them.[64] And why do they seek this? A possible answer might lie in the direction of spiritual healing. SPDC officials accept and see themselves firmly located within the macrocosmology and eschatology of Buddhism. Wrongs must be healed and overcome, including those attached to SLORC/SPDC. Division between the inner self and the community must be treated. Whatever they are, SPDC officials cannot cease to be Buddhist. At the end of the day, they cannot live properly unless they undo the moral, metaphysical and ritual wrongs to which at one time or another they are committed – what Hegel would call the 'unhappy conscience'. All of this can be summed up by the phrase *yadaya chay*, or outwitting fate by prompt action. Nor is this merely confined to state authorities anxious to maintain a grip on power. Some have argued that the current political tension and economic hardship has resulted in a general reliance on the supernatural (Bekker, 1989, 52). The public from time to time also points to omens thought to be cosmic indicators of SLORC/SPDC's venality as well.[65]

To summarize, the SLORC years intensified state control over most religious matters. (SLORC changed its name to the State Peace and Development Council in 1997 but, by including all the ambitious young regional commanders in the policy-making Council, the junta's image of absolute authoritarianisim remains even further entrenched.) Any Buddhist organization that has human or civil rights on its agenda (e.g. the Yahanpyo Aphwe) is forbidden. Further, through a series of state-imposed ecclesiastical Councils, the military has achieved close to full control of the *sangha* hierarchy, structure and education system. Some monks, mostly of an older generation, have gone along with this, yet the majority, professing to be apolitical, support Aung San Suu Kyi and the democracy movement as much now as they did in the dramatic years 1988–90. That brief period provided a glimpse of what they mostly wanted – democratic government and, in the evocative words of Suu Kyi, freedom from fear.

CONCLUSION

Three final observations might be made. First, the twentieth century brought several specific political experiences to Burma – colonialism, Westminster-style parliamentary democracy and military rule. Buddhism has had to adapt to each and, where possible, continue to contribute its moral and spiritual guidance under often indifferent or politically obdurate circumstances. In this matter, the *sangha* has always been the most visible feature of Buddhist life and witness. But whether monk, nun or lay, Burmese Buddhists everywhere, especially those in urban environments, have had many occasions to see their traditional cosmology or world-view confronted or gravely challenged by foreign invasion, modernization and hard-line authoritarian political rule.

Second, the fact that Burma never experienced the intellectual and social renaissance that India arguably did has been identified as a feature that still manifests itself in Burmese Buddhist attitudes. It is true that, because of historical circumstances, Burma did not have the same opportunity as India to adjust itself to modernity, or Buddhism to become somehow a 'modern' religion. Other than during the brief U Nu period (1948–62), there has been little chance for Buddhism in Burma to engage in political, social or economic debate other than on a superficial level. This has perhaps allowed it to be intellectually unchallenged. Apart from some celebrated meditation teachers (e.g. Ledi Sayadaw, We-bu Sayadaw), there have been no prominent social critics or mentors (like Buddhadāsa or Sulak Sivaraksa in neighbouring Thailand). Undoubtedly, however, far-sighted and gifted monks and lay thinkers are there in Burma, waiting for the opportunity so long denied to bring the *dhamma* into a new light.

Third and finally, subdued resistance against colonialism and political authoritarianism involving Buddhist encouragement has been a feature of Burmese life throughout the century. There is no reason to think this spirit diminished. Indeed, there is an essential patience and resolve associated with Burmese Buddhism that lends itself to steadfastness and hope, especially in a time of oppression. As an old Burmese saying so aptly puts it: 'There's no place to go but to religion when you're in trouble' (*pa yar ma ta bar ko kwe yah ma shi*). Faith continues to be strong in a land that has endured so much in the course of just one century.

NOTES

1. Burma's doctrinaire State Law and Order Restoration Council (SLORC) changed the name of the country from Burma to Myanmar in June 1989. The name 'Burma' was a close equivalent of '*Ba-ma*', used by the majority Burmese in everyday language to describe themselves and their country (as, for example, in the 1930 patriotic Dobama Asiayon or 'We Burmans Association'). Myanmar, a traditional name for Burma more often used in literature, is made up of two words: *myan* (strong) and *mar* (hardy). SLORC justifies its use of 'Myanmar' because it reflects the multi-cultural aspect of the country, where minorities may make up as much as 40 per cent of the population. This is regarded as cynical manipulation by most Burmese citizens. The name 'Burma' has been prohibited in any context in Myanmar, and has completely disappeared from public view in that country (unlike, for example, in Sri Lanka, where the name 'Ceylon' survives in many instances and capacities). Enriquez (1933), though it appears dated, is still the best review of Burma's complex ethnic composition. Martin Smith (1991, 27) provides a sound contemporary perspective. The population of Burma in 1995 was estimated at 43.95 million (*Statistical Yearbook*, Government of the Union of Myanmar, Yangon, 1995, 14).
2. There are several pertinent definitions of modernization. The most obvious feature is a scientifically-based modernization identified with European or Western technology and industrialization (Eisenstadt, 1977, 61). Mary Douglas (1982, 6) adds to this the concepts of personal agency, distance from nature and the 'bureaucracy of a mass age' (she disputes the alleged ill effects these have had on traditional societies and cultures). Edward Shils, C.E. Black, R.N. Bellah and others also lead beyond a purely material sense of modernization to see the social, psychological and political ramifications as well (Shils 1981, 1f; Black 1966). For example, Bellah rightly emphasizes that it is not just a matter of technological modernization, but also a 'modernization of the soul' (1965, 196). Latterly, the term 'globalization' has absorbed many of the features contained in the term 'modernization'. So-called 'old globalization' refers to the

Europocentric influences that came to Asia with, for example, the 'three g's' ('gold, gospel and glory'). But although the 'new globalization' bears many hallmarks of the West (including so-called 'junk Westernization'), it is also a very Asian phenomenon. One thing is certain: shortly after World War Two, globalization, modernization and Westernization no longer meant the same thing (Berger 1983, 57). In this chapter, references to modernization will reflect the challenge Burmese society and polity had in coming to grips with recent Western notions.

3. Michael Aung Thwin argues that the Burmese people are more comfortable with rulers who have a military or kingly image, in preference to something borrowed from elsewhere (1985b, 256). He applies this to the 1962 military coup, an event he sees as far more significant than independence in 1948. The coup was 'carried out to resurrect meaningful order in a society that had experienced extreme social and psychological dysfunction – the type of order that neither the colonial system nor the subsequent artificial Parliamentary system had provided'.

4. Aung Thwin notes that the actual period of 'pacification' only lasted from the annexation of Burma to about 1890 (1985b, 246).

5. 'The one single factor which has had the most influence on Burmese culture and civilization is Theravāda Buddhism . . . it has become common to say, 'To be Burmese is to be Buddhist'. Aung San Suu Kyi, in her excellent review of the colonial period (1991, 66, 83).

6. With reference to Buddhism among the minorities, E.R. Leach has written: 'a most important criterion of group identity is that all Shan are Buddhist . . . being Buddhist is symbolically important as a Shan index of sophistication' (1964, 30).

7. H. Fielding Hall's classic text, *The Soul of a People*, London, MacMillan: 1898, was widely circulated among English-speaking Theravāda Buddhists in Ceylon as well as in Burma. He writes (119), 'the inclination to charity is very strong. The Burmans give in charity far more in proportion to their wealth than any other people.'

8. Although the notion of a modern nation, and by extension 'nationalism' is associated in the West only with states that emerged after the Treaty of Westphalia in 1648, it can be argued that in Asia there were important early examples of nations and nationalism. In the case of Sri Lanka, Steven Kemper imaginatively argues that there was a 'full-fledged set of identities' in place centuries before the colonial era that came close to a viable definition of nationalism (1991, 17). Likewise Ernest Gellner, reflecting on traditional Muslim states, writes that nationalism implies a 'culturally homogeneous community, endowed with a state-sustained and endorsed culture' (1984, foreword). These latter sets of conditions apply as well to pre-colonial Burma.

9. The venerable and historic respect for the idea of making good merit is attested to as far back as the earliest of inscriptions found at Pagan, the political and religious centre of tenth- to fourteenth-century Burma. Writing in his introduction to *The Glass Palace Chronicle of the Kings of Burma* (1923, xii), Pe Maung Tin reflects on the Wardak vase associated with Alaungsithu (1113–67): 'the motive of this inscription is the same as that of most of the Pagan inscriptions. The donor desires merit only to share it with others.' Maung Tin then cites Buddhaghosa, the greatest of all Theravāda apostles, who lived in sixth-century Ceylon: 'What then, will there be loss of merit to him who thus shares what he has attained? No. As when from a burning lamp a thousand lamps were lit, it would not be said that the lamp was exhausted; the light, being one with the added lights, becomes increased, thus there is no decrease in our sharing what we have attained; on the contrary there is an increase.'

10. Robert Redfield, 1956, 70, distinguishes between the two polarities in religious life –

the doctrinal, canonical, classical religions of the sages and the literati, and the pursuit of religion at the level of the villager or peasant. In between lies a vast range of religious interpretation and practice.

11. In a recent study of *nat* worship, Yves Rodrigues (1992, 8) writes: 'the Burmese have no god. The Buddha is himself a model of perfection and is only deified by the Mahayana sect. Despite this, they live in a universe populated by mythical and fabulous animals and all kinds of spirits. Among them we find the *nats*.' Originally there were thirty-six *nats* on the 'royal list'. Tradition says Anawrahata, founder of Pagan in 1044, added Thagyamin as the guardian god of Buddhism, the thirty-seventh and last *nat*. There are in addition so-called 'outside' *nats*, spirits not on the 'royal list'. Many *nats* are, then, really Burmanized Hindu deities. (See Spiro 1978, 91; Maung Htin Aung 1959, 83.) Spiro (31) sets down the differences between *nats*, witches, ghosts and demons, arguing that Burmese animism is a completely separate 'religion' from Buddhism, coexisting with the *dhamma* but not embraced by it. Others (Keyes, 1977, 115; Tambiah 1977, 41) claim the opposite, insisting that Buddhism and animism belong to a single religious system. *Nat* worship is still strongly endorsed in Burma. Because they are thought to be irascible and capable of malevolent interference in human affairs, their propitiation is a frequent requirement by even devout Buddhists who might otherwise scorn such superstition. Importantly, *nat* invocation underlies many activities of SPDC officials today in a conspicuous way.

12. The term *gaing* literally means 'group' (Hla Pe 1985, 124, 133), a word that can be used in a political as well as religious sense. Ferguson offers a full explanation when he writes: 'A *gaing*, from the Pāli term *gana* (a chapter of monks) is, sociologically speaking, a group of *taiks* (monasteries) who recognize the somewhat charismatic leadership of a *sayadaw* who is considered the leader. It may at first have practices or beliefs (such as ordination rites, unique textual interpretations) no different from other established sects, but it may develop such differentiating characteristics and become both a self-defined and lay-defined sect, or what is known in Pali as a *nikāya*' (in Mendelson 1973, 86).

13. The best reviews of this topic are in Mendelson (1973, 84), Spiro (1982, 316) and Bechert (1989, 308).

14. Once this relationship was threatened or abolished, Buddhism was in peril of losing one of its major functions, that of legitimating political rule.

15. Cady (1958, 137) notes that the 'sympathetic insurrection which occurred in Lower Burma in 1886–7 developed as a kind of political aggravation of an epidemic of lawlessness dating from 1880'. Sarkisyanz (1965, 102) gives some dreadful details of consequent British oppression. A sporadic guerrilla-style war continued until 1891.

16. The Taunggwin Sayadaw was recognized as 'supreme in all matters relating to the internal administration and control of the Buddhist hierarchy in Upper Burma' (D.E. Smith, 1965, 50).

17. A good example of this was Ceylon. In 1815, the British found it prudent, if not imperative, to accede to the demands that Buddhism be granted state protection. But at home and on the mission front, this initial openness hardened over the years, and by 1853 the Crown withdrew its safeguarding role, provoking a crisis with which the *sangha* was not easily able to cope.

18. 'No concerted effort was made to reassess the past with a view to formulating a viable philosophy for the future. Many Burmese, in the early twentieth century, felt that their patriotic duty required the preservation of old ways without examining them carefully to see if they were fit for the new times' (Aung San Suu Kyi 1991, 119).

19. Sarkisyanz (1965, 130) notes that Kudaw Hmain popularized Burma's historical heritage, writing a secularized panorama of Burmese history in a nationalistic sense. This gave rise to the National School Movement, which, although it did not last very long, nonetheless showed a widening consciousness of Burma's historical traditions among the Burmese intelligentsia.

20. Technically, the founding patriotic organization was the Buddha Sasana Noggaha Association of 1897.

21. Initially, YMBA leadership was Westernized and middle-class. In 1920, it gave founding inspiration to the General Council of Buddhist Associations, which in turn evolved into the General Council of Burmese Associations (GCBA). Buddhist monks, relatively immune from government control, assumed active roles in these bodies, though not without controversy (D.E. Smith 1965, 92).

22. The later Marxist theoretician Thakin Soe, though an ardent critic of Buddhism, used Pāli terms and merged the important Buddhist doctrine of causality, the paṭiccasamuppāda, with dialectical materialism. Taylor notes: 'Soe, the most important left-wing polemicist in colonial Burma, was largely responsible for introducing Marxist-Leninist political concepts through the idiom of Buddhist thought to politically active students before the war' (1987, 238). Sarkisyanz (1965, 174) reflects on the 'Stalinist' leader Thakin Than Tun's celebrated article 'Socialist Ideology and Burmese History' and the search by Burmese Stalinist Marxists for 'continuity with Buddhist political traditions'.

23. Like U Ottama, U Wisera was also jailed by the British in the mid 1930s for his political activism. He became a martyr, however, starving himself to death in prison, protesting the right to wear the saffron robe while in custody. Today he is prominently memorialized by his statue, which stands high over an important Rangoon intersection on the Pyay (Prome) Road.

24. In 1922, the monks established their own General Council of Sangha Sametggi organization, which rejected the more moderate interests of the GCBA and of those who wished to encourage a Western model of political organization in an independent Burma.

25. Sarkisyanz (1965, 148) notes: 'Under British rule, Burma's villages were disrupted, the Burmese local officials disassociated with the populace and the individual released from the restraints of custom and tradition; much of rural Burma became relatively impoverished, while a part of the Buddhist monastic order became demoralized.'

26. The British had encouraged a prodigious immigration of Indians and Chinese to animate their new capitalist economy. Over 1 million Indians were in Burma by the 1930s. In 1931, half of the population of Rangoon was Indian. By 1941, two-thirds of Irrawaddy paddy land was owned by non-agriculturists, mainly Chettiars or Indian money-lenders. This led to landlessness and, in combination with the great depression, widespread impoverishment. Taylor writes: 'The consequences of this migration were not only the creation of the plural society, but also a growing level of tension and conflict between the indigenous population and the migrant labourers. The antagonism between these groups publicly expressed itself in the form of race riots and pogroms, and its political repercussions were still being felt in the 1980s' (1987, 147). Some maintain that the Buddhist 'value system' was perceived by the British as obstructing development (Ling, 1979, 107,111, citing Max Weber's argument that Buddhist values do not find natural expression in a capitalist economy). Sarkisyanz avers that very little of the social justice, humanitarianism or restriction of free enterprise seen in parliamentary Britain overflowed into Burma (1965, 146).

27. 'His effort was associated with a revival of the entire panoply of royal regalia and religious sanctions, Brahman, Buddhist and animist' (Cady 1958, 310). The symbol of the *galon* comes from Hindu mythology, associated with Garuda. Hla Pe (1985, 190) offers a brief review of how and when Indian 'religious cults' entered Burma in the pre-Pagan era.

28. Aung San's assassination was planned and executed at the instigation of U Saw, a former right-wing premier (1940–1). Cady (1958, 421) provides the best account of U Saw's biography, which included internment by the British in Africa during World War Two as a suspected Japanese collaborator. U Saw returned to Burma in early 1946. His motivation to kill Aung San 'was apparently a combination of frustrated ambition, anger and vengeance'. His objective was 'to destroy the existing nationalist government, to blame the crime on the British, and thus to precipitate a general revolution, which his own unscrupulous followers would seek to exploit to their own political advantage'. Graphic accounts of the actual assassination are offered by Bertil Lintner (1989, 40) and Amitav Ghosh (1996, 41). U Saw was convicted and hanged in May 1948.

29. Slim (1986, 516). It should be noted that Churchill's refusal to grant Burma dominion status provoked the all-important Dobama organization to embrace a pro-Soviet strategy. This was a major reason why the British lost Burmese support both during and after the war. Further, despite his self-evident *bona fides*, Aung San was not able to persuade the returning governor of Burma, Sir Reginald Dorman-Smith, to allow his AFPFL control of the Governor's Council after the war. Only with the arrival of the last governor, Major General Hubert Rance, in July 1946, was Aung San appointed Deputy Chairman of a new Executive Council and permitted to negotiate fully the independence of Burma with the government of Clement Attlee.

30. Silverstein (1989, 83) notes that prior to the Panglong Conference, the Shan, Kachin and other ethnic leaders had never met each other or the future leaders of the country such as Aung San and U Nu. The celebrated Article 10 of the Panglong agreement granted the ethnic states the right to secede after ten years, but the Burmese military resisted such compromise. Along with 'primordial ethno-nationalist claims to superiority and conquest', the military showed it had no sympathy for the aspirations of the non-Burmese.

31. Spiro (1982, 134) writes: 'the *pongyi* was the most important instrument by which the independence movement reached the rural masses and gained the adherence of the bulk of the people'.

32. The All Burma Young *Pongyis* Association (Yahanpyo Aphwe), with its headquarters in Mandalay, was formed as a result of anti-Muslim sentiments in 1938. Cady (1958, 393) notes that the group 'included monks who were not amenable to ecclesiastical discipline and who customarily used the yellow robe as a cloak for their political activities so as to escape police interference'. A slightly older Rangoon-based group, the Thathana Mamaka Young Monks Association was similarly engaged in these activities. D.E. Smith (1965, 189) writes that the basic aim of the Yahanpyo Aphwe's founder, U Zawtika, was 'to unify the monkhood in the face of the threat which the Indian Muslims were thought to pose to the Buddhist religion and Burmese culture'.

33. Taylor notes that the only army units to remain loyal to the AFPFL government were Ne Win's 4th Burma Rifles and Karen, Kachin and Chin units which the British had left in place at independence. Some of the ethnic battalions splintered off in due course. At this point, faced with so much disorder as well as by a weak government,

the army 'developed the ability to function independently of civilian control' (1987, 236).

34. Von Der Mehden (1986, 146) points to U Nu's Pyidawtha (Happy Land) Project of 1952, an eight-year plan with the wildly ambitious aim of prosperity for every citizen. The plan aimed to utilize (but not, I think, to manipulate) Buddhism – notably the concept of merit – in order to obtain support in mass self-help projects of one kind or another.

35. In May 1945, the AFPFL's 'supreme council' was enlarged to include a diverse group of representative political leaders, including the so-called Fabian Group led by U Ba Choe. Cady (1958, 520) writes that in 1945, several trade union organizers from Britain assisted the AFPFL socialists in development of their labour programme. The AFPFL also had sympathetic support from Britain's post-war Labour government.

36. Two key architects of the Sasana Council were U Chan Htoon, the Attorney General (later imprisoned for seven years by the military regime) and the respected lay Buddhist spokesman U Win, Minister of Home and Religious Affairs.

37. Buddhism was made the state religion in 1961. There was an almost immediate constitutional amendment guaranteeing freedom of religion, and claims that faith would have nothing to do with the status of Burmese citizenship. Nonetheless, for different reasons, this initiative was ill-interpreted by Buddhist activists (who saw it as a sell-out) and the largely Christian and Muslim ethnic minorities (the reaction of these minority religions took some time to resolve itself). At first, the Anglican and Roman Catholic bishops of Rangoon appeared 'satisfied with the assurances' of continued privileges (for example, church schools). The Muslims were guarded but not openly critical, and the Hindus (theologically and culturally the closest to the Buddhists) completely supportive (D.E. Smith 1958, 246).

38. The All Burma Presiding Monks Association was formed in 1955. Made up largely of older, scholarly monks 'who were recognized heads of monasteries', they greatly assisted U Nu in his plans for the Sixth Great Buddhist Council and for editing the Buddhist scriptures. Writing in 1965 (190), D.E. Smith observed: 'The Presiding Monks Association has been less politically-oriented, has evidenced a deep concern over the problem of monastic in discipline, and has been generally disposed to cooperate with governmental efforts to remedy defects in the *saṅgha.*'

39. Registration of monks became a serious political issue following 1962. The Revolutionary Council's order that all Buddhist monks be part of a national register was rejected by many because it was perceived to be contrary to the tradition of monks as *sannyas*, or 'ones who have left home for homelessness'. Monks attending the 1965 All-Sangha All-Sect Convention at Hmawbi were more conciliatory and allowed for a limited registration, but even this provoked large scale monastic opposition. Registration of monks was not completed until 1981. John Wiant (1981, 63) and Martin Smith (1991, 205) give good accounts. Possibly because of their traditionally accepted superior karmic status, the monks have resented carrying the same kind of identity card as a lay person. In the 1990s, monks carried a multi-page identification that has the appearance of a type of 'passport'.

40. D.E. Smith (1965, 252). Aung Thwin (1985b, 256), writes that the Burmese army 'attempted to do what the British had done, but within a Burmese context and with Burmese priorities: it tried to create a truly secular and modern government within the parameters of a Buddhist society'.

41. The years of Ne Win's direct supervision of government are known as the Ne Win *khit* or Ma Sa La Khit (Ma for Myanmar, Sa for Socialist and La for Lanzin, the name of

Ne Win's political 'party'). Silverstein notes that the although the final years of democratic government in Burma (1960–2) were seen by many as a period of danger and near collapse, there is no evidence of any external threat or internal plot to dismember the country (1980, 98).

42. 'Western educated national leaders had tried to establish links with the countryside through political parties and appointed leaders but they didn't have the stature or ability to unite and transmit a new vision – most used their power only to improve personal wealth and status;' Silverstein (1977, 199).

43. Heinz Bechert indicates how Ne Win identified his political authority and religious policy with that of the old Burmese kings (1967, 34).

44. 'Burmans, through their dread and propitiation of pre-Buddhist Nat spirits, are culturally conditioned in their attitude to physical force as authority'. Sarkisyanz (1965, 236).

45. University students would again show determination in 1974 when they protested against the state's inadequate ceremony marking the funeral of U Thant, former secretary general of the UN.

46. The Revolutionary Council also nationalized schools and hospitals affiliated with Christian denominations and restricted foreign mission work. Taylor maintains, however, that this was not religious discrimination but a result of 'the closing of foreign contacts with indigenous institutions' (1987, 357). At the same time, 'having dissolved the politicized self-governing institutions through which Nu had unsuccessfully tried to control the monkhood, for fifteen years after 1965 the state was unwilling to assault directly the independence of the monkhood'. Wiant (1981, 64) points out that between 1965 and 1974, Ne Win 'apparently turned' to the strict Shwegyin sect 'for guidance' at the Mahagandayou Taik (monastery) in Amarapura.

47. Mya Maung (1991, 99) notes that the 'System of Correlation' (Ar Nya Ma Nya) was really just a reversal of U Nu's vision, which had given priority to spiritual or Buddhist rather than secular or socialist aspects 'in the resurrection of the traditional polity of the Burmese kings'.

48. An important example was the highly respected elderly Mandalay *sayadaw* U Kethaya who launched, as D.E. Smith (1965, 302) writes, a one-man war against Ne Win's policies. Kethaya 'capitalized on the *sangha's* natural political advantages to defy the government', and thoroughly tested the regime by holding illegal mass rallies where he excoriated Ne Win. A long-time leader of the Young Monks Association (despite his venerable age), which had in turn supported the 1958 Ne Win caretaker government, Kethaya (and the YMA) completely switched sides after the 1962 coup.

49. It has always been difficult to ascertain the number of monks in the Burmese *sangha*, partly because of the confusion of names used for the 'different categories of religious practitioners' (Mendelson 1973, 120). The custom of *shinbyu* or ordination to the novitiate for males, most of whom remain in the *sangha* for just a brief period, indicates that many who are in robes are only temporarily engaged in the mendicant life. Estimates of about 130,000 fully ordained monks (usually life-professed *sayadaws* or older monks, and younger monks or *pongyi*) and 190,000 novices (*thamanay* or *samanera*) are considered reliable for the late twentieth century. There are in addition about 20,000 'nuns' (*silashin*, by Theravāda custom, not fully ordained). See Bechert 1967, 26 and 1988, 33; Matthews 1993, 408.

50. Tin Maung (1988, 32) remarks: 'since the introduction of Theravāda Buddhism to Pagan, *Pariyatta Sāsana* (doctrinal teachings of the Buddha preserved in scripture) has enjoyed continuous patronage from the ruling élites of Burma.' Mya Maung

(1991, 4) provides a remarkable review of the way in which tradition and religion are part of the cultural framework by which the military as well as civilian political leaders in post-independence Burma have defined and claimed legitimacy. This sometimes includes an appeal to the old or traditional model of 'absolute despotism' (*padaithayit*, an Old Burmese term probably related to the modern Burmese noun for 'law', *oo pa dai*). From a different but controversial perspective, Lucian Pye (1962, 146) offers a 'psychological' analysis of the relationship between religiosity and power, arguing that 'the fact that Buddhism is a central feature of Burmese life only makes the quest for power more subtle and more indirect'.

51. Cady (1958, 611) gives details of U Nu's 'Buddhist' legislation, acts 'designed to promote religious revival and reform'.

52. Sylvia Fraser-Lu provides a long list of pagodas, temples and former royal palaces that have benefited from SLORC-sponsored 'works of merit' (1997, 4).

53. 'Eight' was considered to be the U Nu regime's most inauspicious number because it marked the termination of the Second Ava dynasty by Shan forces in the Burmese year 888 (1526 CE). 'Eight' is, however, favoured by opposition forces (hence the celebrated 'Four Eights Affair' of 8.8.88 or *Shitlay Loan-A-Yay A-Hkin*). Mya Maung (1991, 221; 1992, 41, 59) shows how the traditional Burmese practice of 'outwitting fate by prompt action' (*yadayah chay*) can be linked with numerology. With Ne Win, and later with SLORC officials, the most powerful number has been nine; hence their use of *koenawin chay*, or rituals that used this numeral. The importance of 'nine' is also seen in the 1987 introduction of banknotes that in one way or another produce the number nine and SLORC's change of the country's name to Myanmar on 18 (1 + 8) June 1989.

54. Sein Lwin (who ordered the shooting of students at the infamous crackdown of July 1962) had replaced Ne Win on 26 July, but was forced to resign as head of state on 19 August. He was succeeded by Maung Maung, a moderate Western-trained lawyer and civilian, who lasted only one month before the pseudo–coup of 18 September-1988 and the end of BSPP rule.

55. Interview, 2 June 1992. Lintner is the Burma correspondent for the *Far Eastern Economic Review*, based in Bangkok. He remains one of the most informed interpreters of Burma's current events and the author of several important books and articles pertaining to Burma's ethnic minority problems.

56. Hla Pe (1985, 123) provides an etymological analysis of *hlut-taw* ('house of representatives') and other Burmese terms for the legislature and branches of government.

57. SLORC report 'Web of conspiracy; complicated stories of treacherous machinations and intrigues of the Burma Communist Party underground and the Democratic Alliance of Burma', set down by Khin Nyunt, Director of Intelligence, December 1990. Bertil Lintner kindly gave me a copy.

58. For a devout or tradition-bound soldier, not to be able to give the clergy alms (*hsoon*) gravely interferes with his ability to make merit (*kutho*) and gain good *karma* (*kan*). Some senior abbots ordered further religious sanctions against the families of the military. Other monks knelt in 'homage' to the Tatmadaw, 'a sacrilegious act to instill fear and shame into the hearts of Buddhist soldiers' (Mya Maung 1992, 184). *Tat* means 'the military', *daw* indicates something big or glorified, hence Tatmadaw refers to a 'respected army'.

59. *Seeds of Peace*, Vol. 8, No. 2, August 1992. The ABYMU, led by the charismatic monk U Khemasara, is part of the Democratic Alliance of Burma. The ABYMU formerly situated its headquarters at Manerplaw, which fell to the military regime in 1995,

along with Kawmoora, the 'capital' of the Karen National Union.

60. For example, in 1997 there were an estimated 1,000 Mon monks from Burma living in Thailand. Because the Mon are also indigenous to west Thailand, some of the Burmese Mon monks find residency in the Thai Mon monasteries. But unless they have the appropriate visa, none is welcomed by the Thai authorities. Much depends on who holds political power in Bangkok. The 1996 government of General Chavalit Yongchaiyudh was disposed to co-operate with SLORC. Chavalit's policy was one of harassment and deportation for exiled Burmese monks. A prominent Mon temple in Bangkok, Wat Prok, is a frequent target. On a raid on 28 January 1997, one hundred Mon monks were arrested and taken to the Burmese border. There, however, they were let loose in a forested area and could make their way back into Burma without detection by SLORC officials. Others hid out for a while and later doubled back into Thailand (interview, near Wat Prok, 27 April 1997). Unfortunately, it is still not safe to mention names, but this and other items of information have come to me in private conversations.

61. There is an interesting but complicated saga associated with this Buddhist protest. Burma is a land of rumours, and facts are often hard to verify, but this incident is backed up by a number of independent sources I spoke to in Burma during March 1997. In October 1996, a secret monks' union (probably related to the Yahanpyo, which had been proscribed) planned for a demonstration on 13 March 1997 to mark an unofficial 'human rights' day to commemorate the lives of sixteen monks who had recently died in custody. In early March, however, just before the planned protest, the senior monk (Pinnyawatha Sayadaw), who oversees the famous Maha Myat Muni Buddha image in Mandalay, discovered a crack in the right shoulder of the statue. Further investigation showed that the *Padamya Myetshin*, the image's legendary interior ruby, along with several kilograms of jewels and gold, had been stolen. Report of the theft prompted a mass meeting of Mandalay monks on the afternoon of 16 March. SLORC officials were implicated because possession of the ruby is said to guarantee victories or power (*hpoan*) to the one who holds it. Trouble spread swiftly, reaching Rangoon on 21 March, just one week before Armed Forces Day, the most important SLORC ritual of the year. It is not possible to corroborate all the details of this event. But it can be shown that the regime immediately took steps to divert the anticipated monastic protest by suddenly magnifying an incident that had actually been dealt with several months before, still simmering just beneath the surface. This involved the molestation of a Buddhist girl by some Muslims in Mandalay. By careful manipulation of this incident, SLORC effectively sidelined the rumour of its involvement with the Maha Muni image. SLORC agents, probably from its auxiliary Union Solidarity Development Association (Kyan Khaing Yea Hnin Hpying Hpyo Yea), masqueraded as monks. All the demonstrators were robed, with heads covered and identity concealed as much as possible. Some were even seen with portable radio transmitters. Unfortunately, some *bona fide* monks were also involved in this maelstrom, vandalizing mosques and desecrating Korans. The rampage slowly burned itself out, with SLORC both blaming the NLD and claiming that the *sangha* itself did this to prevent Burma from being invited into ASEAN, with its powerful member Muslim states. In the end, however, it is possible to conjecture that, although there was *sangha* participation in this sorry event, the underlying cause was *sangha* dissatisfaction with the present state of affairs in Burma.

62. The central responsibility of this directorate is to oversee mission work in tribal areas. It provides essentials for the livelihood of about three hundred monks and seven

hundred Buddhist lay workers in remote areas (Interview, Maung Le, Head of the Directorate, 18 March 1997). It might be mentioned that the Buddhist *sangha* is not particularly well-suited to mission work in areas where merit-making is not customary. Other Directorate responsibilities include relationships with foreign countries where Buddhist matters are concerned, and the award of various Buddhist titles and distinctions, a highly controversial issue in the Theravāda world.

63. The two Buddhist universities (Sasana Takkathe) are open only to monks, who are not permitted to attend secular institutions. In 1997, there were 360 enrolled in Mandalay and 450 in Rangoon. These seminaries were not closed in the March 1997 mass closure of post-secondary universities and institutes. Entrance is restricted to those under thirty and, although a degree takes four years to complete, it is not granted before the graduand serves two years in village ministry. It should, however, be noted that at least 80 per cent of Burma's approximately 300,000 monks and novices are not well educated. Most enter the order at the age of nine or ten with grade 5 education. After that, schooling is desultory and of indifferent quality. For information concerning the origin of Burma's Buddhist universities, see Cady (1958,422) on the 1941 Report of the Pāli University Enquiry Committee, with its aim of reviving scholarship and diminishing 'the growing discord and jealousy prevailing between rival sects'.

64. In early 1997 these 'Victory Spots' were identified with small plots near the Gubyaukgyi and Myazedi temples in Pagan.

65. For example, in 1990 when the Kyauk-daw Gyi Buddha image at the foot of Mandalay Hill became 'swollen' and 'cracked' the credulous believed it to be a sign that the celestial spirits could not bear SLORC's 'desecration' of the Buddhist religion (*The Buddha Sasana and the Burma Military Regime*, ABYMU, 1991, 8). Similarly, in the mid 1990s various Buddha images were reported to have developed breasts, indicative of a coming female ruler (*minlawn*).

BIBLIOGRAPHY

Aung San Suu Kyi (1991) *Freedom from Fear and Other Writings*. New York: Penguin.

Aung Thwin, Michael (1985a) *Pagan: The Origins of Modern Burma*. Honolulu: University of Hawaii Press.

——(1985b) 'The British "Pacification" of Burma: Order Without Meaning', *Journal of Southeast Asian Studies*, September, XVI/(2).

Bechert, Heinz (1967) *Buddhismus, Staat und Gesellschaft in den Ländern des Theravada-Buddhismus*, Band 11. Wiesbaden: Otto Harrassowitz.

——(1988) 'Neue Buddhistische Orthodoxie: Bemerkungen zur Gliederung und zur Reform des Sangha in Birma', *Numen*, 35 (July).

——(1989) 'The Recent Attempt at a Reform of the Buddhist Sangha in Burma and its Implications', *Internationales Asienforum*, 20, 3–4.

Bekker, Sarah (1989) 'Changes and Continuities in Burmese Buddhism', in Silverstein *et al.* (1989).

Bellah, R.N. (1965) *Religion and Progress in Modern Asia*. New York: Free Press.

Berger, Peter (1983) 'Secularity West and East', *This World*, 4.

Black, C.E. (1966) *The Dynamics of Modernization. A Study in Comparative History*. New York: Harper & Row.

Cady, J.F. (1958) *A History of Modern Burma*. Ithaca, NY: Cornell University Press.

Douglas, Mary (1982) 'The Effects of Modernization on Religious Change', *Daedalus*, Winter.

Enriquez, C.M. (1933) *Races of Burma.* Delhi: Government of India Publication.

Eisenstadt, S.N. (1977) 'Sociological Theory and Analysis of the Dynamics of Civilizations and Revolutions', *Daedalus*, Autumn.

Fraser-Lu, Sylvia. (1997) 'A Buddhist Building Boom: Works of Merit Sponsored By the State Law and Order Restoration Council', DeKalb, IL, *Bulletin of the Burma Studies Group*, March.

Gellner, Ernest (1984) *From Nationlism to Revolutionary Islam.* New York: State University Press of New York.

Ghosh, Amitav (1996) 'Burma', *The New Yorker*, 12 August.

Government of the Union of Myanmar, Yangon (1995) *Statistical Yearbook.*

Hla Pe (1985) *Burma: Literature, Historiography, Scholarship, Language, Life and Buddhism.* Singapore: ISEAS.

Kemper, Steven (1991) *The Presence of the Past: Chronicles, Politics and Culture in Sinhala Life.* Ithaca: Cornell University Press.

Keyes, Charles (1977) *The Golden Peninsula: Culture and Adaptation in Mainland Southeast Asia.* NY: Macmillan.

Leach, E.R. (1964) *Political Systems of Highland Burma.* Boston: Beacon Press.

Ling, Trevor (1979) *Buddhism, Imperialism and War.* London: Allen & Unwin.

Lintner, Bertil (1989) *Outrage: Burma's Struggle for Democracy.* Hong Kong: Review Publishing.

Matthews, Bruce (1993) 'Buddhism Under a Military Regime: The Iron Heel in Burma', *Asian Survey*, 33, (4.)

Maung, Mya (1991) *The Burma Road to Poverty.* NY: Praeger.

——(1992) *Totalitarianism in Burma: Prospects for Economic Development.* NY: Paragon.

Maung Htin Aung (1959) *Folk Elements in Burmese Buddhism.* Rangoon: Buddha Sasana Council Press.

Mendelson, M.E. (1973) *Sangha and State in Burma, A Study of Monastic Sectarianism and Leadership*, ed. J.P. Ferguson. Ithaca: Cornell University Press.

Pye, Lucian (1962) *Politics, Personality and Nation Building: Burma's Search for Identity.* New Haven, CT: Yale University Press.

Redfield, Robert (1956) *Peasant Society and Culture.* Chicago: University of Chicago Press.

Rodrigues, Yves (1992) *Nat-Pwe: Burma's Supernatural Sub-Culture.* Gartmore: Paul Strachan, Kiscadale Press.

Sarkisyanz, E. (1965) *Buddhist Backgrounds of the Burmese Revolution.* The Hague: Martinus Nijoff.

Shils, Edward (1981) *Tradition.* Chicago: University of Chicago Press.

Slim, William (1986) *Defeat Unto Victory.* London: Macmillan

Smith, Donald E. (1965) *Religion and Politics in Burma.* Princeton, NJ: Princeton University Press.

Smith, Martin (1991) *Burma: Insurgency and the Politics of Ethnicity.* New Jersey: Zed Books.

Spiro, M.E. (1982) *Buddhism and Society: A Great Tradition and Its Burmese Vicissitudes.* Berkeley CA: University of California.

——(1978) *Burmese Supernaturalism.* Philadelphia, Institute for the Study of Human Issues (first published in 1967).

Silverstein, Josef (1977) *Burma: Military Rule and the Politics of Stagnation.* Ithaca, NY:

Cornell University Press.

——(1980) *Burmese Politics: the Dilemma of National Unity.* New Brunswick, NJ: Rutgers University Press.

——(ed.) (1989) *Independent Burma at Forty Years: Six Assessments.* Ithaca: Cornell University Press.

——(1996) 'The Idea of Freedom in Burma and the Political Thought of Daw Aung San Suu Kyi', *Pacific Affairs.* 69(2).

Steinberg, David (1981) *Burma's Road Towards Development: Growth and Ideology under Military Rule.* Boulder, CO: Westview.

Tambiah, S.J. (1977) *Buddhism and the Spirit Cults in North-East Thailand.* Cambridge: Cambridge University Press.

Taylor, Robert H. (1987) *The State in Burma.* Honolulu: University of Hawaii Press.

The Glass Palace Chronicle of the Kings of Burma (1960), trans. Pe Maung Tin. Rangoon: Burma Research Society.

The Buddha Sasana and the Burma Military Regime (1991) All Burma Young Monks Union, November.

Wiant, John (1981) 'Tradition in the Service of Revolution: The Political Symbolism of Taw-hlan-ye-khit', in *Military Rule in Burma Since 1962*, ed. F.K. Lehman. Singapore: Institute of Southeast Asian Studies.

Tin Maung (1988) 'The Sangha and Sasana in Socialist Burma', *Sojourn.* 31.

Von Der Mehden, Fred (1986) *Religion and Modernization in Southeast Asia.* Syracuse: Syracuse University Press.

'Young Men's Buddhist Association: A Brief Outline of the History of the YMBA', Pazundaung, Yangon, July 1994.

3

BUDDHISM *IN* *EXTREMIS*: THE CASE OF CAMBODIA

IAN HARRIS

Before starting our consideration of Cambodian Buddhism, some points of definition are in order. In Phnom Penh, close proximity to and familiarity with the Court, or more recently with the apparatus of government, has meant that the Buddhist hierarchy has customarily manipulated, or at least been forced to accommodate itself to, prevailing currents of power. In the countryside, on the other hand, and despite an enduring fascination with kingship, power is largely viewed as having occult sources whose manipulations are magical.[1] In other words, the bipolar clerical/shamanic structure observed in Tibet (Samuel 1993) may also hold good for Cambodian Buddhism. This essay, though acknowledging the enormous significance of the second category to most Khmers, will be mainly concerned with the élite urban and clerical part of the equation since this is where explicit politics have their locus.

According to Indic tradition the Kambojas were involved in the Mahābhārata war and subsequently settled in Cambodia, then called Indapata. These may have been the legendary ancestors of the Khmers. Koṇḍañña (fifth century CE), an early king of the country, is said to have been a pious Buddhist although the firm establishment of Buddhism in the country can be dated to the reign of Jayavarman VII (r.1181–1201). At this time Sanskritized 'Mahāyāna' Buddhism coexisted with a variety of Brahmanical beliefs and practices, but a Pāli-based Theravāda spread across the region from the early fourteenth century. Since this time it has been customary to regard Cambodia as a Theravāda country, even though 'Mahāyānist' elements survive down to the present day. An important qualification here is that, in the period between the collapse of the Angkor civilization around 1430 and the beginning of French colonial domination in 1863, Khmer Buddhism, with the exception of Thai connections, was largely isolated from the outside world. It therefore preserved many features not seen in other Theravāda cultures.

From the early seventeenth century Cambodia was subject to the oscillating influences of its two stronger neighbours, Vietnam and Thailand. The royal family, for instance, periodically formed itself into pro-Thai and pro-Vietnamese factions. By and large, the Vietnamese were viewed with more trepidation than the Thai, who at least shared the same Theravāda-based worldview and traditions of orthography. The withdrawal of Vietnam from Cambodia in 1846 (it did not return again until 1979) is marked symbolically by the building by King Duang (r.1848–1860) of seven monasteries with rubble from demolished Vietnamese fortifications near the capital of Udong, and psychologically by an enduring Khmer hostility to all things Vietnamese.

Norodom (r.1860–1904), like Duang before him, had spent time as an acquiescent hostage in Bangkok and was a great supporter of Thai traditions in religion and the arts which were fostered in his new capital of Phnom Penh. Nevertheless, the combined effects of the establishment of the French Protectorate in 1863 and the death of the Thai King Mongkut four years later ensured that Thai influence on Cambodia waned – although it has never completely disappeared – from this point on. Although not a devout Buddhist, Norodom in his will provided funds for the construction of rest houses along the principal roads of the kingdom, perhaps in imitation of the archetypal Buddhist king Asoka, and directed that a golden Buddha image be cast to his own bodily proportions (Osborne 1997, 254). His brother Sisowath (r.1904–27), who came to the throne at the age of 64, seems to have been more religiously observant, and certainly less antagonistic towards the French than his brother. It is difficult to assess the the impact of colonial governance on Cambodian kingship, an important issue since the Theravāda textual tradition regards the king as the linchpin for the entire edifice of organized Buddhism.[2] Some scholars claim that the French actually revived traditional Khmer kingship while others suggest that the actual power of the king decreased, although his symbolic significance increased during this period. Admittedly, the king's power was very narrowly circumscribed during the French Protectorate, but this was probably always the case since rival members of the aristocracy had ensured that he was never an absolute monarch (Thion 1987, 152).

Unlike its neighbour Vietnam which possessed an influential mandarin class, the only sector of Cambodian society with the ability and organizational structure to challenge the powers of the aristocracy was the Buddhist *sangha*. However, the monastic order has been divided into two fraternities since 1864 when Norodom,[3] who had previously been sponsored as a temporary ordinand by the Thai King Mongkut, imported the newly-formed rational reformist, and aristocratic Thommayut (*Dhammayutika Nikāya*) from Thailand through the agency of Preah Saukonn (Pan), a Cambodian monk within Mongkut's spiritual lineage. Norodom had Wat Botum Vaddey constructed adjacent to the new royal palace as the headquarters of the new order, with Maha Pan installed as its *sanghareach* [= *sangharāja*] (Meas-Yang 1978, 38). Subsequently, in 1889 five monks returned from Sri Lanka with Buddha relics and a cutting from the Bodhi Tree as symbols of the implantation of the new order. In fact, the impetus for this development can be traced to Duang's request, shortly before his death, to the Thai king to send a delegation of Dhammayutika monks to his court at Udong. Since this time the Thommayut has enjoyed symbolic prestige, in part because of its close ties with the monarchy but also because of its association with this new concentration of power in Phnom Penh.

Nevertheless, the new order did not enjoy 'unquestioned preeminence' (Keyes 1994, 47) over the older and larger fraternity the Mohanikay (*Mahānikāya*), and when in 1880 Norodom created a national *sangha*,[4] along Thai lines, he appointed the most senior Mohanikay monk, Sanghareach Tieng,[5] to the post of patriarch even though Preah Suakonn was given almost equal footing and, most importantly, the patronage of the royal family. Nevertheless, the Mohanikay has sometimes felt disadvantaged by this arrangement, despite the fact that it enjoys far greater influence in some parts of the country, and rivalry between the two orders has undoubtedly affected the unity of the *sangha* and underlines the distinction between urban élites and the peasantry throughout most of the modern period. Certainly Sisowath was a more vigorous supporter of the reformist order than his brother and seems to have encouraged monastic defections from the Mohanikay to the Thommayut (Osborne 1997, 255). There is also some evidence to suggest that, at the village level, Thommayut lay supporters are wealthier than their Mohanikay fellow-villagers (Ebihara 1968, 381).

It is reliably estimated (Népote and Tranet 1983) that around 2,300 monasteries, including about 400 in the Thai controlled provinces of the north-west, flourished within Cambodia's boundaries at the turn of the century. The vast majority of these were affiliated to the Mohanikay, whose monks were reckoned by the French to exercise a beneficial influence on the populace and towards the Protectorate. Thommayut monks, on the other hand, were regarded as potentially intransigent (Forest 1980, 143). In general, then, the French were more favourably disposed to the traditional 'cosmological' from of Buddhism represented by the Mohanikay than to its 'modernized' Thommayut version, not least because the former was deemed to be deeply rooted in traditional social structures. Unofficial sponsorship of the Mohanikay, then, helped in rendering the country more efficiently administered. This fear of modernity may also have something to do with the generalized romanticism of many French officials in their dealings with Indo-China. To ensure there would be little disturbance from the monastic direction a series of reforms were instituted, notably restrictions on the construction of new monasteries, the introduction of ordination certification, a prohibition on monks learning martial arts and preparing herbal concoctions to gain invulnerability,[6] and improvements to the monastic educational system, ensuring that monks would stay in the country rather than travel to Thailand where it was felt that they would pick up subversive ideas (Forest 1980, 144–7).

There is little to distinguish the two orders in terms of doctrine, yet they disagree over the interpretation of some elements of discipline (*vinaya*), most notably the wearing of robes, the wearing of sandals, the carrying of the begging bowl (*bat*) and the consumption of drinks after midday, and also in their pronunciation of Pāli. The Thommayut believe that their observance of the first three items is more in accord with the Buddha's own practice. Such differences have rarely led to major conflict, though in 1941 King Sihanouk intervened in a dispute over the correct way of wearing the robe by ordering the Committee for the Coordination of Religious Affairs to ban the potentially divisive Thommayut practice of putting the rolled end of the robe over the shoulder (Yang Sam 1987, 18–19). Regulations for the national organization of the *sangha* were formulated in 1943 (in the wake of the so-called 'monks' demonstration' of 1942) and modified in 1948. Both orders have a fully independent *sanghareach* nominated by the Head of State and an elaborate national and provincial hierarchy, the higher reaches of which must traditionally be filled by monks who have spent a minimum of twenty rains-retreats in the order.[7] Both orders also have a tribunal, the *therak sophea* [= *therasabhā*], consisting of monks from the higher echelons of the hierarchy who act as a court of final appeal in matters pertaining to monastic discipline. In extreme cases it is this body that has the authority to defrock a monk and only then turn him over to the secular courts for justice.

Theoretically, and in practice, monks are not eligible to vote or hold political office. Nor may they give evidence in court or witness a legal document.[8] Nevertheless, there is no paucity of evidence of political activity among *saṅgha* members in Cambodia. As early as 1820 a monk named Kai, claiming magical powers and with a vision of a millenial future free of Vietnamese influence, is said to have rebelled against the feeble monarchy of the time and established himself as king at the sacred mountain of Ba Phnom in southeast Cambodia (Chandler 1974). The more serious revolt of 1865–6 against Norodom and his French 'protectors' was incited by Po Kambo, a former monk with a following of some 10,000 including serving monks[9] and various *nak sel* or holy men (Osborne 1978, 238). There seems to have been an element of anti-Catholicism in the revolt, a fact underlined by the beheading of Father Barrea, pastor of Moat Krasas, after Mass on 9 January 1867, who was unable to act on earlier warnings to leave the area (Ponchaud 1990, 80). Probably egged on by the Vietnamese, the rebels rallied significant support in the eastern provinces, particularly around Tay Ninh (Osborne 1997, 187), before being crushed. Although he was actually a Montagnard, Po Kambo claimed to be the grandson of King Ang Chan II (r.1794–1834), a putative royal pedigree being helpful in gaining support in Cambodia at the time. Similarly, we find evidence of monastic involvement in uprisings in 1906, 1909 and in 1916 when a group of Cambodian monks trained in wrestling martial arts, believing that the ingestion of certain herbal medicines would render them invulnerable, cut short their studies in Bangkok to support the claims of Sisowath's exiled son, Prince Yukanthor (Forest 1980, 52, 147, 395). As late as 1925 we hear of an ex-monk, Stung Treng, who gathered a following through the power of a 'golden frog with a human voice' (Chandler 1996, 148).

Peasant protest movements against the tightening colonial grip escalated in the 1920s, many embracing millenial elements derived from Buddhism (Keyes 1994, 48) or the recently founded Cao Dai movement across the border in Cochin China. In 1927 around 30,000 peasants from the eastern provinces of Cambodia travelled across the border to the Cao Dai base at Tay Ninh[10] to pay their respects to the statue of a prince on a white horse who, it was believed, would be reborn imminently to renew the Cambodian nation (Tarling 1992, 239). Various theories about his identity are reported, variously identifying him as the Buddha, Maitreya, a saviour figure of traditional Cambodian mythology, or Prince Yukanthor. In many accounts the identities are conflated. The attraction of Cao Dai to Cambodians was probably related to its self-perception as a form of Indochinese Reformed Buddhism. The announcement of the appearance of a new Khmer king was made at Tay Ninh in June 1928, but by this time it was already too late – the danger, from the perspective of the Cambodian authorities, had already passed (Khy Phanra 1975, 324–5). On 23 May 1927 the Minister of Cults proclaimed that the movement was based on false premises and sought to the exploit the credulity of the untutored. At the end of June in the same year the *sanghareach* of both Buddhist orders ruled that Cao Dai was contrary to the teachings and disciplines of Buddhism and should be rejected. On 26 December 1927 a royal proclamation underlined the movement's heretical nature from the Buddhist perspective, characterizing it as a Vietnamese plot to destabilize the throne, and finally, on 8 February 1928, another royal ordinance declared that involvement in ceremonies contrary to Buddhism and Catholicism [this had been first affirmed in 1863] would be punished. Not surprisingly Cao Daists themselves saw things in a different light and accused the French of interferring in Buddhism, with the Governor-General cast in the role of 'le Pape du Bouddhisme unifié'.[11]

In 1884 King Chulalongkorn had modernized temple schools in Thailand and, by the early twentieth century approximately thirty such schools, in which primary education was dispensed by monks and other teachers 'trained in Bangkok according to modern methods' (Forest 1980, 158–9), flourished in the Thai-controlled Cambodian provinces of the north west. The French were naturally concerned about this since it pointed to both Thai and, more worryingly, British interference in its sphere of influence so, after they had wrested control of the north west from Thailand around 1908, *wat*-based primary education in 'écoles de pagode' was officially encouraged. Students would receive a basic 'franco-cambodian' education and by a royal decree of 1911 (amended the following year) parents not sending boys over the age of eight would be punished. It is not clear that punishment was administered with any vigour but, by 1924, a school inspectorate had been formed and modernization of the system was under way (Delvert 1956, 314; Forest 1980, 159). Nevertheless, there was resistance, particularly amongst monks who seem to have regarded French education as 'a peril for the Buddhist doctrine'.

In 1909 the Mohanikay Sanghareach Tieng founded two modern Pāli high schools, one at Angkor Wat (it only lasted for two years), the other in Phnom Penh. In 1914 the latter was transferred to Wat Preah Keo Morokat (the Silver Pagoda) in the precincts of the Royal Palace before moving to a specially constructed building with a new title, l'École Supérieure de Pāli, which was conferred in 1922. The advantages for the French were obvious. The development of a second tier to the Buddhist educational system reduced the need for monks to travel to Thailand to continue their education. Indeed, a campaign which emphasized the pleasures of being close to one's family and the availability in Cambodia of both indigenous and western medicine in the event of illness (Forest 1980, 146) was launched to convince monks of the advantages of staying in the country. Nevertheless, monastic education had difficulties in rivalling the expanding secular school system as a means for social advancement and by the early 1930s we see a phase of monastic decline accompanied by a deterioration in traditional services associated with monasteries such as basic health care, architectural advice and banking. However, it has been suggested that the reforms of the Protectorate, while they promoted a gulf between secular and religious education, at least ensured that *wat* schools could focus once more on the transmission of Buddhist and Cambodian cultural elements to the population.

The establishment of the Institut Bouddhique in 1930 did much to revive scholarship within the Buddhist tradition. Founded by augmenting the Royal Library of 1925 the Institute, administered by the Ministry of Cults (Meas-Yang 1978, 43) and directed by Suzanne Karpelès, a scholar sympathetic to the fledgling Indochinese independence movement, also sought to 'lessen the influence of Thai Buddhism (and Thai politics) on the Cambodian *sangha* and to substitute more Indo-Chinese loyalties between the Lao *sangha* and their Cambodian counterparts'. (Chandler 1991, 18). This political role was underlined by the fact that monks associated with the Institute were also expected to educate soldiers, particularly the Khmer Krom, in Buddhism in order to keep them in a disciplined frame of mind (Bunchan Mul 1982, 117–18). The Institute was also expected to promote and research into Khmer culture and, as such, produced a Khmer language journal *Kambuja Suriya* [Cambodian Sun] from 1927, which contained articles on folklore and Buddhist texts, and information on the royal family. Perhaps unsurprisingly it became a launching pad for several figures who were to influence the development of Khmer nationalism.

The first overtly political Khmer-language newspaper, *Nagara Vatta*, was founded in 1936 by Pach Chhoen and Sim Var, intellectuals associated with the Institut Bouddhique, who were quickly joined by Son Ngoc Thanh (Chandler 1986, 82f), a Paris-educated magistrate. Aimed at monks and those low-ranking civil servants educated through the monastic school system, rather than the French-educated élite, and with a weekly circulation figure of about 5,000, *Nagara Vatta* championed the cause of moderate Khmer nationalism. Thanh's anti-colonialism placed the newspaper in the vanguard of opposition to a variety of issues, particularly French attempts to romanize the Khmer language and replace the traditional Buddhist lunar system of dating with the Gregorian calendar.

The French attempt to romanize, rationalize and modernize the Khmer writing system consciously followed the Turkish model. However, the system devised by the famous French scholar George Cœdès in the late 1930s led to considerable opposition, particularly from senior monks such as Ven. Hem Chieu,[12] a teacher at l'École Supérieure de Pāli, who saw the reform as an attack on traditional learning and on the status of monastic educators, even though the romanization decree was never intended to be applied to religious texts. Hem Chieu's involvement led to his arrest on 17 July 1942 on charges of plotting a *coup d'état* and translating seditious materials from Thai. He was subsequently imprisoned on Poulo Condore Island (Con Son) where he died in 1943 at the age of 46.

Son Ngoc Thanh used the paper to call for a demonstration (reputed to have been sponsored by the Japanese) to bring about Hem Chieu's release. Part of the anger stirred up by this event was caused by the authorities' insensitivity towards a prominent monk in robes, who was forcibly defrocked after arrest (Bunchan Mul 1982, 119). Traditionally monks may only be arrested after being allowed to ritually disrobe. Around a thousand people were on the march of 20 July, of whom half were umbrella-carrying monks, mainly from Wats Unnalom and Langka in Phnom Penh. The Vietnamese, therefore, coined the term 'The Umbrella War' for the event. After the demonstration *Nagara Vatta* was suppressed by the colonial government. Pach Chhoeun, the editor, was sentenced to death (subsequently commuted to life imprisonment) while Thanh fled to Thailand and then to Tokyo, returning to Cambodia in May 1945. On 20 July 1945 Sihanouk was joined on a platform by Pach Chhoeun and Son Ngoc Thanh in a celebration of the monk's demonstration of 1942 which became the occasion, briefly, for an annual holiday.

With the reimposition of French rule in October 1945, and the granting of permission to found political parties in early 1946, surviving members of the *Nagara Vatta* group founded the Democratic Party (Krom Pracheathipodei), led by Prince Sisowath Yuthevong, with a view to the establishment of a constitutional monarchy along Thai lines. The Party's strength 'came in large part from the Mohanikay sect of the *sangha*, from younger members of the bureaucracy, from supporters of the leftist Issarak [Freedom] movement, and from Cambodia's "intellectual" class' (Chandler 1996, 175). In the Consultative Assembly elections of September 1946 the Party won 50 of the 67 seats, not least because their monastic supporters were in an ideal position to deliver the vote.[13] However, other political forces were also on the move. In April 1950 a Communist-led Unified Issarak Front (UIF) was created by Son Ngoc Minh, also known as Achar Mean,[14] and Tou Samouth (later secretary-general of the Communist Party), both ex-monks though now associated with the Viet Minh. The first meeting of the Front was attended by about two hundred people, of whom 105 are claimed to have been Buddhist monks. The UIF organized a Khmer Buddhist Conference in 1951 at which a play detailing the life of Hem Chieu, now transformed into a national martyr, was performed (Kiernan 1985, 93–4).

The fear of Thai manipulation implicit in the creation of the Institut Bouddhique in part explains the gradual erosion of Thommayut influence[15] as the century progressed. By contrast the Mohanikay, with headquarters at Wat Onnalom, grew in strength and influence, particularly as a result of the work of the scholar monks Ven. Chuon Nath[16] (1883–1969; *sanghareach* 1948–69) and Ven. Huot Tath (1891–1975; headed the order after Chuon Nath's death), members of the so-called Thommakay group (Kiernan 1985, 34). Both monks had been initiated in modern critical scholarship in Hanoi (in 1922–3) by Louis Finot, Director of the École Française d'Extrême-Orient. They became such vehement critics of 'corrupt practices' within the *sangha* that some senior monks Mohanikay lobbied the king who, with French blessings, issued an ordinance specifically referring to the split between 'modernists' and 'traditionalists' and forbidding 'teaching reforms or ... spreading among the faithful modern ideas which conflict with traditional religion',[17] though it did little to deter the modernisers. Chuon Nath also led a team of monks and former monks in the production of the first Khmer dictionary of modern times. First published in 1938 and continually revised through his lifetime, the dictionary created many new words from Pāli, Sanskrit and French sources. As such it became the target of nationalist denunciation, most notably by the French-trained anti-monarchist Keng Vannsak, who argued that it would have been more appropriate to unearth Khmer words from the Angkorian period. Keng Vannsak was also critical of the impact of Pāli and Sanskrit and, indeed, of Buddhism itself since they gave the impression of Cambodia as still part of an 'indianized' sphere of influence – a view later exploited by the Khmer Rouge. Keng Vannsak's ideas[18] were largely supported by the emerging modernized intelligentsia, particularly teachers and students in secular schools, and he was imprisoned for his pains by Sihanouk in 1954 and again in 1968.

Sihanouk's youth (he was only nineteen years old at the time) and 'malleable personality' were felt to be ideal from the French perspective and he came to the throne in 1941 on the death of his grandfather, King Monivong. Styled 'Great Buddhist King' (*dhammika mohareach*) in the constitution of 1947, implying his role as protector of the Buddhist monastic order, Sihanouk has also referred to himself as 'king-monk' (*roi-bonze*).[19] However, he has shown some reluctance in fully exploiting the ancient Mon-Khmer concept of God-king or Buddha-king dating from the Angkorean period, which survived at least until the reign of Norodom.[20] Regrettably, this has not prevented the mass of the population from viewing him in this light, and one of the tragedies of modern Cambodia is the facility with which almost all governments and political groupings have unrealistically sought to identify with the achievements of the Angkorean period.

After leading the country to independence in November 1953 Sihanouk, piqued by the popularity of political parties, abdicated the throne in March 1955 in favour of his father Norodom Suramarit (r.1955–60) in order to launch his Sangkum Reastr Niyum (Popular Socialist Community) which won all the seats in the National Assembly in the elections of September 1955. The Sangkum's 'ramshackle ideology' (Chandler 1996, 199) of Buddhist socialism stressed what Sihanouk regarded as traditional Khmer values, that is the idea of mutual help and promotion of the well-being of the poor, all within a set of Buddhist principles that guided change while avoiding the pitfalls associated with state ownership and collectivization. Coercive wealth redistribution was also avoided in favour of Buddhist ideals where the rich would give to the poor as a merit-making act. Through the heyday of the movement from the late '50s to the early '60s, reservoir, canal and road building was encouraged, expenditure on education rose rapidly,[21] and Sihanouk found many influential monastic supporters, including Chuon Nath himself.

Monastic education benefited from these policies and great efforts were made by the Ministry of Cults and Religious Affairs to develop a coherent Buddhist educational system from elementary to university level. This was accomplished, in part, by ensuring that all applications for the construction of new monasteries included plans for educational provision up to elementary level. Nevertheless Cambodian monks, in comparison with their Thai counterparts, still had limited educational opportunities, with very few progressing beyond the most basic levels. However, in 1955 l'École Supérieure de Pali in Phnom Penh was reorganized as the Lycée Bouddhique Preah Suramarit. This was followed by the establishment of two more Buddhist High Schools in Battambang and Siemreap in the mid 1960s. The Université Bouddhique Preah Sihanoukreach was also founded in the capital on land owned by Sihanouk, admitting its first cohort of students in 1959.[22] Its curriculum covered traditional and modern western subjects including the sciences, although it seems that a significant proportion of monks disrobed at the end of their studies. It was not until 1963 that educational certificates issued by monastic institutions were given equivalence to those awarded by secular schools a policy that seems to have had some effect on halting the erosion of monastic vocations.

At the time some felt that Sihanouk's Buddhist socialism was based on the model already established in Burma, a charge he felt the need to reject vigorously, arguing that the policy emerged naturally from 'Buddhist morality and the religious traditions of our national existence, ... [not] doctrines imported from abroad' (quoted by Zago 1976, 112). Sihanouk argued that Buddhist socialism was an expression of the Khmer spirit yet, shortly before his overthrow in 1970, he was forced to admit the failure of the policy. However, he placed the blame for this on Buddhism itself, with its excessive focus on non-violence, neutrality and compassion. For Sihanouk, these ideals had proved to be insufficient for dealing with the profound corruption and American aggression[23] influencing the country at the time. The views of most Buddhists were somewhat different. They argued that the Buddhist dimension of the policy was only skin deep and were able to cite a variety of violations of basic Buddhist ethics by Sihanouk himself, such as his promotion of casino gambling with resulting high profile suicides due to bankruptcy, and the use of the death penalty for political opponents (Somboon 1993, 138; Yang Sam 1987, 15–16).

Sihanouk was deposed by a coup on 18 March 1970 and the even more incompetent Lon Nol became head of the short-lived Khmer Republic the following November. Given their royalist leanings, Thommayut monks have never fully recovered from this event. A protest march in Phnom Penh planned by senior members of the order immediately after the coup seems only to have been prevented by the swift intervention of Ven. Huot Tath, superior of the Mohanikay (Yang Sam 1987, 42). Lon Nol was himself a firm believer in the message of the Buddha which, he argued, was in accord with the Universal Declaration of Human Rights. To emphasize this point he had the following inscription placed on the Republic's monument outside the royal palace:

Buddhism teaches us to be honest, to reject selfishness and to promote mutual assistance. Above all, it is a symbol of liberty, equality, fraternity, progress and well being. (Zago 1976, 112)

He also identified his administration's anti-communist opposition to the Viet Cong, and the now increasingly active Khmer Rouge, as a battle between Buddhism and the forces of the devil (*thmil* – lit. 'unbeliever'). As head of government he cast himself in the role of Buddhist messiah and the surprisingly prophetic slogan 'If communism comes, Buddhism will be completely eliminated' was much in the air at the time. Predictably, the government employed former Buddhist monks in attempts to counter communist propaganda and Lon Nol made it clear that his aim was to strengthen Buddhism within the country and throughout Asia. He was particularly anxious to demonstrate that Buddhism was more that a match for Christianity and Islam, although he was not averse to studying the missionary strategies of these two religions in an attempt to achieve this goal.[24] The militant Buddhism and anti-Vietnamese rhetoric of the time had the regrettable consequence that many Catholics, most of whom were ethnic Vietnamese, were persecuted with a number of mass shootings occurring around April 1970 (Ponchaud 1990, 136–7). Another unforeseen consequence of the promotion of Buddhism during the Republic was the growing concentration of monks in urban monasteries, many having joined the order as a means of avoiding military conscription. Yet others harboured unrealistic hopes of gaining high level academic qualifications. This inevitably reduced the number of monks engaged in active meditation and led to a sizeable and well-organized constituency of young, vigorous and disgruntled males.

At the annual congress[25] of religious dignitaries of both orders in 1972, the *sangha* passed a motion to the effect that it should avoid involvement in political matters and that this position should be enshrined in the country's new constitution (Zago 1976, 110 & 113). While this accords well with a quietistic reading of Theravāda Buddhist literary traditions it tends to represent an ideal rather than reality. Indeed, the Lon Nol government itself was a prime instrument in the further politicization of the *sangha*. Thus, Hem Chieu's ashes were recovered by Bunchan Mul, Minister of Cults and Religious Affairs, and returned to Phnom Penh in honour in July 1972 by order of Lon Nol himself, thus reinforcing the nationalist significance of the martyr begun by the Issarak movement in 1951.

Khiev Chum, a monastic Umbrella War survivor, became an unconscious apologist for the Republic, arguing that the Buddhist religion should not depend on monarchies since that institution had been rejected by the Buddha himself during his great renunciation.[26] After the 1970 coup he was a frequent broadcaster on National Radio, exhorting his listeners to embrace democratic republicanism which was, to his mind, the basic position of the Buddha. However, his activities were not always as helpful as the government might have hoped. With another scholar-monk, Pang Khat, he encouraged students to protest against some aspects of the regime, seemingly unaware of the fact that many members of his young audience had already been organized by the Khmer Rouge. As the result of complaints regarding his behaviour Huot Tath was forced to reprimand him in 1973. Another monk of the period, the US-educated Kuoch Kileng, agitated for the right of monks to vote in elections.

Lon Nol suffered a stroke in early 1971 and never ruled effectively again, preferring to listen to 'Buddhist mystics who promised magical solutions to [the Vietnam] war' (Chandler 1996, 207). Throughout the period a variety of Buddhist prophecies circulated, one concerning a future Armageddon accompanied by the appearance of a gold and silver castle in which people fought for treasure. Many interpreted this as a reference to Sihanouk's state casino. Another talked of 'A bodhi tree with flat stump, the roots do not grow, a poisonous cobra hides quietly at the same place'. (Yang Sam 1987, 51), a clear reference to the elimination of Buddhism. In retrospect it is easy to identify the cobra with the Khmer Rouge.

Long before the fall of Phnom Penh on 17 April 1975 the Khmer Rouge had been pointing to the burden that around 60,000 unproductive monks placed on the country. Additionally, Buddhism was recast as a foreign, hence 'unpatriotic' religion, with origins in Thailand,[27] and the morality of the monks was openly criticized. During this period Khmer Rouge cadres began to observe a lengthy list of moral precepts, loosely based on the ten monastic precepts of Theravāda Buddhism, to prove that they were more worthy of respect than monks.[28] These arguments were as convincing to some members of the *sangha* as they were to the laity and many monks, who then worked successfully in recruiting peasants, went over to the Khmer Rouge, particularly given Sihanouk's support for the movement as part of a united front against Lon Nol. Some have argued that without these 'patriotic monks' the path to victory would have been much harder to achieve (Chantov Boua 1991, 230).

From March 1970 to June 1973 around a thousand (ie. one third of the total) Buddhist monasteries, particularly in the Khmer Rouge controlled eastern and south-western zones, were put out of action in a variety of ways, 70 per cent of this figure in 1972 alone. The Khmer Rouge have consistently overestimated their 'successes' in this regard but it is clear that during the Civil War all participants found monasteries and their compounds ideal encampments since they were often on higher ground and could be easily defended. The Khmer Rouge and Viet Cong enjoyed another advantage in the use of monasteries, for Republican forces, generally respectful of religious sites, were reluctant to attack them. This is one of the many reasons the Khmer Rouge established themselves early in the sacred area around Angkor.

Before the final victory of the Khmer Rouge in 1975, the majority of monks in the 'liberated' zones fled, usually to government controlled areas. There was no uniformity of treatment of those who remained; indeed there is some evidence that not all cadres were ideologically committed to the eradication of Buddhism (*Ibid.*, 233). Monks were usually reorganized into committees to handle the social, economic and cultural affairs of the *sangha*, severely curtailing the time available for more traditional monastic pursuits, and informing on 'unpatriotic' colleagues was encouraged. The monks were forced to become economically active, mainly in agriculture, and younger monks were selected for re-education, paramedical battleground duties and military service leaving only the odd elderly monk behind in the monastery. Such monks had great difficulty in preserving the link between the laity and the order, not least because Khmer Rouge propaganda had discouraged villagers from inviting monks to perform traditional rites. Indeed, the economic supports of the monasteries rapidly disintegrated, not least because any donations had to be shared with the authorities. In the early 1970s the Khmer Rouge were still aware of the people's strong religious sentiments and tried to avoid explicit persecution. In any case, monks were still needed and occasionally banners extolling Buddhism were displayed alongside Khmer Rouge slogans (Thion and Kiernan 1981, 69).

Pol Pot claimed to have spent six years in a *wat*, two as a monk, although most informed commentators have regarded this as an exaggeration (Kiernan 1985, 26–7). The likelihood is that he served a year as a novice, probably around the age of six, at Wat Botum, the headquarters of the Thommayut order.[29] Likewise Ta Mok, the present Khmer Rouge strongman, is reported as having been a monk until he joined the Khmer resistance around 1942, probably against the background of the Umbrella War disturbances.[30] In one of his early writings Pol Pot wrote approvingly that the 'democratic regime will bring back the Buddhist moralism because our great leader Buddha was the first to have taught [democracy]'.[31] Whatever his early affection for Buddhism, and despite the fact that the Cambodian Communists were heirs to the Buddhist nationalism of the, '40s, by the 1960s the Party had 'begun to shed its Buddhist mantle' (Keyes 1994, 55). Soon after the victory in April 1975 Ieng Sary, the Khmer Rouge Minister for Foreign Affairs, announced that there would be freedom for all religious groups, a freedom underlined by the 1976 Constitution of Democratic Kampuchea (Chapter XV, Article 20). However, this freedom was purely theoretical and needs to be understood in the context of communist thinking on the topic which assumes as primary the freedom not to hold a religious world-view.[32]

The mainly elderly monks who had survived the Civil War were evacuated and forced to walk to a series of distant monasteries where they were placed on meagre rations and hard labour. The monasteries of the capital and other important cities, massively swollen by monks displaced from rural monasteries, were closed.[33] Some distinction between rural and city monks, the former characterized as 'proper and revolutionary', the latter as 'imperialists', seems to have operated in the early Democratic Kampuchea period (Chantou Boua 1991, 229). It is possible that the Khmer Rouge wished to distinguish between Mohanikay and Thommayut monks in this way. Between October and December 1975 almost all monasteries still remaining active in the country were closed.[34] Empty monasteries were physically dismantled to provide building materials, Buddha images were beheaded, stupas smashed, and ancient palm-leaf manuscripts used for rolling cigarettes. Remaining monastic premises became the location for local Khmer Rouge Economic Bureaux (*munti sethakech*) or, if they were remote, torture and execution centres.[35] Particular care was taken in destroying the intellectual inheritance of Buddhism and libraries containing *sūtras* were a special target. From this point on monks unwilling or unable to co-operate were accused of being enemy agents and summarily executed. During the Vietnamese-sponsored trial (15–20 July 1979) of Pol Pot *in absentia*, Tep Vong (the future chairman of the Buddhist order) gave evidence that Pol Pot himself executed 57 monks, including three of his own nephews, in the commune of Chan Sar for this reason (Yang Sam 1987, 69).[36] In 1978 Yun Yat, Minister of Culture, claimed 'Buddhism is dead and the ground has been cleared for the foundations of a new revolutionary culture' and estimates made in 1980 suggest that around 63 per cent of monks died of starvation or were executed by the Pol Pot regime. The rest either escaped the country or disrobed.[37] When Phnom Penh fell to the Vietnamese in January 1979 there were only 100 ordained Cambodian monks in existence, most of these in Vietnamese or Thai exile.[38] Whether cynically or not, the Khmer Rouge began to shift their position on Buddhism after the invasion by Vietnam. Thus Bel Long, a Cambodian monk based in California, was given a warm welcome by Khieu Samphan, when he visited a Khmer Rouge camp on the Thai–Cambodian border in the early '80s (Yang Sam 1987, 91) and recently a conciliatory approach to Khmer Rouge leaders had been fostered by prominent Buddhists. Ven. Tep Vong, for instance, has likened Ieng Sary to Aṅgulimāla,[39] the murderous brigand of canonical Buddhism who was brought to the truth by his contact with the Buddha.

The new People's Republic of Kampuchea (PRK) needed to bolster its own legitimacy but, since Sihanouk quickly entered into an opposition Coalition Government of Democratic Kampuchea (CGDK) with the Khmer Rouge and other anti-Vietnamese groupings, it was unable to play the monarchist card. It therefore turned to the *sangha*, the Vietnam-backed government making the partial restoration of Buddhism one of its first acts on coming to power. International approval for this policy was sought and a delegation of the pro-communist Asian Buddhist Conference for Peace visited the country President Heng Samrin's invitation in April 1979.[40]

Ordination in the early post-Khmer Rouge period proved difficult. Assembling a full quorum of monks for the valid rite was an impossibility. Some took to shaving their head and wearing white and, in this way, Buddhist ceremonies, particularly those commemorating the dead, were performed. In September 1979 seven 'carefully chosen' former monks were reordained with government approval at Wat Unnalom by a Vietnamese monastic contingent headed by Thich Bou Chon, a Khmer who had fled to Vietnam during the previous regime and had become an advisor to the Central Commission of the Vietnamese Theravāda Buddhism. The rest of the delegation consisted of Khmer Krom and Vietnamese monks (Keyes 1994, 60, n.36). The youngest of the ordainees, Ven. Tep Vong, 47 years old at the time, was subsequently appointed head of a unified Cambodian *sangha*. Tep Vong did not employ the traditional title of *Samdech Sanghareach* (king of the *sangha*) as this was regarded as inappropriate in a socialist setting. Instead he was termed chairman or president (*prathean*). The unification of the two *nikāyas* was justified on the grounds that it would eliminate the élitist and monarchical influences of the Thommayut. Indeed, another senior monastic source at the time claimed that, as a result of unification, 'our monks are neither Mohanikay nor Thommayut but Nationalist monks' (Yang Sam 1987, 86).

At about the same time, Tep Vong was elected to the posts of Vice-President of the Khmer National Assembly and Vice-President of the Central Committee of the Khmer United Front for National Construction and Defense (KUFNCD). The latter organization, formed to represent non-Party groupings, encouraged revolutionary endeavour by re-educating Buddhist monks to 'discard the narrow-minded views of dividing themselves into groups and factions'. Not surprisingly, this was not always successful and more recent critics have characterized Tep Vong and other early members of the 'unified' Buddhist hierarchy as 'Vietnamese monks in Khmer robes'.

Despite a more positive attitude to Buddhism the PRK moved cautiously. It forbade the ordination of monks below the age of fifty, ostensibly to maximize economic production but actually to prevent any significant revival. This restriction was lifted in 1988. Monks were limited to one hour every morning in alms collection and the laity [those over fifty] were only permitted to visit monasteries in the evenings after the completion of the day's work. Nevertheless, some younger monks were observed in rural areas even though their ordinations may not have been registered with the Ministry of Cults and Religious Affairs.

A First National Buddhist Monk Conference in May 1982 estimated that there were 2,311 monks in 1,821 monasteries (i.e. fewer than two monks per monastery) at that time, suggesting a decrease of 60,000 monks under the Khmer Rouge. The conference was addressed by Heng Samrin, who extolled Buddhism as a religion in harmony with democratic principles which 'will last forever'. He also praised the positive contribution of Buddhists to society, particularly those with a nationalist outlook like Son Ngoc Minh (Achar Mean) and Achar Hem Chieu,[41] and compared the Khmer Rouge to the hordes of Māra (the Buddhist personification of evil).[42] At a Second Congress of Buddhist monks in 1984, Heng Samrin reminded his audience that they must be prepared to fight to protect the State against its enemies for the existence of the State is the necessary condition for the flourishing of Buddhism itself. They should be particularly vigilant with regard to fellow monks who might be using the ordained state for acts of subversion. Monks were also encouraged to work for good relations with their fellows in Vietnam and Laos. In order for the *sangha* to 'completely discard unhealthy beliefs' (Keyes 1990, 62) eight conditions for its proper regulation were promulgated at this time. They were:

1. to learn the significance of political line
2. to educate the laity with regard to party ideas
3. to model themselves on the Buddha and fight the enemy

4. to preserve and cultivate the patriotic and revolutionary spirit exemplified by Achar Hem Chieu and Achar Mean[43]
5. to preserve the cultural heritage
6. to promote and improve production among the people so that their living standards may be enhanced
7. to assist in building social service establishments
8. to carry out all of the above to achieve victory. (Yang Sam 1987, 85)

The PRK modified its policy on Buddhism in mid 1988 in the light of the planned withdrawal of the last Vietnamese troops (as a consequence of the collapse of USSR) in September 1989. Hun Sen, in a series of talks around the country, notably in Kampot in February 1989 (Ponchaud 1990, 205–6), apologized for the 'government's "mistakes" towards religion' and asked to be pardoned. Since 1988 Radio Phnom Penh has started each day with a broadcast of chanting from a city monastery (Kalab 1994, 67). A tax on temple-monasteries was also abolished around this time and wat-based *Dhammavinaya* and Pāli schools were reopened. Buddhist primary and secondary education re-emerged in the early 1990s. Hun Sen and other leaders have attended Buddhist ceremonies, for example at the Buddha-bone relic stupa (*Preah Sakya Moni Chedi*) outside Phnom Penh railway station, and engaged in conspicuous acts of Buddhist piety since this time. Shrines to those killed by the Khmer Rouge, such as the Vietnam-financed memorial at the killing fields of Choeung Ek on the outskirts of Phnom Penh, architecturally express some aspects of Buddhist cosmological doctrine.

The monastic order increased from around 7,250 in 1987 to 16,400 (including 6,500 novices) in 1990 (Keyes 1994, 62–3). Much of this growth, plus a programme of monastery reconstruction, has been financed by overseas Cambodians. In November 1991 Sihanouk returned to Phnom Penh and resumed the traditional function of supreme patron of the *sangha*. The peace accord of that year also led to the return of refugees, including many monks ordained outside of Cambodia, most notably in Thailand, raising some questions about the seniority of the present ecclesiastical hierarchy. In December the 'unified' order was annulled when Sihanouk re-established the two posts of *sanghareach*. Ven. Tep Vong took control of the Mahanikay and Ven. Bour Kry, a prominent monk in the Paris Cambodian community, became his Thommayut counterpart.[44] The Thommayut remains relatively small, with around 3 per cent of the monastic population in 1995.[45] Even today at Wat Botum, the symbolic centre of the order and home of the *sanghareach*, Thommayut monks are greatly outnumbered by, and somewhat isolated from, their Mohanikay co-religionists. This situation reflects both recent history (all monks at Wat Botum were part of a 'unified,' i.e. basically Mohanikay, order before 1991) and a continuing suspicion of the Thommayut's loyalties on the part of the authorities. Thommayut monks, for instance, once again travel to Thailand for higher ordination (*upasampadā*). Keyes's (1994, 64) remark that the 'modernist approach to Buddhism first championed by the Thommakay faction of the Mohanikay order may be the most favoured in the PRK' still seems appropriate, and despite the re-establishment of a full Thommayut hierarchy some of the places are in fact occupied by prominent Mohanikay monks.[46]

The Buddhist Liberal Democratic Party (BLDP) was one of the parties formed to fight the UN-sponsored election of May 1993. Evolving out of the anti-Communist Khmer People's National Liberation Front (KPNLF)[47] founded by ex-Prime Minister (1967–8) and devout lay Buddhist Son Sann, it won 10 seats in the Constituent Assembly and secured some representation in the coalition government formed in October 1993.[48] The movement has its origins in the anti-Vietnamese resistance movement that flourished in refugee camps, particularly at Prachiburi (Suksamran 1993, 144), along the Thai border from October 1979. Son Sann, convinced that the troubles of the Khmer people lay in their un-Buddhist conduct, had already established a Khmer Buddhist Research Centre, under the guidance of Sirisovanno Pin Sem, incumbent of Rithisen, to revivify and preserve Buddhist traditions, scriptures and scholarship. In the Centre's first publication Son Sann argued for a more socially engaged Buddhism in which monks should leave the security of their monasteries, expand 'their knowledge in political and social questions' and 'exercise influence in regard to motivating the population for the liberation of their country from foreign domination and the Marxist-Leninist ideology' (Son Soubert et al., 1986, 157).

The BLDP has recently been riven by disputes and in July 1995 a faction led by Ieng Mouly separated from Son Sann, ostensibly on the grounds that the latter was too old and too anti-Vietnamese to lead the party. In September of the same year Son Sann's house in Phnom Penh was grenaded and some of his supporters, both lay and monastic, were violently attacked by unknown assailants at Wat Mohamontrey.[49] Subsequently, Ieng Mouly became Minister of Information after behind-the-scenes negotiations with Hun Sen's CPP. Although the BLDP name remains, no obviously Buddhist-oriented movement is now active in national politics.

The formation of the coalition government in the aftermath of the 1993 elections led to the promulgation of a new constitution, re-establishing the monarchy, on 24 September 1993 (Gaillard 1994). In line with most previous Cambodian constitutions, Buddhism is enshrined as the religion of the State[50] and freedom of belief is guaranteed (Article 43). The Kingdom's motto is 'Nation, Religion, King', (Article 4) and the two *sanghareachs* join a six-membered Royal Council of the Throne charged with the responsibility of choosing a new King when necessary (Article 13). Among other provisions, Article 68 states: 'The State shall disseminate and develop the Pāli schools and the Buddhist Institute.'

According to Jennar (1995, 5) all modern Cambodian constitutions represent 'at best, a declaration of intentions', with many provisions reflecting little more than the 'principal preoccupations of the ruling class, including the image of the country they hoped to offer to the outside world'. Nevertheless, the Ministry of Cults and Religious Affairs, re-established in 1992 under Hean Vanniroth (from 1995) as Secretary of State, with responsibilities inherited from the KUFNCD, now consists of four departments responsible for all religions including Buddhism, Buddhist education, the Buddhist Institute and Administration. The specifically Buddhist aims of the Ministry are threefold: to re-establish ecclesiastical structures that existed before 1970, to develop and consolidate monk education, and to republish Buddhist Institute literature (Hean Sokhom 1996, 15). The Institute itself recommenced operations in June 1992 and is currently funded by grants from two foreign NGOs, the Heinrich Böll Foundation (HBF) and the Japanese Sotoshu Relief Committee (JSRC).[51]

In line with Son Sann's prediction, Buddhist social activism has flourished in the last decade. Since 1992 an annual peace march or *dhammayietra* has taken place despite initial opposition from the government and the United Nations. Ven. Mahāghosānanda, a monk from Wat Sampeou Meas, Phnom Penh and an admirer of Gandhi, is one of its architects. Since 1994, when the march came under armed attack, participants, both lay and monastic, have been trained in meditational techniques, particularly the four *brahmavihāras*, as a way of overcoming fear (Moser-Puangsuwan, n.d., 3). The Dhammayietra movement is non-partisan and all banners, undisciplined monks, military uniforms and weapons are forbidden on the march. The aim of the 1995 march was to raise awareness of the issues surrounding landmines and in 1996 the theme was large scale deforestation. Other more localized marches (e.g. against prostitution in Phnom Penh's Toul Kok red-light district and in support of stranded Vietnamese fishing families, a pariah group in contemporary Cambodia[52]) have also been organized by the movement. Mahāghosānanda has become a high profile figure, reports of his activities are carried in the national press, and a film of his message and example circulates throughout the country.[53] In 1994 he was appointed the King's special representative for the protection of the environment. In response to the rising pan-Buddhist environmental agenda of recent years, an Inter-Ministerial Steering Committee for Environmental Education with strong Buddhist representation has produced an environmental manual for primary teachers which will soon be augmented with Buddhist materials. A plan to introduce 'environmental concepts and issues in Buddhist monk education' already exists and a seminar (November 1997) of leading environmental monks, organized by the Buddhist Institute, has produced a White Paper on the topic.

Foreign NGOs have also been active in supporting a variety of Buddhist activities. The German-based Konrad Adenauer Foundation (KAF) entertains serious doubts about the future of Buddhism in Cambodia unless it moves in a more socially engaged direction, and sponsors a 'development-oriented Buddhism'[54] through the Buddhism for Development (BDF) movement based in Anlongvil, Battambang province. Founded in 1990, BDF has its origins in the Son Sann/Pin Sem circle at Rithisen and, until recently, was led by Ven. Heng Monychenda.[55] It has received around $750,000 since 1994. In the field it concentrates on the training of Buddhist monks in rural development work, the establishment of rice and money banks, tree-nurseries and compost making. It also organizes annual national seminars on Buddhism and the Development of Khmer

Society. The KAF also supports the Santi Sena organization led by Ven. Nhim Kim Teng of Wat Prey Chlak, Svay Rieng in forest preservation and similar activities.[56]

It seems that developmentally or environmentally engaged monks are overwhelmingly members of the Mohanikay. This may simply reflect the size and rural nature of the order. However, there is evidence that senior Thommayut monks, despite various inducements, have not participated enthusiastically in such activity. This can be explained in a number of ways. The Thommayut's dedication to strict observance of monastic discipline, particularly the prohibition on handling money and digging the soil, may be a factor. Alternatively, the Thommayut hierarchy may be more meditationally than developmentally oriented. The order's aristocratic character may also be a factor here. A final possibility is that the order is less inclined to accept the well-meaning attentions of foreign, non-Buddhist organizations, although it is too early to tell whether this reluctance represents a faint echo of the order's anti-colonial tendencies during the French Protectorate.

Cambodia Buddhism has clearly experienced considerable turmoil throughout the modern period. Indeed, with the possible exception of Mongolia (and given the recent histories of Buddhism in China, Vietnam and Tibet this is saying quite a lot), no form of Buddhism has come so close to total extinction. However since the nadir of 1975–9 a gradual loosening of restrictions has occurred and there is some reason to hope for a waxing of the *Buddhadhamma* in that benighted country once more. The political situation is still far from stable and present initiatives may not last. Yet Khmer Buddhism has learnt to adapt, and occasionally prosper, in a wide variety of political contexts, be they colonial (whether organised from Paris or Hanoi), monarchical, socialist, republican or doctrinaire Marxist. The visible presence of the *sangha* and its unique significance as the only institution able to operate throughout the country has ensured that almost all governments have felt the need to cultivate it whatever their political philosophy. There is little reason to assume that this situation will change. On a more sombre note, we have seen how Buddhism has regularly taken a leading role by offering 'subdued resistance' to oppressive governance at crucial points in modern Cambodian history. The next few years appear to be shaping into another such climacteric.

NOTES

I would like to thank Olivier de Bernon, David Chandler, David Channer, Penny Edwards and Alain Forest for reading over and commenting on earlier drafts of this essay. Any mistakes or misrepresentations are, of course, my own responsibility alone.

1. The non-orthodox character of Cambodian Buddhism has been well-documented by François Bizot, starting with his first major work *Le figuier à cinq branches* [Recherche sur le bouddhisme khmer, I], Paris: École française d'Extrême-Orient, 1976 [Publications de l'École française d'Extrême-Orient Vol. CVII]. On the more general topic of tantric Theravāda see Cousins (1997).
2. On the question of how important kingship is to the health of Buddhism, see my introductory essay in this volume.

3. Osborne (1997, 177 n.3) was informed by an 'unimpeachable source' that Norodom had also served as a Mohanikay monk in Udong.

4. *Études Cambodgiennes*, 17 (Janvier–Mars 1969), 16.

5. On his life and death see Flaugergues (1914).

6. This is one of the traditional Mon-Khmer occult practices (*vethamon*). A Khmer chronicle of the 1850s distinguishes between the 'cruel' Vietnamese and the Khmer 'people of merit [*nak sel*]' who will remain invincible through recourse to Buddhist ritual, amulets and living according to the Buddha's teachings (Chandler 1996, 121). Lon Nol, in a 1970 decree, recommended that his soldiers cut their skin, in order to allow the Buddha to enter '... [their] body and bring strength' (Becker 1986, 138), and in the 1980s KPNLF troops commonly sported tattoos for apotropaic purposes (*Phnom Penh Post [PPP]*, 8–21 September 1995, Vol. IV, No. 18, 20). Today it is common to hear of soldiers who wear protective amulets or tattoos consisting of mystic diagrams (*yon*) fashioned by shamans (*kru*), many of whom are ex-monks.

7. For a breakdown of the hierarchies of both orders, see Meas-Yang (1978, 39–41) and Martini (1955).

8. see Ministre de l'Information, *Aperçu religieux: le bouddhisme au Cambodge*, Phnom Penh, 1962, 21.

9. A monk by the name of Prak from Tay Ninh is said to have commanded a rebel group and been killed in action during the insurrection.

10. The Tay Ninh region of Cochinchina/Vietnam is still an area rich in ethnic Khmer or Khmer Krom. For a good contemporary source for the events of 1927 see *Gouvernement-général de l'Indochine, direction des affaires politiques et de la sûreté générale. Contribution a l'histoire des mouvements politiques de l'Indochine française*, VII, Le Caodaisme, Hanoi, 1933, 27, 35, 38.

11. *La Griffe*, quoted in Bernardini (1974, 81–2).

12. For a hagiography, see Samphear Kong, *Brah Palat Ghosanag Haem Ciav Virapuras Jati* (Preah Balat Khosaneak Hem Chieu: The National Hero) Phnom Penh, 1972. Others involved in the opposition included Khiev Chum, Pang Khat (a teacher of Sanskrit), So Haiy and Uk Chea.

13. Kalab (1976, 160) reports that during the run-up to the elections of 1966 none of the candidates standing in the village she studied held public meetings. Instead they 'spent their time visiting the abbots in all the local monasteries'.

14. The name appears to be a combination of Son Ngoc Thanh and Ho Chi Minh (Becker 1986, 63). *Achar* is a title held by a senior lay Buddhist.

15. Yang Sam (1987, 17) estimates that in the late 1960s the number of Thommayut monasteries stood at around 107 with the Mohanikay at 3,369. Keyes (1994, 55) gives slightly different figures. All available statistics indicate the Thommayut in steady decline throughout the 1950s and 1960s. Political influences are important here, but one should not neglect the order's strict adherence to the norms of *vinaya* as a contributory factor.

16. For a brief biography see Leang Hap An, *Biographie de Samdech Preach Sanghareach Chuon-Nath, supérieur de l'ordre Mohanikaya*, Phnom Penh: Institut Bouddhique, 1970 [Série de Culture et Civilisation Khmères, Tome 7]. Chuon Nath wrote the words and music to the National Anthem in 1941.

17. Quoted, without attribution, by Keyes (1994, 47). Also mentioned, without a date, by Martini (1955, 418, n.1).

18. See his *Principes de création des mots nouveaux*, Phnom Penh: Faculté des Lettres et des Sciences Humaines, 1966.

19. He spent the rainy season of 1947 as a monk (Yang Sam 1987, 8) and again for a brief period in 1963 after the World Court ruled that the Preah Vihear near the Thai border was the property of Cambodia (Zago 1976, 111; Schecter 1967, 67).

20. Norodom's person was considered so charged with sacrality that, when he once fell from his carriage in Phnom Penh, no native Cambodian felt able to assist him. He was helped to his feet by a passing Frenchman. See Moura, J., *Le Royaume du Cambodge*, Paris, 1883, Vol. I, 226.

21. Sihanouk had been championing the phasing out of French-oriented education with a return to instruction in Khmer since 1945 (Chandler 1986, 85).

22. The Buddhist University was re-established in 1997, taking its first cohort of about forty students from the Buddhist High School. The staff includes three Sri Lankan monks who teach Pāli and Sanskrit.

23. Between March 1969 and July 1973 over half a million tons of American bombs fell on Cambodia.

24. See 'Discours du Maréchal Lon Nol a l'ouverture de l'Assemblée Nationale', *Agence Khmère Presse*, 15 September 1972.

25. Members of the hierarchy customarily gather together in Phnom Penh for Anusamvacchara-Mahāsannipāt, an annual ceremony at the end of January. This event is presided over by the Head of State who addresses all present before they divide for *nikāya*-specific deliberations.

26. For example *Buddhasasana Prajadhipateyy Sadharanaratth* (Buddhism, Democracy, Republic), Phnom Penh: Punloeu Cheat, 1971. For a list of his principal writings see Zago (1976, 118–9, n.33).

27. Ponchaud (1990, 234). This is interesting since only the royalist Thommayut is of Thai origin. Khmer Rouge propaganda accused monks of being leeches on society and of using the doctrine of *karma* to justify the status quo. These have been Asian criticisms of Buddhism since long before the emergence of communism.

28. These precepts, both negative and positive, are listed in Yang Sam (1987, 70). Intriguingly, this strategy was also employed by the Mongolian Communist Party in the late 1920s, see Sarkisyanz, Emanuel, 'Communism and Lamaist Utopianism in Central Asia', *Review of Politics*, 20/4 (1958), 626.

29. David Chandler was told, by Pol Pot's brother, that he spent six months in a *wat* (personal communication, 17 February 1998).

30. Thayer, Nate, 'Forbidden City', *Far Eastern Economic Review*, October 1997, 22.

31. 'Monarchy or Democracy' in *Cambodian Student* (1952), quoted in Becker (1986, 77). Similarly, Khieu Samphan was still calling Cambodia a 'Buddhist country' in 1959 (ibid. 103). Pol Pot is reported as liking to live with a 'Buddhist calm mind' (ibid. 203).

32. The 1976 Constitution also underlines the 'freedom to have no religion'. The Communist Chinese position on freedom of religion is treated in more detail in the Introduction to this volume.

33. Chantou Boua (1991, 230) was told that the number of monks in Wat Unnalom, Phnom Penh had grown from 300 to 1,000 by 1975.

34. The *PPP*, 7–20 May 1993 (Vol. II, No. 11, 20), carried a report on the miraculous salvation of Wat Phnom Sawsia between Kampot and Kep. According to local informants, when the Khmer Rouge tried to destroy it huge snakes appeared from the temple mound and killed them. Subsequent units were too frightened to repeat the actions of their comrades.

35. Ampe Phnom monastery near Kampong Speu was one such centre. Mass graves,

indicating about 5,000 dead, were discovered in September 1980. A room with skeletons and torture implements was also found in a compartment under the temple's floor.

36. David Chandler regards this allegation as a 'wild fiction' (personal communication, 17 February 1998).

37. Evidence suggests that disrobing was very rarely voluntary, even though some monks were, ironically, forced to sign a document certifying the fact that they had 'awoken' to their parasitical status; see Chantou Boua (1991, 235).

38. Keyes 1990, 60. The Ministry of Cults and Religious Affairs gives a much lower figure of 12 (see *Cambodia Report* II/2, March–April 1996, 23).

39. *PPP*, 21 March–3 April 1997 (Vol. VI, No.6, 17). For the Aṅgulimāla sutta, see M.ii.97ff.

40. Sri Lankan monk, Ven. Wipulasara Thero, was a member of the delegation (*PPP*, 9–22 September 1994, (Vol.III, No.18, 8–9). For further information on this organization see Martin Stuart-Fox's contribution to this volume.

41. *Foreign Broadcasting Information Service, Asian and Pacific Daily Report*, 2 June 1982. Hem Chieu was generally referred to by the lay title of *achar* in the PRK period. Representing Buddhist heroes in this way would certainly have been more attractive to the Communist authorities of the time. Some commentators claim that *achars* rather than ordained monks have tended to be in the vanguard of the political resistance movement [Ponchaud 1990, 232]. However, the fluid nature of monkhood in Cambodia means that the same person can be an *achar* and a monk at separate times in their life. Indeed, this seems to have been the case with Hem Chieu, although he was definitely in robes when arrested by the French in 1942. Alain Forest (1992, 88) confirms the association of *achars* and 'mouvements de contestation'.

42. A good account of the speech may be found in Löschmann (1991, 24).

43. Two boulevards in Phnom Penh were renamed in honour of Achar Hem Chieu and Achar Mean after the Vietnamese victory of 1979. They reverted to their Sihanouk-era names in 1993.

44. These dates were supplied by Ven. Bour Kry when I interviewed him at Wat Botum, Phnom Penh on 9 December 1997. The full titles of these dignitaries are Samdech Preah Sumedhādhipati Tep Vong and Samdech Preah Sugundhādhipati Bour Kry.
   On Bour Kry's incumbency at Wat Khemāraram, Paris see Kalab (1994, 61) and, more generally, Ang Chouléan and Tan Yinh Phong (1992).

45. Statistics from the Centre for Advanced Studies and the Ministry of Cults and Religious Affairs published in *Cambodia Report* II/2 (March–April 1996), 23. Ordinations into the Thommayut at Wat Botum seem to have gathered pace since 1992. The *PPP*, 24 July 1992 (Vol. I, No.2, 6) reports the ordination of 150 monks in early July.

46. The second figure in the Thommayut hierarchy is traditionally the Mongol Tepeachar (*mangaladevācārya*). This position is currently held by Ven. Oum Soum, a Mohanikay monk from Wat Mohamontrey, Phnom Penh who is also Inspector General of Buddhist education.

47. PRK soldiers defecting to the KPNLF in the 1980s were required to ordain temporarily and learn 'traditional values and morality' before joining their new army units (Kalab 1994, 70). At Sakeo refugee camp on the Thai border, a pagoda established in 1980 became the centre of opposition to the Khmer Rouge and needed to be protected every night by several hundred men armed with bamboo spears (Ponchaud 1989, 171 n. 7).

48. It was the third largest party after the Cambodia People's Party (CPP) [51 seats] and

FUNCINPEC [58 seats]. Its three ministerial posts were Youth and Sport, Rural Development, and Relations with Parliament. (*PPP*, 2–15 July 1993, Vol II, No. 14, 3.) Son Sann was appointed chairman of the Constituent Assembly and supervised the drafting of the 1993 constitution.

49. *PPP*, 28 July–10 August 1995, Vol. IV, No. 15, 5 and 6–19 October 1995, Vol. IV, No. 20, 1–3. Son Sann retired from active politics in January 1997.

50. A number of monks, eg. Ven Hok Savann, had previously argued for a separation of church and state on the grounds that the *sangha* would lose the people's respect if it was seen to be involved in 'politics instead of practicing the traditional monk's discipline'. Letter to *PPP*, 13–26 August 1993, Vol. II, No. 17, 6.

51. The HBF, linked with the German Party Alliance 90/The Greens, is at the time of writing, in its second three-year, co-operative agreement with the Institute; see Löschmann, Heike, 'Re-establishing the Buddhist Institute' *Cambodia Report* [Special Issue 'Buddhism in Cambodia'] (Vol. II/2 (March–April 1996), 17. The HBF also sponsors the Nuns and Laywomen's Association of Cambodia, inaugurated in 1995 and concerned with the moral and development-oriented education of women and children.

The JSRC as a partner of the Buddhist Institute, has been heavily involved in republishing of materials relating to Buddhism and Khmer culture destroyed during the KR period. For instance, the JSRC has, since 1994, re-established the Institute's quarterly journal *Kambuja Suriya* and in June 1995 presented the King with 1,200 copies of the Khmer Tripitaka for distribution to *wats* and libraries.

Many claim that the entire Buddhist Institute library of around 30,000 titles and 4,000 documents was destroyed after 1975, although whether this was a deliberate and concerted act of vandalism or simply due to foraging for paper, etc. has not been established. Indeed, some informed sources believe that some of the Institute's holdings may still exist at a forgotten location. One further possibility is that some of this material may be preserved at Cornell University (David Chandler, personal communication, 17 February 1998) although I have yet to confirm this. At the present time a new Institute Library is being constructed close to the Royal Palace with money donated by the Japanese Rissho Koseikai Fund for Peace.

52. *PPP*, 11–24 March 1994, Vol. III, No.5, 1 and 8–21 April 1994, Vol. III, No.7, 4.

53. The film is entitled *The Serene Life* (1996), producer David Channer, director Alan Channer. According to David. Channer (personal communication 5 October 1997), Sihanouk has conferred the title of 'International Patriarch', an honour with no precedent in Cambodian history, on Mahāghosānanda.

Two organizations, the Dhammayietra Centre for Peace and Reconciliation in Cambodia and Ponleu Khmer, a coalition of Cambodian human rights and development NGOs, are based at Mahāghosānanda's monastery in Phnom Penh.

54. See *Buddhism and the Development of Khmer Society: Proceedings of the 1st National Seminar on Buddhism and the Development of Khmer Society held in Phnom Penh, 21–23 November 1994*, Anlongvil and Phnom Penh, Buddhism for Development in Cooperation with the Ministry of Cults and Religious Affairs, 1996, 50. Intriguingly, King Sihanouk regards such work as 'an important contribution to the revival of the concept of "Buddhist Socialism" which ... [he] encouraged during the historic Sangkum Reastr Niyum period' (ibid.).

55. Monychenda disrobed in early 1997 to take up a scholarship at Harvard. He has pledged to return to the project in due course. (Interview with Peter Schier, Permanent representative of KAF in Cambodia, 11 December 1997.)

56. Other foreign NGOs include the Deutsche Gesellschaft fur Technische Zusamme-narbeit (GTZ), working mainly through monasteries in Kampong Thom province to encourage community development, and Partage, a French NGO, which sponsors Dhammic Solidarity (*Samakithor*) in Battambang-based community development projects. Some Buddhist monks have also been trained to disseminate human rights information by the Cambodian League for the Promotion and Protection of Human Rights, an organization with links to France and the EEC (*PPP*, 25 September 1992 [Vol.1, No.6,8]).

BIBLIOGRAPHY

Ang Chouléan et Tan Yinh Phong (1992) 'Le monastère Khemararam espace identitaire de la communauté Khmère', in Matras-Guin, J. and C. Taillard (eds.) *Habitations et habitat d'Asie de Sud-Est continentale: practiques et représentations de l'espace.* Paris: l'Har-mattan, 285–302.

Becker, Elizabeth (1986) *When the War Was Over: The Voices of Cambodia's Revolution and its People.* New York: Simon & Schuster.

Bernardini, P. (1974) *Le Caodaisme au Cambodge*, thèse de 3è cycle, Université de Paris VII.

Bunchan Mul (1982) 'The Umbrella War of 1942', in Kiernan, Ben and Chantou Boua (eds) *Peasants and Politics in Kampuchea, 1942–1981.* London: Zed Books.

Chandler, David P. (1974) 'Royally Sponsored Human Sacrifices in Nineteenth Century Cambodia: The Cult of *Me Sa* (Uma Mahisasuramardini) at Ba Phnom', *Journal of the Siam Society* 62/2, 207–21.

Chandler, David P. (1986) The Kingdom of Kampuchea, March–October 1945: Japanese-sponsored Independence in Cambodia in World War II', *Journal of Southeast Asian Studies* XVII/1, 80–93.

Chandler, David P. (1991) *The Tragedy of Cambodian History: Politics, War and Revolution since 1945.* New Haven, CT: Yale University Press.

Chandler, David (1996) *A History of Cambodia, Second Edition – Updated*, Boulder, Col: Westview.

Chantou Boua (1991) 'Genocide of a Religious Group: Pol Pot and Cambodia's Buddhist Monks', in Bushnell, P. Timothy, Vladimir Shlapentokh, Christopher K. Vanderpool and Jeyaratnam Sundram (eds) *State-Organized Terror: The Case of Violent Internal Repression.* Boulder Col: Westview, 227–240.

Choan and Sarin (1970) 'Le venerable chef de la pagode de Tep Pranam' *Bulletin de l'École Française d'Extrême-Orient* 57, 127–54.

Cousins, L.S. (1997) 'Aspects of Esoteric Southern Buddhism', in Connolly, Peter and Sue Hamilton (eds) *Indian Insights: Buddhism, Brahmanism and Bhakti.* London: Luzac Oriental, 185–207.

Delvert, Jean (1956) 'L'œuvre française d'enseignement au Cambodge', *France-Asie* XIII, 125–7, 309–320.

Ebihara, May (1968) 'Svay: A Khmer Village in Cambodia', Unpublished Ph.D. disserta-tion, Columbia University.

Flaugergues, E. (1914) 'La mort du chef suprême des bonzes' and 'La crémation du chef suprême des bonzes', *Revue Indochinoise* [n.s.] 21, 175–182, 481–90.

Forest, Alain (1980) *Le Cambodge et la colonisation Française: Histoire d'une colonisation sans heurts* (1897–1920). Paris: L'Harmattan.

Forest, Alain (1992) *Le culte des génies protecteurs au Cambodge: Analyse et traduction d'un corpus de textes sur les neak ta*. Paris: l'Harmattan.

Gaillard, Maurice (1994) *Démocratie Cambodgienne: la constitution du 24 septembre 1993*. Paris: l'Harmattan.

Hean Sokhom (1996) 'Notes on the Revival of Monk Education', *Cambodia Report* II/2, 14–16.

Jennar, Raoul M. (1995) *The Cambodian Constitutions (1953–1993)*. Bangkok: White Lotus.

Kalab, Milada (1976) 'Monastic Education, Social Mobility, and Village Structure in Cambodia', in Banks, David J. (ed.) *Changing Identities in Modern Southeast Asia*. The Hague: Mouton, 155–69.

Kalab, Milada (1994) 'Cambodian Buddhist Monasteries in Paris: Continuing Tradition and Changing Patterns', in Ebihara, May, Judy Ledgerwood and Carol Mortland (eds) *Cambodian Culture Since 1975: Homeland and Exile*. Ithaca, NY, 57–71.

Keyes, Charles (1990) 'Buddhism and Revolution in Cambodia', *Cultural Survival Quarterly* 14/3, 60–3.

Keyes, Charles F. (1994) 'Communist Revolution and the Buddhist Past in Cambodia', in Keyes, Charles F., Laurel Kendall and Helen Hardacre (eds) *Asian Visions of Authority: Religion and the Modern States of East and Southeast Asia*. Honolulu: University of Hawaii Press, 43–73.

Kiernan, Ben (1985) *How Pol Pot Came to Power: A History of Communism in Kampuchea, 1930–1975*. London: Verso.

Khy Phanra (1975) 'Les origines du Caodaisme au Cambodge (1926–1940)' *Mondes Asiatiques* 3, 315–48.

Löschmann, Heike (1991) 'Buddhismus und gesellschaftliche Entwicklung in Kambodscha seit der Niederschlagung des Pol-Pot-Regimes im Jahre 1979', *Asien* 41, 13–27.

Martini, François (1955) 'L'Organisation du clergé bouddhique au Cambodge', *France-Asie* 12, 416–24.

Meas-Yang, Bhikkhu (1978) *Le Bouddhisme au Cambodge*, Thanh-Long [Études Orientales No. 6].

Moser-Puangsuwan, Yeshua (n.d.) *One Million Kilometers for Peace: Five Years of Walking for Peace and Reconciliation in Cambodia – An Analysis of the Dhammayietra Movement*. Bangkok: Nonviolence International Southeast Asia.

Népote, Jacques et Michel Tranet (1983) 'Deux sources statistiques relative a la situation du monachisme Theravāda au Cambodge a la fin du XIXè siècle', *Seksa Khmer* 6, 39–73.

Osborne, Milton (1978) 'Peasant Politics in Cambodia: The 1916 Affair', *Modern Asian Studies* 12/2, 217–43.

Osborne, Milton E. (1997) *The French Presence in Cochinchina and Cambodia*. Bangkok: White Lotus [reissue of the 1969 edition].

Ponchaud, François (1989) 'Social Change in the Vortex of Revolution', in Jackson, Karl D. *Cambodia 1975–1978: Rendezvous with Death*. Princeton, NJ: Princeton University Press, 151–77.

Ponchaud, François (1990) *La cathédrale de la rizière: 450 ans d'histoire de l'église au Cambodge*. Paris: Fayard.

Samuel, Geoffrey (1993) *Civilized Shamans: Buddhism in Tibetan Societies*. Washington and London: Smithsonian Institution.

Schecter, Jerrold (1967) *The New Face of Buddhism: The Fusion of Religion and Politics in Contemporary Buddhism*. New York: Coward-McCann.

Somboon Suksamran (1993) 'Buddhism, Political Authority, and Legitimacy in Thailand and Cambodia', in Ling, Trevor (ed.) *Buddhist Trends in Southeast Asia.* Singapore: Institute of Southeast Asian Studies.

Son Soubert *et al.* (1986) *Buddhism and the Future of Cambodia.* Rithisen: Khmer Buddhist Research Center.

Tarling, Nicholas (ed.) (1992) *Cambridge History of Southeast Asia,* Vol. 2. Cambridge: Cambridge University Press.

Thion, Serge (1987) 'The Pattern of Cambodian Politics', in Ablin, David A. and Marlow Hood (eds) *The Cambodian Agony.* Armonk NY: M.E.Sharpe, 149–64.

Thion, Serge and Ben Kiernan (1981) *Khmers rouges!: matériaux pour l'histoire du communisme au Cambodge.* Paris: J.-E. Hallier and A. Michel.

Yang Sam (1987) *Khmer Buddhism and Politics from 1954 to 1984.* Newington, CT: Khmer Studies Institute.

Zago, Marcello (1976) 'Contemporary Khmer Buddhism', in H. Dumoulin (ed.) *Buddhism in the Modern World.* New York: Collier Books, 109–119.

4
POLITICS AND AMBEDKAR BUDDHISM IN MAHARASHTRA

TIMOTHY FITZGERALD

INTRODUCTION

In this chapter I am concerned with the Buddhist followers of Dr B. R. Ambedkar, the largest single group of Buddhists in India. Most are members of Ambedkar's own untouchable caste, their ancient name being Mahar. They number around four million, and are situated almost entirely in Maharashtra. The other major group of Buddhists living in India are the Tibetans, who are covered in a different chapter. There are also some Buddhists living in Bangladesh and Bengal,[1] and a group in Agra, the Jatavs.[2] The Mahars and the Jatavs are both untouchable castes and both followers of Ambedkar. However, the other groups have few if any formal connections, belong to entirely different traditions and therefore require different treatment.

Ambedkar Buddhists are by far the most significant group in numbers. They are also politically important, at least in Maharashtra. Yet their low social status tends to reduce their visibility. Members of this caste are located in both urban and rural areas, and though 'untouchable' in ritual terms are made up of a middle class intelligentsia, a rural peasantry and an urban working class.[3] There are also communities of renouncers such as *bhikkhus*[4] and *dhammacharis*.[5]

However, the movement is best approached through its leader Dr B. R. Ambedkar, himself an untouchable, a Ph.D. graduate of Columbia University, New York and the London School of Economics, a London-trained barrister, first Law Minister of independent India, chairman of the Constitutional Drafting Committee and the founder of the movement. Ambedkar first publicly stated that he would not die a Hindu in 1935 at a conference at Yeola after a five-year failed attempt at temple entry in Nasik. He did not finally convert to Buddhism until just before his death in 1956. His public conversion to Buddhism at Deeksha Bhumi in Nagpur, and the subsequent conversion of most Mahars and some non-Mahars, can only be understood in the context of Ambedkar's lifelong struggle to achieve social and political emancipation for the depressed classes in general and the untouchables or scheduled castes in particular. His ideology, including his later interpretation of Buddhism, is an important one in its own right in the modern social and political history of India, and the Buddhist element is not properly comprehensible outside the context of his lifelong political struggle.[6]

DEFINING AMBEDKAR'S GOAL

It might help the reader to focus on the significance of Ambedkar's political struggles, and its relevance to the subject of Buddhism, if I present a summary of what seems to me to be his essential aim. The best way to approach Ambedkar's conversion to Buddhism is to see it as a final attempted solution to the problem with which he had been struggling throughout the 1920s, '30s and '40s. The problem as he conceived it was how to emancipate untouchables from the ritual system known as Hinduism, and following from that, how to create a society based on the values of liberty, equality and fraternity. Caste and the rules underlying caste, which were justified in tradition by such law books as *Manusmṛti*, were the central, institutionalized expression of this problem. For most of his life this was conceived as a social problem requiring a political solution. This does not mean that it had no moral dimension. On the contrary, for Ambedkar the moral issue was fundamental. But he consistently argued that the moral issue would receive no recognition at all from those who controlled power in India until the untouchables themselves had defined a separate political constituency. It was only by defining themselves as a distinct political constituency with a common set of political interests and objectives that the untouchables, and the depressed classes more generally, could negotiate with the various parties from a basis of power.

Ambedkar argued that untouchables were as much a separate and distinct oppressed minority as Muslims. Yet while Muslims were able to negotiate with Congress and with the British from a basis of considerable strength and gain major concessions, the untouchables were not even recognized as having any distinct platform. It was first up to the untouchables to define themselves as a distinct minority constituency and to negotiate with the other interest groups on that basis.

Ambedkar believed that the emergence of politically conscious classes might act as an agent for fundamental change in Indian society. Ambedkar was not a Marxist but he was a democratic socialist insofar as he believed that the redistribution of wealth and opportunity in a society needed some direct government intervention, such as the nationalization of key industries. He also wanted separate electorates as a way round the problem of electoral intimidation and a guaranteed number of seats for backward classes in the legislature; and he wanted an employment and educational policy which actively countered the discriminatory tendencies of traditional caste loyalties. But his long term aim was the creation of a society of morally free and responsible individuals.

In Ambedkar's view the oppressors of untouchables were mainly the high caste Brahmans who controlled Congress and who put the Independence of India above genuine reform. Another group Ambedkar saw as the enemy of the untouchables was the non-Brahman high caste reformers with whom he worked in the earlier years but from whom he became increasingly alienated. But the figure who Ambedkar came to see as the most dangerous to untouchable aspirations was the one who claimed to be the untouchables' leader and emancipator, Gandhi.

Though Gandhi was not himself a Brahman, his influence over both Congress and the non-Brahman reformers was considerable. From Ambedkar's point of view, Gandhi exemplified the problem with high caste reform patronage which he (Ambedkar) constantly experienced throughout his political career. The problem essentially was that the reformers believed that untouchability could be eradicated on the basis of high caste goodwill alone, without giving real power or constitutional rights to untouchables, and without abolishing the caste system or the hierarchical values on which it is founded. As an untouchable himself, Ambedkar had experienced the effects of this system on those who were at the bottom of its hierarchy, and he was in no doubt that untouchability was a fundamental aspect of the very structure of Hindu caste relations. In his view it was impossible simply to remove untouchability by reforming the system. He believed that only through a programme of radical political democratization, involving a revolution in the sphere of values, and the subsequent abolition of caste, could untouchability be removed. All his life he tried to achieve this not merely by moral persuasion but also through constitutional change and political activism. It was this revolution in the sphere of values which he gradually came to identify with Buddhism.

It is one of the many ironies of his situation that he was finally invited by Gandhi and Nehru to chair the Constitutional Committee, which, despite his irritation with this act of high caste patronage, he did with outstanding brilliance. However, his experience as law minister in Nehru's cabinet and the failure of his Hindu Code Bill (1950/1) finally confirmed for him something which he actually already knew, that even constitutional change was insufficient to end untouchability in practice. His eventual conversion to Buddhism in 1956 just before his death was the culmination of this realization, and his final attempt to become free of Hindu culture and society by precipitating the kind of radical change which he believed Gautama Buddha had achieved in ancient India.

THE MAHARS (NOW CALLED BAUDDHA OR BUDDHIST)

Bhimrao Ramji Ambedkar (1891–1956), known as Babasaheb to those who love him, was born an untouchable Mahar. In 1956, on what is now called Dheeksha Bhumi in Nagpur, he publicly converted from Hinduism to Buddhism, accompanied by between 300,000 and 600,000 people (mainly Mahar). Since that time there has been a constant growth in the number of converts. The Mahar (now called Bauddha, or Buddhist) are the largest scheduled caste in Maharashtra, others being Chambhar, Mang (Matang) Dhor and Holare. According to census figures quoted by Karve (1968) the scheduled caste population in Maharashtra dropped between 1951 and 1961 by 45 per cent, that is from just under 4 million (or 12 per cent of the total) to 2,277,000 (5.93 per cent) This happened despite the substantial increase in the population as a whole. In contrast, in the same decade the number of Buddhists rose from 2,500 to 2.8

million. This was the result of the conversions initiated by Ambedkar in 1956, combined with the fact that members of scheduled castes who converted from Hinduism to a religion other than Sikhism lost scheduled caste status and the advantages which that status is supposed to provide in terms of reservations.[7] Fear of losing reservations may have held back even greater numbers from abandoning their formal Hindu identity.

In 1961 three castes accounted for nearly 90 per cent of the scheduled caste population in Maharashtra: the Mahars (35.12 per cent), the Mang (32.65 per cent), and Chambhar (22.06 per cent). But this was the figure after the mass conversions. It does not include the Buddhist population, the vast majority of whom were (and are) Mahar. This brings home the simple numerical sense in which the Mahar-Buddhists dominate the scheduled caste sector. And in the context of the total caste population, only the Maratha-Kunbi complex out-numbers them. By 1971 the Buddhist population of Maharashtra was 3,284,223, being 6.5 per cent of the total population (Kamble 1983, 236: also Hiro 1982).

Untouchable castes were (and still are) residentially separated from the ritually pure part of the village. Thus the area known as *Maharwada* (now *Bauddhawada*) is set aside (*vesakar*) from the main part of the village. All untouchables are thus marginal in multiple senses. And Mahars had a peculiarly symbolic marginality in the society of Maharashtra. Mahars did not have a special skill like Dhor (leather curing), Mang (rope making), or Chambhar (shoe making). Though high in the untouchable hierarchy,[8] they were tradi-tionally village servants who did menial tasks like cutting firewood, digging graves and disposing of dead animals, especially cattle which they ate.[9] Their service was linked to the Mahar *watan*, an arrangement which required Mahars to do service in return for the privilege of working a piece of *watan* land and receiving grain and *roti* from the dominant castes. However, Karve says that despite this right to land it was in fact traditionally tilled by Marathas and Kunbis, not Mahar. Indeed, according to Karve, 'no person from an untouch-able caste did farmwork' though more recently this has changed (Karve 1968, 92). (The practice of *watan* was not abolished until 1959.) Mahar were also traditionally employed as messengers, and this also had polluting connotations insofar as it involved the announcement of deaths. Mahars also had an ancient semi-official function of arbitrating in boundary disputes and mending the village wall. This association with boundaries, walls and margins makes them important not simply as marginal and polluting but as having a special kind of knowledge. Thus there is a suggestion that Mahars may have seen themselves as analogous to Brahmans within the untouchable sub-sector[10]. I have frequently heard it said that their contemporary high evaluation of the importance of education, so much encouraged by Ambedkar, reflects this view of themselves as being in some sense in competition with the Brahmans. The modern Buddhist community certainly has an intelligentsia, being much involved in a modern revival of Marathi literature (Zelliot 1992, 249–333), and in higher education, and also a political awareness and activism as shown in their strong association with the Dalit Panther movement and the Republican Party.

It might be argued that, if the traditional structure of Hindu caste society has been shaken by the impact of 'westernization' and capitalism under British imperialism, the Mahars would be one of the first groups to be loosened and displaced from it. In a way this is true, though the sense in which it is true needs to be carefully spelt out, because the evidence is that despite westernization and other factors, caste hierarchy is in some significant sense still in place. But the Mahars were quick to take opportunities for self-advancement and democratization under British rule. The British found them useful as army recruits, as messengers and servants, and Mahars used these opportunities as escape routes from village life. It also provided them with education; Ambedkar's father and grandfather both served in the British Army, his father was headmaster of an Army school, and Ambedkar himself was educated in Army schools. Another route of escape from their traditional village situation was provided by the British ammunition factories, cotton mills, the railroads and the docks. The 1921 census recorded that, though Mahars maintained strong ties with their ancestral villages, only 13.5 per cent of working Mahars were employed in their original occupations. Whatever the accuracy of these figures, it does suggest that even by that time a Mahar urban industrial workforce had developed. Kamble (1983, 237) suggests that mobility and migration among Mahar-Buddhists have recently still been high.

DR B.R. AMBEDKAR (1891–1956): AN IDEOLOGY IN HISTORICAL CONTEXT

Ambedkar himself was born in a village called Mhow in Ratnagiri district of western Maharashtra. As an untouchable boy he experienced various forms of discrimination from the higher castes at school, including problems over water, food, and commensality generally. One teacher refused to teach him Sanskrit. Yet he managed to pass his Matriculation examination in 1907. With help and encouragement from various interested and reform minded adults – at that time there was a strong reform movement in Maharashtra, mainly due to the non-Brahman movement[11] deriving from Phule (1827–90) in the last century – he went to Elphinstone College, graduated in 1912, and then won a scholarship for higher studies in Economics, Sociology, History and related subjects at Columbia University in New York, where he was awarded an MA in 1915 for his thesis 'Ancient Indian Commerce' and later submitted a Ph.D. thesis on 'The Evolution of Provincial Finance in British India'. In 1916 he presented a paper at the Anthropology Seminar of A.A. Goldenweiser entitled 'Castes in India: their mechanism, genesis and development'. This is an interesting paper and shows that Ambedkar was able to think about his own society with a sociological sophistication which characterizes his most brilliant later polemics, especially *Annihilation of Caste* (1936). In 'Castes in India' he put forward a sociological view that endogamy began historically among Brahman castes, and was designed to protect their purity and their high status. This system of inward marriage became in a sense 'mechanically' replicated among the remaining people who stood outside the Brahman strata, so that the system once started has had a kind of unbreakable propensity towards self-replication. Thus, untouchable castes themselves replicate a hierarchical ranking order and in this way contribute to the continuation of the very system which exploits them.

After Columbia Ambedkar was admitted to the London School of Economics and Political Science and also Gray's Inn where he studied law. This was interrupted because he was forced in 1917 to return to Baroda to serve the Maharaja as part of his contract.

However, caste discrimination on the basis of his untouchability was so severe both in the Baroda State administration and afterwards in the Sydenham College of Commerce and Economics where he was appointed a Professor that he realized that untouchables could never progress unless they began to organize themselves politically and to fight what he considered to be virtually a state of slavery.[12] Therefore in 1920 he founded a Marathi journal *Mooknayak* (Leader of the Dumb). He was helped in this by the Maratha prince Chhatrapati of Kolhapur, who was a leader of the non-Brahman movement and who encouraged Ambedkar's leadership of untouchables.

In his editorials he began to define his position as an untouchable in relation to the other constituencies. Though at this point he was in alliance with, and to some extent dependent on, leaders of the non-Brahman movement, he argued that untouchables were a special and separate class from Brahmans and from non-Brahman Hindus, who had their own interests to defend.

In 1920 he resigned his post and with financial help returned to London to finish his studies where he was awarded an M.Sc. in the University of London and where he also succeeded in qualifying as a barrister at Gray's Inn. He then returned to India as one of the most highly qualified people in the country, but still an untouchable. He began practising as a barrister in the High Court in Bombay but again experienced severe discrimination. Therefore in 1924 he started *Bahishkrit Hitkarini Sabha* (Association for the Welfare of the Depressed Classes). This was a continuation of the alliance with the non-Brahman movement, for the society had a reformist platform with Parsis and high caste Hindus in prominent positions. However, the real activists were untouchables, including Ambedkar, who stated the objectives of the association which included the necessity to develop a consciousness of social struggle and to overcome inertia and indifference. It was at this time that Ambedkar coined the slogan 'Educate, Organize, Agitate' which he repeated again at the All India Depressed Classes Conference in 1942.[13] The implication of his speech (and it is an important one) is that Mahars and other untouchables have for centuries been exploited by the system, yet they have not until this historical point been properly conscious of this fact, but have accepted it and even in a sense contributed to their own exploitation through their passive acceptance. This is consistent with Ambedkar's eventual rejection of high caste political patronage, which he distrusted.

The first really important challenge to the status quo in the form of direct action came at the Mahad Conference in March 1927. This conference ended with a march on the Chowdar water tank in 1927. Four years earlier the Mahad municipal authorities had opened the tank for use by untouchables, but the high caste Hindus had refused to allow them to drink the water. In his speech before the drinking ceremony, Ambedkar criticized the British government for stopping recruitment of Mahars into the British army under pressure from higher castes. He denounced this as ingratitude. Secondly he urged on his followers the importance of education and financial independence to break the hold of the traditional village system of servitude. This attempt to break free from traditional duties is still a major issue for the Buddhists. He also publicly stated the view that the untouchables were capable of fighting their own political battles and did not need the often condescending leadership of outsiders.

After the conference speeches about 10,000 protesters, mainly untouchables though with some progressive Brahman and non-Brahman reformers, marched to the tank and Ambedkar and others drank water from it. There were reprisals from the high caste Hindus, many men, women and children being attacked and beaten. The high caste Hindus then performed water-purification rites using 108 pots of curd, cow-dung, cow-urine and so on. Meanwhile, to the fury of the protesters, the Mahad Municipality revoked the original liberalization in the name of public order.

The following month, April 1927, Ambedkar began publishing a new periodical in Marathi, *Bahishkrit Bharat*, which came out intermittently over a period of two years. In his editorials his views on high caste reformism came strongly into focus. They foreshadow his attacks on Gandhi.

In his first editorial he denounced the hypocrisy of high caste 'reform' leaders who he argued did nothing themselves actively to promote the rights of untouchables but merely paid lip-service, and when the untouchables themselves took matters into their own hands most of these reformers stood on the sidelines and advised caution. He also asserted the right of untouchables to enter the Hindu temple.[14] Still more importantly, in one editorial he warned the high castes:

> We want equal rights in society. We will achieve them as far as possible while remaining within the Hindu fold or, if necessary, by kicking away this worthless Hindu identity. And if it becomes necessary to give up Hinduism it would no longer be necessary for us to bother about temples. (quoted in Gore 1993, 91)

This radical threat to 'kick away' Hindu identity shocked Hindu society and eventually led Ambedkar to Buddhism. Ambedkar also argued in various editorials that untouchability was contrary to the principles of justice instituted by the British administration, which therefore had a legal and ethical duty to defend the rights of untouchables. He further suggested in tactical terms that untouchables had enough political strength to mediate Hindu–Muslim relations by threatening to convert to Islam, if only they (the untouchables) would realize their strength.

Ambedkar was trying to develop a movement of protest. He frequently used the Marathi word *pratikar*, meaning something like protest or resistance, an assertion of natural rights against oppression. He also stressed the importance for all untouchables, of whatever caste, of overcoming their own caste differences and uniting in a common cause. This appeal to common interests was an attempt to define a *class* interest. It was aimed especially at Mang, who are the second largest untouchable caste. Though in recent times some Mang have been involved in Dalit politics, they have tended to remain within the traditional Hindu ideology.

In a speech in November 1927 Ambedkar specifically advocated *satyagraha*, and it was this that led to the second march on the Mahad Chowdar water tank. In a speech he proclaimed that the march was not simply for the right to drink water; it was a call for a fundamental social revolution, and he likened their collective goal to the Charter of Human Rights of the French Revolution.[15] However, the most controversial demonstration of this rejection of caste inequality was the public burning of a copy of the ancient and sacred Hindu law book, the *Manusmṛti*, a text which symbolizes the values of orthodoxy.

In the same year the Governor of Bombay nominated Ambedkar to the Bombay Legislative Council, and in 1928 he was appointed Professor in the Government Law College, Bombay. The last issue of *Bahishkrit Bharat* appeared in November 1929. One important point which he made in the final editorial concerned *swaraj* (self-rule). He expressed the view that from the point of view of the untouchables *swaraj* might be a 'calamity' because it was unbelievable that once the British had left the scene the high castes would continue voluntarily with reform.

He was also invited by the British to appear before the Simon Commission on constitutional reform, on which occasion he demanded among other things reserved places for the untouchables in government offices, on legislative councils and in education. The Simon Report, published in 1930, incorporated Ambedkar's proposals, but drew strong opposition from conservatives and therefore the British Government convened the Round Table Conferences in London to continue to try to find a settlement on the future constitution. At the first conference Ambedkar made a strong representation on behalf of untouchables, this time arguing for both reserved seats *and* separate electorates for untouchables, in this way emphasizing his basic political demand that untouchables should be treated as a distinct constituency. He also raised the issue of *swaraj*. We have seen that Ambedkar had already expressed the view that reform should come before *swaraj* because he fundamentally doubted the ability or willingness of the Congress to take the case of untouchables seriously once the British had left India. But on the other hand it was not clear to him how far the British were prepared to go on the untouchables' behalf, so at the London conference he put pressure on the British government by arguing that they had so far failed to bring far-reaching reforms, in which case the untouchables seemed to have no alternative but to support *swaraj*.

Gandhi attended the second of the conferences as the Representative of the

Congress. Ambedkar again proposed special political representation for untouchables and was supported by Ramsay Macdonald, who subsequently proposed the granting of separate electorates to the untouchables in the Communal Award (1932). However, Gandhi opposed separate electorates, at least for untouchables, and having lost the argument at the Round Table Conference he resorted to fast-until-death tactics to get his own way. This resulted in the Poona Pact of 1932, in which Ambedkar was forced to compromise in order to save either Gandhi's life or the fate of India from political turmoil.

Two years earlier Dr Ambedkar had been involved in organizing a temple entry *satyagraha* in the town of Nasik. Ambedkar no longer believed temple entries to be as important as securing political rights for untouchables through constitutional change (Gore, 1993, 124; Zelliot, 1992, 131). In any case he had little time for supernaturalism, and he was already formulating his opposition to the worship of gods, which was much later to be expressed in his interpretation of Buddhism and in his twenty-two vows, which were designed to accompany induction into the practise of Buddhism. Nevertheless, the failure of this long-drawn-out campaign (it went on for five years) angered him, for it indicated in graphic form how little the caste Hindus were really prepared to concede, and at the Yeola Conference in 1935 he made the famous statement that, though unfortunate enough to be born a Hindu, he certainly would not die one (Gore, 1993, 126; Ahir, 1989, 136; Ahir, 1990, 20).

One of the most important statements of Ambedkar's views was *Annihilation of Caste* (1936). This was originally written as a speech which he had been invited to deliver by the Jat Pat Todak Mandal of Lahore, a high caste reform group. When they read it they found it too dangerous so they cancelled the event. This merely confirmed Ambedkar's often expressed conviction that high caste reformers were not genuinely committed to the emancipation of the untouchables, since every time a genuine note of protest was struck they drew back and advised caution. Consequently Ambedkar published the speech as a pamphlet instead. This drew a response from Gandhi, 'A Vindication of Caste', published in the *Harijan* (15 August 1936). Ambedkar replied in a second edition which included a preface, Gandhi's *Vindication*, and Ambedkar's reply to Gandhi.

The published correspondence makes it clear that the reason the Mandal cancelled the speech was that Ambedkar refused to cut what he considered to be the essential point of his argument, which they variously found to be either irrelevant or too dangerous, namely that the real method of breaking up the caste system was not to bring about inter-caste dinners and inter-caste marriages but to destroy the religious notions on which caste is founded (1936, 49).

The religious notions he was referring to were of course the traditional Hindu ideology of rank based on purity and untouchability, and which manifested itself in caste, in ritualism, and in the suppression of autonomous individuality. Ambedkar's argument can be summarized thus: political and constitutional reform cannot succeed unless it is preceded by social reform aimed at the eradication of untouchability. But social reform can only mean abolition of caste, because untouchability is a defining feature of caste. In reality, caste cannot be reformed (contrary to Gandhi's hope), only annihilated. And the annihilation of caste implies the abolition of Hindu ideology, particularly as it is formulated in the *Śāstras* and *Smṛtis*. Caste is fundamentally 'a state of mind' (he meant this both collectively and individually), which is systematized in these texts, while endogamy is what he calls the 'mechanism' of caste. It is Hindu dogma that prohibits intermarriage, and therefore ultimately it is the Hindu values that must be destroyed:

> ... it must be recognised that the Hindus observe caste not because they are inhuman or wrong-headed. They observe caste because they are deeply religious ... the enemy you must grapple with is not the people who observe caste, but the Shastras that teach them this religion of caste. (1936, 111)

Ambedkar called for the replacement of Hindu ideology based on hierarchy and pollution with the fundamental principles of liberty, equality and fraternity (1936; 9, 128). For him these were *religious* principles. Furthermore, he wanted to bring this alternative tradition into line with traditional Indian ways of thinking, which in effect meant identifying a strand of his own indigenous culture which could legitimately be presented as a critique of Hindu ritual orthodoxy. Near the end of the *Annihilation of Caste* he suggested in a footnote that the values of liberty, equality and fraternity could be found in the *Upaniṣads* (1936, 128), though he does not pursue this tantalizing statement. Later, he found it in Buddhism. In both cases it is with the renouncer where he identifies the universal values which can replace the Hindu ritual system.

The argument with Gandhi exemplifies Ambedkar's criticisms of high caste reformism in general. Most reformists claimed to want to abolish untouchability but they did not want to abolish caste as such. Gandhi was among these. Some of his views changed over the years. For instance, in 1920 he was advocating the traditional bar on inter-marriage and inter-dining between castes, but by 1946 he was encouraging inter-caste marriages (Zelliot 1992, 153). What did not change much was his commitment to *caturvarṇya*, the ideal *varṇa* system, also known as *varṇāśramadharma*. He believed this division according to different functions is inherent in human nature, is essential in all societies, and was the original order of Hindu society from which the present system had degenerated. He was also consistent in his condemnation of untouchability, which he saw as a degeneration from the original ideal division of social functions. He claimed that this ideal did not imply hierarchy, which was a subsequent development, saying he deplored the fact that different functions had come to confer superiority and inferiority. All occupations are equally honourable: 'The calling of a Brahmin ... and a scavenger are equal' (*A Vindication of Caste*, 1936, 138). Yet he also upheld the birthright of *varṇa* and indeed the birth duty. People must follow their hereditary occupations: 'One born a scavenger must earn his livelihood by being a scavenger, and then he can do whatever else he likes' (Gandhi in 1937, quoted by Zelliot 1992, 154).

Nobody could doubt that Gandhi genuinely wanted to abolish untouchability. But it is difficult to see how Gandhi imagined that superiority and inferiority could be kept out of such a picture. Ambedkar hit back, and any reader who wishes to feel the power of Ambedkar's rhetoric is well advised to read his *A Reply to the Mahatma* (1936, 143–60), where he systematically shreds Gandhi's arguments and exposes their hypocrisy. Among his many arguments, he points out that if Gandhi was consistent, he would be fulfilling the merchant duties of his own *Bania* (*vaisya*) caste, and not meddling in politics.

In Ambedkar's view such high caste defence of a reformed orthodoxy constituted the main obstacle to his ambition to unite different castes into one interest group and thus to ensure that the untouchables were a real party in any constitutional arrangements. Though Ambedkar was now known throughout the country, nevertheless he had no effective organization outside the Marathi-speaking areas. By 1942 the Independent Labour Party, which Ambedkar had formed in 1936 and which he had hoped would develop into a class-based, rather than a caste-based, political platform, collapsed. The party had done well in the 1927 elections to the new Bombay legislature, but in the country as a whole untouchables had tended to support Congress. The inherent divisiveness of caste, even among untouchables themselves, made it almost impossible to form a class-based nationwide platform defined by common interests of depressed classes. This innate feature of Hindu society and culture was furthermore deepened by the very people who claimed to want reform, Gandhi in particular. By setting himself up as the leader of the nationalist movement and thus of the Indian people, and by claiming to have the authority to bring about reform, Gandhi was able to sabotage Ambedkar's leadership more effectively than any other single leader or interest group.[16] Ambedkar travelled around India extensively and emphasized the class dimensions of political issues, appealing to the shared interests of all depressed classes whether urban or agricultural. Yet in a speech at the All India Depressed Classes Conference in Nagpur in July 1942 Ambedkar seems to return to his role as leader of the untouchables as though he sensed the failure of the broader appeal. He reiterated that his fundamental political objective was that untouchables were not a subsection of Hindu society but a separate constituency, as distinct from Hindu society as were the Muslims.

It was at this conference that the Scheduled Castes Federation was formed, in effect taking over from the earlier and less narrowly defined Depressed Classes Movement. Ambedkar reiterated that Gandhi was the greatest opponent of the untouchables. He ended his speech by repeating his slogan 'educate, organize, agitate'.

When war broke out, Ambedkar had encouraged untouchable youth to join the army and at his insistence the British allowed a Mahar battalion to be formed. He criticized the nationalists for putting independence before the war effort and opposed Gandhi's 'Quit India' subversion campaign which the Mahatma had begun in 1942. He was appointed by the British to serve on the Executive Council of the Viceroy of India, and this and his continued support of the British war effort made him unpopular with many people of all classes.

Ambedkar's dislike of Gandhi steadily increased. He argued that Gandhi was unfit to be a political leader. He criticized his representation of India at the Round Table Conferences, and he questioned his real motives for wanting to undermine Britain and for gaining independence. Finally, he demanded that Gandhi explain his true war aims. He pointed out that while the Hindus had been ready to conciliate with Muslims and Sikhs, they did everything they could to ignore the demands of the untouchables. In his address in January 1943 to the members of the Deccan Sabha on the 101st anniversary of the birth of the reformer Ranade (1842–1901)[17], and again in his book *What Congress and Gandhi Have Done to the Untouchables* (1945), Ambedkar strongly denounced Gandhi and other high caste reformers, arguing that they had only harmed, not furthered, the interests of the untouchables. In one chapter he pleaded with foreigners not to be taken in by the claims of Congress to represent the interests of all Indians, and pleaded with the British in particular not to allow Congress to turn formally democratic institutions into a tyranny over minorities.

In 1946 the new British Labour Government instituted the election of a new constitution-making body, the Constituent Assembly, and Congress and the League won decisively in their respective areas. The Scheduled Caste Federation was badly defeated. Ambedkar, knowing his current unpopularity, did not even bother to stand. It appeared from the election results that the Scheduled Castes Federation only had influence in Bombay and Central Provinces, but that elsewhere members of the scheduled castes had overwhelmingly voted for Congress. Despite this, Ambedkar continued to argue that untouchables are a distinct minority constituency, and should be recognized as such. In 1947 the Constituent Assembly did adopt a formal resolution abolishing untouchability. Ironically this was greeted with cries of 'Victory of Mahatma Gandhi' even though Gandhi had always opposed legal measures and instead claimed that change must come from the heart. Ambedkar was the one who had always seen that the heart was not enough in these matters, and that law was profoundly important.

The Constituent Assembly elected Ambedkar chairman of the Constitution Drafting committee, and as such he was more responsible than any other single individual for the drafting of the Constitution and for steering it through the Assembly. Though he hoped to secure the interests of the scheduled castes and other minorities, he also had a wider vision of the polity which won him esteem and approval. The Constitution did in fact establish a number of provisions for scheduled castes, including recognition that scheduled castes and tribes suffered from special disadvantages; the need for certain protective measures such as reservation of seats in legislatures, education and government service; the empowerment of states to undertake special provision of assistance and welfare; and the creation of a special Commissioner for scheduled castes and tribes. But the Constitution did not provide for separate electorates.

Though the Constitution, which was passed by the Constituent Assembly in early 1950, provided a legal framework of equality and social justice, Ambedkar was aware, and warned the Assembly, that juridical equality was in contradiction to *de facto* social and economic inequality. Ambedkar knew, for all his hard work on the Constitution, that it was not sufficient. As far back as 1936, in *Annihilation of Caste*, he had argued that the ending of untouchability required a fundamental revolution in the sphere of values. This warning in a sense became a prophecy when he attempted to get his Hindu Code Bill through the Assembly. The aim of the bill was, among other reforms, the equality of women. For example, it sought to make forms of marriage other than monogamy illegal. It sought to confer on women rights of property, inheritance, divorce and adoption. Though Nehru supported the Bill it drew increasing degrees of hostility from Hindus and Nehru dropped it. Ambedkar argued that the provisions of the Bill were deducible from the principles laid down in the Constitution, but he could not overcome hostility from orthodox Hindus.[18]

Other reasons for his resignation were his failing health and his dislike of the élitist way in which Nehru ran his cabinet, with a small inner group discussing and deciding issues before they had been considered by the wider Cabinet. But the deepest reason was undoubtedly the vicious attacks made against him by orthodox Hindus for his attempt to introduce the Hindu Code Bill.[19]

AMBEDKAR AND BUDDHISM

It is sometimes claimed that a Buddhist revival was already under way in India long before Ambedkar converted. Macy and Zelliot and also Ahir refer to a 'revival' whose roots included archaeological discoveries in the nineteenth century; the translation of Buddhist texts; the foundation of the Maha Bodhi society by Anagārika Dharmapāla; the conversion in the early part of the century of some Tamil-speaking Pariahs; and the influence of important Indian Buddhist scholars such as Mahāpaṇḍita Rahula Sanskrityayan, Ven Anand Kausalyayan[20] and Ven. Jagdish Kashyap (Macy and Zelliot 1980, 134; Ahir 1989). Undoubtedly some of these factors influenced Ambedkar, for he did not turn to Buddhism in a vacuum. But when the word 'revival' is used, it must be borne in mind that the numbers of Buddhists in India are tiny in the context of the whole population.

After his resignation Ambedkar devoted time to thinking, speaking and writing about Buddhism. In 1950 he published a pamphlet, *The Buddha and the Future of His Religion*. In 1950 he addressed the Young Man's Buddhist Association in Colombo and his talk was to form the basis of a book, *Revolution and Counter-Revolution in Ancient India*, which remained unpublished during his lifetime.[21] He also began writing his book *The Buddha and His Dhamma* in this year. It was to be published posthumously in 1957.

His most dramatic action, on 14 October 1956, was publicly to take *deeksha* in Nagpur with his wife Savita on what is now called *Deeksha Bhumi*, conducted by the Burmese monk U Chandramani, who spoke the refuges and the precepts in Pāli. Nagpur may have been chosen for its symbolic connection with the Nagas. In his book *The Untouchables: Who They Were, and Why They Became Untouchables*, first published in 1948, Ambedkar argued that the Nagas were the aboriginal people of India, who were suppressed by the invading Aryans, turned to Buddhism, and were consequently turned into 'broken men' (outcastes) by the Brahmins.[22] After U Chandramani had performed the *deeksha* rites, Ambedkar then publicly took his own specially formulated twenty-two vows, which included a renunciation of Hinduism and all Hindu gods, and an affirmation of the principle of equality and of the truth of Buddhism. Ambedkar then himself inducted 400,000 others into Buddhism on the same day (Sangharakshita 1986, 134ff).[23] It is ironic that by renouncing Hinduism and converting to Buddhism, the members of the scheduled castes who converted lost their rights to reservations (see Macy and Zelliot 1980, 134).

The Meaning of Buddhism

Macy and Zelliot (1980, 135) have rightly pointed out that Ambedkar's interpretation of Buddhism is highly rationalistic in its rejection of anything that might look like supernaturalism or superstition. It would be fair also to say that, according to Ambedkar's understanding, *Buddhadhamma* is essentially morality. By morality he means compassion, caring for one's fellow human and for the natural world, feeling a sense of responsibility and commitment, being actively committed to the well-being of the world. Morality, unlike the ritual obligations which permeate Hinduism, springs from the heart of the individual and is based on a sense of brotherhood and sisterhood. Buddhism, on this line of reasoning, becomes the basis of the new egalitarian society, the structural equivalent of hierarchy as the basis of Hindu society.

There is no doubt that Ambedkar was an intensely religious man, in the sense of having a deep commitment to values and principles such as compassion, justice and equality. But he needed a religion which made a difference in this world, a religion which could change society and empower the backward classes. As a soteriology (doctrine of salvation), Buddhism has always been concerned with the fate of the individual, but in the sense of release (*nirvāṇa*) from this world (*saṃsāra*) through the self-discipline of the four noble truths and the eightfold path. For Ambedkar the four noble truths and the eightfold path were crucial. But he was critical of those forms of Buddhist practice which tend towards detachment from the world. This does not mean that he rejected what he called the 'self-cultivation' of the *bhikkhus*, by which he meant their moral and intellectual development as human individuals. What he criticized was the sharp distinction in traditional forms of Buddhism between the *saṅgha* on the one hand and the *upāsaka* (lay Buddhist) on the other (Ambedkar 1957, 80, 328; see also Macy and Zelliot 1980, 138). For Ambedkar, soteriology has a strong social and political component.

Though Ambedkar certainly believed in the liberation of the individual, he saw clearly that in the modern world the priority must be institutional liberation. The struggle for liberation, traditionally symbolized by the solitary renouncer in the forest, or by Gotama Buddha sitting alone beneath the *bodhi* tree, had to be transformed into a struggle against institutionalized bondage. I use the word bondage here deliberately, because even today there is bonded labour in parts of Maharashtra such as Marathawada (Pandit 1990; Fitzgerald 1993, 1996) and this modern form of bonded labour is seen by many Buddhists and Dalits as a continuation of the traditional system of village duties in a different guise. Thus for Ambedkar, and for many of his followers today, 'fetters' were not only those karmic hindrances which conditioned the individual's consciousness from one lifetime to another. They were also institutionalized realities which required a political solution.

Ambedkar believed that *bhikkhus* should not be renouncers in the sense of withdrawing from the world. They should be socially and politically committed to justice. He was attracted by the Mahāyāna concept of the *bodhisattva*, who delays his own liberation out of compassion for less fortunate or less advanced beings. Furthermore, the *bodhisattva* ideal lends itself more easily to modern concepts of democracy, human rights and social justice, for it can easily be seen as a compassionate activity in favour of the oppressed and the fight against social and political injustice. Salvation is conceived in terms of the struggle for emancipation and dignity of the oppressed classes of Hindu society.

Ambedkar's interpretation in *The Buddha and His Dhamma* (1957) is very much concerned with human morality as taught by the Buddha. It is also strongly flavoured with rationalism.[24] On the basis of moral principles and values it tends to emphasize an interpretation of Buddhist liberation as a social and political liberation, rather than as traditional individual enlightenment. For example, he equates *nirvāṇa* (the Buddhist concept of the transcendent) with the Eight-fold Path (which in traditional Buddhism is the way, the practice, by which one obtains *nirvāṇa*) (1957, 288); and the Eight-Fold Path's most important aspect, 'right outlook', is in turn defined as the recognition of cause and effect (291). This is almost like saying that *nirvāṇa* is equivalent to scientific rationality. But 'cause and effect' is also suggestive of an analysis where caste is identified as the cause, suffering (untouchability and exploitation) as effect, and rational political action, motivated by loving kindness, the means for ending that suffering. In this kind of way, Ambedkar attempts to present traditional Indian Buddhism as fully consistent with materialism, with scientific rationality, with political reform, with representative democracy, with the principles of equality, fraternity, liberty. This does not mean that he was not concerned about traditional concepts of personal enlightenment, only that his goal was conceived in terms of institutional liberation (liberation from the institution of untouchability and ritual pollution) as a necessary condition of any personal freedom.

Contemporary Political Buddhism

It seems significant that on almost all Buddhist shrines in Maharashtra one finds two pictures. One is of the Buddha sitting cross-legged in the rags of the renouncer meditating beneath the bodhi tree and achieving enlightenment. In the other one sees Ambedkar, dressed in a modern blue business suit, wearing heavy rimmed glasses, and holding a large book which represents literacy, education, and also perhaps the egalitarian Constitution of India. Here are two conceptions of the meaning of enlightenment side by side, the traditional and the modernist, seen by many (but not all) Buddhists as different and legitimate aspects of the one process.

Concepts such as *mokṣa* (liberation), *nirvāṇa* (enlightenment), *prajñā* (wisdom) and *karuṇā* (compassion) are multivalent. They can and do carry different nuances of meaning simultaneously in Ambedkar's writing and in the minds of Buddhists today. Today, the concept of Ambedkar as a *bodhisattva* or enlightened being who brings liberation to all backward classes is widespread among Buddhists. Of course, many Buddhists worship Ambedkar and Buddha much as they worship the old Hindu gods, and for some these may be merely significant additions to the supernatural pantheon. However, Ambedkar himself was entirely against supernaturalism, seeing it as a form of dependency induced by the traditional oppression of Hindu caste culture. And the dominant understanding of present day Buddhists, especially more educated Buddhists, is explicitly against the idea that Ambedkar is a supernatural being, just as Ambedkar was against the idea that Śākyamuni was anything other than human. Some Buddhists believe Ambedkar was enlightened or partially enlightened in a way similar to traditional Theravāda interpretations of Gotama Buddha's enlightenment, which stresses his humanity and refrains from turning him into a god. When such Buddhists perform *pūja*, they are recalling Gotama Buddha's and Ambedkar's outstanding lives and example. Many educated Buddhists interpret Ambedkar's enlightenment as the product of education and the full realization of his potential as a human being, not in a transcendental way.

Buddhist Intellectuals and the Dalit Movement

This interpretation of Buddhism, which places the emphasis on morality and scientific rationality, and which tends to be oriented towards socio-political liberation from institutionalized bondage, is well-represented among intellectuals today. In August 1991 I interviewed a number of lecturers at the Nagpur Deeksha Bhumi Dr Ambedkar College in Nagpur.[25] These were eight highly educated and articulate men who are committed Buddhists and who are personally knowledgeable about Ambedkar's writings. Since there are many colleges in Maharashtra which carry Ambedkar's name, and which have a high percentage of Buddhist professors, the facts about these men and their families give a valuable glimpse into a sector of the middle classes within the untouchable caste. Their parents had been Mahar up till the 1956 conversion, at which point they had become Buddhists and stopped using the name Mahar. Six said their parents had been illiterate agricultural workers; in one case the father had got to fourth grade, and in the other both parents had got to third grade. In contrast to their parents these men all had at least one Master's degree; some had two, and some three. Out of six wives, three matriculated to tenth or twelfth standard, two had BSc's, and one had two Master's degrees.

All eight lecturers were critical of caste endogamy, saying that it was an old tradition and no longer relevant now that they were Buddhists. Yet of the six who were married, all married women of Buddhist families; four of the six married into the same sub-caste, and one told me that his father would probably choose a wife for him from the same sub-caste. At one level this seems obviously to contradict Ambedkar's values, because he himself identified endogamy as the main mechanism of caste.[26] Yet in reality these men are trapped by the all-pervasive endogamous system. It may contradict the ideals in practice, but does not necessarily contradict them in intention. The possibility of caste inter-marriage is very restricted for all castes.

When asked what was the most valuable thing Dr Ambedkar gave to the Buddhists, six of the lecturers quoted the slogan 'educate, organize, agitate'. For them this was almost a summary of the meaning of Buddhist doctrine. For them Buddhism can be summarized as follows: Buddhism means equality, human dignity, self-help and self-reliance, rejection of caste and inequality, rejection of reliance on supernatural agencies, along with the acceptance of scientific rationality, modern education, democracy, and the rights of the individual. These men always interpreted traditional concepts of Buddhism in materialistic and non-mystical ways. For instance, I was frequently told that *karma* has no meaning, or alternatively that it means 'action which has social consequences'. The concept of *nirvāṇa* had no clear meaning for any of these men; and on the subject of meditation only two had a slight acquaintance with it, while the other six showed no interest or were positively dismissive. Also, rebirth is unambiguously rejected in its traditional form, but it is interpreted in two different ways. One is in the theoretically diluted way and materialistic sense given to it by Ambedkar (1957, 236): as the natural process whereby the physical elements which make up the body return to undifferentiated nature at death, and then are recombined to form a new body at birth. The other is in the entirely different sense of the awakening of human dignity, of their own control over their destiny, of escape from the sense of subordination and dependency and ritual denigration.

This sentiment is frequently expressed in Dalit political writing and Dalit poetry (Zelliot 1992), and it would be a mistake to misunderstand the intensity of feeling that accompanies this understanding, or the intensity of the devotion felt by these men towards Ambedkar and his ideals. This is a conscious, deliberate and well-articulated counter-ideology of fundamental democratic change. It finds its more formal political expression in the Republican Party of India (RPI), and its most militant form in the Dalit Panthers.

Before his death Ambedkar was planning the transformation of the older Scheduled Castes Federation into a new Republican Party of India. However, this only became a reality after he died. The Party has provided the formal political focus, but the most militant activism has been the Dalit (down-trodden) movement, which is a generally scheduled caste militant movement dominated by the Buddhists and known as Dalit Panthers or Dalit Black Panthers.[27] The Panthers were particularly active in the 1970s and early '80s, partly in reaction to the Marathawada pogroms (Zelliot 1992, 179–80; 314).[28] Much of this political activism has its literary counterpart in novelists and poets writing in Marathi (see Zelliot 1992; Joshi 1986; Rajshekar 1987). Some of this literature draws direct parallels between the position of the Dalits in India and the position of blacks in America. One difference is that, whereas blacks were taken to America as slaves, the Dalits follow Ambedkar's theory (1948) and identify themselves as the black aboriginals of India who were enslaved by the invading Aryans.

Ambedkar's hope that the Republican Party would develop into a broadly based party has not transpired. For one thing castes have tended to form *political associations* in the context of modern politics, thus inhibiting the formation of classes.[29] Also the party has been beset by factionalism. Insofar as the Party is a political force at all in Maharashtra it has had to make its way through alliances with the bigger parties. Ambedkar's grandson Prakash Ambedkar entered politics in 1983 when he called a meeting of activists to unify the RPI, then splintered into three main factions;[30] but although he is respected by some he is by no means the undisputed leader. He has been criticized for never being actively involved in Dalit agitation. For example, he did not participate in the campaign in the late 1970s to get Marathawada University renamed Dr Babasaheb Ambedkar University. His chief rival, Ramdas Athavale, made an alliance with Congress (I) and gained a post in the cabinet of the Maharashtra State Minister Sharad Pawar, thus suggesting that many Buddhists and Dalits may tactically vote Congress (I). Prakash Ambedkar has been involved in alliances with Janata Dal, with Muslims, with leaders of tribes, with Christian organizations, and also with OBCs (other backward castes apart from scheduled castes). However, his attempt to follow his forebear into a broader-based alliance with non-scheduled castes has been criticized by militant Dalits on the grounds that OBCs often look down on Dalits, and sometimes have even participated in atrocities against them.[31]

Buddhist Transcendentalism

To these intellectuals, Buddhism is an explicit commitment to social, economic and political liberation from their status as untouchables and from the Hindu ideology which justifies that status. Furthermore, it is clear that despite the perpetuation of caste identity through endogamy this commitment has a wider reference to democratic change in India as a whole. For other Buddhists this same commitment is also combined with a degree of transcendentalism more closely connected to traditional doctrine concerning a personal revolution in consciousness through meditation.[32] There are various soteriological organizations in Maharashtra today claiming to represent Buddhism,[33] but the only one that I know well is the *Trailokya Bauddha Mahasangha* (TBMSG) in Pune.[34] This organization acknowledges two spiritual founders, Dr Ambedkar, and the

English monk Sangharakshita who met Ambedkar a few times before he died and subsequently was involved in the early conversion movement (Sangharakshita 1986; 1988, 51–4).[35] This is not a *bhikkhu saṅgha* in the Theravāda sense since its full time members, called *dharmacharis* and *dharmacharinis*, are allowed to marry and have children.[36] It does, however, claim to be in the main stream of Buddhism, and to unite the social revolutionary message of Ambedkar with a detailed interpretation of Buddhist doctrine. It organizes retreats, teaches the reading of Buddhist scripture and meditation, and runs medical services, education for children and adults, homes for orphans, and a very active and well-supported temple in a poor district of Pune.

The doctrine and practice of TBMSG, though not political in the sense that the Dalit movement is political, is nevertheless closely identified with Ambedkar. The organization has his picture on all its shrines alongside the Buddha, and sells all his writings from its own bookshops along with traditional Buddhist texts and the commentaries of Sangharakshita. Committed members of TBMSG implicitly accept that key Buddhist terms such as *dhamma, nirvāṇa, karunā and bodhisattva* are multivalent or have gradations of legitimate meaning. For example, the '*dhamma* revolution' means both the mental and moral revolution of individual enlightenment and also the ending of caste and the establishment of a democratic society through committed socio-political action. The two are seen as different emphases within the same process. It also discourages supernaturalism and believes that self-reliance in both the moral and political spheres can be strengthened through meditation and spiritual discipline.

Village Buddhists[37]

So far I have suggested a spectrum of interpretations of Ambedkar's legacy among Buddhist intellectuals, Dalits, and the committed members of one soteriological organization. But these are mainly urbanites. The actual situation of Buddhists in village contexts is complex. On the one hand, caste is still a visible, inescapable and dominating feature of villages in Maharashtra. The villages are dominated by powerful Maratha, Kunbi and other landowning clans; Brahmans are still ritually the most prestigious, and other ritually pure castes, such as Lingayat Wani, Sutar (carpenters), Kumbhar (potters), Koli, Navi, Sonar (goldsmiths) and Lohar (blacksmiths), consider themselves relatively high and practice vegetarianism. Buddhists and other untouchables still live in separate parts of the village. They are only allowed into the ritually pure part of the village if servicing a higher caste, must use separate water wells, and cannot stand on the *par* (platform) of the village temple (*mandir*). Though the ancient *balutedari* system of services[38] has largely been replaced by a cash economy, nevertheless it is still operating in a different form, and members of different castes still perform services for the higher (especially Maratha) castes and indeed for the village as a whole on special days such as festivals. These services are rewarded with annual and special gifts of grain, *roti*, cash and other items.

Untouchable services such as night-soil removal, sweeping, grave-digging, dragging the carcasses of dead animals and so on are still performed by most castes, even though they also work for cash as labourers. Furthermore, Dhor communities still practise leather curing,[39] some Mang still make rope, Chambhar still make shoes. There is also evidence that, in the rural areas, untouchables still practice hierarchy and even untouchability among themselves, and that, for example, Buddhists consider Mang beneath them and even polluting.[40]

On the other hand, there is also strong evidence that since the 1956 mass conversion Buddhists have gradually been refusing to perform many of their traditional services, and instead work only for cash, usually as agricultural labourers, though sometimes as tailors, barbers or other acquired skills.[41] This has provoked periodic pogroms against them, but the Buddhists and Dalits are well organized politically and have defended themselves. There is also evidence that Buddhists have tended to withdraw from high-caste dominated village festivals such as *nagpanchami* (snake-god festivals) and perform their own alternative celebrations. There is some evidence that their refusal to participate in traditional activities has aroused resentment among the high castes and even other untouchable castes such as Mang, despite the fact that Mang seem to have benefited economically from this. By the same token, what in one light may look like untouchability practised by Buddhists against Mang in another light looks like disdain because Mang insist on conforming with the system that exploits them and do not support Buddhists in their wider bid for emancipation.

Buddhists are undoubtedly still involved in worship of the goddess Mariai and other gods such as Khandoba. However, I have suggested elsewhere that this might be explained pragmatically by the widespread fear of *kadak* deities who are believed to bring disease and death. Though more research needs to be done, it may be that Buddhists, despite their continued worship of deities such as Mariai, have quite widely withdrawn from those collective ritual activities most strongly associated with the dominance of the Marathas and the caste hierarchy.

We are here talking about a *de facto* lifestyle which many people who are proud to identify themselves as Buddhists practise by default. For example, sub-caste endogamy is widespread among all categories of Buddhists, at least in certain areas such as Nagpur and Marathawada. It is therefore part and parcel of contemporary Buddhist identity, even though Buddhists themselves deplore it.

CONCLUSION

Despite the apparent inability of the Buddhists and Dalits to form a coherent political party, there is nevertheless a distinctive counter-culture and ideology deriving from Ambedkar and motivating large numbers of Dalits, mainly Buddhists but also members of other scheduled castes. What is notable about all these different categories of Buddhists, urban and rural, illiterate or literate, is the high degree of consciousness that exists about Ambedkar's writings, his political and soteriological goals, in short of the meaning of Ambedkar Buddhism.

The democratic Buddhist values and political philosophy of Ambedkar are widely disseminated among Buddhists throughout Maharashtra. Even in remote villages with a high percentage of illiteracy, these values are disseminated in *vihāras* and meeting places, from large, highly organized temples which provide training in Ambedkar Buddhism to small temples and *vihāras* in city neighbourhoods and in large and small villages.[42] In many villages and urban neighbourhoods there is a local person such as a schoolteacher who may have done a training course in one of the larger organizations and who acts as leader of simple rituals (though he is not in any sense like a Brahman priest), organizes meetings, and teaches Ambedkar Buddhism. Thus these values are not merely subjectively held in the minds of a few individuals, but have acquired a shared, public reality which has led to significant changes in social relations. Examples of this are a widespread refusal to perform traditional polluting duties such as scavenging, and a widespread refusal to participate in *certain kinds* of Hindu ritual. The sharing of egalitarian values is directly and explicitly linked to Ambedkar's work on the Republican Constitution, and his work as an advocate in a judicial system founded on the principle of equality before the law; the centrality of his call for the annihilation of caste; and his interpretation of Buddhism. Further factors are a high rate of literacy and political consciousness among Buddhists, a willingness to work only for cash, and a militant resistance to the power of Brahmans and dominant landowners such as Maratha.

NOTES

1. Zelliot (1992, 235–7).
2. The Jatavs of Agra City are an untouchable caste who converted from Hinduism. See Lynch (1969). Like the Mahars, they considered Ambedkar to be the true leader of the untouchables, not Gandhi.
3. The term 'class' is problematic. Ambedkar strove to create a class consciousness among the scheduled castes and other 'backward classes' based on a perception of shared interests and transcending caste loyalties, but it is problematic to what extent this has been achieved.
4. The traditional name for a Buddhist monk (also *bhikṣu*).
5. *Dhammacharis* (also dharmachari) are renouncers who belong to the Trailokya Bauddha Mahasangha Sahayaka Gana based in Pune. I discuss this group below.
6. The most comprehensive collection of Ambedkar's writings and speeches is the Government of Maharashtra series of several volumes edited by Moon (1979, 1982, 1987, 1989, 1990). One of the best recent discussions of Ambedkar's ideology in social and political context is Gore (1993). A standard biography is Keer (1962). During the 1960s and early '70s a spate of articles were written by American scholars such as Eleanor Zelliot, Adele M. Fiske, Owen Lynch and Robert Miller, all contributors to the volume on untouchables in India edited by Mahar (1972). Zelliot in particular is essential reading, and her essays published since that time have been

conveniently collected in Zelliot (1992). There are historical books by Kamble (1983) and Ramteke (1983). Karve (1968) is an anthropologist of Maharashtra and her work includes some reference to Mahars/Buddhists. There are also several books by Ahir (1989, 1990, 1991). A fairly comprehensive discussion of the available literature can be found in Fitzgerald (1989).

7. 'Reservations' refers to the policy of reserving a fixed percentage of seats in local and national assemblies, and jobs in government agencies, for members of backward classes and scheduled castes. Competition for such seats and jobs means that a great deal hangs on who is defined as 'backward', etc.

8. Higher than Mang, Dhor or Holare, but probably considered untouchable by Chambhar (Patwardhan 1973, 59, 187). The Chambhar shoemaker in one village where I visited stayed in the house of a clean caste carpenter in the clean part of the village, suggesting that in that area at least Chambhar are only marginally untouchable.

9. Kamble (1983, 66–92) lists traditional Mahar duties in some interesting detail.

10. Wilkinson (1972, 82) says that, like the Brahmans, the Mahar had a traditional occupation as astrologers.

11. The Non-Brahman movement was a social reform movement started by members of mainly middle-ranking castes in the nineteenth century and aimed against the Brahman monopoly of social privileges. See O'Hanlon (1985) and Omvedt (1976).

12. The reader can find vivid descriptions of this discrimination in Ambedkar's *Waiting for a Visa: Reminiscences*, published by Siddharth Publications (People's Education Society), 1990.

13. It was repeated to me again by Nagpur intellectuals in 1992 as an integral part of the meaning of Buddhism, with connotations of self-reliance and intelligent struggle.

14. This right has still not been won. In all the villages I visited in Marathawada untouchables are still not allowed on to the platform (*par*) of the main temple, usually a *maruti* (Hanuman) *mandir* (temple).

15. The claims of the untouchables to use the Chowdar tank were not legally granted until 1937.

16. This sabotage on the part of high caste sympathizers continues. For example, Nanda (1985), in a book ostensibly about Gandhi and his critics, mentions Ambedkar only once in the index, and lists none of his works in the chapter-by-chapter bibliographies.

17. He compared Ranade favourably with both Gandhi and Jinnah; the speech was published: see Ambedkar (undated).

18. The Hindu Code Bill (1950/1) did in a sense become law in the shape of four separate Acts of Congress.

19. For example, Jere Shastri, one of the Shankaracharyas, viciously attacked Ambedkar as an untouchable who dared to interfere with orthodox Hindu practices (Gore, 1993, 189). In 1969 the Shankaracharya of Puri publicly defended untouchability (Zelliot 1992, 175.)

20. In 1983–4 I was fortunate enough to have met the latter before he died in his training centre for *bhikkhus* in Nagpur. He told me that he wanted to find an intellectual convergence between Buddhism and Marxism.

21. This has recently been published in Moon, 1987, Vol.3.

22. He also claimed that the Nagas and the Dravidians were the same people (Ambedkar, 1948, 1977, 66). This idea has fed into the thinking of the Dalit 'Black' Panthers, who sometimes identify themselves as the dark-skinned original people suppressed by the fair-skinned Aryans(See Rajshekar 1987).

23. U Chandramani had lived in India for fifty years and was India's senior (longest serving) Buddhist monk. There were also Sinhalese Buddhist monks present. Sangharakshita's sympathetic account points out that for a layman to administer *deeksha*, especially in front of monks, is a break with tradition.

24. This book was not completed before his death, and was assembled by the editors from extensive notes which he had written when ill.

25. This is the site of Ambedkar's public conversion and therefore has profound symbolic value for all Buddhists. A *stūpa* is in process of being constructed to house Babasaheb's ashes. Elsewhere I discuss the connection in Ambedkar's mind between Nagpur (city of the Nagas) and early Buddhism.

26. Ambedkar's second wife, who is still living, is in fact Brahman.

27. Rajshekar (1987), who wishes to combine a Marxist analysis with Ambedkar's thought, also uses the term 'black untouchables'; he draws a parallel between the position of blacks in America dominated by Anglo-Saxons and untouchables in India dominated by Brahmans. This links with Ambedkar's (1948) argument that the untouchables were the aboriginals of India, who were suppressed by the Aryans, were the first Buddhists, and were consequently outcast. Rajshekar also argues for a black untouchable homeland, Dalitastan (pp. 74).

28. Joshi (1986, 141–7) includes the Dalit Panthers Manifesto, published in Bombay, 1973.

29. See Dumont (1980, 220–2) for a discussion of this phenomenon, and his concept of the *substantialization* of castes.

30. See the interview of Prakash Ambedkar by Lina Mathias in Engineer (ed.), 1991, 346ff).

31. I am grateful to Professor Eleanor Zelliot for sending me some interesting details of the most recent (1997) elections which have relevance to the political situation of the Buddhists and Dalits. The RPI (Republican Party of India) aligned itself with the Congress Party in Maharashtra with the over-riding aim of defeating the Shiv Sena/BJP (Bharatiya Janata Party). The RPI put up four candidates in Maharashtra and all four were elected. These were Prakash Ambedkar, R.S. Gawal, Professor Jogendra Kawade and Ramdas Athawale.

32. This transcendentalist element is not accepted by all Buddhist-Dalit sympathizers. See for example Guru Gopal (1991), who sees it as mystification. On the other hand, I have met Dalits who engaged in violent struggle but who are now meditating *dharmacharis* in the TBMSG.

33. For example All India Bhikkhu Sangha, Bharatiya Bauddha Mahasangha, Sramana Upasaka Prachar Sangha, Bharat Brahman Bhikkhu Sangha. There is also a temple in Nagpur run by a Japanese monk, Shurei Sasai.

34. I have extensively interviewed its members; most are Indian but some are Western.

35. Sangharakshita is also the founder of the Friends of the Western Buddhist Order [FWBO] On the TBMSG and Sangharakshita, in addition to the other works listed the reader's attention is drawn to the following works: Sponberg (1996) and Pilchick (1986). Unfortunately I was unable to obtain them prior to writing this chapter.

36. Celibacy is considered to be an extra spiritual discipline freely entered into for a limited period of time.

37. I give more details in Fitzgerald (1993).

38. The *balutedari* system can be compared in some respects with the *jajmāni* system of northern India, though they are different in certain respects. Originally there were

twelve *balutedars* whose duty was to serve the whole village, though the system functioned under the patronage of the powerful land-owning castes, especially the Marathas. See Fitzgerald (1997).

39. I have visited two such Dhor communities, and have seen the traditional process in action.

40. There is a difficulty of interpretation: when Buddhists refuse to allow Mang to share their well on the grounds that Mang are still scavenging, are the Buddhists actually practising untouchability against Mang? Or are they expressing disappointment and contempt that Mang still conform to the Hindu system and refuse to join Buddhists in their rejection of that system? See Fitzgerald (1997).

41. Carter (1974, 53–4) notes that in western Maharashtra Mahars refuse to perform their traditional duties.

42. I should also mention the *mahila mandalas* or women's groups which Dalits and Buddhists are involved in organizing in cities and villages. These groups disseminate information and give mutual support between women concerning specifically female issues to do with rape, abuse, disease and medicine, dowry, abandonment, work, etc.

BIBLIOGRAPHY

Ahir, D.C. (1989) *The Pioneers of Buddhist Revival In India.* Delhi: Sri Sat Guru Publications.

Ahir, D.C. (1990) *The Legacy of Dr Ambedkar.* Delhi: BR Publishing.

Ahir, D.C. (1991) *Buddhism in Modern India.* Delhi: Sri Sat Guru Publications.

Ambedkar, B.R. (1916) [1936] 'Castes in India: Their Mechanism, Genesis and Development', in *Annihilation of Caste.* Jallandhar City: Bheema Patrika Publications.

Ambedkar, B.R. (1936) *Annihilation of Caste.* Jallandhar City: Bheema Patrika Publications.

Ambedkar, B.R. (undated) *Ranade, Gandhi and Jinnah: Address delivered on the 101st Birthday Celebration of Mahadev Govind Ranade, 1943,* Jallandhar City: Bheema Patrika Publications.

Ambedkar, B.R. (1945) *What Congress and Gandhi Have Done to the Untouchables.* Bombay: Thacker.

Ambedkar, B.R. (1977) [1948] *The Untouchables: Who They Were and Why They Became Untouchables,* 3rd edn. Shravasti, Balrampur: Bharatiya Bauddha Shiksha Parishad.

Ambedkar, B.R. (1950) *The Buddha and the Future of His Religion.* Jallandhar City: Bheema Patrika Publications.

Ambedkar, B.R. (1957) *The Buddha and His Dhamma.* Bombay: People's Education Society.

Ambedkar, B.R. (1990) *Waiting for a Visa: Reminiscences.* Bombay: Siddharth Publications (People's Education Society).

Carter, A.T. (1974) *Elite Politics in Rural India: Political Stratification and Political Alliances in Western Maharashtra.* Cambridge: Cambridge University Press.

Dumont, Louis, (1980) *Homo Hierarchicus: The Caste System and its Implications.* Chicago: University of Chicago Press.

Engineer, Asghar Ali (ed.) (1991) *Mandal Commission Controversy.* Delhi: Ajanta Publications.

Fitzgerald, T. (1989) 'Buddhism and Social Change in Maharashtra', in *Bulletin of Humanities, Aichi Gakuin University*, 50–73.

Fitzgerald, T. (1990) 'B.R. Ambedkar on Caste and Buddhism', in *Bulletin of Humanities, Aichi Gakuin University*, 54–67.

Fitzgerald, T. (1993) 'Ritual, Politics and Soteriology in Ambedkar Buddhism', *Indian Journal of Buddhist Studies*, 5/1, 25–44.

Fitzgerald, T. (1996) 'Ambedkar, Dumont and Buddhism', *Contributions to Indian Sociology*, (n.s.) 30/2 273–88.

Fitzgerald, T. (1997) 'Ambedkar Buddhism in Maharashtra since 1956', in *Contributions to Indian Sociology* (n.s.), 31/2.

Gore, M.S. (1993) *The Social Context of an Ideology: Ambedkar's Political and Social Thought.* New Delhi and London: Sage.

Guru Gopal. (1991) 'The Hinduisation of Ambedkar', *Economic and Political Weekly*, 20 Febuary.

Hiro, D. (1982) *The Untouchables of India.* London: Minority Rights Group.

Joshi, Barbara R. (ed.) (1986) *Untouchable! Voices of the Dalit Liberation Movement.* London: Zed Books, Minority Rights Group.

Kamble, N.D. (1983) *Deprived Castes and their Struggle for Equality.* New Delhi: Ashish.

Karve, I. (1968) *Maharashtra: The Land and its People.* Bombay: Maharashtra State Gazetteers General Series.

Keer, D. (1962) *Dr Ambedkar, Life and Mission.* Bombay: Popular Prakashan.

Lynch, Owen M. (1969) *The Politics of Untouchability: Social Mobility and Social Change in a City in India.* New York and London: Columbia University Press.

Macy, J.R. and Zelliot, E. (1980) 'Tradition and Innovation in Contemporary Buddhism', in Narain, A.K. (ed.) *Studies in History of Buddhism.* Delhi: B.R. Publishing Corporation, 133–51.

Mahar, J.M. (ed.) (1972) *The Untouchables in Contemporary India.* Arizona: University of Arizona Press.

Mathias, Lina. (1991) 'Punch in the Nose Backwards', interview with Prakash Ambedkar, originally published in *The Independent*, reprinted in Engineer, 1991, 346–50.

Moon, Vasant (ed.) (1979, 1982, 1987, 1989, 1990) *Dr Babasaheb Ambedkar: Writings and Speeches*, Bombay: Dept of Education, Govt of Maharashtra, Vols 1–8.

Nanda, B.R. (1985) *Gandhi and His Critics.* Oxford: Oxford University Press.

O'Hanlon, R. (1985) *Caste, Conflict and Ideology: Jyotiba Phule and Low Caste Social Protest in the Nineteenth Century.* Cambridge: Cambridge University Press.

Omvedt, Gail, (1976) *Cultural Revolt in a Colonial Society.* Bombay: Scientific Socialist Education Trust.

Pandit, Vivek, (1990) *Report of the Campaign for Human Rights.* Bombay: Vidhayak Sansad.

Patwardhan, S. (1973) *Change Among India's Harijans: Maharashtra, A Case Study.* Delhi: Orient Longman.

Pilchick, Terry, (1986) *Jai Bhim! Dispatches from a Peaceful Revolution.* Glasgow: Windhorse.

Rajshekar, V.T. (1987) *Dalit: The Black Untouchables of India.* Atlanta/Ottawa: Clarity Press.

Ramteke, D.L. (1983) *Revival of Buddhism in Modern India.* Delhi: Deep & Deep.

Sangharakshita, Ven. (1980) *A Survey of Buddhism.* Boulder, Col: Shambala and Glasgow: Windhorse.

Sangharakshita, Ven. (1986) *Ambedkar and Buddhism.* Glasgow: Windhorse.

Sangharakshita, Ven. (1988) *The History of My Going for Refuge.* Glasgow: Windhorse.

Sponberg, Alan, (1996) 'TBMSG: A Dhamma Revolution in Contemporary India', in Queen, Chrishopher S. and Sallie B. King (eds) *Engaged Buddhism: Buddhist Liberation Movements in Asia.* Albany, NY: State University of New York Press, 73–120.

Wilkinson, T.S. (ed.) (1972) *Ambedkar and the Neo-Buddhist Movement.* Madras: Christian Literature Society.

Zelliot, E. (1966) 'Buddhism and Politics in Maharashtra', in Zelliot, 1992, 126–49.

Zelliot, E. (1972) 'Gandhi and Ambedkar: A Study in Leadership', in Zelliot 1992, 150–78.

Zelliot, E. (1992) *From Untouchable to Dalit: Essays on the Ambedkar Movement.* Manohar, New Delhi.

5

JAPANESE NATIONALISM AND THE UNIVERSAL DHARMA*

HIROKO KAWANAMI

INTRODUCTION

When Japan came out of its long political seclusion in the late nineteenth century, Buddhism had been upholding the social cohesion of the Tokugawa Shogunate for more than 250 years. Buddhist temples had acted as local instruments and priests conducted rituals to maintain the cohesion of the community and family. However, as Japan entered a new political climate in the early twentieth century, State Shintō was introduced to counter the threat of Western military powers and to accelerate the process of nation building. This period of modernization was characterized by an increasingly oppressive regime which resulted in the persecution of many religious organizations. In order to survive, Buddhism attempted to reconcile its universalist teaching with a national ideology, in which process the Buddhist Law (*dharma*) had to find ways to co-exist with Emperor (*cakravartin*) worship. Some sects revised their religious teaching in the struggle to maintain doctrinal authority against the overwhelming influence of the secular power. In this climate, the majority of Buddhist sects, aiming to protect their interests, actively catered for the needs of the state by propagating the imperial ideology of State Shintō. However, there were also Buddhist individuals who fought for religious and social reform, and honoured their responsibilities in the face of mounting social problems in the early part of the twentieth century.

After defeat in the Second World War, Japan entered a new era with the introduction of democratic principles administered by the American occupation. Clause 20 of the new Constitution (1947) stipulated religious freedom to be one of the fundamental rights of Japanese citizens for the first time. It allowed religious activities to become the private domain of the individual and henceforth protected from any political influence. However, in the spiritual vacuum created by the consequent defeat of State Shintō, established Buddhist sects in general did little to provide for new spiritual directions. They continued to pursue their traditional ways in performing rituals for the family and ancestors in spite of the increasing calls for modernization, while, from the 1960s, urbanization accelerated the break up of rural village communities and hence eroded the

* The author would like to express her thanks to the Nuffield Foundation Social Science Small Grants Scheme for funding a research visit to Japan that contributed to the completion of this paper.

sects' traditional economic foundations. In contrast, new Buddhist organizations such as Sōka Gakkai, Reiyūkai and Risshō Kōseikai steadily consolidated their positions in the cities and among Japanese abroad, and numerous 'new religions' mushroomed in the postwar period, rapidly becoming a focus for a new religiosity in the latter part of the twentieth century.

STATE SHINTŌ AND STRUCTURE OF OPPRESSION

The period of turmoil that followed the collapse of the old feudal government and the restoration of the imperial court in the late 1860s brought about a movement called *Haibutsu Kishaku* (Movement to Abolish Buddhism).[1] During this period Buddhism underwent waves of persecution. Temples were plundered, statues destroyed, and Buddhist priests had their lands confiscated; events precipitated by the long dominance of the Buddhist temples and the frustrations of the people who resented the power of the priests who had historically acted as political tentacles for the ruling power. As the state quickly shifted its former patronage to Shintō, the Buddhist establishment was obliged to take a cautious and pragmatic approach in its dealings with the imperial authority. Nevertheless, instead of turning this ordeal into a self-reflexive exercise which might have led to a revival of its religious autonomy, Buddhist sects sought more patronage and closer relationship with the state for protection. Simultaneously, they continued to exert day-to-day influence on the population through *danka-seido*, parish system established in the Tokugawa period, and 'as before, the people largely continued to maintain temple affiliations, based on funerals, grave sites, and ancestral memorial rites performed by temple priests' (Hardacre 1991, 28). In other words, traditional Buddhism continued to cater for the needs of the establishment by never attempting to divorce itself from the collective system of the family and ancestors, and by not taking any initiatives in encouraging people to pursue individual religiosity, it continued to 'remain pre-modern and feudal in its fundamental characteristics' (Murakami 1980, 73).

As Japan embarked on its course of modernization in the late nineteenth century, the indigenous worship of nature and ancestors was transformed into a systematic belief system equipped with a world-view to suit its national goals. The Imperial Constitution promulgated in 1889[2], provided its legal framework, and the Education Decree (Kyōiku Chokugo) of 1890 gave a moral foundation to the project. An ideology of State Shintō was created in which the descendants of the Sun Goddess, Amaterasu Ōmikami ruled the land, thereby providing mythological justification for the divine origins of the imperial lineage on which the legitimacy of the Emperor was based. In the face of demands for a separation of politics and religion, the government took the view that State Shintō was not a religion, emphasizing the distinction between private and public practices of religious beliefs (Hardacre 1991, 115–21). Nevertheless, its status remained ambiguous, as was the general understanding of the definition of 'religion'; consequently, State Shintō was granted a 'trans-religious' status whose primary role was to perform rites and rituals for the state. The supreme authority reverted to the Imperial Court, and the Emperor became deified as '*Arahito-gami*' (the living Man-God), who integrated the role of shaman and political authority in his role as the supreme 'officiator'. In this process, the religious arm of Shintō classified as Kyōha Shintō or Sect Shintō[3] was separated from State Shintō, and became officially registered as 'religion' along with other religions such as Buddhism and Christianity. By becoming 'religions' however, they were designated to the lower ranks and became officially subordinated in the imperial political hierarchy. Simultaneously, the legal framework for State Shintō was successively implemented. The Police Preservation Law (Chian Keisatsu-hō), issued in 1900, forbade all religious persons including priests and monks from participating in political activities and their rights to be elected were taken away.[4] The notorious Peace Preservation Law (Chian Iji-hō), enacted in 1925[5], came into effect in 1929. These laws granted the state authority sweeping powers and were effectively used to support the imperial system in order to oppress any type of anti-imperial movement and 'dangerous thoughts'.

The main enemy of the establishment was international communism, but religious groups were not excluded from persecution. Buddhist sects also came under scrutiny, and even the patriotic Nichiren sect was criticized for upholding Amaterasu the Sun Goddess as the patron saint of the *Lotus Sūtra*. As such it was ordered to delete some of the terms from the scriptures believed by its devotees to have been written by Nichiren.[6] Some sects such as Jōdo Shinshū, had to modify irreverent terms and revise their original religious doctrine, while others, desperate to save their position, became increasingly co-operative in serving the state.[7] The notion of *Hakkō Ichiu*[8] resulted in the annexation of Korea in 1910 and the colonization of Manchuria, which heightened a general mood of patriotism. Nihonzan Myōhōji, established in 1917 by Fijii Nittatsu, advanced into Manchuria and spearheaded nationalist missionary work to propagate the doctrine of the Emperor among local people, Japanese expatriates and soldiers.[9] Additionally, the sense of doom evoked by the Kantō earthquake (1923) in Tokyo and the world economic depression triggered one of the worst decades of economic crisis and social instability. The general sense of urgency created an environment for the mushrooming of 'new religions'.[10] The 1930s and '40s were an exceptionally dark period which saw accelerated oppression and tighter controls over speech, thought, and beliefs. The Religious Organizations Law (Shūkyō Dantai-hō) issued in 1939, was implemented to control all religious organizations, and subsequently religious groups, the majority of which were 'new religious' and also Christian sects came under severe persecution. Most of the Buddhist sects[11] nevertheless actively supported Japanese imperialism and continued to send their priests and nuns to China and the Korean Peninsula, and became increasingly involved in nationalistic proselytizing.[12]

THE LIBERAL UNDERCURRENT IN THE EARLY TWENTIETH CENTURY

There was a new Buddhist movement in the early part of the twentieth century that led to a break between reformers and the establishment. A new Buddhist organization, called Bukkyō Seito Dōshikai (Association of Buddhist Purists),[13] was originally founded in 1899 as a result of an increasing disappointment with the complacency of traditional Buddhist sects. It represented a 'consistent effort to propagate and organize the New Buddhism as a radical alternative to traditional Buddhism' (Thelle 1987, 209). New Buddhists were influenced by the activities of Protestant Christianity (especially Unitarianism) which involved itself with social issues,[14] and attempted to seek a more socially engaged type of Buddhism suited for the needs of a modern civic society. This was also the time when Japan seized the opportunity to acquire a monopoly of the Chinese market whilst World War I saw the momentary retreat of the European powers from the Chinese Continent. Japan expanded its domestic markets significantly but the monopoly of industrialists and *zaibatsu* (financial and industrial corporate dynasties) had created high inflation, uneven distribution of wealth, and unwaged migrants pouring into the cities. This situation brought about frequent unrest and strikes, and in 1918 the high price of rice caused riots throughout Japan. The problem of poverty and injustice was taken up by the socialists[15] who formed the Socialist Liberal Party in 1901. The movement presented a major threat to the imperial administration, and many of the socialists who advocated social reform came under severe persecution; some of them were Buddhist monks who were executed under the Peace Preservation Law.[16]

In the meantime, the development of industrial capital and the growth of a middle class laid a foundation for a new civil society. The era was characterized by an advocacy of individualism, liberal sentiments, and strong demands for a better quality of life. It was also characterized by a liberal and humanistic undercurrent, referred to as the era of 'Taishō Democracy'. This liberal climate led to an interaction between traditional Buddhist thought and modern philosophy, and saw a popularization of Buddhist literature. The philosopher Nishida Kitarō (1870–1945), who published *Zen no Kenkyū* (The Study of Goodness) in 1911, was deeply influenced by his lifelong friend and Zen teacher Suzuki Daisetsu (1870–1966) and became the driving force behind the Kyōto School of Philosophy. He was influential in promoting an East–West synthesis which incorporated Buddhist doctrine with the modes of analysis and argumentation borrowed from the traditions of Western scholarship.[17]

The Buddhist establishment was also not free from the influence of the time, and modern Buddhist studies came to be taught in many of the newly established Buddhist universities.[18] Academics such as Anesaki Masaharu (1873–1949) called for the revival of Buddhism and advocated a return to the spirit of primitive Buddhism. Kiyosawa Manshi (1863–1903), who criticized the corrupt lifestyle of Jōdo Shinshū Honganji priests, preached 'inner spirituality' and tried to revert to the earlier forms of Buddhist spirituality which he understood to be innately personal. His contemporary Itō Shōshin, an ex-monk of the Jōdo Shinshū Ōtani sect, who emphasized the ideals of altruism and loving kindness, advocated a spiritual life devoted to social work. Finally, Ōuchi Seiran (1845–1918) preached Buddhism for lay householders and called for a departure from the monastic community. There was also a growing mass culture and an increased interest in arts and entertainment. Buddhist literature such as *Shukke to Sono Deshi* (The Renouncer and his Disciple), written by Kurata Hyakuzō (1891–1943) caught the imagination of the general public and became a major best-seller.[19] It was a humane depiction of Shinran (1173–1262), the founder of Jōdo Shinshū, and his disciple Yuien, and their personal struggle in overcoming lust and greed in an attempt to find the ultimate spiritual path. The book became a large scale cultural phenomenon which was performed in theatres all over the country. But the Jōdo Shinshū sect was outraged, claming that the saintly image of their founder had been tainted. This incident, however, exposed their conservative and feudal outlook and the limitations on the part of the Buddhist establishment in understanding public sentiments and accepting the social climate of the time.

NICHIREN BUDDHISM UNDER THE NATIONAL POLITY

The most active and nationalistic strands of Japanese Buddhism derived their inspiration from the teachings of the thirteenth-century saint, Nichiren, who based his religious philosophy on the *Lotus Sūtra*. Tanaka Chigaku (1861–1939), formerly a monk of the Nichiren sect, had become dissatisfied with his own sectarian affiliation. In his *Risshō Ankokuron* (Treatise on Establishing True Dharma and Securing Peace in the Nation) Nichiren (1260) wrote that a stable and peaceful society could be established only if the political power accepted and practised the 'right Buddhist law', in other words, worshipped the canon of the *Lotus Sūtra* (Murata 1971, 34). Tanaka elaborated Nichiren's religious ideal into a unique 'Nichirenism' and established a neo-Nichiren doctrine in 1902[20]. He actively supported the imperial polity by arguing that the Imperial Constitution was an ideal manifestation of Nichiren's religious teaching, in which the unity between *dharma* and the absolute authority of the Emperor could be fully realized. Tanaka involved himself in actively inspiring lay Buddhists, and formed the Rengekai, which became Risshō Ankokukai (Association for Establishing True Dharma and Securing Peace in the Nation) in 1885. Subsequently he founded another organization, Kokuchūkai (Nation's Pillar Society), in 1914. There were several strands and interpretations of the teachings of Nichiren in the early twentieth-century. However, Tanaka, who referred to his own theory as 'pure Nichirenism', advocated a religious ideology that was relevant to the political climate of the time. It was profoundly nationalistic, and was devoid of the spiritual egalitarianism[21] or criticism originally expounded by Nichiren towards the secular power of the political establishment, but Tanaka's ultimate aim was to establish a doctrine which could amalgamate state religious ideology with the principles of the *Lotus Sūtra*.[22] He held that unquestioned political authority over the Japanese people and their 'brothers' in the Greater East Asia Co-Prosperity Sphere lay in the hands of the Emperor and the imperial family. Religion would be the tool for ensuring the success of this project.[22] Tanaka won support among nationalistic Buddhists and right wing politicians, and consequently exerted considerable influence upon prominent people of his generation (Nishiyama 1990, 47).[23] In 1923 he founded Rikken Yōseikai (Constitutional Development Society) as the political wing of Kokuchūkai to promote his beliefs and ideology. He also stood as a candidate for the Lower House in 1924, with a motive of converting the whole nation to Nichiren Buddhism. In order to achieve this, he advocated the founding of *Kokuritsu Kaidan*, the national ordination platform,[24] to ordain priests independently dedicated for the worship of the *Lotus Sūtra*. He even attempted to have a Parliamentary bill on the matter passed. If his project was fully realised, in his view, the Emperor would become a righteous Buddhist king (*cakravartin*)[25] who would eventually rule the world.

The strands of Nichiren Buddhism which supplied much of the more ardent teachings in the Buddhist revival in the early twentieth century tended towards ultra-nationalism. However, there were also movements initiated by the followers of Nichiren whose message was trans-national and universal. In 1931, the Manchuria Incident took place[26] and after this the Japanese army was increasingly drawn into Chinese affairs. In the same year, Senō Girō (1889–1961), a Nichiren lay activist, founded Shinkō Bukkyō Seinen Dōmei (New Buddhist Youth League).[27] He addressed the question of how to practise and live the *dharma* in an unjust and corrupt world. He advocated the realization of a society based on the Buddhist ideals of sharing, equality and compassion, and called for individual responsibility and social action. He also emphasized the universal and humanistic aspect of the Buddha's doctrine and pointed out that nationalistic tendencies did not constitute Nichiren's essential teaching. Senō was fiercely critical of the Japanese invasion of China, denouncing this imperialist aggression as selfish and as representing nothing more than the quest for power of the capitalist class. He was anti-capitalist, anti-fascist, anti-war, and asked his followers to resist conscription. However, he was ultimately not against the Emperor. Senō differed from other Buddhist teachers of the time in underlining the need for personal responsibility, placing equal emphasis on the ruler and the ruled alike, and advocating that the imperial and the national conscience should come together in realizing the true *dharma*. In 1933 he published his masterpiece, *Shakai Henkaku Tojō no Shinkō Bukkyō* (New Buddhism on a Path to Social Reform). The six principal ideas described in the book provided the guidelines for his Buddhist movement,[28] which challenged the political climate of the time through its affinity with the 'downtrodden'. Senō also sharply criticized the élite classes and formed alliances on many occasions with anarchists, socialists, and outcasts.[29] As a result, his movement came to be seen as anti-social and dangerous and it was forced to disband in 1937.

NEW BUDDHIST ORGANIZATIONS

Many of the newer Buddhist organizations arose out of similar types of concern addressed by Buddhist liberals. These reformist movements which spread mainly in the 1930s included Reiyūkai, Risshō Kōseikai, Sōka Gakkai, Nenpō Shinkyō (affiliated to the Tendai school), Kōdō Kyōdan, Gedatsukai (affiliated to Shingon), Shinnyoen, Myōchikai Kyōdan, Bussho Gonenkai Kyōdan, and Nakayama Shingo Shōshū. The majority of them were Nichiren sub-sects, led primarily by lay devotees who were critical of the corruption and lack of concern for the general public displayed by the priests. Ordinary people were attracted to their religious practices due to their strong this-worldly orientation (*genze riyaku*) which promised immediate relief from daily problems and miscellaneous worldly benefits. Everyday concerns such as health, family problems, social relations and financial difficulties were dealt with, and the prospects for promotion, good marriage, and success in life were guaranteed in return for commitment. New Buddhist organizations also inherited values and religious techniques from traditional Buddhism, however they differed in their emphasis on the role and responsibility of the individuals in opposition to that of the former, where religiosity was the responsibility of the family collective.

Reiyūkai (Society of Friends of the Spirits) started as a lay Buddhist organization founded by Kubo Kakutarō and Kotani Kimi in 1930. Kubo[30] was a devout follower of the *Lotus Sūtra* and believed that the only solution to social problems and hardship could be found in the combined teachings of this text and the effective practice of *senzo kuyō* (remembering and worshipping the ancestors).[31] He became convinced of the need to move away from the traditional practice of relying on the priests to conduct rituals for the afterlife, and of restoring to individuals the authority to take responsibility for and to improve their own spirituality. Simultaneously, he maintained the significance of family relationships by preaching the concept of *karma*; that an individual's karmic position could be enhanced by propitiating one's ancestors and parents. Members were encouraged to mutually support themselves through confraternities, called *kō*, in times of economic difficulties. During the oppressive period of State Shintō, Reiyūkai reached an accommodation with the cult of the Emperor by installing a president related to the imperial family, and by taking an active role in a series of public services to aid the war effort. As such it survived the difficult period as one of the least adversely affected religious organizations. In the post-war turmoil, members rapidly increased among those who had moved away from their traditional communities and were alienated in the cities. Kotani Kimi, in her role as a charismatic faith healer, initially attracted isolated housewives, the unemployed and the downcast, and by 1948, led one of the largest new religions in the immediate postwar period. However, during her later years of leadership in the 1950s, members became involved in a series of legal battles due to financial mismanagement, bribery and corruption, and, as a result, internal disputes intensified. On the other hand, the construction of new religious centres, Mirokusan (Future Buddha Mountain) in 1964 and Shakaden (Buddha Palace) in 1975, fulfilled the aim of Kubo, the original founder, to establish a national ordination platform. After Kotani's death in 1971, the task of reconciliation and recovery were thrust upon her successor Kubo Tsugunari, an academic and a liberal. He played down the superstitious tone and replaced traditional healing practices with the notion of individual responsibility and personal development. He initiated ventures such as the 'Inner Trip Movement' in the 1970s and the 'Inner Self Development Movement' in the 1980s. Reiyūkai refocused the latter in the 1990s by launching the 'Life–a Dynamic Exchange' concept to promote the understanding of interdependence and the totality of one's being.[32] However, some members saw these ventures as 'more style than substance' (Hardacre 1984, 51) and the difference in views subsequently created divisions, manifesting a wide gap between traditionalists in the western regions, many of whom lived around Ōsaka, and the liberal headquarters in Tokyo.[33] The rift pointed to the dilemma faced by many religious organizations founded before the war, whose membership was based on traditional hierarchical bonds, relying heavily on conservative values such as loyalty and obedience. Yet simultaneously, movements had to be steered in more democratic and egalitarian directions to attract younger members and attune themselves to the changing demands of the outside world.

There were several groups that broke away from the Reiyūkai.[34] These were Kōdō Kyōdan, Sankai Kyōdan, Shishinkai, Risshō Kōseikai, Myōchikai, Busshogonenkai, Kuonkai, Hōshikai, Daieikai, Myōdōkai Kyōdan, Daijikai, Seigikai and Kisinkai. Risshō Kōseikai (Society for Establishing True Dharma and Harmony for Believers Who Seek Perfection), which grew to become the largest organization among them, was founded by Niwano Nikkyō and Naganuma Myōkō in 1938. They retained much of the doctrine, religious practices and rituals from Reiyūkai, particularly the worship of the *Lotus Sūtra* and the ancestors, and they similarly emphasized the importance of discipline and the need for the spiritual development of individuals. Niwano drew upon a variety of traditional folk practices of divination based on *rokuyō* (calendrical omens), *kyūsei* (an astrology in which the numbers 1 to 9 are connected to colours and planets), *shichishin* (divination of the seven gods), geomancy and onomancy. Risshō Kōseikai successfully expanded its influence as a lay Buddhist organization among urban housewives by adopting a method called *hōza*, a type of group counselling led by a leader who encouraged participants to discuss their experiences and problems. Like Reiyūkai, it upheld traditional values such as respect for parents and old people, but it also insisted on personal virtues such as modesty and tolerance as a prerequisite for personal development. These values allowed its members to adapt to a new middle-class domesticity based around the nuclear family, whilst maintaining the essence of traditional family values and gender roles. Risshō Kōseikai increased its influence rapidly, and, by the middle of the 1950s, it had its own educational institutions, training facilities, hospital, cemetery, and newspaper. This expansion culminated in the erection of a statue of the eternal Buddha in the Great Sacred Hall at Suginami-ku in Tokyo in 1964. Having entered a stable period, Risshō Kōseikai extended its energy in co-operating with other religious organizations, joining the Peace Delegation of Religious Leaders against Atomic Weapons in 1963, and sending a delegation to visit Pope Paul VI in the Vatican in 1965. From the 1960s onwards, their missionary work focused on evangelizing Japanese expatriates in Brazil, Hawaii and California. In 1978, the Niwano Peace Foundation was established to promote peace activities, with an emphasis on inter-religious co-operation.

One of the most influential new Buddhist groups, Sōka Gakkai (Value Creating Academic Society), previously known as Sōka Kyoiku Gakkai (Value Creating Education Society), was established in 1930 by Makiguchi Tsunesaburō. Having started as a lay offshoot of Nichiren Shoshū,[35] it's founder's initial aim was to incorporate educational values with both the doctrine of the *Lotus Sūtra* and the teachings of Nichiren. However, the movement overstepped the confines of State Shintō during the 1940s, by preaching that the true *dharma* of the divine king could be achieved only if the Emperor converted to the *Lotus Sūtra*, thereby addressing the question of the superiority of the *Lotus Sūtra* over the religious authority of the Emperor. In 1943, under the Peace Preservation Law (Clause 21), executive members were arrested and Makiguchi died in prison. His principal disciple Toda Jōsei survived the ordeal and re-established the organization in 1946 under the new name of Sōka Gakkai. The organization expanded its influence by an aggressive practice of proselytism called *shakubuku*,[36] preaching that Nichiren Shoshū presented the only true *dharma* (*shōbō*) and rejecting all other religious organizations as heresies.[37] It also challenged the traditional Nichiren sect and other Buddhist sects as corrupt, commercial, and anti-spiritual. By so doing it appealed to many disenchanted souls in the immediate postwar period who were attracted by the promise of an immediate improvement in their quality of life. In the early 1950s as the Korean War intensified, a major 'Save Japan, Save Asia' campaign was launched by Sōka Gakkai to address the general sense of anxiety. In contrast to other neo-Buddhist organizations such as Reiyūkai or Risshō Kōseikai, which continued to support the conservative politicians affiliated with the Liberal Democratic Party while not involving themselves directly in politics, Sōka Gakkai was fiercely independent in its political orientation. As the movement gained in fervour and pace, members sought political means to convert the whole population. In 1955, Sōka Gakkai members stood as independent candidates in the local elections and won 53 seats. In the following year three members were elected to the Lower House, then six were elected in 1959. During the protest movement against the renewal of the US–Japan Security Treaty in 1960, Sōka Gakkai consolidated its position as a political force. As the organization became more politicized, an extensive network extending from a central administration to regional branches and smaller study units was established, incorporating the urban lower middle class housewives and salaried men, providing a platform for those who were dissatisfied with their political parties.

In 1960 Ikeda Daisaku became the third President. Under his leadership, the traditional religious authority of Nichiren Shoshū gradually became subordinated to the secular authority of its lay association.[38] At the same time the establishment of a political organization, Kōmei Seiji Renmei (League of Fair Politics), allowed Sōka Gakkai to formulate its own policies more effectively. Their political ideals, based on Buddhist democratic principles, were against all forms of corruption, they advocated fair elections, and wanted to achieve a true parliamentary democracy. In practice, their ultimate objective was to realise a mass welfare state and a prosperous economy, which was 'neither wholly materialistic nor wholly spiritual' (Murata 1971, 169), but based on a synthesis of capitalism and socialism. Slogans with terms such as human socialism, *dharma* democracy, global ethnicity, complete neutralism and so on, were frequently used to stress the universality of Sōka Gakkai's political ideals. They increased their influence by offering day-to-day counselling, gathering direct feedback from constituents, and representing the political interests of the self-employed and owners of small and family owned businesses and manufactures. Sōka Gakkai entered a period of stability in the 1960s and in 1964 Kōmei Seiji Renmei became a full political party, Kōmeito (Clean Government Party). It continued to send its candidates into both the House of Representatives (Lower House) and the House of Councillors (Upper House) of the National Diet. By 1969, Kōmeito 'had twenty-four seats in the 250-seat House of Councillors and twenty-five seats in the 486-seat House of Representatives' (*ibid.*, 19). It had become the fourth ranking party in the Upper House and the third in the Lower House, which consolidated its influence as a middle party controlling the balance between the Liberal Democratic Party and the Socialist Party.[39] In the multi-party politics of the 1970s, Kōmeito competed for second position as the party of opposition with the Liberal Socialists, whilst the two major parties struggled with internal disputes and declined in power and popularity.

Kōmeito had become the first Japanese political party with its foundation resting on a huge religious organization. However, it was different from European political parties, such as the Christian Democrats, because its religious wing was directly in control of the political party. As Sōka Gakkai became increasingly criticized for theocracy in 1970, President Ikeda announced its separation from Kōmeito. Intent on increasing its influence as a serious political force, Kōmeito attempted to underplay its religious flavour to the extent of eliminating all religious terminology from its statutes. However, it remained the political party of Sōka Gakkai, in which the President was the actual party leader. Sōka Gakkai itself put more emphasis on activities related to the promotion of education, cultural activities, and the peace movement in its attempt to distance itself from mainstream politics in the 1970s;[40] in the 1980s it went on to expand its influence abroad by setting up more than 100 international branches. Nevertheless, Sōka Gakkai had become too powerful, and consequently the relationship with the Buddhist priests of Nichiren Shoshū deteriorated. In 1990 Sōka Gakkai was excommunicated by the Nichiren Shoshū sect, and Ikeda was removed from his position as representative of Nichiren Shoshū's lay association. This resulted in an acrimonious situation which left the issue of the spiritual afterlife of its lay members unresolved.

RELIGIOUS FREEDOM IN THE POSTWAR PERIOD

After the defeat of Japan in 1945, the Japanese saw a clause in the Potsdam Declaration which stipulated the freedom of religions. State Shintō came to an end with the Shintō Directive of 1945, prohibiting all state support and patronage for Shintō, since the occupying army was adamant that the nationalistic tendencies of State Shintō should be completely dismantled. Under the supervision of the Americans, all legal constraints that had restricted the freedom of political and civil rights, and of beliefs and thoughts, were abolished. The sudden freedom granted was appreciated, but the loss of traditional values had created disorientation and a widespread spiritual vacuum. The new religions that were founded during this period appealed to the secular and immediate needs of the general population. They reiterated the traditional values such as harmony in the family and good relationship with others, simultaneously appealing to the values of prosperity and stability, and a life devoid of poverty and conflicts through their pragmatic teachings of *genze riyaku* (this-worldly benefit). Traditional Buddhist sects continued to decline as the democratic policies of the occupation threatened the economic foundation and the authority of Buddhist temples. The land reform which took place in 1946 shook the landlord class from its pedestal, and as their material support dwindled, the economic foundation and the authority of the temples were further eroded. The cohesion of traditional village communities and family units, a fundamental *raison d'être* for the temples, was breaking up. The effect of the land reform was particularly severe in Buddhist sects such as Shingon, Sōtō, Nichiren and Jōdo, which had all relied heavily on tenancy income from rural land holdings. Out of necessity, many temples turned to practical ways of making ends meet, running nurseries, Sunday schools, old people's homes, car parks and restaurants on their compounds. Many priests went to work as part-timers to supplement their dwindling income.[41]

Along with the economic crisis, internal problems increasingly manifested themselves in the Buddhist sects of Jōdo, Jōdo Shinshū, Sōtō, Nichiren, Shingon, and Tendai. They all experienced conflicts and factional upheavals, and Shingon and Nichiren sects saw the numerous proliferation of break away subsects. This was in large part the result of dissolving the previous legal framework that had forced many sects to stay under one umbrella, thus hindering free religious expression. However, as the urge for democratization gained momentum in the postwar euphoria, sub-sects gained strength and factions increasingly asserted their independence. In 1948, Western Honganji temple of Jōdo Shinshū sect saw the formation of the first religious trade union by its staff and temple employees. Such upheaval, nevertheless, did not result in an overall reform or change in the fundamental structure of Japanese Buddhism. The established Buddhist sects continued to preserve their position as the religion of the family, conducting funerals and rituals for the ancestors, and clinging to the traditional relationships with their lay donors. Nevertheless, priests themselves could not ignore the changing needs of their lay devotees who were willing to take a more active part in the running of their temple institutions. Yet allowing them to become more involved led to a further erosion of traditional authority, whilst these Buddhist priests failed to inspire their lay congregation with a new type of spirituality.

BUDDHIST MOVEMENTS IN THE POST-WAR PERIOD

In the years following the war, some lay members of the Buddhist community began to question the war responsibilities of the Buddhist sects. Other issues that preoccupied them at this time included the demand to improve working conditions for employees of Buddhist institutions, the promotion of inter-religious dialogue with other religious traditions, and the search for new roles for Buddhist priests. In 1946, Senō Girō and Mibu Shōjun, previously members of Shinkō Bukkyō Seinen Dōmei, which, as we have already noted, was active in the 1930s, formed Bukkyō Shakaishugi Dōmei (Buddhist Socialist Alliance), to be renamed Bukkyō Shakai Dōmei (Buddhist Society Alliance) in 1949. Senō continued to call for a united front of all Buddhists against oppression, and although he succeeded in forming Zenkoku Bukkyō Kakushin Renmei (National Buddhist Liberal Alliance) with the co-operation of some priests of the Jōdo Shinshū Honganji sect, he failed to get the support from the majority of the established Buddhist sects. In the years that followed he became increasingly disillusioned with the limitations of his religious movement, and came to the conclusion that social revolution was the only way to realise social change and liberate the masses from the ills of the capitalist system. Senō managed to form a brief alliance with the Socialist Party in the 1950s, but after becoming more disillusioned with their infighting dominated by conflicting ideologies, he ultimately joined the Communist Party at the end of 1959 (Kōkoku 1987, 225).

Throughout the 1950s Buddhist organizations attempted to seek more active collaboration with Shintō, Christianity and the 'new religions' in order to achieve the collective goal of world peace. Thus, Bukkyōsha Heiwa Kondankai (Buddhists' Peace Discussion Group), which initiated the Shūkyōsha Heiwa Undō Kyōgikai (Committee for the Religious Persons' Peace Movement), issued an influential peace statement in 1951. These disarmament movements tended to build up good levels of co-operation and some, such as the Heiwa Suishin Kokumin Kaigi (People's Assembly for the Promotion of Peace), worked closely with Sōhyō, the Socialist Party Trade Union. In 1954, Zaike Bukkyō Kyōkai (Lay Buddhists Association) was founded under the initiative of Buddhist scholars and lay activists[42], and in this new era of democratization and

116

secularization, the voices of lay Buddhists came increasingly to be heard. The liberal section of the Buddhist community, who were more open to new ideas, formed the Zenichi Bukkyō Undō (United Buddhist Movement), which aimed to cut across the sectarian divide by promoting active communication between priests and the laity. They were supported by the association of traditional priests, Bukkyō Rengōkai, which later developed into the Zen-Nihon Bukkyō-kai[43] (National Japanese Buddhists Society) whose first conference was held on the initiative of the Shingon sect at Mt. Kōya in 1953. Following the First World Fellowship of Buddhists (WFB) Conference in Colombo, Ceylon (1950), Zen-ichi Bukkyō Undō organized the second WFB Conference in Tokyo in 1952, initiating a new relationship with other Asian Buddhist countries. As a result of these contacts the Buddhist establishment helped to facilitate the return of bones of Chinese prisoners of war who had died as victims of forced labour during the Japanese occupation, thus starting an active postwar relationship with Chinese Buddhists. The 1960s, and '70s saw closer co-operation between Japanese Buddhist groups, with the Bukkyōsha Heiwa Kyōgikai (Buddhist Peace Council) acting as a link, and Buddhists were seen demonstrating together during national rallies against the renewal of the US–Japan Security Treaty and at peace protests during the Vietnam War. Nihonzan Myōhōji, which as a result of postwar defeat had lost its base in China, now abandoned its nationalist tendencies and adopted a new doctrine of non-violence and absolute peace based on Gandhi's teachings. Along with Ōmoto-kyo, it had become one of the major Buddhist forces in the anti-nuclear peace rallies, and chanting Nihonzan Myōhōji monks dressed in yellow robes accompanied by lay devotees with large fans and drums participating in the anti-American base movement of the 1960s, became a common sight. In 1976, the Fourth Asian Buddhist Conference for Peace was held in Tokyo, and a resolution was passed known as the 'Tokyo Appeal', asking for the abolition of all nuclear weapons. The success of the conference led to the founding of the ABCP Japan Center in 1977, which became a non-sectarian organization for the promotion of world peace.

REFORM, CONFLICT, AND ATTEMPTS FOR REVIVAL

Traditional Buddhist sects which were struggling to maintain their influence continued to be faced with aggressive proselytizing and rapid expansion of new Buddhist organizations in the urban areas, and a waning power base in the countryside owing to urbanization and rapid economic growth, which accelerated from the mid 1960s. Nevertheless, they were eager to introduce moderate and effective reforms to improve relationships within the organization. One of the largest, the Jōdo Shinshu Honganji sect[44], for example, successfully turned the dissatisfaction and antagonism expressed by the regional branch temples towards the head temple into a reform programme. In 1961, in commemoration of the 700th anniversary of Shinran's death, the *Monshintokai*

Undō (Movement of the Faithful) was initiated. The movement concentrated on strengthening the functions of branch temples while, at the same time, reaffirming the control of the head temple. It also promoted activities aimed at gaining younger members, and improved the training of both priests and lay teachers. The Movement certainly seems to have stimulated the active participation of the lay congregation in promoting reform. However, there was an underlying danger that such an attempt would, by dividing up the organization into further factions, develop into a major conflict. This did in fact occur within the Jōdo Shinshū Ōtani sect, where traditionalists upheld Ōtani Kōchō, the Abbot (*zasu*), while reformists wanted to bring in new blood and modernize the sect by shifting the locus of religious practice back to individual devotees. Naturally, the traditionalists resented such a challenge to their authority. They asserted that the blood lineage from its founder Shinran was their most valuable source of legitimacy and argued that the authority of the *Hōshu* (literally the person who preaches the *dharma*, equivalent to the Pope) was absolute, and the trinity of *Hōshu*, *Kanchō* (head of sect administration) and *Zasu* (abbot) of the main Honganji temple resided in one person, who was the direct successor of Shinran. However, the reformers desired more participation in the decision-making process of the organization. In the course of time, the shift of authority to the individual members became increasingly evident, to the extent that the Ōtani family could no longer continue to claim to be the sole authority by virtue of their inherited lineage. By the 1970s, the reformists were in the majority, and in 1978 they elected a new *Kanchō* which led to the resignation of Ōtani Kōchō, who fiercely disapproved of this turn of events. This in turn led to his breaking away[45] from the family sect and a rather impotent declaration of his own absolute authority.

In this period we witness a variety of off-shoots of established Buddhism which began to challenge the doctrine and authority of the Buddhist sect from which they had emerged. One of them, Jōdo Shinshū Shinrankai, was established in 1958, having broken away from the Jōdo Shinshū Honganji sect. Its founder Takamori Kentetsu was born into a family which traditionally administered a Jōdo Shinshū Honganji sect temple in Toyama prefecture. He graduated from one of the Hoganiji sect universities in Kyōto, but became increasingly sceptical of the corruption and materialistic lifestyle of the priests of the Honganji head temple. He denounced them and became an ardent lay activist, propagating the return to the original spirit of its founder Shinran. Shinrankai's members are united in the belief that the contemporary religious practices of Honganji temple have departed from the original words of Shinran (1173–1262) and his successor Rennyo (1415–99). The fact that its members are generally young is a distinguishing feature since other traditional Buddhist sects are eager but not always successful in attracting young followers. The activities of Shinrankai are concentrated around the study and learning of the scriptures as well as listening to the sermons given by Takamori at regular meetings. Its criticisms of the Honganji sect intensified in the mid 1980s and violent clashes referred to as *hōsen* (*dharma* war) by its followers were reported. The aggressive nature of these anti-Honganji protests has had some scholars referring to Shinrankai as a group of 'Shinshū fundamentalists' (Yokoyama 1997, 199).

In spite of the general criticism that traditional Buddhism had become *sōshiki Bukkyō* (Buddhism involved with funeral rites), catering only for matters connected with death and ancestral rites,[46] with little relevance to the spiritual life of contemporary Japanese people, many of the traditional sects such as Jōdo, Tendai, Nichiren, Sōtō, and Rinzai have attempted to revive their spiritual roots by engaging in structural modification of their organizations. Thus, the Nichiren sect[47] sought to achieve renewal by setting new programmes for the education of its priests and seeking alternative sources of funding. The Jōdo sect on the other hand, promoted the *Otetsugi Undō* (Join Hands Movement) in the early 1960s to strengthen local and regional ties with the head temple through encouraging devotees to play a more active role in planning and carrying out activities in their parish temples. Finally, Sōtō, the largest of all Buddhist sects in number of temples and devotees,[48] began a ten-year project in 1965 to improve the quality of its priests and promote better training. In addition, since 1981 it has encouraged the faithful to become fully initiated into the Buddhist community by taking the Three Refuges and observing the five precepts (Azuma 1993, 24–5). Most traditional sects, then, are seeking to revive the spirit of Buddhism by the provision of better training for priests and the fostering of lay participation. However, their traditional rural foundation continues to dwindle, while, in the cities the more aggressive proselytizing of 'new' Buddhist groups creates practical difficulties, particularly those associated with finding sites to establish new temples. Their endeavours to achieve reform, and acquire new urban premises, do not seem to be readily successful.

CONCLUSION

In the Buddhist teaching, the *dharma* is considered to be above and beyond the political affairs of the secular world. However, ever since the time of its arrival in Japan in the sixth century, Buddhism has been patronized by aristocrats and as a result, its role changed to one of providing a moral and spiritual foundation for the nation and securing the welfare of the ruling class. As a consequence, Japanese Buddhism became subordinated to the state and appropriated as an effective tool for the political power. Although medieval Japan saw sporadic periods during which Buddhist forces, such as those of the Jōdo Shinshū and Nichiren sects, formed alliances with the peasants and rose to challenge the establishment, tighter controls imposed on Buddhist organizations through the *danka seido* (parish system) during the Tokugawa period, followed by the oppressive period of State Shintō, seemed to have sapped the religious spirit of Japanese Buddhism. However, since the late 1970s up to the time of writing (1998), Japan has witnessed a remarkable proliferation of 'new religions' and 'new new' religious sects. Their growth notably contrasts with the decline of established Buddhism, which is seen to have become commercial, worldly, and unspiritual in the eyes of its critics. Furthermore, new Buddhist organizations such as Sōka Gakkai have expanded their religious influence and have steadily established a solid political power base to realize their religious ideals. Recurrent political corruption and scandals fill the headlines, leaving people overwhelmingly indifferent to national politics. Just as politicians are seen as self-serving and have fallen in public estimation, many members of the Buddhist priesthood have also failed to command the devotion and respect of their erstwhile constituencies. In modern day Japan, people can afford a wider variety of religious techniques and spiritual attractions, with multiple religious choices being offered to suit their tastes and orientation. Some of the newer religious organizations concentrate on religious techniques of empowerment and practices such as fasting, special diets and rigorous meditation, whilst others emphasize the importance of personal development in the style of counselling, group therapy and self-reflection. Many of these techniques have been appropriated from the ascetic practices of traditional Buddhism. In this sense, we may be seeing the traditional Buddhist spirit emerging in new religious contexts. It can also be said that in this age of disenchantment, people are reacting by discovering ways of providing themselves with a type of inner strength, a feeling of self-valuation, and a sense of belonging in a society which no longer believes that party politics and the religious establishment have much to offer.

NOTES

1. The movement occurred as the result of an Order issued in 1868 which aimed to separate Shintō from Buddhism and to raise the status of the former. As a result, Buddhist temples throughout the country were destroyed or abolished through the consolidation period. Inagaki (1993, 61) says that the statistics from Toyama prefecture show that only seven temples survived out of 1,639 temples belonging to seven sects.
2. The Imperial Constitution stipulates that 'people are free to choose their own religion on condition that they do not disrupt the order and peace of the country and neglect their social duties' (Article 28). This Article in fact limited rather than encouraged the freedom of choice of religions and beliefs.
3. There were thirteen sub-sects that were affiliated with Sect Shintō.
4. Murakami (1970, 164).
5. In the same year, the Universal Manhood Suffrage Bill was passed giving all male subjects above the age of 25 the right to vote.
6. Satō (1989, 318).
7. In the early 1930s, Marxists criticized the Buddhist establishment for their feudalistic tendencies, their eagerness to serve the authority, and their reactionary role in society.
8. The concept of *Hakkō Ichiu* emphasized the supremacy of the Japanese race, and its sacred mission to spread its way of life to other nations in Asia by establishing the 'Greater East Asian Co-Prosperity Sphere'. The ideology was essential to justify the military invasion of China and other parts of Southeast Asia. *Hakkō* signified the 'Eight directions', in other words, the whole world, and *Ichiu*, 'to become one family',

      implying that the Japanese race which upheld the Emperor as a symbolic patriarch had a mission to rule Asia conceived as one harmonious family.

9. Both the Jōdo Shinshū Honganji sect and the Ōtani sect had been sending their missionary priests to Korea and China since the Sino-Japanese War in 1894. After 1910, their missionary work spread to the whole of the Korean Peninsula and the number of missionaries increased dramatically. The Honganji sect, however, focused their missionary work mainly on the Japanese soldiers to preach them the importance of loyalty and of performing their duties to the imperial state in this life so that they would receive peaceful enlightenment in the next (Mitō 1987, 68). For a consideration of this issue from the Korean perspective, see Sørensen's essay in this volume.

10. The government however, did not acknowledge these new religious organisations as 'proper religions' and put them in a legal category of 'pseudo-religions'. Many of them such as Ōmotokyō, Hitonomichi, Honmichi and Seichō no Ie came under severe persecution in the 1930s.

11. Buddhism was restructured into 13 sects and 28 sub-sects (from 56 sub-sects) at this time.

12. Very few Buddhists advocated pacifism during this period. The most important pacifist must be Itō Shōshin (1876–1963) who devoted his life to the *Muga-ai Undō* (Altruistic Movement), which aimed to liberate humankind from selfishness and craving.

13. It later came to be known as Shin Bukkyōto Dōshikai (New Buddhists Fellowship). The movement continued until 1915 and its members consisted of students and Buddhist scholars of the Nishi Honganji School.

14. They actively exchanged views about social reform and roles in society with the Unitarians in their journal *Shin Bukkyō* (New Buddhists).

15. Some of them such as Katayama Sen who formed the first trade union, and Kinoshita Naoe were Christians, and Abe Isoo, Kishimoto Nobuta were Unitarians.

16. When Kōtoku Shūsui was arrested in 1910 for his alleged leadership in the plot to assassinate the Emperor, there were several Buddhist monks in his group. They were Uchiyama Gudō (Sōtō, executed), Mineo Setsudō (Rinzai, life), Takagi Kenmyō (Shinshū Ōtani sect, life).

17. Tanabe Hajime, a direct disciple of Nishida and Watsuji Tetsurō, was also influenced by the School. Nishitani Keiji and Takeuchi Hitoshi were members of the second wave.

18. Komazawa University was founded in 1925 by the Sōtō Zen sect to promote and modernise Buddhist studies beyond the learning of rituals and textual translations. It was also meant to introduce modern Buddhist education for priests, their families and the general public.

19. Popular Buddhist literature followed such as *Shunkan* by Kikuchi Kan, *En no Gyōja* by Tsubouchi Shōyō, *Hōnen* by Mitsui Masashi, *Kōbō Daishi* by Watanabe Katei, *Nichiren Shōnin to Nihonkoku* by Takayama Chogyū.

20. Tanaka was credited as the founder of the School of Japanese Imperial Polity (*Kokutai-gaku*). His major work *Honge Myōshu Shikimoku*, develops a unique interpretation of Nichiren Buddhism.

21. Nichiren preached the spiritual equality of all sentient beings regardless of position and status before the absolute authority of the Buddha. The political authority was viewed merely as a means of realising the eternal *dharma*.

22. Nishiyama (1990, 53), asserts that Tanaka's teaching was very close to placing the

authority of the *dharma* based on the *Lotus Sūtra* above the concept of the national polity of the Emperor

23. Among them were the literary figures Miyazawa Kenji, Takayama Chogyū (although he saw the influence of Nichiren beyond the confines of the imperial polity), scholar Anesaki Masaharu, army general Ishiwara Kanji, and right-wing terrorist Inoue Nisshō who was the founding member of a fascist group called Ketsumeidan (Blood Alliance League). In March 1932 they assassinated Inoue Junnosuke, the former Minister of Finance, Dan Takuma of the Mitsui financial group, and in May of the same year, they assassinated the last pre-war party prime minister, Inukai, at his official residence.

24. Reiyūkai in 1931, and Sōka Gakkai in the 1950s, proposed the same concept of *Kokuritsu Kaidan*, but it was Tanaka Chigaku who originally presented the idea.

25. The political ideology of upholding the king as the supreme and righteous leader gained popularity at the end of thirteenth century Japan among followers of the Nichiren and Jōdo Shinshū sects (Satō 1989, 332–3).

26. The Japanese Kwantung Army, alarmed that the establishment of a new Chinese government under the nationalists in 1928 would threaten Japan's special privileges in southern Manchuria, created a sabotage incident in 1931. This triggered a full scale military action in Manchuria which was without the sanction of the civilian government in Tokyo. By 1932, Manchuria was under the control of the Japanese army and the state of Manchuko was created.

27. The massacre of several million Koreans in the aftermath of the Kantō Earthquake (1923) was a turning point for Senō. He fully awoke to the impermanence, self-ishness and materialism that he believed had been predominant in people's lives. He had also witnessed the suffering and misery of tenant peasants in the villages, and had been involved in many peasant uprisings. These factors led to a search for a better society which entailed some measure for social reform (Inagaki 1993: 89).

28. The six principles are as follows. (1) Buddhism does not believe in a permanent almighty existence. Ego must be discarded and everyone must work towards realizing an ideal society where mutual development is possible; (2) There is no soul that survives into the afterlife; (3) Buddhism in the past has confined the people to an abstract concept of 'salvation' without providing them with an actual direction to overcome their everyday problems. But Buddhism does not preach spirituality at the expense of an economic life. A comfortable and humane lifestyle can be achieved before any type of spirituality; (4) The traditional *saṅgha* symbolizes a communal lifestyle with no private property or selfish interests. A true Buddhist should work selflessly to establish a better society, a model of which is provided by the *saṅgha*; (5) The true teaching of Buddhism should aim for the liberation of humanity and should not be confined to a narrow framework of a nation-state. This type of nationalism does not profit the people but only gives an opportunity for the capitalist entrepreneurs to accumulate capital for their selfish gains. The old Buddhist establishment since *Haibutsu Kishaku* has become too nationalistic, which is wrong. There should be disarmament and an effort for world peace; (6) The movement is a non-sectarian Buddhist movement, which unifies Buddhism. The going back to the original teachings of the Buddha, that of the Three Jewels, is the guiding principle of the organization.

29. He also worked very closely with Suiheisha (Horizontal Society), a political organiza-tion established in 1922 which represented the interests of Japanese untouchables (*burakurnin*) in their aim to abolish social discrimination. Descendants of *burakumin*

who engaged in certain types of occupation such as killing of animals, tanning leather, and collecting rubbish, had been discriminated against and segregated from the rest of the population.

30. Kubo was originally trained by Masuko Yūkichi who was a follower of Tanaka Chigaku, the founder of Kokuchūkai, mentioned earlier. But the teachings of Nishida Mugaku on the power of the ancestors to save the nation may also have had a determining influence upon him.

31. The practice of ancestor worship traditionally implied the propitiation of patrilineal ancestors by the family. Reiyūkai honoured both patrilineal and matrilineal ancestors and preached that the relationship with them was an individual matter. It shifted the responsibility of *senzo kuyō* from the sole duty of the first-born son to every member of the family.

32. Members were encouraged to perceive that they were just a part of 'the myriad life forms that existed on the earth' and that people lived and received life 'amidst innumerable human relationships sustained by the blessing of nature' (Reiyukai 1990, 25).

33. Kubo Tsugunari was ousted in 1996 from the position of President.

34. In its existence for more than 60 years, 'fourteen bodies have split off including at least one that has surpassed that parent organisation in size and influence' (Hardacre 1984, 4).

35. Nichiren Shōshū started by one of Nichiren's chief disciples Nikkō differs from other Nichiren sects in its interpretation of the *Lotus Sūtra*, and worships Nichiren as a reincarnation of the historical Buddha.

36. *Shakubuku* was a conversion method advocated by Nichiren himself as highly appropriate in the 'age of the extinction of the right Law' (*mappō*). It literally means to 'break and subdue' any religious convictions which were held previously.

37. One of the most serious religious debates to take place in the postwar period (1955) between Sōka Gakkai and the Nichiren sect were the Otaru Dialogues. Sōka Gakkai's proselytizing strategy involved attacking the subject's previously held convictions, forcing potential converts to cut all ties with their family temples, and converting them to Nichiren Shōshū. This created severe tension between Sōka Gakkai members and their family temples. Buddhist priests were outraged by the attitude of Sōka Gakkai, which not only presented a grave challenge to their traditional source of authority but was also seen as destroying the traditional relationship between the temple and its village congregation. In the early 1960s, temples all over the country refused burial of the deceased family members of Sōka Gakkai members who had previously left their religious affiliation. The courts finally ruled in favour of the temples, asserting that those who managed the graveyards had the right to refuse burial on the grounds that the applicant was not an affiliated member of their Buddhist organization.

38. Their relations came to a halt in 1990, when Nichiren Shōshū denounced Sōka Gakkai and cut off its members from the Buddhist congregation. This incident posed an interesting question as to whether a lay Buddhist organization could survive without the backing and legitimation of a traditional religious authority (Astley 1992, Metraux 1992).

39. In 1966, their seats had increased to almost 1,800. This figure includes national, prefectural and municipal seats.

40. Ikeda initiated Sōka Gakkai's involvement in peace activities, asserting its strong position for the abolishment of all nuclear weapons. Its Youth Section has been

involved in helping the refugees in Southeast Asia, sending relief goods to areas in Africa affected by famine, and publishing anti-war materials.

41. In postwar Japan, Buddhist temples have increasingly come to rely on income from tourists (including pilgrims who visit on pilgrimage tours) and others, by devising a variety of ventures such as '*mizuko kuyō*' (conducting special ceremony for the aborted foetus) to attract the general public. Tendai sect, for instance, have appealed to the imagination of the general public by reviving the traditional ascetic practice called '*kaihō-gyō*' (mountain sojourn practice of walking meditation). With the help of publicity generated by the media, they have attracted a large number of new devotees and secured financial income.

42. It was led by Watanabe Shōkō, Masutani Fumio and Masunaga Reiō, and its Buddhist journal 'Zaike Bukkyō' (Lay Buddhism) has been second in circulation after 'Daihōrin' (Big Wheel of the Dharma).

43. The organization also won the support of the association of traditional Buddhist priests' Bukkyō Rengōkai (Buddhist United Party).

44. Honganji sect venerates Shinran as its founder but after the death of the eleventh abbot, Rennyo, in the sixteenth century, difficulties arose. By the beginning of the seventeenth century, Shinran's followers had organized themselves into two different sects, Shinshū Honganji-ha (West Honganji sect) and Shinshū Ōtani-ha (East Honganji sect).

45. More than 30 regional temples displayed their loyalty and followed Ōtani Kōchō in his move to declare independence.

46. Most Buddhist temples have become largely dependent on the income fees paid for 'services connected with death and ancestors', in which priests are 'regarded as little more than ritualists to be consulted in conncection with death' (Reader, 1991: 88).

47. In 1966, it initiated a movement called *Nichirenshū Gōhō Undō* (Movement to Promote the Observance of Nichiren's Teachings).

48. In 1992, the Sōtō sect had 14,746 temples and 6,940,814 registered devotees, followed closely by Jōdo and then Shingon sects (Bunka-chō 1992).

BIBLIOGRAPHY

Secondary sources in English

Astley, Trevor (1992) 'A Matter of Principles: A Note on the Recent Conflict between Nichiren Shōshū and Sōka Gakkai', *Japanese Religions* 17, 167–75.

Bailey, P.J. (1996) *Postwar Japan: 1945 to the Present.* Oxford: Blackwell.

Beaseley, W.G. (1990) *The Rise of Modern Japan.* London: Weidenfeld & Nicolson.

Blacker, Carmen (1975) *The Catalpa Bow: a Study of Shamanistic Practices in Japan.* London: Allen & Unwin.

Collcutt, Martin (1986) 'Buddhism: the Threat of Eradication', in *Japan in Transition: from Tokugawa to Meiji*, eds. Marius Jansen and Gilbert Rozman. Princeton, N.J.; Princeton University Press.

Hardacre, Helen (1984) *Lay Buddhism in Contemporary Japan.* Princeton, NJ: Princeton University Press.

Hardacre, Helen (1991) *Shinto and the State: 1868–1988.* Princeton, NJ: Princeton University Press.

Heisig, J. and Maraldo J. (1994) *Rude Awakenings: Zen, the Kyoto School and the Question of Nationalism*. Honolulu: University of Hawaii Press.

Ienaga, Saburō (1965) 'Japan's Modernization and Buddhism', *Contemporary Religions in Japan* 6, 1–41.

Kiyota, Minoru (1969) 'Buddhism in Postwar Japan: a Critical Survey', *Monumenta Nipponica* 24, 113–36.

Lee, Edwin B. (1975) 'Nichiren and Nationalism: the Religious Patriotism of Tanaka Chigaku', *Monumenta Nipponica* 30, 19–35.

Metraux, Daniel A. (1988) *The History and Theology of Sōka Gakkai*. New York: Edwin Mellen Press.

Metraux, Daniel A. (1992) 'The Dispute between the Sōka Gakkai and the Nichiren Shōshū Priesthood: a Lay Revolution against a Conservative Clergy', *Japanese Journal of Religious Studies* 19, 325–36.

Mullins, M.R. *et al.* (eds) (1993) *Religion and Society in Modern Japan: Selected Readings*. Berkeley, CA: Asian Humanities Press.

Murakami, Shigeyoshi (1980) *Japanese Religion in the Modern Century*, trans. Byron H. Earhart. Tokyo: University of Tokyo Press.

Murata, Kioaki (1969) [1971] *Japan's New Buddhism: an Objective Account of Sōka Gakkai*. New York: John Weatherhill.

Reader, I. (1991), *Religion in Contemporary Japan*. London: Macmillan.

Reiyūkai Movement (1990). Tokyo: The Reiyūkai.

Risshō Kōseikai (1966). Tokyo: Kōsei Publishing.

Rogers, Minor L. and Ann T. (1991) *Rennyo: the Second Founder of Shin Buddhism*. Berkeley, CA: Asian Humanities Press.

Smethurst, Richard (1974) *A Social Basis for Prewar Japanese Militarism*. Berkeley, CA: University of California Press.

Thelle, N.R. (1987) *Buddhism and Christianity in Japan: from Conflict to Dialogue 1854–1899*. Honolulu: University of Hawaii Press.

Wagatsuma, Hiroshi (1977) 'Some Aspects of the Contemporary Japanese Family: Once Confucian, Now Fatherless', *Daedalus* 106, 181–210.

Woodard, William P. (1972) *The Allied Occupation of Japan 1945–1952 and Japanese Religions*. Leiden: E.J. Brill.

Secondary sources in Japanese

Azuma, Ryūshin (1993) 'Bukkyōsō wa Nanio Subekika' (What Is Expected of the Buddhist Monk), *Daihōrin* 3, 22–27.

Bunka-chō (Ministry of Culture) (1992) *Shūkyō Nenkan* (Religious Registry). Tokyo: Bunka-chō.

Gendai Bukkyō o Shiru Daijiten Henshū Iinkai (ed.) (1980). *Gendai Bukkyō o Shiru Daijiten* (The Big Dictionary for Understanding Contemporary Buddhism). Kyoto: Kinka-sha.

Ikeda, Eishun (1976) 'Meiji no Bukkyō: Sono Kokoro to Shisō' (Buddhism of Meiji Period: its Spirit and Ideology), in *Nihonjin no Kōdō to Shisō*, vol. 31. Tokyo: Hyōron-sha.

Inagaki, Masami (1974) *Budda o Seoite Gaitō e* (To the Streets Carrying the Buddha on My Back). Tokyo: Iwanami Shinsho.

Inagaki, Masami, (1975) [1993] *Kindai Bukkyō no Henkakusha* (Buddhist Reformers in the Modern Period). Tokyo: Ōkura Shuppan.

Inoue, Kiyoshi (1966) [1981] *Nihon no Rekishi* (The History of Japan), vol. 3. Tokyo: Iwanami Shinso.

Kashiwahara, Yūsen (1990) *Nihon Bukkyōshi Kindai* (The History of Japanese Buddhism: Modern Period). Tokyo: Yoshikawa Kōbunkan.

Kōkoku, Junkei (1987) 'Senō Girō ni Tsuite: Sengo no Katsudō o Chūshin ni' (Senō Girō: with Emphasis on his Postwar Activities), in *Kindai Shinshū Kyōdanshi Kenkyū*, ed. Takamaro Shigaraki, Kyōto: Hōzōkan.

Mitō, Ryō (1987) 'Shinshū no Chōsen Fukyō' (Propagation of the Shinshū Sect in the Korean Peninsula), in *Kindai Shinshū Kyōdanshi Kenkyū*, ed. Takamaro Shigaraki Kyōto: Hōzōkan.

Murakami, Shigeyoshi (1970) *Kokka Shintō* (State Shintō). Tokyo: Iwanami Shinsho.

Murakami, Shigeyoshi (1976) 'Chian Iji-hō ni yoru Shūkyō Danatsu' (Religious Persecution under the Peace Preservation Law), *Kikan Gendaishi* 7, 135–46.

Murakami, Shigeyoshi (1980) *Kindai Nihon no Shūkyō* (Religion in Modern Japan). Tokyo: Kōdansha Gendai Shinsho.

Nakamura, Hajime, *et al.* (1989) [1994] *Iwanami Bukkyō Jiten* (Iwanami Dictionary of Buddhism). Tokyo: Iwanami Shoten.

Narakura, Tetsuzō (1989) 'Haibutsu Kishaku to Minshū' (Persecution of Buddhism and the Populace), in *Bukkyō to Nihonjin*, vol. 10, ed. Shigeyoshi Murakami, Tokyo: Shinjūsha.

Nichirenshū Gendai Shukyō Kenkyūjo (1996) *Nichirenshū no Kin-Gendai* (The Modern and Contemporary for the Nichiren Sect). Tokyo: Nichirenshū Shūmuin.

Nishiyama, Shigeru (1985) 'Nihon no Kin-Gendai ni okeru Kokutairon-teki Nichirenshugi no Tenkai: Ishiwara Kanji to Kokuchūkai' (The Development of Nichirenism in Modern-Contemporary Japan: Ishiwara Kanji and Kokuchūkai), in *Ishiwara Kanji Senshū*, vol. 1, ed. Kanji Ishiwara, Tokyo: Tamairabō.

Nishiyama, Shigeru (1990) 'Nihon Kindai to Bukkyō' (Japan in the Modern Era and Buddhism), *Agama* 107, 46–59.

Okudaira, Yasuhiro (1976) 'Chian Iji-hō Kaisei no Rekishi' (The History of Revisions of the Peace Preservation Law), *Kikan Gendaishi* 7, 38–67.

Satō, Hirō (1989) 'Kindai Nationalism to Bukkyō' (Modern Nationalism and Buddhism), in *Bukkyō to Nihonjin*, vol. 2, ed. Toshio Kuroda Tokyo: Shunjūsha.

Tamura, Yoshirō (1969) [1979] *Nihon Bukkyōshi Nyūmon* (Introduction to the History of Japanese Buddhism). Tokyo: Kadokawa Sensho.

Yokoyama, Masataka (1997) 'Sōka Gakkai', in *Shin Shūkyō Jidai*, ed. Sanpei Deguchi *et al.* Tokyo: Okura Shuppan.

Yokoyama, Masataka (1997) 'Jōdo Shinshū Shinrankai', in *Shin Shūkyo Jidai*, ed. Sanpei Deguchi *et al.* Tokyo: Okura Shuppan.

6
BUDDHISM AND SECULAR POWER IN TWENTIETH-CENTURY KOREA*

HENRIK H. SØRENSEN

INTRODUCTION

The relationship between the state and the religious traditions that developed in Korea during the dynastic period has in many ways followed a pattern that can also be seen as having obtained in such countries as China, Japan and, to a certain extent, Vietnam. Like Korea, these countries were governed by absolute sovereigns, who sat at the peak of a powerful bureaucratic structure staffed by government officials steeped in the Confucian tradition, a system of thought and behaviour that combined within itself ethics, philosophy, religious beliefs, and the right to implement the correct social norm. In some of these countries the Confucian governments also saw it as their duty and right to decide on issues of orthodoxy and heterodoxy in relation to other types of faith and practices. Since Buddhism was an extremely powerful force within the whole of East Asia, most of the cases involving control of religious activity by the governments inevitably led to a confrontation – in some cases violent – between the state and Buddhism. Of course, the presence of certain local variants and particular cultural traits and characteristics of these countries somewhat temper these rather broad statements. It should also be remembered that the legalistic aspect of Confucianism has survived up to this day within all the cultures and political systems in East Asia, and it can therefore be said to continue to exercise its 'ideological' tyranny through contemporary political structures.

In the Korean case, Buddhism had enjoyed an absolutely unrivalled position as the leading ideology and national faith since its introduction to the Peninsula during the fourth century and up to the very end of the Koryŏ dynasty (918–1392). Buddhism had not only supplied the basic tenets of belief and modes of religious practice of the Korean people, but had been the single most important ideological foundation on which the Korean kings and their government built their national and cultural ideologies.

* I should here like to thank my Buddhist friends in Sŏnggwang Temple, South Chŏlla province, for supporting me with valuable information on the current situation of Korean Buddhism, and Professor Kim Youngho of Inha University for sharing his insights with me. Thanks are also due to the Korea Research Foundation for its support over the years.

Following an almost five-hundred-year-long period of prosperity and influence that spanned the major part of the Koryŏ dynasty, Buddhism and its supporters among the nobility lost out to the rising force of Confucianism at the end of the fourteenth century.[1] With the establishment of the Chosŏn dynasty (1392–1910) the new Korean government became dominated by Confucianism, which monopolized the political, social and economic apparatus of the country. At the beginning of the dynasty a series of anti-Buddhist edicts were formulated with the dual purpose of diminishing the economic power of the temples through the confiscation of temple lands, and of preventing Buddhist monks from meddling in national politics as had been their custom during the preceding dynasty.[2]

During the first two hundred years of the Chosŏn dynasty Buddhism continued to exert some influence on the higher strata of Korean society, including members of the royal court. However, following the Imjin War of 1592–8 it began a gradual but steady decline, not only economically but also spiritually. Many temples throughout the country fell into disrepair or were simply abandoned.[3]

It was only towards the end of the nineteenth century, at a time when foreign missionaries were already becoming established on the Peninsula, that an orthodox revival of Buddhism took place through the efforts of the monk Kyŏnghŏ (1849–1912),[4] a master of Sŏn.[5] Under his influence a number of lay Buddhist societies were established, which were in large part responsible for stimulating and rekindling the interest in Buddhism among the common people in the large provincial towns.[6] Furthermore, Kyŏnghŏ is also noteworthy for being the master of several influential disciples, many of whom played important roles in the development and modernization of Korean Buddhism during the twentieth century.[7]

THE IMPACT OF JAPANESE BUDDHISM DURING THE EARLY COLONIAL PERIOD

In the aftermath of the Unyōmaru incident of August of 1875, the first 'opening' of Korea, the 'Hermit Kingdom', was initiated by the Japanese through the joint signing of the Kanghwa Treaty in the following year. According to text of the treaty, Korea was to allow the Japanese to trade from three ports on the Peninsula chosen by themselves.[8] Immediately after the treaty was signed Japanese immigrants and traders began to arrive, and in their wake came the first Buddhist missionaries. The original task of these Japanese priests was to take care of the spiritual needs of the Japanese residing in Korea. However, they were soon actively engaged in securing converts among the Korean population. It appears that the Japanese government actively supported this trend, as it directly served its interests on the Peninsula. Prior to the Sino-Japanese War of 1894–5 it was mainly missionaries from the Jōdo Shinshū School who worked among the Koreans. However, priests of the Nichiren School were also present in Korea from 1881 onwards.[9]

Owing to the growing importance and influence of the Japanese Buddhist missionaries in Korean society, the Tokyo government naturally saw the old anti-Buddhist laws upheld by the Korean government as being contrary to their plan of using the religion as a tool of colonization. For this reason the Japanese government sought to have the anti-Buddhist law forbidding monks and nuns to live and work in Seoul abolished. To this end they covertly backed the efforts of Sano Zenrei (1864–1917),[10] a missionary priest of the Nichiren School, who petitioned the Korean government to allow members of the Buddhist clergy to operate in the capital. Sano was successful in his endeavours – undoubtedly due to strong Japanese pressure – and Buddhist monks and nuns were once again able to propagate their faith freely in Seoul.[11] With this new situation in their favour, not only were the various Japanese schools of Buddhism represented on the Peninsula able to strengthen their missionary efforts and to win new converts for their cause, but Korean Buddhism itself got a much-needed boost of goodwill and prestige in society at large.[12]

After the ban on the Buddhist clergy entering the capital had been lifted Sano and his assistant priest Shibuya (n.d.) set about converting Korean monks to their brand of Buddhism. With the help of these new Korean monks the Japanese missionaries established their headquarters in Chunghung Temple on Mt Pukhan. Following a meeting which Sano organized in Seoul, a number of local temples joined the Nichiren Sect.[13] The success of the Nichiren Sect was short-lived, however. When the Korean monks realized that they had virtually submitted themselves to a highly sectarian and nationalistic Japanese brand of Buddhism, many chose to abandon the affiliation with Sano. Eventually this first Japanese attempt at incorporating and subsuming Korean Buddhism under one of its Buddhist schools proved to be a failure.[14]

Whereas the rejection by the Korean Buddhists of the Nichiren sect was indirectly a setback for the Japanese colonial power, Korean Buddhism as such began to thrive after more than 300 years of suppression. The effects of Sano's efforts on behalf of Buddhism, along with further reforms, were quickly felt among the Korean followers of the religion. Almost overnight Korean Buddhism embarked on a process of modernization and reform inspired by the Japanese, a development which coincided with a renewal of practice within the tradition itself.

Following the revoking of the anti-Buddhist laws and regulations, a series of new laws were formulated by the Korean government in the years following. Of greatest importance and consequence were the new regulations of 1899, 1902 and 1904, which reinstated much temple land to the respective monasteries, and returned much of the control of the running of the temples to the Buddhists themselves.[15]

In 1899 a new government office was set up within the royal palace for the specific purpose of overseeing Buddhism. Wŏnhŭng Temple in Seoul was made the official headquarters and administrative centre of Korean Buddhism. Under the revised temple law of 1902 sixteen major temples in the country were designated as head temples under the administrative centre in Seoul, and they controlled all the lesser temples in Korea. By 1904, after the Japanese had in effect gained supreme control of the Korean government, official involvement with the running of the temples ceased. For the next six years the temples and monasteries were free to run their own affairs, and a certain decentralization of Buddhism took place.

In the same year a large scale attempt at absorbing Korean Buddhism into another Japanese Buddhist school took place. At that time a number of Korean temples such as Pongwŏn Temple, Wŏnhŭng Temple and Hwagye Temple co-operated with the missionaries of the Japanese Jōdo School and succeeded in establishing the Buddhist Research Association (Pulgyo Yŏngu Sahoe) and a school for Buddhist education. When the Japanese missionaries sought to gain control over the Association, they failed, and all the pro-Japanese Korean monks were forced to resign from their posts. The Association was temporarily discontinued.

By 1908 a need was felt among leading abbots of the main temples in Korea for a new, centralized form of organization, and a large scale meeting was convened at Wŏnhŭng Temple where fifty-two representatives from various leading temples assembled. The monks participating in this meeting did not represent the whole of the Korean Buddhist sangha, but mainly consisted of abbots with pro-Japanese views. The man behind this meeting was Yi Hoegwang (1862–1933),[16] who was then abbot of Haein Temple. His purpose was to unite all the various lineages and temple-families in the country into one single organized body. This led to the establishment in 1910 of the Wŏn School of Korean Buddhism, with its headquarters in the newly built Kakwang Temple in Seoul, and the election of a chief abbot representing all Korean Buddhists. Yi Hoegwang, then abbot of Haein Temple, was elected to this important and influential position, and Kwŏn Sangno became head of the administration of the order. Both men were strong supporters of the Japanese and sought to establish close ties with Japan.

Earlier, Yi Hoegwang had befriended a Japanese Sōtō Zen priest, Takeda Hanshi (d.u.), who had worked as a political agent for the Japanese in Korea during the 1890s. In 1895 he had been involved in the conspiracy that led to the assassination of Queen Min.[17] He had been officially placed under custody in Japan, but had returned to Korea in 1906 in the capacity of missionary priest.[18] In collusion with Takeda, Yi Hoegwang secretly sought to merge the newly founded Wŏn School with the Sōtō School, a merger that would eventually lead to the assimilation of Korean Buddhism.[19] While this was taking place, the Jōdo Shinshū and the Jōdo School, both of which were strongly represented by mission-temples in Korea, also had plans to absorb the Wŏn School into their respective organizations. However, Yi rejected their overtures on the grounds that there were irreconcilable differences between the doctrines of Pure Land Buddhism and those of Sŏn, which had been the Buddhist mainstream in Korea since the Chosŏn dynasty. Shortly after the Japanese occupation of the Korean

Peninsula in 1910 Yi Hoegwang went to Japan in the company of Takeda to negotiate the details of the merger with the head of the Sōtō School. Evidently Yi believed that he could effect a merger on an equal standing. Of course, the Sōtō School had absolutely no interest in such an accommodation. What it wanted was to absorb the Wŏn School into itself with the aim of eventually gaining control over all the major temples in Korea. In the end Yi accepted an agreement in which Korean Buddhism was incorporated into the Sōtō Zen School. When it became known in the Korean Buddhist community that Yi had accepted such a merger he became the target for intense criticism and protests.

In protest over Yi Hoegwang's manipulation, and having a well-founded fear of being brought under the administration of a Japanese School of Buddhism, the conservative and anti-Japanese faction of Korean monks organized themselves as the reformed Imje School during the same year. They first established their headquarters in Sŏnggwang Temple in South Chŏlla province, but later moved to Pŏmŏ Temple in Pusan. With the implementation of the Temple Ordinance the following year the dividing line between the pro- and anti-Japanese factions became even more accentuated as it heralded the beginning of a prolonged strugle for control over the main temples.[20]

A growing number of educated Koreans, who rejected Christianity and Western values, came to look at Buddhism as an ideological source of inspiration. One main reason for this was that an Eastern tradition that had existed in Korea for more than 1,500 years was thought to be better suited to the Oriental mind than Christianity.[21] Another reason was that it was seen as a more obvious rallying point for those nuturing a growing sense of nationalism. Furthermore, since many Korean intellectuals saw Japan as a modern nation comparable to the USA and European countries, but with strong roots in Buddhism, their choice was obvious.

During the years 1900 to 1910 many Korean intellectuals went to Japan to study at the modern universities in Tokyo and elsewhere. Among those who went were Yi Nŭnghwa (1869–1943), Pak Hanyŏng (1870–1948), a highly respected scholar-monk from Sŏnun Temple, Han Yongun (1879–1944), etc., all of whom became warm advocates of the reform of Korean Buddhism following, more or less, the established pattern that had shaped religion in Japan following the Meiji restoration.[22]

Interestingly, this development, which can be spoken of as the 'japanization' of Korean Buddhism, had relatively little to do with the Japanese Buddhist schools in Korea. There are virtually no records to speak of that indicate active participation by Japanese priests in this development, and it would appear that Korean Buddhists were mainly consolidating their own institutions. The Japanese Buddhist priests appear to have been uniformly uninterested in Korean Buddhism as such, and Korean monks, even those positively inclined towards what they saw as a modernized form of Buddhism, were basically not interested in converting to Japanese Buddhism. It seems that there was not much interaction between Japanese missionaries and Korean monks after the annexation of Korea was effected in 1910; in any case, direct co-operation or joint projects were never engaged in after this time.

KOREAN BUDDHISM UNDER JAPANESE COLONIAL RULE

Up to the time of the annexation of Korea in 1910, Korean Buddhists in general had benefited greatly from the presence and influence of the Japanese on the Peninsula. However, this situation was not to last. During the following year the Japanese governor-general and his administration implemented a new set of regulations, the so-called Temple Ordinance (Kor. *sach'al yong*, Jap. *jisetsu rei*) of 1911. In accordance with this elaborate document the Korean Buddhist community, including all the temples, temple lands and other property, was placed under the direct control of the office of the governor-general.[23] All Korean abbots were elected by this office without any consultation with monks living in the temples. It goes without saying that only monks who had demonstrated a support for Imperial Japan stood a chance of being elected to such a post.[24] In effect this made the appointed abbots into virtual 'owners' of the temples in which they resided, and gave them authority to dispose of the temples' property as they saw fit and to throw out those who opposed them. Such a policy was in direct conflict with traditional Korean temple organization, under which the *sangha*, living in a given monastery or temple, ran it as a collective enterprise. Authority was vested in the residents according to a mixed system of spiritual merit and seniority. Under the old system it was not possible for any individual to sell the temple lands or other property. The new Japanese regulations, combined with the fact that many of the pro-Japanese abbots married and begat children with rights of inheritance, severely undercut the temples and monasteries as centres of training for the traditionally celibate Korean *sangha*.[25]

Each New Year the abbots of the thirty main temples were required to go to Seoul to meet with the Japanese governor-general.[26] At these meetings they were seated at a sumptuous banquet and required to swear an oath of fidelity to the Japanese Emperor. In consequence, the degree to which Buddhism was able to function in Korean society was closely connected with the support of the colonial government.

The reaction of the Korean Buddhists to the Japanese occupation was a mixed one. Some monks openly favoured the new power and influence which Buddhism was now enjoying. Others were more sceptical, and again there were many who rightly felt that Japan had occupied their country against the will of the Korean people, and who therefore resented everything they stood for. Accordingly, Korean Buddhists became divided on this issue, and at least four major groups developed, as follows:

1. The traditionalists, a minority group consisting of conservative and celibate monks, who sought, on the one hand, to revive traditional Korean Buddhist

practices, and, on the other hand, to remain independent of the colonial government and its influence.

2. The pro-Japanese priests, mainly consisting of the abbots of the main temples and their cohorts. Most of these were not celibate, but maintained families in or near the temples thus complicating the lives of the traditional monks.

3. The reformers led by Han Yongŭn, mainly consisting of younger monks. This group advocated modernization of the Korean monastic system, including marriage. Despite the fact that they borrowed many of their ideas from reformed Japanese Buddhism, this group was strongly nationalistic. However, several of them, like many members of the pro-Japanese faction, were not celibate.

4. Lay Buddhist intellectuals like Yi Nŭnghwa, etc., who sometimes supported the colonial government and sometimes did not. This group maintained links with both the reformers and and the conservative factions within the clergy.

One of the ways in which the Japanese colonial powers attempted to gain political control over the Korean *saṅgha* was through secularization. This ploy had worked effectively in bringing Japanese Buddhism under the political and economic control of the government during the Meiji reforms, and was to prove equally effective against Korean Buddhism. During the first decade of the Japanese occupation, many Korean monks gave up their vows of celibacy and took wives. Some did this secretly, others were more open about it.[27] Despite the fact that Han Yongun sided with the anti-Japanese group during the factional infighting that took place during the first decade of the colonial period, his position as a self-proclaimed reformer and modernist brought him into direct confrontation with the traditionalists. With the publication of his major work, *Chosŏn pulgyo yusillon* (Treatise on the Reformation of Korean Buddhism),[28] first published in 1913, Han openly challenged the values and structures of traditional Korean Buddhism, and in this manner indirectly assisted the Japanese government in undermining resistance to reform and co-operation. One might think that Han Yongun must have realized the dangers of supporting the Japanese Buddhist model of a married clergy as openly as he did since it was obvious to everyone that it would mean a radical restructuring of traditional Buddhism, as had happened in Meiji Japan, but apparently that was not the case. On the contrary, he remained in an ambivalent position as a patriotic Korean Buddhist, who nevertheless advocated reforms that worked counter to the interests of the majority of his co-religionists. He, thereby, ended up assisting the colonial government in its task of controlling the clergy and their temples.[29]

As part of the modernization of Korean Buddhism there was a veritable spate in the publication of Buddhist journals and periodicals during the first decade of the Japanese occupation of Korea. As many as seven such journals appeared in rapid succession over a short period of eight years. The target audience for the journals was Korean Buddhists in general – including both the clergy and members of the rapidly growing lay community. Interestingly, the intellectual level of the material in all the journals was very high, despite the fact that the articles were written in a mixture of *Hangul*, the Korean alphabet and *Hanja* (Chinese characters). Clearly, these journals were meant for people with a considerable level of classical education and understanding of Buddhist doctrines and practice. Nevertheless, they served as organs for the promotion of a contemporary and modern form of Buddhism. It is unclear who funded these publications, but it is certain that they would not have appeared if the colonial government had not approved of them beforehand. Some of the journals may have been funded by various Buddhist groups, but it is certain that some were at least partly funded by the Japanese. In any case, several of them carried political messages from the Japanese governor-general to the Korean Buddhist congregations, and nearly all of them contained pro-Japanese material, even down to the vignettes. Some, such as the *Chosŏn pulgyo wŏlbo* (Korean Buddhist Monthly), appear to have been more political (i.e. pro-Japanese) than others.[30]

As far as the political line of the editors and contributors of these journals went, it is evident that they represented the whole spectrum of Korean Buddhists, including staunch supporters of the Japanese colonial cause like Yi Hoegwang and Kwŏn Sangno (1879–1965),[31] through moderates such as Yi Nŭnghwa, to members of the anti-Japanese faction and nationalists like Pak Hanyŏng, Han Yongun, and others. At least, such was the case in the journals that appeared between 1911 and 1918. Whereas the pro-Japanese editors openly and frequently flaunted their loyalty to the Japanese Emperor, the moderates and the more patriotic contributors generally kept a low political profile, and remained occupied with traditional Buddhist topics which would not bring them into trouble with the government. However, it appears that the Japanese government kept a constant lookout for anti-colonial elements, and even over the course of a few years one sees great changes in the editorial boards of the various journals. This may be taken as a fairly sure indication that the colonial power was highly sensitive to overt changes in the professed loyalty to its cause on the parts of the editors. The relatively brief publication span of these early journals may have been directly caused by interference from the colonial government, which must have made the editorial process highly complicated for an editor with any degree of patriotic or nationalist sentiments.[32]

During the winter of 1919–20, Yi Hoegwang, still the abbot of Haein Temple, again sought to unite the Wŏn School with a Japanese Zen school, this time the Myōshin-ji branch of the Rinzai School. In February 1920 he returned to Korea with the signed agreement of a merger without having informed his compatriots. The seven points of the merger were published in the Japanese newspaper *Chūgai Nippō* on the 6th of April of that year. Political issues aside, the rationale behind Yi's argument for a merger with the Rinzai School was that; since the Sŏn tradition in Korea, i.e. the lineage descending from T'aego (1301–82) and Naong (1320–76), had inherited the orthodox Linji transmission from China, and that the same held true for Rinzai, both schools shared a common spiritual ancestry and thus were compatible. It is obvious that by this move Yi sought to gain a powerful position within the Korean Buddhist hierarchy. Furthermore, he 'forgot' to inform his fellow Buddhists that the merger would effectively place the Korean temples and monasteries under the control of the Rinzai School and the Japanese colonial government. However, Yi's attempt was foiled by the majority of Wŏn adherents led by Kang Taeryŏn (1875–1942), abbot of Yongju Temple in Sŭwŏn. This happened despite the fact that Kang was strongly pro-Japanese and the officially appointed head of the national temple organization controlling all the main temples (*ponsan*) in Korea. Undoubtedly strong personal motivations played a decisive part here.[33]

Following the March the First Movement's (Samil Undong) demonstrations for independence in 1919, and the subsequent clamp-down on followers of the nationalist cause, the highly unpopular governor-general was recalled to Tokyo, and a new, more moderate, sucessor was appointed in his place. The failure to prevent the nationalist demonstrations from taking place was undoubtedly a major reason for the removal of the old governor-general.[34] In any event, the colonial government recognized that its policy of suppression and control had been too harsh. By playing their cards unsuccessfully the Japanese had succeeded in alienating a significant portion of the intelligentsia, including many religious leaders. The colonial power was aware that the independence movement was mainly led and organized by religious groups, and it now tried to implement a less repressive method of integration and enforcement of co-operation. This change in attitude was also felt within Buddhist circles, and although the colonial government remained in effective control of the temples and their economy, monks began to enjoy a greater sense of autonomy in their day-to-day operations.[35]

The excesses of the pro-Japanese abbots had also proved too embarrassing, and in 1920 the new Japanese governor-general revised the Temple Ordinance. In response to this situation the Japanese reorganized their temple administration and a new office was set up in Kakwang Temple in Seoul to oversee the thirty-one main temples in the country. The criticism of the old system was that too much power had been invested in the abbots, who had the authority to run temples as virtual businesses. This had caused severe problems and conflicts within the *sangha*. In addition these powerful appointees were found to have spent too much money on personal affairs. Two years later, Han Yongŭn and his group of followers founded the Pulgyo Yushin Hoe (the Buddhist Reform Association). This movement was generally hostile towards the colonial government and its supporters among the Korean *sangha*, and during the same year they had Kang Taeryŏn, one of the leading pro-Japanese abbots, forcefully removed from this post.[36] At the same time Korean Buddhism was restructured into Sŏn and Kyo (i.e. meditation and doctrinal branches of Buddhism) in accordance with the system prevalent during the Chosŏn. In 1929 Korean Buddhism became established as one order, with the name Chosŏn Pulgyo.[37]

Later, in 1926, Paek Yongsŏng (1864–1940), a leading reform-minded monk within the conservative faction, presented a petition to the governor-general urging him to prohibit monks from marrying. He argued that by allowing monks to marry in accordance with the Japanese custom dissent and factionalism were caused within the Korean *saṅgha*. However, Pack's memorandum was neither officially recognized nor its suggestions implemented. On the contrary, the official prohibition against clerical marriage that had remained in token effect prior to that time was abolished. By the end of the 1920s the majority of men within the Korean Buddhist *saṅgha* were married or maintained mistresses, and in many temples the secularized priests were living with their families. Even anti-Japanese monks eventually took wives, and the number of celibate monks declined yearly up to the end of the colonial period.

A new Buddhist journal, *Pulgyo* (Buddhism),[38] edited by Han Yongun, saw the light of day in 1924, and was allowed to continue publication until 1933.[39] This journal was less erudite than earlier journals, and the editor used it as a platform for his ideas for modernizing Korean Buddhism. The calls for modernization and reform were useful to the Japanese as a means of breaking the ideological support for traditional Korean Buddhism expressed by the majority of the monks within the anti-Japanese faction of the *saṅgha*, and they were generally supportive of Han's endeavours.

During the 1930s, when Japan was earnestly engaged in the war against China, control of the religious institutions in Korea became increasingly harsh. Buddhism and its institutions were still allowed a high degree of freedom, since most of its administrative leaders had been placed in their posts by the colonial government. Nevertheless, there were growing numbers of nationalist or simply conservative monks, who resented Japanese control and the undermining of the traditional monastic system by married priests residing with their families in the temples. Many of the monks opposing the Japanese, and Korean sycophants within the *saṅgha*, chose to leave the large temples and monasteries in order to live in small hermitages and newly constructed temples located in the remote countryside beyond the effective control of the government. This group of monks would eventually form the backbone of the Chogye Order that emerged after 1945.

With the Japanese invasion of China in 1937, and the subsequent outbreak of World War Two, control of Korean Buddhism became increasingly severe. Any form of opposition or lack of co-operation was forbidden, and at public religious sermons in temples officiating monks were obliged to support the Japanese war effort by including prayers for the Emperor and the success of the imperial army.

During this final phase of colonial rule in Korea, Buddhist journals such as *Shin Pulgyo* (New Buddhism)[40] and *Pulgyo Sibo* (The Buddhist Periodical) were utilized by the government in its war effort, and pro-Japanese authors wrote propaganda articles in order to make the Korean population rally to the Japanese cause. Such publications included calls for Buddhists to enrol in the Imperial Japanese army and to surrender valuables, including art treasures from the temples, to the government.[41] The fact that Han Yongun served as editor of

Shin Pulgyo from 1937 until his death in 1944 shows that his highly acclaimed patriotism did not exclude continued co-operation with Imperial Japan.[42]

KOREAN BUDDHISM UNDER THE FIRST REPUBLIC

After the liberation in 1945, Korean Buddhism emerged as a growing religion, albeit split into several groups, often with highly diverse doctrinal and historical backgrounds.[43] While most of these had their roots in the Korean tradition, a number of new sects, some with a clear Japanese background, arose within a few years of the start of the Republican period. Today more than thirty established schools of Buddhism exist in Korea, reflecting a wide spectrum of Mahāyāna beliefs and practices. Common to most of these schools are their strong sectarian attitudes, which are rarely grounded in serious doctrinal differences, but which mainly rest on economic, social or regional issues. This is all the more evident since they all rely on support from essentially the same prospective followers, the majority of whom are women.[44]

The Chogye Order is the largest Buddhist denomination in contemporary Korea.[45] Having historical roots that extend back to the mid-Chosŏn,[46] the order was only officially established as late as 1941 with its headquarters in Chogye Temple in Seoul. Its monastic adherents were made up of a motley crowd of monks and nuns formed by members of the old Imje and Wŏn denominations that were founded at the beginning of the colonial period. It encompasses both married priests and celibate monks and nuns. In terms of practice it includes both meditative and scholar monks, as well as ritual specialists. During the first decade following liberation from the Japanese, internal strife broke out between the celibate and the previously anti-Japanese monks, on the one hand, and the formerly pro-Japanese married priests, on the other. This power struggle over control of the temples was a direct outcome of the situation that had prevailed during the colonial period as mentioned above. By the late 1950s, the President of the First Republic, Syngman Rhee (Yi Sŭngman, ruled 1948–60), eventually intervened on the side of the celibate monks who, with official backing, were able to gain full control of nearly all the major monasteries in the country. The present Chogye Order was officially founded in 1962 as the Chogye Chonglim following the official ousting of the faction of married priests.[47] Being vastly outnumbered, the married priests and their followers were allowed to occupy a handful of lesser temples, and only remained in control of a few important monasteries. Eventually this group broke away from the Chogye Order to form their own denomination, the T'aego School, in 1970.[48]

It is interesting to observe that many of the 'new Buddhist groups' (i.e. those that were founded during the Japanese occupation or immediately after 1945) all retain strong elements of Japanese Buddhism. While this is most clearly seen in such movements as Wŏn Buddhism, the Chin'gak School, the Chinŏn School and the Kwanŭm School, even within such major denominations as the Chogye and T'aego schools there are still many vestiges, mainly structural and physical, that to a certain degree still reflect the legacy of the Japanese occupation.

Shortly after the Japanese capitulation the Communists took power in the northern part of the Korean Peninsula, eventually proclaming the People's Democratic Republic of Korea in 1948. Being anything but democratic the new regime, under the leadership of Kim Ilsung (r.1945–93), set about reforming Korean society according to a Stalinist model. In effect his rule became a uniquely odd politico-religious mixture, consisting of a twisted totalitarian socialism and hyper-nationalism, with a racist element that still remains unmatched in the world. All religious institutions including Buddhist temples, Christian churches, Confucian schools and Shamanist shrines within its borders were subjected to government control, and eventually closed on a variety of pretexts. Many believers were prosecuted as foreign spies or subversive elements, and thousands were either killed or imprisoned. In the period 1945–50, Buddhism was essentially exterminated as a living religious tradition in North Korea. With the outbreak of the Korean War (1950–3), the Korean Peninsula became the first testing ground in the struggle for world domination that initiated the Cold War. During the war, many Buddhist temples in the South were destroyed or damaged, and an unknown number of monks and nuns were killed by invading Communists from the North.[49] Since the 1960s, a select number of Buddhist temples and monasteries, mostly located in scenic places such as Mt Kŭmgang and Mt Myŏhyang, have been rebuilt and reopened for the public as museums. Whatever, 'religious' activity remains in North Korea is nothing but the 'cultural' branch of the government.[50]

PARK CHUNGHEE AND BUDDHISM

Despite his staunch nationalistic stance and strong support from the USA, Syngman Rhee was never a popular president. Having lived in exile during the entire colonial period he lacked sufficient support from a local power base, and was, moreover, dependent on economic support from the well-to-do. In 1962, in the aftermath of a lengthy and serious student uprising against his rule a military strongman rose to power. This was Park Chunghee (r.1962–79), an ultra-Conservative nationalist. He initiated a tradition in which the next three Korean presidents were all 'recruited' from the Military Academy in Seoul. Although he was a ruthless dictator and strict authoritarian, Park considered himself a pious Buddhist and often went out of his way to support various temples. As a nationalist he sought to capitalize on Korea's glorious past as a Buddhist nation, and was responsible for renovating many Buddhist monuments and sanctuaries including the famous Pulguk Temple and the Sŏkkuram, both situated in Kyŏngju, the old capital of the Silla kingdom.[51] In 1961 a new law governing Buddhist temples and their ownership, the much hated *Pulgyo chaesan kwalli pŏp* (Law for the Control of Buddhist Property) was promulgated. The law gave the government the right to interfere in the workings of the temples, including their economy, and to maintain police agents there.

Although Buddhism as such was supported, sometimes on the direct orders of the President himself, in the long run the close affinity between the military government and religion proved disruptive and worked against the interests of the latter. Among the many ills that resulted from this relationship was that Buddhist monks were drafted alongside other young men into the nation's armed forces.[52] Furthermore, in supporting a dictatorial President, Buddhists were accused of abandoning their basic principles of compassion and equality. One example of such support is furnished by Lee Hurak, a self-proclaimed Buddhist and a notorious right-wing extremist. This man was the chief of the KCIA (Korea's version of the CIA) during Park's heyday. In the course of his period in power many dissidents and enemies of Park Chunghee's regime were imprisoned and tortured, or simply dissappeared at the hand of this well-meaning 'bodhisattva'. After he fell from power on corruption charges, Lee became a patron of Buddhism and served as the protector of various religious journals.

Due to the widespread paranoia and dissent that characterized the entire span of Park's rule, Buddhist leaders were often carted up to Seoul where they were forced to swear their allegiance and loyalty to the President and his regime in much the same manner as the Japanese governor-generals had done during the colonial period. Those who refused were harrassed and in some cases removed from their monastic positions. It was also during this period that the first dissident monks arose within the sangha, something that would eventually grow into a major religious and political force within the Chogye Order during the reign of Chun Doohwan. Among these was Pŏpchŏng, a Chogye monk and leading intellectual from Sŏnggwang Temple in South Chŏlla province. Pŏpchŏng was in open opposition to the authoritarian and despotic rule of Park Chunghee, and as a popular speaker among students, as well as a prolific writer of both prose and poetry, he was considered dangerous by the government. Eventually he was forbidden to speak publicly and was placed under house arrest in a small hermitage above his home-temple for almost a decade.

KOREAN BUDDHISM UNDER THE FIFTH REPUBLIC

Following the assasination of Park Chunghee in 1979 and the subsequent rise to power of Chun Doohwan and his cohorts the following year, Korean Buddhism effectively entered a new era. Gone was the active support from an over-zealous and ultra-nationalist president with dictatorial status. The new president, again a scion of the Military Academy, was a Presbyterian Christian and a staunch anti-Buddhist, who sought to undermine and restrain Buddhist activities as much as possible. From Chun's perspective, Buddhism was a conservative and backward religion that had no place in modern Korean society. Like Park, Chun Doohwan was well aware that Buddhism commanded the largest percentage of the religiously active part of the population and he, therefore, felt it necessary either to control or to weaken it. One of the ways of achieving this aim was to turn the temples and their scenic locations into resorts for tourists. Hitherto the temples had been allowed to control the entrance fees to their domains, but by turning the monastic estates into national parks, the government at one stroke deprived the temples of a significant source of income. In addition, as the temples were now situated within national parks run by the government, they could only look on helplessly as extensive tourist resorts complete with hotels, brothels and bars were build right at their front gates. In the weekends and on public holidays thousands of tourists flocked to the most popular temples, becoming a nusiance for the monks and nuns in training, in addition to being a burden on the natural environment. Needless to say, many Buddhists resented the rule of the new president and his anti-Buddhist attitude, and monks, especially those connected with the Chogye Order, were highly critical of the government. The reason for this was that they stood to lose a good deal in terms of land, income and semi-autonomy.

The first serious confrontation between the new military government and the Chogye Order took place in the Fall of 1980 after a layman had burned himself alive at Hŭngryun Temple in Kyŏngju in protest at the moral condition of the *sangha*. Chun's government used this incident as an excuse to harass Buddhism, and the Chogye Order in particular. Accordingly, the government demanded that the *sangha* should be purged of 'undesirable elements'. On 30 October the government ordered the military into several of the major temples in the country, including the Chogye Temple in the capital, to search the premises for anti-government elements. In connection with these searches and investigations the government employed thugs, and several monks were injured or otherwise brutalized. Many were arrested on false charges and eventually a large number of monks and lay people were prosecuted for conspiracy, or for being pro-Communist. Following this, the Buddhist community, and the Chogye Order in particular, came under the strict surveillance of government agents.[53]

The political strain between Chun Doohwan's government and Buddhism continued, but only came to the fore in earnest in 1986 when monks and nuns from the Chogye Order joined in popular uprisings against the government in all the large cities nationwide. An anti-government rally was held on 9 July in Haein Temple, in which monks attempted to thwart the government control of temple lands on the basis of the much resented *Pulgyo chaesan kwalli pŏp* of 1961. The meeting also addressed earlier attempts at harassing the Chogye Order such as those that took place in 1980, referred to above. Accordingly, several monks were arrested by the police.[54] Eventually, it became impossible to silence the protesters, who enjoyed tremendous support in the population at large and the president was forced to step down, thus permitting the first democratic elections ever to take place in the history of Korea.

Interestingly, the rule of Chun Doohwan was a major contributory factor in the modernization of Korean Buddhism. Due to rapid economic development and rising living standards the Buddhist sects and their temples have grown rich. Many of the large monasteries have been renovated at enormous cost, and many new temples have sprung up, both in the countryside and in the big cities.

There can be little doubt that the increasing individual wealth of many ordained members of the Korean *sangha* has contributed greatly to a degeneration of the quality of religious practices, such as rituals and meditation, not to mention the keeping of the precepts. Many monks in the Chogye Order – and even some nuns – no longer maintain celibacy, but oddly enough this trend has not affected the numbers seeking to join the married clergy of the T'aego Order. There is also a tendency for monks and nuns, who in various ways have amassed sufficient personal wealth, to move out of the temples and set themselves up in private houses in residental areas, sometimes even with their own cars.

Another factor in this degeneration is the continuation of the draft system for monks. This practice, which involves monks learning to maim and kill, in addition to being subjected to a diet of meat and to alcohol, contributes greatly to the undermining of monastic discipline, and in particular the upholding of the precepts as set down in the *vinaya.*

The traditional monastic education must also be held accountable for the current debasement of Buddhist doctrines. While almost all other aspects of Korean Buddhism have undergone modernization and reform, monastic education has remained virtually unchanged. Somehow the conservatives have retained control over this highly important facet of monastic training, with the result that many monks and nuns only have a rote-learning attitude to the Buddhist scriptures. This means that while they may be able to recite lengthy passages of text, actual understanding of its contents is often insignificant, and in many cases entirely lacking.[55]

KOREAN BUDDHISM AND POLITICS ON THE THRESHOLD OF THE TWENTY-FIRST CENTURY

Although Buddhist politics and inter-sectarian issues cannot be limited to one single denomination, here focus will be placed on the Chogye Order, which accounts for the vast majority of followers in the country. At present the Chogye Order, with its headquarters in the Chogye Temple in Seoul, controls the vast majority of temples in South Korea, including most of the important historical monuments. It also accounts for the greatest activity among the laity, including missionary work abroad.[56] From an economic perspective the Order is fairly strong, although its infrastructure and executive power are often weakened by the diverse and contradictory interests of the various lineages and temple families which constitute it. The Chogye Order is essentially an umbrella organization for several Sŏn lineages and their temples, and has been able to set up only an overall administrative structure for co-operation and general regulations governing its followers. In practice the individual lineages of transmission within the Order enjoy considerable autonomy and manage their own economy. Sectarian strife among the various lineages and temple families within the order is not uncommon.[57] Furthermore, there is a high degree of tension between major factions within the order, an issue to which we shall return below. The head of the order, the so-called 'Supreme Patriarch', is a senior monk, usually a highly respected Sŏn master, who is chosen for his spiritual merits by a board of delegates. These delegates, usually abbots and senior monks of a certain spiritual standing, represent the major temple families. Administration of the Chogye School, including the task of pacifying and manipulating various factions, as well as the handling of the order's finances, is carried out at the headquarters in Chogye Temple in Seoul. This institution, which is mainly bureaucratic in function, is headed by an administrative chief, whose actual power equals and sometimes even exceeds that of the Supreme Patriarch.

One example of sectarian infighting within the order has been the recent crusade of Sŏngch'ŏl (1912–93), a Sŏn master from Haein Temple, against the teachings of Chinul (1158–1210),[58] who is considered the founder and spiritual forefather of the temple family based at Sŏnggwang Temple in South Chŏlla province. In 1981 Sŏngch'ŏl was elected to the position of Supreme Patriarch, and soon after began to harass the followers of this lineage by attempting to discredit the tradition of sudden enlightenment, gradual cultivation advocated by Chinul.[59] There can be little doubt that the Supreme Patriarch was sincere in his attempt at discrediting the legacy of Chinul from a doctrinal standpoint. However, it should also be noted that he began his campaign at a time when the Songgwang temple family had recently lost its dynamic leader, and was therefore spiritually and politically weakened. It is obvious that Sŏngch'ŏl was aware that the other lineage had strong support among the laity, and was moreover well-known for its Western followers. By undermining it he stood to gain prestige for himself, as well as being in a position to attract new followers. Although there may have been short term political and economic benefits to be gained by Sŏngch'ŏl and his followers, in the long run his attacks brought unrest and dissent within the very order he was supposed to represent.

The political turmoil that occurred at the Chogye Temple in March and April of 1994 was to a large degree occasioned by the late Supreme Patriarch's decade-long neglect of the administrative problems of the order. This had led to a usurpation of power by the chief of administration, a monk of ill-repute named Sŏ Yihyŏn, who was able to run the political and economic affairs of the order as he pleased for a succession of terms in office. Eventually his excesses became too much for the majority of monks and nuns, and he was ousted after prolonged fighting in and around the Chogye Temple in March and April of that year. One of the things that brought about the downfall of Sŏ Yihyŏn was a scandal in which it was alleged that he had illegally contributed ten million US dollars from the temple coffers to the campaign-fund of President Kim Young-sam during the presidental elections of 1992.[60] Fear that these allegations would be investigated publicly may also have accounted for the fact that the President and his ministers first sought to assist Sŏ. For several days police fought against protesters at the Chogye Temple, many of whom were beaten up and arrested. In the end the reform party prevailed and Sŏ Yihyŏn was forced to leave office. The full extent of Sŏ's administrative and economic irregularities have never been fully discovered. The government officially apologized to the Chogye Order for its poor handling of the matter, which had involved active police involvement on the side of the ousted administrative head, and a settlement was eventually reached with the new administration of the Order.[61] However, a lid was placed over the matter, much to the relief of the ruling party, and Sŏ Yihyŏn's dubious connections with the government were glossed over and forgotten.[62]

In addition to temple politics, there is a growing tendency towards actual political organization within the Chogye Order transcending mere temple politics and issues of lineage. There are currently three leading, and numerous smaller, factions within the Order. The still-dominant and major group consists of older monks and nuns who wish to maintain the status quo in terms of organization and seniority. They are largely non-political as far as party politics go, but wish to maintain control of the Order both administratively and spiritually. One means of achieving this is by providing uncritical support for the various governments, even though this often compromises fundamental Buddhist ethics. On the reform side are the young monks and nuns, mainly from the Saṅgha College in Seoul, who insist on a thorough reformation of Korean Buddhism along modern lines. They tend to be politically active and consider themselves supporters of democracy and an open society. For these reasons they are often branded 'activist monks' by the government, which sees them as a potentially subversive factor on a par with the radical student movement. Many in this grouping support the abolition of the vow of celibacy for monks and nuns. Another reform faction consists of monks based at Ch'ilbul Hermitage on Mt Chiri. In contrast to the reform party in Saṅgha College, this group seeks to rid the order of various excesses so that it may return to traditional monasticism and meditation. In addition they seek a system of authority based on spiritual merit not on seniority, a left-over from Confucianism. Interestingly, this more conservative reform party fought alongside the young monks from the Saṅgha College during the ousting of Sŏ Yihyŏn and his cohorts from Chogye Temple in the Spring of 1994.

Other non-political Buddhist groups include the Pure Land Movement, a Buddhist environmentalist group headed by the monk Pŏpchŏng, who became famous as a reformer and political figure in opposition to Park Chunghee. Recently he has become involved in environmental issues, and has established an activist movement that seeks to combat widespread pollution and protect the natural resources of the country.[63] Movements such as this, in which monks and civilians work closely together, are becoming increasingly common in Korean society, and in the years to come may spell the demise of Korean Buddhism as a religion of seclusion and non-involvement in secular matters.[64]

CONCLUSION

With the collapse of the Korean Kingdom in 1910 and the Japanese takeover of power in Korea, Buddhism embarked on a new period of modernization and reform. However, the price of these gains was heavy indeed. Korean temples became secularized and Korean Buddhism was to a large extent harnessed to the Imperial Japanese wagon. Although temples enjoyed a prosperity unheard of during the Chosŏn dynasty, and monks and nuns came to enjoy a much more respectable position in Korean society at large, freedom of speech and movement became restricted, and unquestioned submission to the secular powers represented by the colonial government was obligatory. In this sense Korean Buddhism became more politically involved than ever before in its 1,500-year-plus history in the country, but without being able to exercise a political role of its own choosing.

In 1945 Korea was liberated from the Japanese and a new period of religious prosperity and diversity set in. While Buddhism more or less dissappeared from North Korea during the 1950s, many Buddhist denominations prospered in the South with little interference from the secular powers. During the following three decades the fortunes of Korean Buddhism have been intimately connected with the current political powers, which without exception have influenced the development of the religion greatly in ways that have been both positive and negative. With the founding of the Third Republic, by Park Chunghee in 1962, Buddhism entered a new phase. It was, once again, elevated to a position amounting to that of a national ideology, although this also meant that it became publicly associated with the legitimizing of the government of the day.

While Buddhism, and in particular the temples, faced stiff opposition from the 1980 government of Chun Doohwan, it nevertheless reached a level of prosperity unheard of previously. Despite the fact that the government of the Sixth Republic under No Taewoo signified a continuation of presidents that had graduated from the Military Academy, the new government was in fact the first real 'civil' government that Korea had ever enjoyed. Under No, who came from a family of Buddhists himself, Buddhism continued to prosper and was allowed to become increasingly engaged in social activities. Towards the end of the 1980s Buddhists established their own TV channel, the Buddhist Broadcasting System, which enabled them to reach a wider audience nationwide.

The relationship between Buddhism and the government of Kim Youngsam was tenuous and shaky. As a result of recent events in which the government actively took sides in the inter-sectarian conflict within the Chogye Order, many Buddhists place little faith in the President. No doubt the problems are partly caused by the fact that the current president is a Christian with little sympathy for those belonging to other faiths. However, the government has now realized that to challenge the Buddhist community of Korea openly may be political suicide. In modern Korea political opposition is not so easily bullied into silence as it was once. Buddhists are still the largest group of religious believers in the nation, and a government that works against their faith stands little chance of getting elected.[65]

NOTES

1. For a brief description of this crucial phase in the history of Korean Buddhism, see U Chŏngsang and Kim Yongt'ae, (1968, 134–8). See also Takahashi Tōru (1929, 30–55). For additional information on the formation of Confucian ideology during the period in question, see Duncan (1994).
2. For an interesting study of the anti-Buddhist measures during the early Chosŏn, see John I. Goulde, 'Anti-Buddhist Polemic in Fourteen and Fifteen Century Korea: The Emergence of Confucian Exclusivism', doctoral thesis, Harvard University, Cambridge, Massachusets 1985. See also Han T'akkun, (1993).
3. For a survey of the state of Korean Buddhism during the latter half of the Chosŏn dynasty see Kim Duk-Hwang, (1988, 227–37).
4. For additional information on this remarkable monk see Sørensen, (1983).
5. For a useful survey of the renaissance of Sŏn Buddhism during the nineteenth century see Han Kidu 1984a. See also Sok Do-ryun, (1965).
6. Yi Sŏngt'a (1993, Vol. 1, 425–36).
7. Among these were Mangong (1872–1946), Suwŏl (1855–1928), Yongun (1878–1944) and Hanam (1876–1951). See Sok Do-ryun Vol. 5:4 (1965), 17–22. A more detailed presentation can be found in Han Kidu (1984a).
8. See Lee Ki-baik, *A New History of Korea* (trans. Edward W. Wagner and Edward J. Shultz) Seoul: Ilchokak, 1984, 268–70.
9. See Sørensen (1991, 46–62.)
10. For a biographical outline of this important figure, see Takahashi (1929, 890–1).
11. See ibid., 892–902.
12. See Sørensen *op.cit*. See also Chŏng Kwangho (1982, 385–484).
13. See Takahashi, (1929, 892–6).
14. Kang, Wi Jo (1979, 42–7).
15. For a discussion of these laws, see U Chŏngsang and Kim Yongt'ae (1968, 175–8).
16. For his activities, see Im Hyebong (1993, Vol. 2, 459–72).
17. For a brief description of the episode, see Lee Ki-baik, *op.cit.*, 293–5.
18. See Kang, Wi Jo (1979, 42–7 (esp. 44–5)).
19. Takahashi (1929, 918–33).
20. See Kang Sŏkchu and Pak Kyŏnghyŏn (1980, 39–52).
21. For further information on the strained relationship between Buddhism and Christianity in Korea see Sørensen (1988, 25–31)
22. Part of the Meiji reforms were aimed at curtailing the power of the Buddhist temples by undermining their internal structures, governance and economy. This was chiefly brought about by institutionalizing the marriage of the Buddhist monks. With the formal abolition of celibacy for the *saṅgha*, the majority of monks became caretakers of small temples which were run as family enterprises. Hence, the modernized form of Buddhism the Japanese missionaries represented in Korea was one of married priests, an academic schooling for its clergy, and an economy based on what amounted to parish temples. In other words, the Japanese Buddhists were generally less dependent on voluntary offerings from the faithful, or on growing their own crops – as was the case in Korea – but were used to earning their own money for the

services they performed in society. For a highly informative study of the Buddhist reforms under the Meiji government, and as such of great importance for an understanding of the Buddhist revival in Korea, see Ketelaar (1990).

23. The full text of the ordinance is reproduced in U Chŏngsang and Kim Yongt'ae (1968, 175–89).
24. Sŏ Kyŏngsu, (1982, 87–112).
25. Although these regulations were not officially implemented before 1926, in fact many Korean monks were married or otherwise had mistresses more or less openly previous to this time. Han Yongun, for one, is said to have secretly kept a mistress.
26. The system of organizing the temples into thirty main temples and nearly 1,000 secondary ones was implemented in 1915. See U Chŏngsang and Kim Yongt'ae, (1968, 189–90).
27. So far the most useful account of the problems that occurred over the married clergy in Korean Buddhism can be found in Buswell (1992, 25–30).
28. See Han Yongun, (1913, reprinted 1978).
29. Ch'ŏe Pyŏnghŏn (1984, Vol. 1, 451–8.)
30. This is apparent in both its style and its layout. The issues often feature the portraits of Japanese officials, including the governor-general, drawings that show Korea as a part of the greater Japanese Empire, and vignettes with the Japanese flag, etc. Kwŏn Sangno (1879–1965), the editor, was a strong and influential supporter of the Japanese. See also Michael E. Robinson, 'Colonial Publication Policy and the Korean Nationalist Movement', in *The Japanese Colonial Empire*, Meyers, Ramon H. and Mark R. Peattie (ed.), Princeton: Princeton University Press, 1984, 312–43.
31. For a study of his views on Buddhism see Yang Nangyong, (1993, Vol. 1, 437–50.) Following the liberation from Japan in 1945 this influential monk, scholar and politician continued to be active in Buddhist circles. For his pro-Japanese activities, see Im Hyebong, (1993, Vol. 2, 509–22).
32. The journals have been republished in *Han guk Pulgyo chapchi ch'ŏngsŏ* (The Complete Books of Korean Buddhist Periodicals), Vols 1–18, Seoul: Poyŏn Kak, 1976. For a study of these journals see. Sørensen, (1990, 17–27).
33. See Kang Sŏkchu and Pak Kyŏnghyŏn (1980, 79–83).
34. See Lee Ki-baik (1984, 340–4).
35. See Sørensen (1993, 49–69).
36. See Kang Sŏkchu and Pak Kyŏnghyŏn (1980, 93–6).
37. See U Chŏngsang and Kim Yongt'ae (1968, 190).
38. For more information on this journal see Kang Sŏkju and Pak Kyŏnghyŏn (1980, 203–6.)
39. This magazine was first published on 15 July 1924 and the last issue appeared on the 1 August 1933. Altogether 108 issues appeared.
40. This journal was first published on 3 March 1937 and the last issue was put out on 1 August 1944.
41. See Im Hyebong (1993). A full list of this material is included in the bibliography, 607–21.
42. The ambivalence and inconsequence of Han Yongun's behaviour is further underscored when seen in relation to his view on the relationship between politics and religion. For an illuminating article on this aspect of his thought, see Sŏ Kyŏngsu, (1985, 63–79).
43. The best information on the Buddhist sects in modern Korea is found in the *Han'guk chonggyo yŏn'gam* (Eng. subtitle: *The Yearbook of Korean Religions*). This is a large and

detailed handbook on all the religions in the country. It is edited by the Han'guk Chonggyo sahŭi Yŏn'guso, and has been published by Koryŏ Halimwŏn since 1993. For a slightly outdated survey see also Mok Chŏng-bae, (1983, 19–27).

44. For a working model with which to deal with contemporary Korean Buddhism, see the essay by Shim Jae-ryong, (1993, 50–55). See also Lee Young-ja (Yi Yŏngcha) (1983, 28–37). For details of Buddhist practice and belief in contemporary Korea, see Sørensen, 1999.

45. The Chogye Order is sometimes considered as having originated in the mid-Koryŏ due to a misunderstanding of the name which it shares with a Sŏn Buddhist lineage of that period.

46. An attempt at establishing a direct historical link with the Sŏn tradition of the mid and late Koryŏ is not only irrelevant in the light of modern Korean Buddhism, but is apt to confuse the sectarian reality of the present order. The Chogye Order is in fact primarily a political and sectarian amalgamation of several collateral lines of transmission, all of which descend from the Sŏn Buddhist tradition prevalent during the latter half of the Chosŏn. For the primary source materials pertaining to this important Buddhist school, see *Chogye chong sa* (1989).

47. For a discussion of these events, see Buswell, (1992, 30–3).

48. The strained relationship between the Chogye Order and the T'aego School was eventually resolved in 1982 at a meeting attended by representatives of both denominations. See *Korea Newsreview*, August 28 (1982), 24.

49. See. Kang Sŏkchu and Pak Kyŏnghyŏn, (1980, 235–6).

50. Information on the fate of Buddhism in North Korea can be had from *Pukhan sach'al yonggŭ* (1993).

51. Among the nationalist-*cum*-Buddhist institutions Park launched was the re-establishment of the Hwarang, a youth corps that was trained in a mixture of military skills, patriotic fervour and Buddhist piety. Originally the Hwarang had been a special military unit under the old Silla dynasty (c. 300–668). Park's training centre has since been closed down.

52. For material on this see *Chogye chong sa* (1989, 59–64).

53. Kim Chongch'an (1986, 298–316)

54. See ibid.

55. For a discussion of the current state of Korean Buddhism, and in particular the impact of modernity, see Lee Eun-Yun (1992, 56–61). See also Shim Jae-ryong (1991, 165–76); and (1996, 107–13); and Sørensen, (1996, 159–90). A recent compilation of various articles on the current situation of Buddhism in Korea – mainly seen from within the tradition – can be found in *Yisipil segi munmyŏng kwa pulgyo* (1996).

56. This situation is slowly changing, and a number of the new Buddhist sects – including the Ch'ŏnt'ae School – is growing rapidly.

57. For a brief and somewhat nativistic discussion of the recent history of Korean Buddhism with emphasis on the Chogye Order, see Mok Chŏng-bae, (1993, 23–49).

58. The majority of Chinul's writings can be found in *The Korean Approach to Zen: The Collected Works of Chinu*, Buswell, Robert E. (trans.), Honolulu: University of Hawaii Press, 1983.

59. Most of Sŏngch'ŏl's attacks are formulated in his *Sŏnmun chŏngno* (The Correct Way of Sŏn Buddhism), Seoul: Pulgwang, 1987. For a sober and detailed discussion of the doctrinal issues involved, see Robert E. Buswell, 'The Debate Concerning Moderate Radical Subitism in Korean Sŏn Buddhism', in *HCSCC*, Vol. 1, 489–519 (esp. 509–16). See also Mueller (1992, 105–26). Although well-written and factual, this

article is slightly biased in favour of Sŏngch'ŏl's position.

60. See *Korea Herald*, 5 April 1994, 1, 3, 9.
61. See Cho Sang-hee, 'Buddhist Elders Not Satisfied with Choi's Apologetic Visit', *Korea Herald*, Saturday 25 June 1994.
62. For illuminating journalistic treatment of this interesting episode, see Kim Nanggi, (1994, 12–21). See also Kwak Pyŏngch'an *et al.*, (1994, 8–13). Prof. Kim Yongho of Inha University kindly provided me with this material.
63. See Cho Sang-hee, 'Supra-Sectarian Campaign: Monk Initiates' "Pure Land Drive"', *Korea Herald* 31/3 (1994).
64. See also 'Monk Operates Farming Community to Teach Buddhism through Labour', *Korea Herald*, Saturday 6 August 1994.
65. For further details on Buddhism in present-day Korea, see Sørensen (1996, 159–90); 1998 (forthcoming).

APPENDIX

Governments in Korea from the Chosŏn to the present

Chosŏn 1392–1910
Japanese Colonial Period 1910–1945
First Republic 1949–1960   Democratic People's Republic of Korea 1949–
Second Republic 1960–1962
Third Republic 1962–1972
Fourth Republic 1972–1980
Fifth Republic 1980–1987
Sixth Republic 1987–1992
Seventh Republic 1992–1997
Eighth Republic 1997–

BIBLIOGRAPHY

Note the following abbreviations are used:

Hanguk chonggyo sasang ŭi chae chomyong	HCSCC
Hanguk kŭndae chonggyo sasang sal	HKCSS
Hanguk pulgyo chapchi chongsŏ	HPCC
Hanguk Pulgyo kwange nonmun sonjip	HPSKRS
Hanguk pulgyo sasang sa	HPSS
Korea Journal	KJ
Kŭndae Hanguk pulgyo saron	KHPS
Pulgyo hakbo	PH
Seoul Journal of Korean Studies	SJKS
Yisipil segi munmyŏng kwa pulgyo [English subtitle: *Buddhism and Civilization in the Twenty-first Century*]	YSMP

An Pŏng-jik, (1979) 'Han Yong-un's Liberalism: An Analysis of the *Reformation of Korean Buddhism*', *KJ* 19/12, 13–18.
Buswell, Robert E. (1992) *The Zen Monastic Experience: Buddhist Practice in Contemporary Korea*. Princeton, NJ: Princeton University Press.

——— (1996) 'Is There a "Korean Buddhism" in the Pre-National Age?', *YSMP*, Seoul: Dongguk University, 617–39.

Chinsan Han Kidu paksa hwagap kinyon [Festschrift Commemorating the Sixtieth Birthday of Chinsan, Professor Han Kidu] (1993) *Hanguk chonggyo sasang ŭi chae chomyong* [New Light on Korean Religious Thought] [*HCSCC*], 2 vols. Comp. Chinsan Han Kidu paksa hwagap kinyon non munjip kanhaeng ŭiwŏn hoe. Iri: Wongwang taehakkyo ch'ulp'an kuk.

Chogye chong sa [The History of the Chogye School] (1989) Comp. by Sŏ Chongbŏm. Seoul: private publication.

Ch'ŏe Pyŏnghŏn, (1984) 'Ilje pulgyo ŭi ch'imt'u kwa Han Yongun ŭi *Chosŏn pulgyo yusillon* [On the Penetration of Japanese Buddhism and Han Yongun's *Chosŏn pulgyo yusillon*]', in *HCSCC* Vol. 1, 451–8.

Chŏng Kwangho, (1982) 'Ilje ŭi chonggyo chŏngch'aek kwa sikmin chi pulgyo [Imperial Japan's Policy of Religious Administration and Buddhist Colonization]', in *Hanguk Pulgyo kwange ronmun sonjip* [Collection of Articles on Korean Buddhist History] [*HPSKRS*], ed. Chungang Sungga Taehak, Seoul, 385–484.

Chŏng Sŭnil, 'Han Yongŭn ŭi pulgyo sasang', *HKCSS*, 417–36.

Cozin, Mark, (1987) 'Wŏn Buddhism: Origin and Growth of a New Korean Religion', *Religion and Ritual in Korean Society*, Laurel Kendall and Griffin Dix, *Korea Research Monograph* 12. Berkeley; CA: UC, 171–84.

Duncan John, (1994) 'Confucianism in the Late Koryŏ and the Early Chosŏn', *Korean Studies* 18, 76–102.

Dumoulin, Heinrich (1976), 'Contemporary Buddhism in Korea', in *Buddhism in the Modern World*, ed. Heinrich Dumoulin and John C. Maraldo. New York and London: Collier Macmillan, 202–14.

Han Chongman, 'Paek Yongsŏng ŭi taegak kyo sasang', *HKCSS*, 369–92.

Kidu, (1976) '*Pulgyo yushin non* kwa *Pulgyo hyŏksin non,*' Ch'angchak kwa pip'yŏng 11/1, 233–57.

——— (1984a) 'Kŭndae Hanguk ŭi sŏn sasang [The Sŏn Thought of Modern Korea]', in *HKCSS*, Iri: 201–22.

——— (1984b) 'Chosŏn malgi ŭi sŏn non', *Hanguk sŏn sasang yŏngu*, ed. Pulgyo munhwa yŏnguwŏn. Seoul: Tongguk Taehakkyo ch'ulp'an, 411–81.

Han T'akkun (1993) *Yugyo chŏngch'i wa pulgyo* [Confucian Politics and Buddhism]. Seoul: Ilcho Kak.

Han Yongŭn (1978) *Chosŏn pulgyo yushin non.* Keijō (Seoul): Pulgyo sŏgwan, 1913 (reprint; Seoul: Poryŏn Kak).

Han'guk chonggyo yŏn'gam [Eng. subtitle: The Yearbook of Korean Religions]. (1993– Ed. the Han'guk Chonggyo sahŭi Yŏn'guso. Seoul: Koryŏ Halimwŏn.

Han'guk kŭndae pulgyo paengnyŏn sa 2 vols. Minjŏk Sa (Seoul). No date of publication given.

Han'guk pulgyo chapchi ch'ŏngsŏ [The Complete Books of Korean Buddhist Periodicals] [*HPCC*] (1976) Vols. 1–18. Seoul: Poryŏn Kak.

Han'guk pulgyo inmyŏng sajon [English subtitle: The Korean Buddhist Biographical Dictionary] (1993) Comp. Yi Chŏng, Seoul: Pulgyo sidaesa.

Im Hyebong (1993) *Ch'inil pulgyo non* [A Discussion of Pro-Japanese Buddhism] 2 vols. Seoul: Minjoksa.

Kang Kun-ki (1996) 'The Present Situation and Prospects of Korean Buddhism in the World', *YSMP*, Seoul: Dongguk University, 585–96.

Kang Sŏkchu and Pak Kyŏnghyŏn (1980) *Pulgyo kŭnse paengnyŏn.* Chungang Ilbo

[Buddhism in the Recent One Hundred Years], Seoul, 39–52.

Kang, Wi Jo (1979) 'The Secularization of Korean Buddhism under the Japanese Colonialism', *Korea Journal* 19/7, 42–7.

Ketelaar James Edward (1990) *Of Heretics and Martyrs in Meiji Japan: Buddhism and Its Persecution.* Princeton, NJ: Princeton University Press.

Kim Chongch'an (1986) 'Tae Han Pulgyo Chogye chong ŭl haebu handa [The Rebellion of the Great Korean Buddhist Chogye Order]', *Sindong A* [New East Monthly] Nov. 298–316.

Kim Duk-Hwang (1988) *A History of Religions in Korea.* Seoul: Daeji Moonhwa-sa.

Kim Nanggi (1994) 'Minju tang, 80 ŏkwŏn haengbang ch'achwa kukchu kwŏn paldong,' [The Disturbance concerning the Scandal involving the Democratic Party and the missing 80 billion Wŏn) *Chugan Chosŏn* (Chosŏn Weekly) 21 April, 12–21.

Kim Sŏngbae (1977) 'Han Yŏngun p'yŏn pulgyo kyoyŭk pulgyo hanmun tokbon e' taehan yŏngu', *PH* 14, 173–84.

Kim Uchang (1979) 'Han Yong-un and Buddhism', *KJ* Vol. 19/12, 19–27.

Kim Yŏngt'ae (1988) 'Kundae pulgyo ŭi chongt'ong chongmaek', *in KHPN,* ed. Pulgyo Sahakhoe. Seoul: Minjoksa, 183–208.

Kim Youngho (1995) 'Yi Nŭnghwa's Approaches to the History of Religions in Korea and to the Comparative Study of Religion', in *Religions in Traditional Korea,* ed. Henrik H. Sørensen. *SBS Monographs* 3. Copenhagen, 131–55.

Kŭndae Hanguk pulgyo saron (1988) [*KHPS*], ed. Pulgyo sahak hoe Minjok sa. Seoul.

Kusan Sunim (1985) *The Way of Korean Zen,* trans. by Martine Fages. New York and Tokyo: Weatherhill.

Kwak Pyŏngch'an *et al.,* (1994) 'Pan YS esŏ kaegukkong sin uro', [New Quarrels over Anti-YS Attacks] *Han Kyorae Weekly News Magazine* 21, 8–13.

Lee Eun-Yun, (1992) 'Issues Confronting Korean Buddhism Today', *Koreana* 6/4, 56–61.

Lee Ki-baik, (1984) *A New History of Korea.* Seoul: Ilchokak.

Mok Chŏng-bae (1983) 'Korean Buddhist Sects and Temple Operations', *KJ* 23/9, 19–27.

—— (1993) (Mok Jeong-bae) 'Buddhism in Modern Korea', *KJ* 33/3, 23–49.

Mueller, Mark (1992) 'Sŏngch'ŏl's Radical Subitism', *Seoul Journal of Korean Studies* 5, 105–26.

Nam Toryŏng, 'Kŭndae pulgyo ŭi kyoryuk hwaldong', *HKCSS,* 275–319.

No Kwŏnryŏng 'Pak Hanyŏng ŭi pulgyo sasang kwa yushin ŭndong', *HKCSS,* 393–416.

Pak Kyŏnghyŏn, 'Kŭndae pulgyo ŭi yŏngu', *KHPS,* 15–68.

—— (1981) 'Buddhism in Modern Korea', *KJ* 21/8, 32–40.

Park Sun-young (1983) 'Buddhist Schools and Their Educational Ideologies', *KJ* 23/9, 38–45.

Pukhan sach'al yonggŭ [A Study of the Temples in North Korea] (1993) Comp. Sach'al munhwa yongŭ wŏn. Seoul: Hanguk pulgyo chong tanhyŏp ŭi hoe.

Shim Jae-ryong (1993) 'Buddhist Responses to Modern Transformation of Society in Korea', *KJ* 33/3, 50–5.

—— (1991) 'Modernity and Religiosity of Korean People Today', *SJKS* 4, 165–76.

—— (1996) 'Buddhism and Information Society', *YSMP,* Seoul: Dongguk University, 107–13.

Sŏ Kyŏngsu (1982) 'Ilje ŭi pulgyo chŏngch'aek [The Buddhist Policy of Imperial Japan]', *PH* 19, 87–112.

—— (1985) 'Han Yongun ŭi chŏnggyo pŭni non e taehayŏ [Han Yongun's Arguments in

Favour of the Separation of Politics and Religion]', *PH* 22, 63–79.

Sok Do-ryun (1965) 'Modern Son Buddhism in Korea', *KJ* 5/1, 26–30; 5/2, 27–32; and 5/4, 17–22.

Sŏngch'ŏl (1987) *Sŏnmun chŏngno* [The Correct Way of Sŏn Buddhism] Seoul: Pulgwang.

Sungsan Pak Kil-jin paksa kohi kinyŏm: Hanguk kŭndae chonggyo sasang sa [The History of Contemporary Religious Thought in Korea] (1984) [*HKCSS*]. Iri: Wŏngwang t'aehakkyo ch'ulp'ansa.

Sørensen, Henrik H. (1983) 'The Life and Thought of the Korean Sŏn Master Kyŏnghŏ', *Korean Studies* 7, 9–33.

—— (1988) 'The Conflict between Buddhism and Christianity in Korea', in *East Asian Institute Occasional Papers* 1, 25–31.

—— (1990) 'Korean Buddhist Journals during the Early Japanese Colonial Rule', *Korea Journal* 30/1, 17–27.

—— (1991) 'Japanese Buddhist Missionaries and Their Impact on the Revival of Korean Buddhism at the Close of the Chosŏn Dynasty', *Perspectives on Japan and Korea* ed. Arne Kalland and Henrik H. Sørensen. *Nordic Proceedings in Asian Studies* No. 1. Copenhagen, 46–62.

—— (1993) 'The Attitude of the Japanese Colonial Government Towards Religions in Korea from 1910–1919', *Copenhagen Papers of East and Southeast Asian Studies* 8, 49–69.

—— (1996) 'Korean Buddhism on the Threshold of the 21st Century', in *100 Years of Modernization in Korea: Toward the 21st Century: Selected Papers of the 9th International Conference on Korean Studies*. Seoul: Academy of Korean Studies, 159–90.

—— (1999) 'Korean Buddhism: The Pre-Modern and Modern Period', in *Buddhist Spirituality 2. World Spirituality* Vol. 9, ed. Paul Swanson *et al.* New York: Crossroad Publishing Co. (forthcoming).

Takahashi Tōru (1976) *Richō bukkyō*. [Buddhism under the Yi Dynasty] Keijō (Seoul); reprint, Tokyo: Kokusho Kankōkai, [1929].

The Scripture of Won Buddhism (1988) (Won Pulgyo Kyojon) trans. Pal Kohn Chon, 2nd edn. Iri: Won Kwang.

T'uigyŏng Tang Sangno paksa ch'ŏnsŏ (1990) Vol. 5. Seoul: T'uigyŏng Tang Sangno paksa ch'ŏnsŏ kanhaeng ŭiwŏnhoe.

U Chŏngsang and Kim Yongt'ae 'Hanguk pulgyo sa [The History of Korean Buddhism]', [*HPSS*] (1968) Seoul: Chinsu Tang.

Wŏn pulgyo chŏnsŏ. Comp. Wŏn pulgyo chŏnghwa sa (1992) Iri: Wŏn pulgyo ch'ulp'an sa.

Yang Nangyong (1993), 'Kwŏn Sangno Chosŏn pulgyo kaehyŏk sasang ŭi yŏngu [A Study of Kwŏn Sangno's Thought on the Reform of Korean Buddhism]', in *HCSCC* 1, 437–50.

Yi Nŭnghwa (1918) *Chosŏn pulgyo t'ongsa*, 2 vols. Keijō (reprint, Poryŏn kak, 1976).

Yi Pongchun (1991) 'Chosŏn Sŏngchong cho ŭi yugyo chŏngch'i wa paebul chŏngch'aek', *PH* 28, 259–90.

—— (1992) 'Yŏnsan cho ŭi paebul ch'aek kwa kŭ ch'ui ŭi sŏnggyŏk', *PH* 29, 355–76.

Yi Sŏngt'a (1993) 'Kyŏnghŏ sidac ŭi sŏn kwa kyŏlsa [Sŏn in Kyŏnghŏ's Time and [Buddhist] Associations]', in *HCSCC* 1, 425–36.

Yi Yŏngcha (1984) 'Chosŏn chung hugi ŭi sŏnp'ung', *Hanguk sŏn sasang yŏngu*, ed. Pulgyo munhwa yŏnguwŏn. Seoul: Tongguk Taehakkyo ch'ulp'an pu, 339–410

—— 'Kŭndae kŏsa pugyo sasang', *HKCSS*, 223–48.

—— (1983) (Lee Young-ja), 'Current State of Buddhism Among Women in Korea', *KJ* 23/9, 28–37.

Yisipil segi nunmyŏng kwa pulgyo [Eng. Subtitle: Buddhism and Civilization in the 21st Century] [*YSMP*] (1996) Proceeding of The International Conference on Buddhist Studies Commemorating the 90th Anniversary of Dongguk University. Seoul: Dongguk University.

Yŭ Pyŏngdŏk, 'Ilje sidae ŭi pulgyo', (1975) in Sungsan Pak Kilchin paksa hwagap kinyŏm, *Hanguk pulgyo sasang sa.* Iri: Wongwang taehakkyŏ ch'ulp'an kŭk, 1,159–87

Yun sa-sun (1984) 'Won Buddhism and Practical Learning (The Influence of Practical Learning on Salvation Consciousness)', *KJ* 24/6, 40–9.

7
LAOS: FROM BUDDHIST KINGDOM TO MARXIST STATE[1]

MARTIN STUART-FOX

INTRODUCTION

The interrelationship between Buddhism and politics in Laos has deep historical roots. The earliest traces of Buddhism within what are now the geographical limits of the modern Lao state date back to the sixth or seventh centuries on the plain of Viang Chan (Vientiane), and some form of Buddhism was known in Luang Phrabāng well before the founding of the Lao kingdom of Lān Xāng in the mid fourteenth-century (Gagneux 1972; Lévy 1940).[2]

The political importance of Buddhism throughout the classical period of Lao history derived from the legitimation it provided for the exercise of power at all levels of Lao society. Theravāda Buddhism, the form practised in Laos, legitimized monarchical rule by subsuming the earlier basis of legitimation through descent from Khun Bôrom mythical ancestor of the Lao race, and the worship of powerful territorial spirits (*phī meuang*) within a universalized Lao-Buddhist world-view.

Introductory parts of various Lao chronicles told how the Buddha himself had visited Laos, leaving the imprint of his footstep here and there, and prophesying that in this land in the future the *dhamma* would flourish. It was the concepts of *kamma* and rebirth, however, that both provided the basis for legitimation of power and structured the Lao-Buddhist world-view. Kings were reborn into the royal line as a result of their accumulated *kamma*. The power they exercised was thus theirs by right through the working out of universal law. In a similar way, Buddhism legitimized the entire hierarchical Lao social order, for whether one was noble or commoner, free or slave, also depended on *kamma* (Stuart-Fox 1983, 1996).

While Buddhism thus legitimized the exercise of power, however, that power was not arbitrary. The king was expected to rule as a *Thammarāxa* (*Dhammarāja*) in accordance with the *Thammaxāt*, rules of kingly behaviour based on Buddhist moral principles. Moreover, though Buddhism justified the rigidity of the social hierarchy, the *saṅgha* itself provided a means of social mobility for the talented and ambitious. To be a monk brought with it honour and status. Monks officiated on state occasions, advised kings, and often took the lead in resolving political crises (including succession disputes). Senior abbots were royal appointees, and the relationship between the monarchy and the *saṅgha* was close and mutually supportive (Stuart-Fox 1998).

The nineteenth-century marked the nadir of Lao fortunes, both politically and for the Lao *sangha*. Two centuries earlier, Viang Chan, then capital of the extensive Lao kingdom of Lān Xāng, had attracted monks from throughout Buddhist Southeast Asia to study at its monasteries. A visiting Dutch merchant at the time remarked that monks in Viang Chan were 'more numerous than the soldiers of the Emperor of Germany'. But the division of Lān Xāng, into three separate kingdoms early in the eighteenth century condemned all three to become tributaries of Siam. When in 1827 the last king of Viang Chan attempted to throw off Siamese suzerainty, his capital was sacked and destroyed. Only one pagoda (*vat*) and the stupa of Thāt Luang were spared. Thereafter only in Luang Phrabāng did limited royal patronage maintain some semblance of Buddhist scholarship, ceremonial and art.

THE FRENCH ASCENDANCY

In 1893 French gunboat diplomacy forced Siam to part with all Lao territory east of the Mekong. A further treaty in 1907 established the borders of the modern Lao state. For the French, however, Laos was little more than a hinterland for Vietnam, 'rounding out' as they put it, French Indochina. First priorities for the French when they took control of Laos were administration and taxation (Stuart-Fox 1995). Interest in Buddhism was minimal, for religion could safely be left to the Lao. If the Lao *sangha* was in a parlous state, then that was a problem for the Lao: it warranted no official French concern.

French colonialism was more insidious in its impact, however, than benign neglect might suggest, for French rule effectively eliminated any political influence for Buddhism in Laos. In part this was due to the separation of *sangha* and state, but other factors were also at play. To begin with, the choice of Viang Chan as the seat of colonial administration left the king of Luang Phrabāng as little more than a marginalized puppet symbolically ruling in a nominal protectorate. Moreover, since evidently the king ruled not by karmic right but by benevolent permission of the French Résident Supérieur, religious ritual legitimizing his right to rule was reduced to little more than entertainment, in the eyes of some, at least, of the French-educated Lao élite. Buddhism may have retained a nostalgic cultural significance (Abhay 1959), but it almost entirely lost its political legitimizing function. Political power was exercised in colonial Laos solely on the basis of French law backed by French force.

Buddhism was further marginalized in the colonial state by being deprived of its primary educative role, at least in the centres of power. Some attempt was made to use the *sangha* as an inexpensive means of providing rudimentary primary education in Lao (in preference to introducing a costly comprehensive state education system) through so-called 'pagoda schools'. Some training for monk-teachers and minimal facilities were provided, but the project was not an educational success. Moreover, it relegated Buddhism to the status of second class provider for the state, since anyone with ambitions for their children preferred to send them to secular French-language schools.

Two developments in the 1920s and 1930s did something to retrieve the fortunes of Lao Buddhism. One was growing interest in Lao archaeology and history encouraged by the work of the École Française d'Extrême-Orient; the other was the impact on Lao Buddhism *per se* resulting from establishment of a Buddhist Institute in Phnom Penh. In both French scholars took the lead, enthusiastically encouraged in Laos by the senior Lao figure in the colonial administration, Prince Phetsarāt Rattanavongsā, and his personal secretary, Sila Vīravong. While historical studies began to reveal something of the greatness of the Kingdom of Lān Xāng, of greater symbolic significance was the reconstruction of the Thāt Luang (damaged by Chinese bandits digging for treasure in the 1870s) and the rebuilding of Vat Phra Kaeo (temple of the Emerald Buddha in Viang Chan before it was carried off to Bangkok in 1779). Several young monks were sent to Phnom Penh to pursue higher Buddhist studies, while courses in Pāli began to be taught in Viang Chan and Luang Phrabāng. The quality of monastic education and discipline were also improved through a new set of statutes reorganizing the structure of the *sangha* and its administration (Meyer 1931, 53).

By the late 1930s Lao Buddhism had experienced something of a 'renaissance' (Zago 1973, 133). While the level of knowledge and discipline in rural monasteries still left much to be desired, in the urban areas new *vat* were constructed and old ones repaired. In 1937 a College of Pāli was established in Viang Chan. By 1940, there were in round figures 4,000 monks and novices (i.e. aged less than 20) in the Lao *sangha* (Zago 1973, 135, n.14). Buddhism was thus in a position to play some part in the development of nationalist sentiment through the activities of the National Renovation Movement of the early 1940s.[3] Monks were among those strongly opposed to French moves to write Lao using Roman script, a project defeated largely through the opposition of Prince Phetsarāt. Buddhism figured too in the rediscovery of Lao history and culture celebrated in the pages of the Movement's news-sheet, *Lao Nyai.*

While the *sangha* played no direct role in the dramatic events of 1945 (internment of the French, declaration of Lao independence, Japan's surrender, establishment of an independent Lao government), monks were among the eager supporters of the Lao Issara (Free Laos) movement. With the French reconquest of Laos in May 1946, the Lao Issara government was forced into exile in Thailand and it was left to monks who remained behind to fan nationalist sentiments, and surreptitiously raise funds at Buddhist festivals to support the independence movement (Khamtan Thepbualī 1975, 36). Most were stongly nationalistic, opposing both continued French influence and the Viet Minh. So when in 1949 the Lao Issara divided into moderates and radical Marxists (the Pathēt Lao), only a handful of activist monks left the *sangha* to join the revolutionary movement.

THE KINGDOM OF LAOS

In 1946 the protectorate of Luang Phrabāng was combined with the directly administered provinces of central and southern Laos to form a single unified Kingdom of Laos, but it was not until 1949 that Laos gained a measure of real independence. Not until October 1953, under pressure from events in Vietnam, did France agree to full Lao independence. By that time, in part perhaps due to the uncertainties of war and fear of conscription, the number of monks and novices had increased to 13,500, more than three times the number in 1940 (Zago 1973, 135, n.14).

Under Article 5 of the 1947 constitution, Buddhism was declared the state religion, but it was not clear what role, beyond a purely ceremonial one, the *sangha* would play in Lao politics. The politicians handed power by France were almost without exception members of powerful families and clans from the three regions – north, centre and south – into which the country naturally divided. Moreover, they were French-educated, with a respect for French secular institutions. The King of Luang Phrabāng had been proclaimed King of Laos, but he was to be a constitutional monarch, safely removed (in Luang Phrabāng) from the centre of political power (in Viang Chan where the National Assembly met). Lao politicians looked not to the *sangha* for political legitimation, but to the constitution and the electorate.

But this was only part of the story, for in the popular mind the high social status of those elected to parliament or public office was still underwritten by a Buddhist world-view. Social status depended in part on family connections, in part on education, but it was belief in *kamma* that enabled such men to claim political office, for their positions of wealth and social prestige were implicitly accepted as theirs by right of their own accumulated merit. Conceptions that were essentially Buddhist thus continued to influence the shape of Lao politics, by reinforcing the claims of a conservative social élite to wield political power.

For three years after the Geneva Agreements of 1954 brought an end to the First Indochina war, negotiations continued between the Royal Lao government and the Pathēt Lao revolutionary movement aimed at reintegrating Pathēt Lao controlled areas into the Royal Lao administration. At last in November 1957, a Provisional (First) Coalition government was formed in which the Pathēt Lao were given two ministries, one of which was Religious Affairs. It was a fateful decision, one that set new parameters for the relationship between Buddhism and politics in Laos.

The incongruity of a communist minister, Phūmī Vongvichit, taking charge of the religion portfolio should not obscure the Pathēt Lao rationale for accepting it. The Ministry of Religious Affairs was responsible for supervising the *sangha*, the only nationwide organization independent of the civil administration that penetrated down to the village level. Moreover, as anyone could become a monk, the Pathēt Lao could easily infiltrate the *sangha* to propagate its message of 'true' national independence and anti-imperialism (aimed by then primarily at the United States). Not only did the *sangha* provide an ideal communications network, the Ministry itself used government funds to bring monks to Viang Chan to attend seminars, nominally to discuss religious matters, but in fact providing a forum discussion of social and political affairs.

So effective was Phūmī Vongvichit's politicization of the *sangha* that one of the primary tasks of the right-wing government that took power after the collapse of the First Coalition was to subordinate the *sangha* to much closer government control. Under the terms of Royal Ordinance 160, promulgated on 25 May 1959, monastic organization was brought into line with the civil administration of province, district, canton and village. Officials at each level of the *sangha*, from the abbot of a monastery on up, were henceforth appointed by the chief monk at the next highest level, with the endorsement of his administrative counterpart – who was thus in a position to veto any nominee to whom the government objected. Election of the *Sangharāja* to head the Order was by secret ballot among senior monks, from nominees vetted by the Ministry of Religious Affairs. No one over the age of 18 could join the *sangha* without the written permission of the district chief, and had to carry a government-issued identity card. Civil authorities had to be notified not only when a monk left the *sangha*, but whenever he travelled beyond the district where his *vat* was located (Kruong Pathoumxad 1959). In fact, all monastic correspondence had to be forwarded through the secular authorities, who were also represented on monastic disciplinary tribunals.

This heavy-handed government response aimed not just to eliminate Pathēt Lao influence in the *sangha*, but to replace it with overt government control. With the backing, and on the advice, of the United States, since 1954 the dominant foreign power and principal aid-giver in Laos, the right-wing government attempted to use the *sangha* as the Pathēt Lao had done, as an instrument of government policy. In pursuit of this aim, the government attempted to involve the *sangha* not just in preaching anti-Pathēt Lao propaganda, but in actively supporting and working for government policies and programmes. It also encouraged extension, especially in southern Laos, of the strongly anti-communist Thai school of Theravāda Buddhism known as the Thammanyut-nikāy (though by far the majority of Lao monks belonged to the rival Mahā-nikāy).[4]

These moves provoked considerable opposition from within the *sangha*, leading to formation of two clandestine movements: one of 'novices in defence of their rights'; the other of 'young monks opposed to the Thai Thammanyut-nikāy'. While the former demanded improved and more relevant education for novices, including the right to read newspapers and discuss politics, the latter aimed to reduce Thai influence in Laos. Most of the agitation occurred in Viang Chan, and centred on demands for a return to the pre-1959 organization of the *sangha*, reinstatement of monks and senior lay officials dismissed for political reasons, including the *Sangharāja* and the principal of the Pāli school, and a return to monastic control of monastic affairs (Lao People's Democratic Republic 1979, 27–8). For the first time ever, in February 1960 a group of monks mounted a placard-waving demonstration, which rightist politicians denounced and leftists supported. Government attempts to smother dissent thus enabled the Pathēt Lao to pose as champions of monastic autonomy, and of the protection of Buddhism as the national religion and guardian of Lao culture (Halpern 1964, 57–8).

Just how politicized the Lao *sangha* had become was evident from the popular response that greeted the August 1960 *coup d'état*. Captain Kônglae's call for an end to civil conflict and return to a policy of strict neutrality with respect to Cold War divisions immediately struck sympathetic chords among younger monks and novices. Once again monks took to the streets to demonstrate in favour of national reconciliation, neutrality, and an end to political corruption. Monks also often took the lead in the intense political discussions to which the *coup* gave rise. When rightist forces retook Viang Chan four months later, many monks retreated north with the neutralists. Those who remained or subsequently returned to their *vat* retained their sympathies for the neutralist cause.

During the next year and a half until the signing in July 1962 of the Geneva Agreements on the neutrality of Laos, the Pathēt Lao, in alliance with the neutralists, gained considerable sympathy and support within the *sangha*. There were several reasons for this (discussed at greater length in Stuart-Fox and Bucknell 1982). One was what has been called the *sangha's* 'inverse class structure' (Halpern 1964, 60), in large part a legacy of colonial education and language policy. As French remained the language of government (officially until 1962, but even thereafter), the élite sent their children to French-language schools. Children from poor rural families, however, could only afford an education by joining the *sangha*, where the education they received in the vernacular hardly equipped them for government service. Thus the only alternative for the more ambitious was to seek promotion within the *sangha*. As a result, most of the monastic hierarchy came from poorer backgrounds and could thus more readily relate to Pathēt Lao class propaganda.

A related reason for Pathēt Lao influence in the *sangha* had to do with the political marginalization of Buddhism. This had occurred under the French but continued under the Royal Lao regime. Though Buddhism was the state religion, it had lost much of its legitimizing role. Government leaders did not seek the advice of senior monks as earlier kings had done, and though monks continued to perform a ceremonial role in such secular celebrations as Independence Day and Constitution Day, this was more show than substance. As a result, senior figures in the *sangha* hierarchy tended to busy themselves with purely religious affairs or withdraw into contemplative isolation, so leaving the way open for younger, politicized, activist monks to exert greater influence, both within the Order and among the lay community.

Other factors playing into Pathēt Lao hands included the division into Thammanyut and Mahā-nikāy, which led to dissension within the *sangha*. The low level of Buddhist education and lax discipline, especially in rural areas, permitted some *vat* to become centres of political agitation (Niehoff, 1964, p. 110); while the *sangha's* own conception of its cultural and moral responsibilities, especially in the face of increasing American influence and declining standards of public morality,'led some monks at least to question government policy (Halpern 1964, 60). Little surprise, therefore, that Pathēt Lao calls for social revolution and moral renewal should strike a responsive chord with many younger monks.[5]

Under the impact of the war in Vietnam, the Second Coalition government in Laos collapsed as rapidly as had the First. In the decade during which the Indochina War engulfed much of the country, the struggle for influence within the Lao *sangha* intensified, with both sides attempting to win over influential monks to their cause. At the Second National Congress of the Lao Patriotic Front (LPF) held in Xam Neua in April 1964, point nine of the action programme called upon all Lao people 'to respect freedom of belief; oppose all schemes to sabotage and split up religions; and protect pagodas and respect Buddhist monks' (quoted in Zasloff 1973, 124). Activities of the Pathēt Lao organized National Association of Lao Buddhists, a member organization of the Lao Patriotic Front, were publicized over Radio Pathēt Lao, including the holding of seminars to denounce American intervention in Laos, and the rebuilding of pagodas destroyed by American bombing.[6]

The extent to which Buddhism became drawn into the revolutionary struggle in Pathēt Lao areas is evident from a captured PL document dated 14 January 1968, which reports the dispatch of thirty-three monks to various districts 'to preach revolutionary ethics . . . to protect Buddhism, to revive the real morality, to explain the revolutionary tasks to the people, and to resist the psychological warfare of the American imperialists and their reactionary lackeys' (Zasloff 1973, 61). Thus did politics and religion combine, to the extent that in the Pathēt Lao zone the latter became little more than the vehicle for the former.

The LPF held its Third National Congress in October 1968, at which a twelve-point political programme was adopted. Point three on this programme is worth quoting in full for the light it sheds on the increasing politicization of the *sangha*:

A. To respect and protect Buddhism, and unite with all religions, thus contributing to realizing national unity and strengthening the national forces against US aggression;

B. To oppose all acts of sabotage by the US imperialists and their henchmen against Buddhism, such as distorting Buddhist catechism,[7] controlling Buddhist monks and forcing them to serve criminal schemes, destroying pagodas or using them to preach decadent American culture, sowing discord among various Buddhist factions, etc.;

C. To respect and defend Buddhism, preserve the purity of monks and their right to practise Buddhism, protect pagodas, encourage unity and mutual assistance among monks and believers of various Buddhist factions, and encourage solidarity among priests and followers of other religions. (Zasloff 1973, 124)

Reading between the lines, one can discern not only the extent to which the Pathēt Lao were using Buddhism to advance their own political agenda, but also their concern over the Viang Chan government's attempt to do the same. After the breakdown of the Second Coalition, the Royal Lao government made a concerted attempt to use the *sangha* as a vehicle for its own policies and propaganda. Lao-speaking Thammanyut monks from north-eastern Thailand were encouraged to come to Laos to spread their anti-communist message, while Lao monks were sent to study in Thailand. Meanwhile monks of both schools were recruited to promote government development programmes. How such policies were pursued and how effective they were are worth examining for the impact they had on the politicization of the Lao *sangha*.

In the early 1960s American officials working in rural development were arguing that Buddhism in Thailand and Laos could be a vehicle for the technical changes which they believed it was necessary to introduce in rural areas in order to raise living standards and so reduce the appeal of communism. More specifically, Buddhist monks could supply the village level leadership required to get small scale community development projects off the ground (as they had in Laos in the village self-help programme of 1959, when it was discovered that financing for more than half the projects was going to construct monastic buildings) (Niehoff 1964, 110).

This suggestion was taken up by two government agencies, the Commission for Rural Affairs and the Ministry of Religious Affairs, which together in 1970 organized the first of a series of seminars for monks on community development. At the time a monastic census placed the total number of monks in government controlled villages at 6,348, of whom 42.8 per cent were aged between 20 and 25 (Vongsavanh Boutasvath and Chapelier 1973, 4). The decision to involve the *sangha* was taken not only because of the leadership role of monks in rural communities, but also because of their openness to modernization – especially where the *sangha* itself benefited.

More seminars followed. Most of the (screened) monks who attended became enthusiastic once they understood the programme and were convinced its aims were compatible with Buddhist teachings. An evaluation of the programme found that monks who had attended seminars spoke up in favour of community development on public occasions, though few took any initiative in promoting new projects. For that they relied on government officials, who in turn were reluctant to request active participation by senior monks (Vongsavanh Boutsavath and Chapelier 1973, 36–7). Monks showing most initiative were singled out and sent to Thailand for further training.

In the zone under Royal Lao government control from 1964 to 1975, which included all major population centres, the 1959 regulations ensured government control of the *sangha* as an organization, but failed to gain its whole hearted support for government policies, let alone the war effort. As the war dragged on, the *sangha* became increasingly critical of the impact of Americanization on Lao culture and morality. Conspicuous consumption by those who profited from the war, the adoption of a Western lifestyle by their children, prostitution and drug addiction, all contrasted adversely with everything that Buddhism stood for. When the cease-fire of 1973 led to formation of the Third

Coalition government, most monks welcomed the opportunity for peace and national reconciliation.

THE TRANSITION OF POWER

In May 1974, at Pathēt Lao urging, the National Political Consultative Council meeting in Luang Phrabāng unanimously endorsed what came to be known as the 'eighteen-point political programme' the fifth point of which committed the Coalition government 'to respect Buddhism and other religions; preserve pagodas and temples and other historic sites; and defend the right to worship of Buddhist monks and other religious believers' (National Political Programme 1975). These guarantees reflected the liberal and democratic tone of the document as a whole, which was widely welcomed as providing the political basis for national unity and reconstruction.

Peace and reconciliation were themes eagerly taken up by the *sangha*, encouraged by the new Minister of Religious Affairs, a pro-Pathēt Lao neutralist by the name of Ku Suvannamēthī, himself a former monk. Buddhist monks actively popularized the eighteen points, welcomed the 'liberation' of the Mekong towns in 1975, and were among the first to volunteer to attend political seminars conducted by the Pathēt Lao. The *Sangharāja* called on all monks to work closely with the new regime for the good of the nation, while Pathēt Lao cadres respectfully visited pagodas to explain their policies.

The strategy of the Pathēt Lao was twofold: to argue that Buddhism and socialism were compatible beliefs; and (given the shortage of trained PL cadres) to make use of monks to explain and justify the policies of the new regime to the people. In political seminars, monks were told that Buddhism and socialism both taught the essential equality of all people, and the promotion of happiness through elimination of suffering. The Buddha, they were told, was socially progressive because he had rejected the class into which he had been born out of compassion for the common people (Lafont 1982, 150). He was a great man, but then so were Marx and Lenin (Becker 1979).

A more sophisticated argument for the compatibility of Buddhism and socialism was advanced by Khamtan Thepbualī, the former monk whom the Pathēt Lao placed in charge of their religious policy (under the direction of Politburo member Phūmī Vongvichit). The timeless core of Buddhism had survived through the ages, according to Khamtan, through a process of adaptation to new social and political circumstances. Under capitalism, however, it had become corrupted and used in support of an unjust and exploitative social order. Under socialism, it would be purified of all superstition and unnecessary dogma to become a vehicle for moral and social progress (Khamtan Thepbualī 1975, 46–8; and interview with Khamtan Thepbualī, Viang Chan, 6 December 1980).

Among those superstitions of which Lao Marxists set out to purge Buddhism were its outdated cosmology and belief that *kamma* depended on accumulation of merit (*bun*). Buddhist belief in multiple heavens and hells above and below a flat earth was ridiculed by reference to modern science. Space probes had demonstrated conclusively that the earth was round, and had failed to locate any heavens. Deep oil drilling had been equally unable to discover any hell. As for merit, it was absurd to imagine that this could be gained by feeding monks or giving donations to temples, or that it could be transferred by pouring holy water (Interview with Bhikkhu Sāthukhamfan, Bangkok, 19 November 1978). And just as the great Lao Buddhist king Phōthisārāt had proscribed the worship of the innumerable spirits (*phī*) which figure so prominently in Lao popular belief, so too did the new Marxist regime forbid their worship – with about the same nugatory effect.[8]

Even purged of such superstitions, however, Marxism and Buddhism in fact sought very different goals. While Buddhism offered the hope of individual salvation through eventual escape from the cycle of rebirth Lao Marxism proclaimed the transformation of society through the 'three revolutions' – in production, technology and consciousness (Doré 1982). The 'new socialist person' who would lead the struggle to build socialism in Laos was a world apart from the traditional Lao peasant resigned to acceptance of things as they are in the hope of a 'better' rebirth. Moreover, an essential contradiction existed between Marxist justification of revolutionary violence and Buddhist compassion for all sentient beings.

The contradictions evident in Pathēt Lao attempts to create some common intellectual ground between Marxism and Buddhism as a basis on which to use Buddhism for its own ends were paralleled by contradictions in its attempts both to destroy the social influence of the *sangha* and to make use of it to promote socialist policies. Just as the Royal Lao government, on American urging, had attempted to use the social status of Buddhist monks to promote community development, so the Pathēt Lao attempted to use monastic influence at the village level to gain acceptance of its socialist programme.

At the same time, however, the Lao People's Revolutionary Party which emerged from the shadows towards the end of 1975 was even more determined than the Royal Lao government had been to limit and control the independence of the *sangha*. For in the eyes of the Party, as the only vertically structured organization in Lao society reaching down to the village level, the *sangha* posed a potential threat, since it was believed capable, like the Catholic church in Poland, of serving as a focus of anti-Party resistance. (Incidentally, all foreign Catholic priests working in Laos were expelled in September 1975.)

Throughout 1975, therefore, as the Lao People's Revolutionary Party slowly tightened its grip on power, it both used and undermined the *sangha*. The very practice of requiring young monks, whether more or less committed, to spread Pathēt Lao propaganda steadily reduced the prestige of the Order by making it appear a pliant instrument of the Party. Not that monks had much option, for they were usually accompanied by cadres who listened to, and even recorded, their every word. Some were even accompanied by armed guards as they went from village to village, ostensibly for their own protection. Any monk who failed to proclaim the Pathēt Lao message sufficiently enthusiastically would be sent for political re-education (Mahā Kanlā Tanbualī 1977, 48–9).

The independence of the *sangha* was formally destroyed in 1976 when, in an unprecedented move, the large ivory-handled ceremonial fans carried by senior members of the hierarchy as emblems of their rank were symbolically broken (Mahā Kanlā Tanbualī 1977, 58–9). Under close Party supervision, the *sangha* was restructured as the Lao United (Unified) Buddhists Association to include both the Mahā-nikāy and Thammanyut-nikāy schools (though many Thammanyut monks had already fled to Thailand). All executive positions in the new organization were filled by monks acceptable to the Party.

At the level of the *vat*, pressures were exerted on young monks to leave the Order and serve the revolution. Those who remained were required to perform some socially useful task – as teachers, or as health workers preparing and administering traditional medicines – and so earn their own livelihood. The *pātimokkha*, the fortnightly recitation in Pāli of the 227 precepts a monk must live by, was transformed in to a self-criticism session in Lao during which shortcomings, especially failure to follow the Party line, were admitted and publicly criticized (interview with Bhikkhu Vanna Buaphaphong, Nôngkhāy, 18 November 1978).

Despite the heavy hand by which the Party brought the *sangha* under its control, Buddhism was never a target for massive repression in Laos, as it was in Cambodia under the Khmer Rouge, or in China during the Cultural Revolution. The Party was careful in its Buddhist policy, especially during the crucial transition to power in 1975, not to provide a target for popular resentment or political opposition. In this it was assisted both by poor morale and a crisis of identity in the *sangha* itself, and by increasing popular cynicism over the opportunist political role played by a number of Buddhist monks. In retrospect, one can only endorse the admission of one senior Lao monk that 'the fall of Laos to the communists was partly the fault of the *sangha*, because the *sangha* had many weak points which made it an easy target for the communists' attack' (Mahā Kanlā Tanbualī 1977, 70).

BUDDHISM IN THE EARLY YEARS OF THE LAO PEOPLE'S DEMOCRATIC REPUBLIC

Six 'revolutionary monks' occupied a prominent position in the front row of delegates to the Congress of People's Representatives that met in Viang Chan on 2 December 1975 to accept King Savāngvatthanā's abdication and declare the formation of the Lao People's Democratic Republic. Yet there are only two references to Buddhism in the documents of the Congress. One, in the action programme, stipulated freedom of religion, but warned that monastic schools would be 'given directives whereby they will function in conformity with the orientation of national education'. In other words, religious teaching was to be controlled by the Party. The other reference came in the political report of

Kaisôn Phomvihān, Secretary-General of the LPRP. Monks, Kaisôn said, would be expected

> to contribute actively to reviving the spirit of patriotic unity, to encourage the population to activate production and economize, [and] to help people in their education in order to raise the cultural level and contribute to persuading, education and correcting those who take the wrong path or who do not behave properly so they may become good citizens. (*Documents du Congrès National des Représentants du Peuple* 1976, 25)

Political expectations of the *saṅgha* under the new regime could not have been stated more clearly. It was to act as an arm of the Party in promoting Party policies and educating a compliant citizenry. Apart from that, it had no clear religious or spiritual role to play in Lao society.

In the harsh years of 1976 and 1977 as the economy collapsed, drought ravaged the rice crop, and the regime struggled to enforce its power, new pressures were brought to bear on Buddhism. At first the Party tried to limit celebration of Buddhist festivals on the grounds that they were a waste of scarce national resources (JPRS 1976a), but as popular resentment mounted the policy was reversed. (The prohibition on mass celebration of the 1976 Rocket Festival (*bun bang fai*), traditionally associated with fertility, was widely blamed for the drought of the following year.) People were actively discouraged from visiting their local *vat* to make offerings, though this too was relaxed after it led in some places to potentially damaging confrontations.[9]

Even so, the government went out of its way to demonstrate that those monks who conformed to what was expected would be properly rewarded. Monks were invited to attend all state occasions, including Lao National Day and even May Day celebrations, where they were invariably seated in places of honour and mentioned first in any address. Phūmī Vongvichit, as Minister of Education, Sport and Religious Affairs, attended major Buddhist ceremonies, while another member of the Politburo, Deputy Prime Minister Nūhak Phūmsavan, headed the official party at the 1976 Thāt Luang festival. Monks officiated even at state funerals for Party members, and at the dedication of the memorial to Pathēt Lao cadres and soldiers who died in the revolutionary struggle.

While such outward forms were observed, however, the Party made it abundantly clear that it was in control. All monks were required to attend classes in political education, in order to know what to teach in their sermons. Their duties were to educate, to provide health care, to contribute to national development, and to propagandize on behalf of the regime. In the words of the 1976 Action Plan of the Lao United Buddhists Association, monks were to

> contribute effectively ... to the national task, to participate in the progressive mass movement and be determined to wipe out all traces of the former backward regime and thwart all of the enemy's undermining maneuvers with respect to the fatherland and religion. (JPRS 1976b, 20)

Phūmī Vongvichit was even more specific in his address to Buddhist teachers (monks) attending a training course in Viang Chan in October 1976. Party policy, he told his audience, was

> to request Buddhist monks to give sermons to teach the people and encourage them to understand that all policies and lines of the Party and government are in line with the teachings of the Lord Buddha so that the people will be willing to follow them. (FBIS 1976)

Attendance at such 'training sessions in political and religious morality' was compulsory. Seminars typically lasted for a week or more, and were addressed by the regime's trusted henchmen. Monks who failed to display a properly compliant attitude were sent for longer periods of political re-education. In the region of Viang Chan, this seems to have been the extent of repression, but reports from southern Laos were more disturbing. There the Thammanyut school was more strongly entrenched,[10] and methods resorted to by the Party to enforce its political will more harsh. Monks whom the authorities suspected of being anti-communist were arrested, and a number were reportedly executed (interview with Bhikkhu Vanna, Nôngkhāy, 18 November 1978). If such reports were true, it may be that the government held some monks responsible for popular resistance, strongest in the south, to its abortive attempt to collectivize agriculture.[11]

In March 1979 the government established a new mass organization, the Lao Front for National Construction (LFNC), to act as a broad umbrella bringing together all officially sanctioned associations, including the Lao United Buddhists Association. The seventh point in the Front action programme committed it to ensure freedom of religious belief and protection of places of worship 'while resolutely countering all attempts to use religions to oppose the national interest or destroy the socialist regime' (Lao Front for National Construction 1979). The same month the 87-year-old former *Saṅgharāja*, who had been confined to his *vat* and forbidden to preach, escaped to Thailand on a raft of inflated inner car tyre tubes, bringing with him more reports of official repression.

As a member of the LFNC, the *saṅgha* was expected to promote not only the political line of the Party internally, but also its foreign policy externally. Lao Buddhists attended communist bloc orchestrated world conferences for peace, and were prominent in the Asian Buddhist Council for Peace.[12] At such venues they regularly denounced warmongering imperialists and other enemies of the regime. When Viang Chan moved to improve relations with Bangkok, a delegation of Lao Buddhists was dispatched to attend the festival of the Thāt Phanom, the most sacred shrine in north-eastern Thailand.

By the late 1970s vastly different estimates were being provided by government officials and monks who had escaped to Thailand on the state of Buddhism in Laos. According to official figures, the number of monks and novices (17,000) had actually increased since 1974 (Peagam 1977). Other estimates put the figure at around one tenth as many (interview with Bhikkhu Mahā Bunkong, Bangkok, 13 November 1978). What was clear, however, was that the *saṅgha* as an organization had been reduced to an instrument of the Lao People's Revolutionary Party. From being primarily an organization ministering to the religious and spiritual needs of the Lao people, it had become a mouthpiece for the political and social policies of the new regime. The morality it taught was no longer to assist people on their path towards ultimate enlightenment, but rather to encourage them to become 'new Lao socialist men and women' and participate in the building of socialism.

Or so Party ideologues hoped. For the vast majority of the Lao people, however, Buddhist conceptions of *kamma* and merit still shaped their view of the world. Even in the face of political pressure, women in particular had stubbornly continued to give food to monks and attend their local *vat*. So when the Party was forced to relax its hardline policies in the face of the failure of agricultural co-operativization, the conditions were present for a return to Buddhist observances (see Peachey and Peachey 1983).

In an interview with the author in Viang Chan in December 1980, Khamtan Thepbualī, Director of the Department of Religious Affairs, pointed out that religion in the Soviet Union continued to exist, even after sixty years of socialism. So Buddhism would continue to be practised in Laos. In fact it was unthinkable, he implied, that Laos should ever cease to be Buddhist. It was a theme repeated by other Lao friends and contacts: to be Lao was to be Buddhist, irrespective of the regime in power.

BUDDHISM AND POLITICS IN CONTEMPORARY LAOS

By the late 1980s both internal and external pressures were forcing the Party to modify its policies. Building socialism in Laos was not something that was going to happen in a hurry. As the Soviet Union began to count the cost of its support for Vietnamese domination of Cambodia (and Laos), the countries of Indochina were forced to rethink their relations with the region. In Laos economic reforms introduced as part of the so-called 'new economic mechanism' effectively dismantled centralized economic controls to allow a freer play of market forces and foreign economic investment. So while the collapse of communism in the Soviet Union and eastern Europe was a 'nightmare' for the Lao Party, it yet proved resilient enough to ride out the resulting political turbulence.

The political and economic model for Laos, and Vietnam, in the 1990s has been the People's Republic of China. So while it has permitted considerable liberalization of the economy, the Party has been determined to retain authoritarian control of political processes. When some younger Western-educated middle level officials began agitating for the introduction of multi-party democracy in Laos, three ringleaders were arrested and sentenced to long gaol sentences. None, it should be noted, apparently made any reference to Buddhism in their defence (Amnesty International 1996).

Social liberalization falls somewhere between the economic and the political. The Party has been very reluctant to permit any organization to be established over which it might not exercise full control. All officially endorsed organizations continue to be members of, and thus under the direction of, the Lao Front for National Construction – including the Lao United Buddhists Association. In fact, civil society in the form of citizen organizations functioning outside of government (i.e. Party) control hardly exists at all in the Lao case.

That said, acceptance of Buddhism as having a vital role to play in Lao social and cultural life has come a long way since the early years of the regime. While monks remaining for long periods in the *sangha* cannot be members of the LPRP, the earlier limitation on Party members entering the Order as a mark of respect, and to make merit, for a deceased parent has been relaxed. Party members, from the Politburo on down, regularly attend Buddhist ceremonies.

The sight of the 'communist' (and one can argue over whether this is any longer an appropriate term to use) power élite down on their knees before senior monks carries with it a symbolic message that is hardly lost on the Lao people. Even political leaders, it is widely conceded, are Buddhists first and socialists second. This is borne out by a visit to the former residence, now a revolutionary museum, of Kaisôn Phomvihān, founding Secretary-General and later President of the LPRP. For there in his private study stands a glass case containing a number of Buddha images, before which is an incense burner. Asked about the half-burnt sticks of incense, the guide explains, rather defensively, that Kaisôn did not actually light them himself: a servant did it for him. Moreover, it is openly acknowledged that in the year before he died, Kaisôn regularly meditated with a senior monk from a monastery just outside Viang Chan, and that 'senior leaders' invite monks to conduct Buddhist ceremonies in their own homes (interview with Phra Vichit Singālat, Viang Chan, 14 January 1997).

Just how important the Party considered Buddhism to be by the early 1990s is illustrated by the pomp and ceremony accompanying the state funeral for Mahā Thongkhūn Anantasunthôn, Chairman of the Lao United Buddhists Association. Not only did 'thousands' of monks attend, but so did three senior members of the Politburo, including the ailing State President, Suphānuvong (FBIS 1991). And in an interview with the author in December 1993, a month before his death, Politburo member Phūmī Vongvichit spoke warmly of the need to impart Buddhist morality to the younger generation who lacked the dedication and discipline of those who had carried out the revolution.

Buddhism has clearly regained much of the social position it temporarily lost during the early years of the regime. Throughout the Lao People's Democratic Republic lines of monks daily undertake their dawn 'begging' round and large crowds attend all major Buddhist festivities. The number of monks and novices combined has increased, though many have joined the *sangha* primarily to improve their educational prospects. (Monks attending the monastic high school at Thāt Luang in Viang Chan come overwhelmingly from the provinces.)

In rural areas, where there is still on average only one *vat* per five villages, nuns may outnumber monks (Miehlau, 1996, 50–1).

The *sangha* may have recovered much of its former popular standing, but links with the Party still remain close and it seems unlikely to regain greater independence. At its Sixth Congress, however, the Party acknowledged the need to upgrade monastic education. Loss of senior monks since 1975, through death or migration, and the emphasis given to political rather than religious education of younger monks has seriously reduced educational standards. Knowledge of Pāli in particular has declined to 1930s levels, with many monks able to chant by rote only the few phrases needed in commonly performed ceremonies. A new tertiary level Buddhist College has been established at Vat Ong Teu, providing a three-year degree. Students undertake compulsory studies in Buddhist *dhamma*, and a choice of either pedagogy (to become teachers) or linguistics (including Pāli and English). One difficulty has been to find qualified Lao teachers, as the *sangha* hierarchy, no doubt on Party instructions, does not want to rely on Thai monks (interview with Phra Vichit Singālat, Viang Chan, 14 January 1997).

A possible new political role for Buddhism seems now to be emerging in Laos; one that carries with it some dangers for the regime. It is obvious that Marxism as a political ideology has proved incapable of animating the Lao people. The problem for the regime, therefore, is what to replace it with. The Party justifies its monopoly of power on the grounds that it led the Lao revolution to its victorious conclusion. But as that event fades, and the suspicion grows that the revolution succeeded only in replacing one corrupt élite by another, the Party must seek some additional justification.

Here Buddhism would not appear to be of much help. Accumulated merit may reinforce the institution of monarchy and a hierarchical social order, but it hardly does much to justify who comes out on top in Party power struggles or proclaim egalitarianism and the 'self-mastery' of the masses. Where Buddhism does figure, however, is in its centrality to Lao nationalism as this is expressed both in Lao history and in Lao cultural identity. And it is towards Lao nationalism that the Party seems increasingly to be looking to shore up its political position.[13]

The danger of using Lao nationalism is that ethnic Lao constitute not much more than half the population of Laos, and that most of the hundred-odd ethnic minority groups and sub-groups are not Buddhist.[14] While revolutionary justification for the seizure and exercise of power rests on uniting all ethnic groups through concepts of resistance and struggle, nationalist justification would tend to reinforce historic ethnic Lao élitism, especially if combined with active missionizing. Buddhism could thus inadvertently promote social division.

It is not obvious to an observer that the secretive LPRP has any clear idea of where it is heading. The recent decision to establish the Ong Teu higher school of Buddhism which will attempt to resuscitate higher studies in Pāli and Buddhist exegesis might indicate recognition of the need to improve monastic knowledge and discipline; but it might also aim to reduce growing reliance on Thailand. In the late 1990s as many as sixty Lao monks were studying in Thai monastic schools (plus another nine in Burma).[15] Moreover, as members of the Thai royal family enjoyed considerable respect in Laos, close ties between the Thai and Lao *sangha* could actually undermine Lao sovereignty.

CONCLUSION

Buddhism in Laos traditionally provided powerful legitimation for the exercise of political authority. Though the Buddhist *sangha* was effectively marginalized during the colonial period, both sides in the civil conflict that engulfed Laos from 1945 until the victory of the Pathēt Lao in 1975 attempted to make political use of Buddhism in support of their rival positions. Once victory was achieved, however, the Lao People's Revolutionary Party systematically reduced the *sangha* to an instrument of its political will.[16] With the collapse of communism in the late 1980s, the LPRP has adopted a policy of economic liberalization and political authoritarianism which requires new forms of legitimation. In place of revolutionary justification for the exercise of political power, the Party is reverting to nationalism. It is in this context that Buddhism is experiencing a resurgence in popularity, even though the *sangha* remains under tight Party control. Whether or not its social influence will permit the Order to regain a degree of institutional independence thus remains to be seen.

NOTES

1. This article was written before publication of Grant Evans, (1998) *The Politics of Ritual and Remembrance: Laos Since 1975*. Chiang Mai, Silkworm Books, in which he argues that 'a re-Buddhification of the Lao state' (67) is presently underway as the central plank in 'a retraditionalized nationalism' (162). Much more controversially, Evans argues that the best way to overcome the malaise in Lao political culture would be to restore the monarchy, a proposition unlikely ever to be entertained while the Lao People's Revolutionary Party holds power.
2. The system of transliteration used in this chapter is taken from Martin Stuart-Fox (1997) *History of Laos*, Melbourne: Cambridge University Press.
3. The movement was led by a group of young French-educated Lao intellectuals whose cultural nationalism gained French backing as a counterweight to pan-Thai propaganda from Bangkok.
4. The stricter Thammanyut-nikāy was founded by King Mongkut of Siam in the mid nineteenth century, whereas the Mahā-nikāy, though doctrinally similar to the Thai school of the same name, was organizationally independent.
5. The parallel between Buddhist asceticism and the selfless dedication of the revolutionary was one the Pathēt Lao deliberately fostered (Halpern 1967, 215).
6. This did not prevent local cadres from discouraging religious observance (Chapelier and van Malderghem 1971, 69–71).

7. This refers to attempts to interpret Buddhist scripture as powerfully opposed to Marxism.

8. The Party was still battling superstition years later. (See *Viang Chan Mai*, 14 May 1983 (JPRS 1983)). Today it no longer bothers (Miehlau 1996, 50).

9. Restrictions depended very much on the whim of local Party cadres, and varied considerably throughout the country.

10. Siamese influence was always stronger in southern Laos where the ruling family owed allegiance, after the Lao–Siamese war of 1827–8, to Bangkok.

11. On the role of Buddhism in peasant resistance to socialization of the rural economy, see Evans 1993.

12. The Council was a markedly left-wing communist front organization.

13. In January 1997, the government sponsored a three-day conference of scholars and Party officials on Chau Anuvong, the last king of Viang Chan, who died fighting for Lao independence not from the United States or France, but from Siam.

14. Actually 130 different ethnic groups and sub-groups have been identified in Laos, which the government groups as Lao Lum (Lao of the lowlands), Lao Thoeng (Lao of the mountain slopes) and Lao Sūng (Lao of the mountain tops).

15. In an interview with the author in January 1997, four senior monks indicated that the *sangha* hierarchy would prefer to send Lao monks to study in India (as a number did before 1975).

16. Whether this has pushed Lao Buddhism in the direction of Mahāyānist 'themes', as P-B. Lafont argues, seems unlikely, however (Lafont 1990, 161).

BIBLIOGRAPHY

Abhay, Thao Nhouy (1959) 'Buddhism in Laos', in René de Berval (ed.) *Kingdom of Laos*. Saigon: France-Asie, 237–56.

Amnesty International (1996) 'Lao People's Democratic Republic: Prisoners of Conscience Suffering in Isolation'. London, November.

Becker, Elizabeth (1979) 'Buddhism in Laos Adapts to Communist Tenets', *Washington Post*, 8 May.

Chapelier, Georges and van Malderghem, Josyane (1971) 'Plain of Jars: Social Changes under Five Years of Pathet Lao Administration', *Asia Quarterly* 1, 61–89.

Documents du Congrès National des Représentants du Peuple (1976). [Viang Chan]: Lao Hak Xāt.

Doré, Amphay (1982) 'The Three Revolutions in Laos', in Martin Stuart-Fox (ed.) *Contemporary Laos: Studies in the Politics and Society of the Lao People's Denocratic Republic*. St Lucia: University of Queensland Press, pp. 101–15.

Evans, Grant (1993) 'Buddhism and Economic Action in Socialist Laos', in C. M. Hann (ed.) *Socialism: Ideals, Ideologies, and Local Practice*. London: Routledge, 132–47.

Evans, Grant (1998) *The Politics of Ritual and Remembrance: Laos since 1975*. Chiang Mai: Silkworm Books.

Foreign Broadcasts Information Service (FBIS) (1976) 'Speech to Buddhist Teachers', 28 October.

Foreign Broadcasts Information Service (FBIS) (1991) 'Leaders Attend Cremation of Senior Buddhist Monk', 20 March.

Gagneux, Pierre M. (1972) 'Vers une Révolution dans l'Archéologie Indochinoise', *Bulletin des Amis du Royaume du Laos* 7/8: 83–105.

Halpern, Joel M. (1964) *Government, Politics, and Social Structure in Laos: A Study of Tradition and Innovation*. New Haven, CA: Yale.

Halpern, Joel M. (1967) 'American Policy in Laos', *Michigan Alumni Quarterly Review* 67, May, 213–19.

Joint Publications Research Service (JPRS) (1976a) 'Regulations Issued on Performing Religious Functions', Translations on Southeast Asia 638, 10 May.

Joint Publications Research Service (JPRS) (1976b) 'Lao Unified Buddhists Association Action Program Defined', Translations on Southeast Asia 651, 21 July.

Joint Publications Research Service (JPRS) (1983) 'Columnist Discusses Superstitious Practices', Translations on Southeast Asia 1,318, 28 July.

Khamtan Thepbualī (1975) *Pha Song Lao kap kān Pativat* [The Lao Sangha and the Revolution]. Viang Chan: Naeo Lao Hak Xāt.

Kruong Pathoumxad (1959) 'Organization of the Sangha', in René de Berval (ed.) *Kingdom of Laos*. Saigon: France-Asie, 257–67.

Lafont, Pierre-Bernard (1982) 'Buddhism in Conterrmporary Laos', in M. Stuart-Fox (ed.) *Contemporary Laos: Studies in the Politics and Society of the Lao People's Democratic Republic*. St Lucia: University of Queensland, 148–62.

Lafont, Pierre-Bernard (1990) 'Transformations Politiques et Évolution du Bouddhisme au Laos depuis 1960', in A. Forest *et al.* (eds) *Bouddhismes et Sociétés Asiatiques: Clergés, Sociétés et Pouvoirs*. Paris: L'Harmattan, 155–62.

Lao Front for National Construction (1979) Action Program. *Khaosān Pathēt Lao, Bulletin Quotidien*, 7 March.

Lao People's Democratic Republic (1979) 'The Important Role Played by the Lao Buddhist Monks in the Field of Revolution', mimeograph, Viang Chan, 15 June.

Lévy, Paul (1940) 'Les Traces de l'Introduction du Bouddhisme à Luang Prabang', *Bulletin de l'École Française d'Extrême-Orient* 40, 411–24.

Mahā Kanlā Tanbualī (1977) *Sathāna Phra-Phuttha-Sāsanā nai Prathēt Sāthāranarat Prachā-thipatai Prachāchon Lau* [The State of the Buddhist Religion in the Lao People's Democratic Republic] Bangkok: Khana Sasanikachon.

Meyer, Roland (1931) *Le Laos*. Hanoi: Imprimerie d'Extrême-Orient.

Miehlau, Sabine (1996) 'Hochkonjunktur von Geisterglauben: Buddhismus in Laos', in Roland Platz and Gerd Rieger (eds) *Südostasien im Wandel*. Stuttgart: Schmetterling, 45–52.

'National Political Programme for Building a Peaceful, Independent, Neutral, Democratic, United and Prosperous Laos' (1975) *Lao News*, 12 February.

Niehoff, Arthur (1964) 'Theravada Buddhism: A Vehicle for Technical Change', *Human Organization* 23: 108–12.

Peachey, Linda and Peachey, Titus (1983) 'Religion in Socialist Laos', *Southeast Asia Chronicle* 91, 16–19.

Peagam, Norman (1977) 'Buddhism Retaining Major Role in Laos', *New York Times*, 26 April.

Phouvong Phimmasone (1973) 'L'Organisation du Bouddhisme au Laos', *Bulletin des Amis du Royaume Lao* 9, 120–9.

Stuart-Fox, Martin (1983) 'Marxism and Theravada Buddhism: The Legitimation of Political Authority in Laos', *Pacific Affairs* 56, 428–54.

Stuart-Fox, Martin (1995) 'The French in Laos, 1887–1945', *Modern Asian Studies* 29, 111–39.

Stuart-Fox, Martin (1996) *Buddhist Kingdom, Marxist State: The Making of Modern Laos*. Bangkok: White Lotus.

Stuart-Fox, Martin (1998) *The Lao Kingdom of Lān Xāng: Rise and Decline*. Bangkok: White Lotus.

Stuart-Fox, Martin and Rod Bucknell (1982) 'Politicization of the Buddhist Sangha in Laos', *Journal of Southeast Asian Studies* 13, 60–80.

Vongsavanh Boutsavath and Georges Chapelier (1973) 'Lao Popular Buddhism and Community Development', *Journal of the Siam Society* 69/2, 1–38.

Zago, Marcel (1973) 'Bouddhisme Lao Contemporain', *Bulletin des Amis du Royaume Lao* 9, 130–7.

Zasloff, Joseph J. (1973) *The Pathet Lao: Leadership and Organization*. Lexington, MA: Heath.

8

FIRST AMONG EQUALS: BUDDHISM AND THE SRI LANKAN STATE

TESSA BARTHOLOMEUSZ

INTRODUCTION

The second, or 1972, constitution of post-independence Sri Lanka privileged Buddhism, Sri Lanka's majority religion, as 'foremost' among the religions of the island. At the same time, it guaranteed each of Sri Lanka's traditions (i.e. Buddhism, Hinduism, Islam and Christianity) equal protection under the law. In other words, Buddhism was ensconced in the 1972 constitution as first among equals, and it has retained its peerless yet parallel status as Sri Lanka marches into the twenty-first-century. Though the politics of Sri Lanka's present president, Chandrika Bandaranaike Kumaranatunga, have been informed by secular ideology, the constitution that her party drafted in 1997 further enhances Buddhism's relationship with the state. According to clause 7 of this draft constitution, the President must appoint a Supreme Advisory Council composed of Buddhist monks and lay people to assist in legislating laws, thereby magnifying the earlier constitutional status of Buddhism.

Sri Lanka's post-independence constitutional policies concerning Buddhism have a history that reaches back to the late nineteenth century. At that time, Sinhalas, the majority of whom are Buddhist, began to hone an ideology in which they were closely associated with the political history and territory of the island. Based on interpretations of the *Mahāvaṃsa*, a fifth-century chronicle of Buddhism in Sri Lanka, the ideology established the Sinhala-Buddhist people, as the sole and rightful heirs to the island (Spencer 1990, 1–16). In the colonial situation, the rediscovery of the *Mahāvaṃsa* provided Sinhalas with proof that they, like their colonizers, were Aryan, and that Sri Lanka (then called Ceylon) could boast a long, glorious Buddhist civilization that could rival Europe's. Interpretations of the *Mahāvaṃsa* that rendered the island as authentically Buddhist and Sinhala fostered a sense of pride that equated nationality, Buddhism and territory (Gunawardana 1990, 76–7). While some have urged that only Sinhalas and Buddhists have rights to the island, thereby excluding minority ethnic and religious groups, most Sinhalas, at least since the late nineteenth century, have argued for the primacy of the Sinhalas in political, religious and cultural life. Despite differences in attitudes towards minority ethnic and religious groups, both ends of this ideological spectrum define Sri Lanka in Sinhala-Buddhist terms (Kemper 1991, 16). To one degree or another, the *Mahāvaṃsa's* charter for the Sinhalas, Buddhism and its relationship to Sri Lanka echoes in three of the four post-independence constitutions. Notwithstanding the emphasis of all four on Sri Lanka as a secular state, the minority religions of the island have, to varying degrees, been compelled to accept their paradoxical status as secondary yet equivalent to Buddhism. Indeed, Sri Lanka's version of secularism warrants further exploration in order to clarify the relationship between Buddhism and the state. To this end, this chapter will pay careful attention to the following four issues: the history of the relationship between religion, politics and the state in the late nineteenth century; the intersection of Buddhism and politics in the early 1900s up until independence; Buddhism and the state in post-independence Sri Lanka; and the meaning of secularism in the post-independence period.

RELIGION, POLITICS AND THE STATE IN THE LATE 1800s

In the final decades of the nineteenth century, when Buddhist Sinhalas began to forge an identity that equated being Sinhala with having rights to the entire island, doubtless a form of cultural resistance to the British, the island's largest ethnic minority, the Tamils, began to boast that they too had an unassailable bond with Sri Lanka. Dagmar-Hellman Rajanayagam (1994, 76), in a study of Sri Lankan Tamil identity, has argued that late nineteenth-century Tamils used historical sources to prove that they, like the Sinhala people, had 'a right to be' in Sri Lanka. Tamils had to prove, under pressure from the architects of the emerging Sinhala-Buddhist identity, that they also could claim the island as a homeland, that they were not Indian, and that they had a right to exist as part of the legitimate population of Sri Lanka. In short, from the late nineteenth century, Sri Lanka's ethnic majority and largest ethnic minority carved out identities in relationship to each other and to the colonial power. Despite scholarship that suggests that the Sinhala-Tamil ethnic conflict is centuries old,[1] its roots can be traced to the end of the last century, when the issues of ethnicity, religion and territory began to take centre stage in the political drama of the island. With burgeoning Sinhala and Tamil nationalisms that were wedded to Buddhism and Hinduism respectively, politics in Sri Lanka was reinvented and, in appeals to the indigenous past in a contemporary situation of foreign domination, both Sinhalas and Tamils asserted the need for religious values as part of their political activity. Thus, the Tamil-Hindu revival movement, headed by Armugam Navalar (1822–79), directed the attention of Tamils towards education (C.R. de Silva 1977, 389), which (just as it did for the Buddhists) remained a rallying cry for the island's Tamil politicians throughout the mid twentieth century.

While the centre for the Tamil revival movements was Jaffna, Sinhala-Buddhist activity was concentrated in the 'low country', that is the south-eastern coastal area near Colombo, where local élites, who considered Buddhism to be in danger of perishing after centuries of foreign domination, spearheaded the campaign to resuscitate it. Beginning in the 1880s, patriots, such as Anagārika Dharmapāla, with the *Mahāvaṃsa* as their guide, equated Buddhism and nationalism (Bond 1988, 55). At the same time, the Sinhala = Buddhist equation became part of the discourse of identity politics. The rhetoric surrounding the appointment of representatives to the Legislative Council, which in 1883 established a uniform judicial system, attests to the power of the new Sinhala-Buddhist identity. Thus, one Buddhist writer in 1889 was scandalized to learn that the Sinhala representative was a non-Buddhist. In this overt criticism of the Sinhala Christian, the Sinhala = Buddhist equation resonates loud and clear.[2] Only a small step was required to create the final link in the formula, namely nation = Sinhala = Buddhist. That step was taken by Dharmapāla, as has been well-described elsewhere (Tambiah 1992, 6–8).

As is well-known, Dharmapāla motivated Sinhalas to restore Buddhism to its former glory as described in the *Mahāvaṃsa*. Referring to this fifth-century text, he vaunted the triumphal history of his people: 'There exists no race on this earth today that has had a more glorious, triumphant record of victory than the Sinhalese ... who alone have a "Mahavamsa"' (Guruge 1991, 481). Arguing that Buddhism had suffered immensely under the influence of Christianity, Dharmapāla highlighted the plight of the Sinhala people:

> Buddhism prohibits alcoholic drinks and drugs, and in Ceylon where the religion has flourished for nearly 2000 years, since the British advent, we see all old traditions being wiped off by the introduction of Western abominations ... Consequently, we see the noble Religion of the Tathagata [Buddha] slowly disappearing from the Island where it had so long flourished. There is no way to prevent it, and as long as the religion of the pagans influences the Sinhalese Buddhists, so long will Buddhism decline and not prosper. (Guruge 1991, 106)

To stem the tide of corruption, Dharmapāla urged Buddhists to become agitators 'for the preservation of our nation, our literature, our land, and our most glorious religion at whose source our forefathers drank deep for nearly seventy generations'.[3] As the first person in the modern period to link his nation's role to the preservation of Buddhism, Dharmapāla underscored the sacred mission of the island: 'Ceylon, the home of the Dhamma, sacred to the Buddhists, hallowed by the touch of the blessed feet of the all-compassionate Lord, has become the beacon light to future Humanity' (Guruge 1991, 677). In this reference to the *Mahāvaṃsa's* story of the Buddha's magical journey to consecrate the island, Dharmapāla helped to seal Sri Lanka's fate as a Buddhist 'promised-land'. He also helped to establish a significant ideology, namely Sinhala-Buddhist fundamentalism (Bartholomeusz and de Silva 1998), which in the 1950s changed the course of Sri Lankan politics for ever.

The promised-land ideology that Dharmapāla and others helped to fashion in the 1880s and 1890s is fundamentalist in that it relies on religion as its source for identity. In its interpretations of the quasi-religious text, the *Mahāvaṃsa*, the ideology sets boundaries that determine who belongs to the island and who does not, promulgates dramatic eschatologies that reveal a unique destiny for the Sinhalas and their island, and dramatizes and mythologizes enemies, namely, any group or people opposed to the hegemony of the Sinhala Buddhist.[4] Late nineteenth-century Sinhala-Buddhist fundamentalists, then, identified the Buddhist Sinhalas as the people who had been charged by the Buddha himself to maintain and protect Buddhism. In addition, they identified the island of Sri Lanka as *dhammadīpa*, the island (*dīpa*) of the *dhamma*, the Buddhist teachings.

Political interpretations of the *Mahāvaṃsa*, such as Dharmapāla's, shaped attitudes about Buddhism and the island's destiny in the early decades of the twentieth century. The temperance movement, which had begun in the final decades of the nineteenth century, became in the 1910s and 1920s a focus for Buddhist sentiments (K.M. de Silva 1977, 75) which reflected the *dhammadīpa* ideology. The movement, which provided a focal point for those interested in promoting Buddhist values against foreign vices, was also political in nature, becoming the training ground for many nationalist and labour leaders (Jayawardena 1972, 115), including the significant figure of D. Baron Jayatilake. Although the first temperance organizations were established in Ceylon by Christian groups in the 1880s, both Christians and Buddhists saw the problem of alcohol as a 'curse' brought to the island by 'English rule' (Jayawardena 1972, 86–97). For Buddhists, the promotion of Buddhist ethical injunctions on the consumption of alcohol, for instance, was closely related to the preservation of Sri Lanka as *dhammadīpa*. According to Dharmapāla, the Buddha himself made this point on one of his visits to Sri Lanka. From this perspective Europeans and Tamils (and other non-Buddhist people who corrupt Buddhist culture and threaten its values) are invaders, whose claims to the island are fraudulent. Indeed, Dharmapāla specifically listed Tamils among other 'foreign' plunderers of the sacred Buddhist island (Guruge 1991, 207).

The degree to which 'the *Mahāvaṃsa*-view' of history (Seneviratne 1989, 5), or Sinhala-Buddhist fundamentalism, percolated in the low country is difficult to assess.[5] Yet it is clear that the new Buddhist consciousness heightened the awareness of many in the 1880s and 1890s who came to view themselves as inhabiting a sacred Buddhist isle. This was as true for Buddhists as it was for non-Buddhists. Indeed, the new Buddhist consciousness also made an impact on the religious and ethnic minorities of the island and discussions of the preservation of the special character of the country were prevalent in the English-language newspapers and publications of the period, which drew their readership from a large cross-section of society. As we have already seen, *dhammadīpa* rhetoric helped to shape Tamil nationalism. British Christian missionary publications also tried to keep abreast of Buddhist publications and activities, especially attempts at establishing quality Buddhist schools for Buddhist children. Citing the Buddhist agenda to educate girls as a reason to persevere in converting the 'heathen', Christian missionaries also endeavoured to undermine the new Buddhist consciousness (Bartholomeusz 1991, 45).

Evidence from periodicals of the late nineteenth century suggest that non-

Sinhalas worked for the Buddhist cause. Among these were some Tamils and Burghers (descendants of the Portuguese and the Dutch) who rallied for Buddhism, not least because uniting for Buddhism called attention to the plight of all locals under British rule.[6] Thus, while the plight of Buddhism had already awakened Sinhalas to a new national pride, it also, more generally, represented the debased condition of the nation. In short, even some non-Buddhists were swept into the tide of Sinhala nationalism, intertwined as it was with Buddhism. Others, on the other hand, responded to Sinhala pride by creating rival nationalisms.

By the end of the nineteenth century, Buddhists had made large strides in 'resuscitating' their religion. Perceiving Buddhism to be on the brink of destruction, they established printing presses in both Sinhala and English to disseminate news of their progress. They founded a Buddhist Defence Committee to air grievances to the colonial government and they established schools that eventually rivalled the best British institutions on the island (C.R. de Silva 1977, 404). Finally, they turned their attention towards the promotion of traditional Sinhala literature, music and art (Halpe and Dharmadasa 1977, 434–5). Thus, in addition to bringing into prominence traditional religion and culture, the Sinhala Buddhist revival was also a form of cultural resistance against the British.

The emphasis on Sinhala literature as a protest against Western culture was especially marked in the writings of the novelist Piyadasa Sirisena (1875–1946), who doubtless responded to the powerful presence of English as the language of the ruling power and also of the local intelligentsia, the effect of which had been to relegate Sinhala to second-class status. The Sinhala literary revival generated a sense of pride in being Sinhala. Moreover, inasmuch as Sirisena and others wrote about religion and politics, the literature of the 1880s and 1890s was used to achieve specific political ends while promoting Buddhism (R. Obeyesekere 1984, 75). While their style may have been inspired by Western forms, the themes of their literature were local. In this wedding of Western and local, the focus on vernacular language, Buddhism and Sinhala national pride, so marked in the early writings of Sirisena, was to sharpen in the twentieth century. Nevertheless, 'while the drive for the political movement came from the religious and literary revival spear-headed by the Sinhala-speaking intelligentsia, the political victory went in fact to the English educated élites' (R. Obeyesekere 1984, 45).

Though some among the English-educated élite, such as Dharmapāla, rallied for the recovery of a national consciousness, linked to Buddhist fundamentalism, this new Buddhist consciousness had little demonstrable impact on the formal political élite. Despite Dharmapāla's efforts religion and politics, as spheres of activity, remained separate in turn-of-the-century Sri Lanka. Moreover, in the early decades of the twentieth century, 'the Buddhist movement lacked an institutional apparatus which might have been converted into a political organisation' (K.M. de Silva 1977, 75). However, by the beginning of the twentieth century the Buddhist movement had permeated all levels of

Sinhala society (including the *sangha*, or the order of monks). In the decades to follow, this movement would play important roles in fostering Sinhala-Buddhist fundamentalism and furthering the conflation of Buddhism and Sinhala identity, especially after the granting of universal suffrage in 1931.

BUDDHISM AND POLITICS: THE TWENTIETH CENTURY TO 1948

In the early twentieth century, while Sinhalas, such as Dharmapāla and Sirisena, on the one hand and Tamils, on the other, contested what it meant to be Ceylonese, the British managed to withstand the pressures of local élites for a share in the administration of the country. The situation began to change in the 1920s, when the British, under pressure, began to share power with representatives of the Sinhala, Tamil, Muslim and Burgher communities (K.M. de Silva 1977, 76). Although Buddhist activism was muted in the first two decades of the new century, ethnic politics manifested itself in a variety of causes, such as the temperance movement (as we have seen), and in a variety of organizations and pressure groups designed to foster Buddhism (Bartholomeusz 1994). Among the most important of these was an organization of lay Buddhists, the All Ceylon Buddhist Congress (ACBC), whose goal was 'to promote, foster and protect the interest of Buddhism and of the Buddhists and to safeguard the rights and privileges of the Buddhists' (Tambiah 1992, 13). Sir D. Baron Jayatilake, a politician and co-founder of the ACBC in 1919, argued that '... the Sinhala Buddhist population ... has no organisation other than the ACBC to look after their interests unless the democratically elected government takes up that responsibility.'[8] As these words suggest, Jayatilake believed that the state had a responsibility to foster Buddhism, in line with the hard interpretation of the *Mahāvaṃsa*. In this way, he recapitulated the discourse of *dhammadīpa*. Yet at the same time, like most Westernized Buddhist revivalists of the period, Jayatilake supported a Western secular constitutional ideology (Tambiah 1992, 12). Indeed, like the Sinhala-speaking novelists of the late nineteenth century, who drew on both Western and local literature to create their own 'traditional' artistic styles, Jayatilake combined both Western and local ideas about the state and religion in the creation of his political thought.

A few years after the founding of the ACBC, during the elections of 1924, 'the cry of "Buddhism in danger" echoed throughout several constituencies in which Buddhist candidates faced Christian opponents' (K.M. de Silva 1993, 306). Indeed, Christians and Buddhists continued to vie for power in the decades immediately prior to independence. Christianity, aligned as it was with the colonial powers, became the focus of many Buddhist politicians, who criticized it as a Western front and as a threat to the integrity of *dhammadīpa*. Slowly but surely, it became politically advantageous to be a Buddhist. Yet, despite the interest that some had in fostering Buddhism, Jayatilake, D.S. Senanayake and other élite politicians resisted the notion of a Sinhala-Buddhist polity (K.M. de Silva 1993, 307). Rather, in the years leading to Sri Lanka's independence, politicians addressed Buddhist grievances obliquely by focusing on issues, foremost among them education, which called for a challenge to the dominance of Christian schools.

There are a number of additional developments that are crucial to a full understanding of Sri Lanka's move towards independence, even when we acknowledge Sinhala-Buddhist nationalism which remained brimming on the surface of Sri Lankan politics. The achievement of universal adult franchise in 1931 introduced into the political process a vast number of Sinhala voters, ensuring an effective future Sinhala hegemony. Indeed, the 'grant[ing] of universal suffrage was a measure which was to have the most profound effects on the country's politics' (K.M. de Silva 1977, 80). With the establishment of this new electorate in the elections for the State Council that soon followed, Sinhala voters for the first time obtained an absolute legislative majority over the representatives of the other ethnic groups (Tambiah 1992, 10).

Another factor that had a profound effect on Sri Lanka's politics in the period was the issue of language which, as we have seen, had already been a factor in the Sinhala cultural revival of the late nineteenth century. By the early 1940s, however, the issue of language moved from the cultural to the political sphere, where J.R. Jayewardene, who would become prime minister in 1977, introduced a bill which established Sinhala and Tamil as the national languages of the island (de Silva and Wriggins 1994, 7). Although Jayewardene eventually acceded to Sinhala demands that Sinhala should be the only official language of Sri Lanka, his 1942 bill politicized language for the first time. Still, while the language issue would take centre stage in early post-independence politics, the most hotly contested issue in the immediate pre-independence period was not language; rather, it was the state's protection of Buddhism.

During the 1930s and 1940s, as Sinhala, Tamil, Muslim and Burgher politicians debated secular matters such as proper forms of representation, a second discourse, based largely on the Buddhist rhetoric of the late nineteenth century, re-emerged. Fostered by Buddhist monks, this rhetoric became so pervasive in the 1940s that, without a doubt, it shaped the early post-independence political process. Among the main actors, a group of influential monks, namely the Vidyalankara group based at the monastic university of the same name, supported by some influential laymen, argued that monks had always been responsible for the welfare of the people. Additionally, they were charged with protecting the Buddha's teaching. This meant that monks were obliged to involve themselves in politics (Phadnis 1976, 164). Prominent among these monks was Walpola Rahula (1907–1997), who claimed, in his 1946 treatise *The Heritage of the Bhikkhu*, that monks had a right, indeed a duty, to engage actively in the politics of the island. In Rahula's assessment, Buddhism had, until the colonial period, been the 'national' religion of the Sinhalas. Citing the *Mahā-vamsa* as his source, Rahula urged 'religio-patriotism' and the like, thus augmenting the earlier Buddhist fundamentalism from the monastic perspective. Moreover, enshrined in Rahula's rhetoric about the island and its Buddhist mission was a Buddhist justification for violence. In his reflections on a *Mahāvaṃsa* story about Buddhist enlightened beings, or *arahants*, who assuage a king's grief for having taken life in protecting Buddhism, Rahula promoted a Buddhist just-war theory:

> Working for the freedom and uplift of the religion and the country was recognized as so important and noble that the Sinhalese in the 5th century A.C., both laity and *Sangha*, seemed to have believed that *arahants* themselves had accepted the idea that even the destruction of human beings for that purpose was not a very grave crime. What is evident from this is that the *bhikkhus* at that time considered it their sacred duty to engage themselves in the service of their country as much as in the service of their religion.[9]

This served to renew the call for Buddhist restoration. Thus, Buddhist fundamentalist notions about the island and Buddhism, coupled with charges against the Sinhala political élite (such as Senanayake and Jayatilake) who were characterized as unsympathetic to religious issues, helped to narrow the range of issues which Sri Lankan politics would address in the post-independence period (Tambiah 1992, 19). Education, too, continued to occupy the minds of many who sought to underscore the state's relationship with Buddhism. In particular the demand that the state do something to end the Christian dominance of schools was heard more frequently. Thus, on the heels of independence in 1948, Sinhala-Buddhist nationalism reappeared, this time with sharper focus and mass mobilization and support, urging the state to guarantee a variety of rights.

THE TWENTIETH CENTURY: FROM 1948 TO 1997

In 1948, Jayatilake and other Sinhala politicians, including D.S. Senanayake, independent Sri Lanka's first prime minister, achieved the ultimate reward for their linking of Buddhist concerns and secular politics: independence. From 1948 until 1956, Senanayake's United National Party (UNP) maintained a secular stance towards religion and politics in the island even though there were clear indications that the Sri Lankan Buddhist populace expected more from the newly-elected, allegedly Buddhist post-independence leaders.

The local élites, who had been groomed by the British and who were comfortable enacting Western, rationalist policies in regard to religious matters, assumed power upon Sri Lanka's winning independence from Britain in 1948. Mention of the relevance of Buddhism to the island, (as contained in the speeches of political monks as well as in ordinary Buddhists' concerns), was strikingly absent from the government rhetoric and actions during the early post-independence period. To be sure, in the decades surrounding independence, many Buddhist politicians involved themselves in Buddhist activities, such as establishing convents (Bartholomeusz 1994, 124), yet for the most part, they displayed this religiosity in the religious, rather than the political, arena.

In the meantime, that is, from 1948 until 1956, issues relating to Buddhism and the state suffused the public consciousness. For instance, in 1951 the ACBC sent to the prime minister, D.S. Senanayake, a memorandum stressing: 'It is incumbent upon the present government of Free Lanka to protect and maintain Buddhism' (quoted in K.M. de Silva 1993, 315). As the ideological heirs of Dharmapāla, Sirisena and other Buddhist revivalists of the late nineteenth and early twentieth century, the Sinhala populace, guided by organizations such as the ACBC, continued to exert their 'rights'. These rights and other expectations revealed themselves most pointedly in *The Betrayal of Buddhism*, a 1956 treatise that explored the relationship between Buddhism and the state, and alleged an unassailable link between Buddhism, the state, and the Sinhala people.[10] Outlining their grievances as well as their recommendations, the monk and lay authors of the treatise pointed to sections 28 and 29 of the Soulbury Constitution, the section that protects the integrity of each of the religions of the island, as being detrimental to Buddhism. For the *Betrayal*'s authors, sections 28 and 29 of the Constitution 'managed to safeguard [Christianity] and attain a status unparalleled in any other land' (1956, 27), enabling Christianity, which to all intents and purposes was the state religion in the British period, to maintain its position in the post-independence period. Implicitly critiquing the British-groomed politicians who embraced the secular ideology of the island's first post-independence constitution, the Soulbury Constitution, the authors of *The Betrayal of Buddhism* demanded that Buddhists reinvent politics in Sri Lanka. The 'Buddha Sasana Commission Report', produced by 590 co-authors, both monk and lay, followed soon after the publication of *The Betrayal of Buddhism*, complete with recommendations which it challenged the government to accept. Among them was 'the establishment of a Buddha Sasana Council for the purpose of promoting the welfare of the Buddha Sasana' in the island.[11]

As an alternative to the vision offered in *The Betrayal of Buddhism* and the Commission Report, a Buddhist layman, A.T. Ariyaratne, inspired by Gandhian notions, began to advance a reinterpretation of Buddhism designed to meet the political, social and economic challenges of the modern world. His movement, Sarvodaya Shramadana, founded in 1958, has focused on the liberation of individuals as the first step in the liberation of society, thus shifting the focus from nation to person. For Sarvodaya, which has maintained a grass-roots, folksy orientation since its inception, Sri Lanka, can be home to people of a variety of faiths and races while at the same time maintaining its status as *dhammadīpa*,[12] no doubt reflecting one perspective within the Buddhism of the early post-independence period.

Ironically, it was one of the most Westernized persons among the political intelligentsia in the mid 1950s, S.W.R.D. Bandaranaike, who seized upon popular sentiments. Around this time some Buddhist monks, convinced of the decline of Buddhism and Sinhala culture, formed a monastic political party, the Eksath Bhikkhu Peramuna (EBP), which helped to promote Sinhala-Buddhist nationalism. Like that of its lay counterparts, the EBP's war cry was a 'Sinhala only' language policy, which was also seized upon by Bandaranaike. With Bandaranaike at its helm, the Mahajana Eksath Peramuna (MEP), a grass-roots political group of Buddhist monks and laity galvanized by demands for a 'Sinhala only' language policy, won the 1956 elections, marking a new departure for secular Sri Lankan politics. The MEP received 37.54 per cent of the votes, 10 per cent more than the incumbent United National Party (Manor 1989, 242). The electoral upset seemed to point to the UNP's complacency in its attitude towards the relationship between the state, the Sinhala people and Buddhism, a situation that would no longer be tolerated by many Buddhist monks and lay people. Reflecting on the 1956 elections in 1958, one Buddhist monk, Seelawansa Thero, claimed for the *sangha* the credit for the overthrow of the UNP.[13] The *sangha* and the MEP have continued to carry the banner of Sinhala-Buddhist concerns, framed in the revivalist rhetoric of Bandaranaike's earliest oratory, down to the present.

Bandaranaike's victory was facilitated by the potent meaning of the year 1956 in Buddhist history. This year marked the Buddha Jayanti, or the 2,500th anniversary of the final passing of the Buddha. Buddhist activists, both lay and *bhikkhu*, took advantage of the event as they appealed to popular sentiments regarding the position of Buddhism in the political process.

Since 1956, nationalism based on language and religion has continued to hold sway in Sri Lanka's politics. Bandaranaike had come to power on a powerful wave of Sinhala-Buddhist emotion. In the years that followed, Bandaranaike's political outlook, with its roots in the late nineteenth century, would continue to inform Sri Lanka's politics and become enshrined in constitutional law. For instance, the constitution of 1972 unequivocally consolidated the 'Sinhala only' policy of the earlier period, and gave constitutional protection to Buddhism, granting it special recognition. At the same time, however, it guaranteed the protection of all Sri Lanka's religions. While the framers of the 1978 constitution sought a more conciliatory language policy, and accommodated Tamil as an 'official' language of Sri Lanka (K.M. de Silva 1996, 37), they further enshrined Buddhism as the state religion, while at the same time guaranteeing the legal protection of all the religions of the island. Though it may be true that the former prime minister, J.R. Jayewardene, the architect of the 1978 constitution, sought constitutional reforms to repair 'the damage to ethnic harmony that the constitution of 1972 had caused' with the inclusion of an extensive charter of fundamental rights (de Silva and Wriggins 1994, 381), it is also the case that the 1978 constitution guaranteed the state's special obligation towards Buddhism. Moreover, the Sixth Amendment of the 1978 constitution, taken on Jayewardene's initiative, requires parliamentarians and other officers of the law, to take an oath that they 'will not, directly or indirectly, in or outside Sri Lanka, support, espouse, promote, finance [or] encourage the establishment of a separate State within the territory of Sri Lanka'. The irony is that, while Jayewardene was criticized for not being 'traditional' enough, for he had imbibed much of the ideology of the British regarding the economy, trade etc., the subtext of the Sixth Amendment further conflated the unity of the

Buddhist religion and the entirety of the island. *Dhammadīpa* belonged to the Sinhala Buddhists and was not to be violated. The unparalleled ethnic violence towards Tamils in 1983 was, in part, a consequence of this view.

Buddhist fundamentalist politics continued to shape the platforms of politicians in the 1980s and well into the 1990s. For instance, one of President Premadasa's first acts when he took his oaths of office in 1989 was to establish and preside over a Ministry of Buddha Sasana (religion) (K.M. de Silva 1993, 34), thereby strengthening the link between Buddhism and the state in Sri Lanka.[14] Yet the presidential election of 1994, and the local government polls of 1997,[15] suggest that a countervailing tendency in Sri Lanka's politics, that is, a type of secular politics, in part bequeathed by the British, has re-emerged as a viable alternative to Buddhist fundamentalism. In both 1994 and 1997, long-standing political parties, such as the MEP, were superseded and defeated by Kumaranatunga's People's Alliance (PA), which took a stance similar to that of the UNP soon after independence. The PA patronized Buddhism, yet it offered to protect all the religions and ethnic communities of the island. Moreover, in her version of secular politics, Kumaranatunga, daughter of the murdered architect of the MEP and rival of the UNP, S.W.R.D. Bandaranaike, paradoxically demonstrates how Sri Lanka has come full circle in its attitudes towards Buddhism. Yet as Kumaranatunga's constitutional Supreme Advisory Council made up of Buddhist monks and laity suggests, her attitude towards religion has also been shaped by Buddhist pressure groups, which have informed constitutional politics since the early twentieth century.

THE MEANING OF CONSTITUTIONAL SECULARISM IN SRI LANKA

Sri Lanka's post-independence politics have in large measure been guided by an élite groomed by the British to govern after they ceded power to locals in 1948. As we have seen, the attitude of the UNP government of 1947–56 to the religious and cultural question was one of avoidance. While it is true that UNP ministers patronized Buddhist occasions, they took the position that Buddhism required no special protection or any specific constitutional guarantees; for UNP politicians, religion was a private matter (Wilson 1977, 298).

Much like their counterparts in other former British colonies, Sri Lankan political élites have tended to accommodate both local and global ideas about the relationship between religion and politics. However, since the 1940s, they have been keenly aware that it is politic to underscore the state's obligation towards Buddhism while also remaining aware that secularism is part of the fabric of Sri Lanka's constitutional history. Thus, in response to pressures from a significant proportion of the populace for the protection of Buddhism, a new definition of secularism has emerged that encompasses both national and transnational concerns; and while the new definition of secularism synthesizes both, the concerns are in conflict and are contested. On the one hand, responding to local ideology that postulates an unbreakable link between the island, the Sinhalas and Buddhism, the élite since 1972 have crafted constitutional laws which, as we have seen, grant Buddhism the pre-eminent position among all the religions of the island. On the other hand, each of the four constitutions of post-independent Sri Lanka have underscored the secular nature of the state, which links Sri Lanka to the 'enlightened' nations of the world. In this 'Buddhist secularism', a phrase I have coined to highlight the verbal sleight-of-hand regarding religion in Sri Lanka's post-independence constitutions, Buddhism can enjoy privileges in an otherwise temporal society.

Like Sri Lanka, India has had to grapple with the meaning of secularism in its own neo-colonial world. Indian ideas on secularism also hinge on local and global definitions (Nandy 1990). Moreover, in both Sri Lanka and India, the élite, while imbibing European notions about religion and politics, have had to adjust their definition of the modern state to accord with traditional categories of religion.

Since at least the early nineteenth century, religion in Europe and in South Asia has been forced to account for itself and to justify its existence. The intellectual endeavour that fuelled this predicament engaged some of the most influential figures in the British political tradition. Concomitantly, Sri Lankans, whether Buddhists, Hindus, Muslims or Christians, defended their 'rights' as members of religious communities and as Sri Lankans. At the same time, by the late nineteenth century, the debate about the 'religious' and the 'secular' constituted much of Europe's and South Asia's political and social discourse. Additionally, the politics of secularism became inextricably linked to the politics of ethnicity, so much so that to discuss secularism without reference to ethnicity is to disregard altogether the potent nature of the secular, particularly in South Asia.

By the late nineteenth century in Europe, debates about the meaning of secularism, a term which already had a long history, had resulted in two distinct definitions. On the one hand, the term, as defined by Owen Chadwick, denoted an 'essential antagonism that existed between it and religion', in which religion is opposed to science and 'is gradually dispensed with, both as a source for explanations about the world, its creation and operations, and as a basis for morality' (Crimmins 1989, 3). In this new relationship, there is no place for religion in public life. Religion has been replaced by reason and science and identity leans toward homogeneity rather than pluralism. On the other hand, for others, such as Edmund Burke, secularism meant quite simply a 'response to the changing conditions of life and thought', in which religion 'remains an integral and vital part of social and intellectual activity' (Crimmins 1989, 3). In this scenario, 'religion' and 'state' may share a healthy alliance, religious diversity and coexistence are stressed, even in the public domain, and identity is fluid. Secularism in our first definition calls for what Nandy has described as 'the abolition of religion from the public sphere' (1990, 74), while the latter model is 'accommodative and pluralistic' (1990, 74).

Nandy argues that the accommodative model is more compatible with the meaning most Indians ascribe to the term 'secularism' (1990, 74). Yet he adds that the rational, scientific and European sense has been internalized by India's westernized intelligentsia, which has created competition between secularists on the contemporary scene. In Sri Lanka, the clash of 'secularisms' has generally involved these two basic categories. There are, however, three competing definitions of secularism among the westernized Sri Lankan community, the third being a sort of Buddhist secularism, unique to the island, which Schalk (1990, 280) calls 'dharmacracy', that is, a fusion of secular politics with Buddhism.

The first use of secularism, the European style, is best illustrated by reference to the Soulbury Constitution of Sri Lanka, drafted in 1948. Section 29 of that document guarantees that laws shall neither 'prohibit [n]or restrict the free exercise of any religion', nor shall they 'confer on persons of any community or religion any privilege or advantage which is not conferred on persons of other communities or religions.[16]' The work of this first constitution was undertaken by D.S. Senanayake who, as we have seen, became Sri Lanka's first prime minister, and the British constitutional expert Sir Ivor Jennings (Wilson 1977, 289). Together they crafted a Westminster-style constitution that protected the rights of minority groups from discrimination, and, by divorcing politics from religion, granted no special privileges to Buddhism.

The second (1972) and third (1978) post-independence constitutions, however, compromised the nature of the first constitution by creating a uniquely Sri Lankan view of secularism. Sirima Bandaranaike, then prime minister and widow of the slain Buddhist S.W.R.D. Bandaranaike, promulgated a new constitution in 1972 which accorded Buddhism the 'foremost place' among Sri Lankan's religions. In addition, the document declared Sinhala to be Sri Lanka's official language. By linking religious and linguistic nationalisms, Sirima Bandaranaike's 1972 constitution pointed to Buddhism's status as Sri Lanka's state religion, while at the same time unifying and privileging Sri Lanka's Sinhala speakers as a special linguistic group.

The third constitution, drafted in 1978, further enhanced Buddhism's relation to the state. Article 9, for instance, assured freedom of conscience to all, yet it also provided Buddhism with special protections which, according to one jurist, has rendered Sri Lanka 'neither a theocratic nor a secular state'.[17] Despite that, article 9 of the 1978 constitution is regularly cited as the foundation of Sri Lanka's secular society.[18] One 1994 writer, debating the merits of the island's presidential candidates, and aware of the seemingly contradictory nature of the place of the other religions *vis-à-vis* Buddhism in the 1972 and 1978 constitutions, argued that secularism had not been compromised in the post-independence period. From his perspective, other countries have much to learn about religious harmony from Sri Lanka's example:

> It is difficult to think of any other state in the world where the people of a country with [a] predominant majority of people belonging to one religious group have permitted the holy days of other religious groups also to be declared as national holidays. In Sri

Lanka the holy days of Hindus, Muslims, Catholics and other Christians are all national and public holidays along with the holy days of the Buddhists.[19]

Former President Premadasa, who served as prime minister under President Jayewardene, and who consciously and publicly defended Buddhism while patronizing all religions on the model of Asoka,[20] advocated a *dharmishta* society in which Buddhism informs the polity, and symbolizes the tension between definitions and redefinitions of the 'secular' in Sri Lanka. While some Sri Lankans criticized Premadasa for what they considered to be his exploitation of Buddhism, others lauded his efforts to privilege Buddhism while patronizing other faiths, that is, to maintain a secularism unique to Sri Lanka, namely Buddhist secularism.

The contest in Sri Lanka over what constitutes a secular society, even after Premadasa's death, has remained a continuous theme in the English-medium newspapers.[21] The battle was most noticeable in 1994 and 1995, and then again, in 1997. In 1994, for example, *The Island* focused on the impending presidential elections, Christian proselytization, and the meaning of national identity, all of which brought into focus the relationship between Buddhism and the Sri Lankan state. Again, in early 1997, while President Kumaranatunga called for a federal system for Sri Lanka as she and the Presidential Assembly drafted a new constitution, the question of the integrity of the island, of *dhammadīpa*, helped to fuel newspaper discussions on the meaning of secularism. These 1994 and 1997 discussions, spurred on by separate pressures, have provoked a variety of responses, all of which reflect the contested nature of a modern Buddhist culture. For instance, one Buddhist, writing in October 1994, just prior to the presidential election, argued for a 'society free of discrimination on the basis of race, [and] religion'. At the same time, he urged the government to protect Buddhism, stating that such protection would fall within the limits of 'secular governance'. For that writer:

> Protecting Buddhism is not anti other religion. ... What the Buddhists expect from the government is [that] in addition to the constitutional protection, it should protect Buddhism from the unethical conversions of Buddhists by all kinds of organizations.[22]

In his tacit critique of Christian missionary methods in Sri Lanka, he expressed the view that secularism need not exclude the privileging of one religion over another.

The Buddhist–Christian relationship has indeed fuelled the debate over what constitutes a secular society in Sri Lanka. In that debate at least one Buddhist has alleged that Christians should understand that protection of Buddhism in Sri Lanka is a fundamental right, and that such protection does not mean that Buddhists are hostile to Christians.[23] According to this writer, Christians should understand that freedom of opinion and expression includes the right to critique religions publicly:

Criticism of religion is not precluded from this fundamental human right. Also, in terms of Article 18 of the Universal Declaration [of the 1978 constitution] everyone has the 'right to freedom of thought, conscience and religion.' The implication of this right is that everyone has the right to examine the credentials of any religion and to criticise it.[24]

Here, state maintenance of Buddhism and the liberty to practise any religion are deemed to be compatible. One should be free to be a Christian, but it is the government's duty to protect Buddhism from Christianity. For this writer, 'the question at issue is not one of the denial of the right to the freedom of religion ... it is the abuse of that democratic freedom by certain Christian Churches ... in their questionable methods in propagating the Gospel.'[25] In other words, Sri Lanka's secular democracy demands the government's controlling hand in matters relating to Buddhism, even at the expense of other religions.

The 'question of whether Sri Lanka [is] a secular state or not' was asked often in 1994 in *The Island*. Lauding President Kumaranatunga's allegedly neutral position on religion, one editorial considers the role of the government in a secular society:

> Separating politics and religion should not mean that government should divorce itself from religion. It only implies that it should not make political mileage out of religion. President Kumara[na]tunga not attempting to sell Buddha, Hindu gods, Christ or Mohammed for political gain is a refreshing deviation in Sri Lankan politics.[26]

From this perspective, secularism amounts to 'private' rather than 'public' religious diversity in a setting where politicians work for the good of the many without politicizing religion. Kumaranatunga, then, is a truly secular leader for she remains neutral with regard to religion. However, this version of secularism is not compromised by granting Buddhism a special place in the constitution. On the contrary, its prominence is a natural outcome of the history of Buddhism in Sri Lanka.[27]

In 1994, *The Island* also contained articles that pushed for a homogeneous Sri Lankan identity, one that does not privilege Buddhism or any religion. In a letter to the editor, a Sinhala writer encouraged people to forget about their ethnic and religious identity in order to craft a national identity for the good of the whole:

> At the risk of being called an idealist, let me say that the solution will come only when we think of ourselves really and truly as Sri Lankans. . . . Let's hope the new trend that emerged at [the parliamentary] election will grow until we all truly begin to think nationally.[28]

Think nationally, the Sinhala writer urges Sri Lankans: trade in religious and ethnic identities for a national one. In short, exchange fluid self-identity, religious, cultural and linguistic for national identity, and internalize the

European idea of secularism. Put differently, maintain separate realms for the political and the religious, and diminish the importance of religion.[29]

The 1994 and 1995 issues of *The Island* abound with letters from Sinhala, and presumably Buddhist, Sri Lankans on the subject of secularism and Buddhism. In one such letter, a critique of a previous editorial, the writer expresses, in an ironic tone, his disdain for Sinhala Buddhists who expect to be privileged in Sri Lankan society:

> So, [his] principle is the Sinhalese, the Tamils, the Muslims, the Burghers and even the Veddas (why not) are equal, but the Sinhalese are *seniores priores*, more equal than the others.[30]

Responding to Sinhala-Buddhist fundamentalism, this writer argues that neither Buddhists nor the Sinhala people deserve special treatment in a truly secular, non-discriminatory society.

On balance, then, while voices were heard in 1994 and 1995 which urged that privileging Buddhism does not compromise the secular nature of the government, there were just as many voices extolling a multi-religious, multi-ethnic secular society, where all people are equal, and where self-identity and its expression may be enacted in public dialogue. The same is true for 1997, the year in which the fourth constitution of independent Sri Lanka occupied the minds of many.

In 1997, as Kumaranatunga drafted a new constitution and promoted a federal system that would undermine the powers granted to the majority community in the 1972 and 1978 constitutions, the meaning of secularism was, once again, an issue for the English-language press. Kumaranatunga's attitudes towards Buddhism, and towards the island, are complex. As we saw in the introduction to this chapter, clause 7 of the proposed constitution grants: 'The State shall consult the Supreme Council in all matters pertaining to the protection and fostering of the Buddha Sasana.' The Supreme Advisory Council was the brainchild of former president Premadasa, whose public patronage of Buddhism came under attack from European-style secularists. Established in September 1990, the Council was initially made up of twenty-five members, sixteen of whom were monks (including the *mahānayake* of each monastic fraternity (*nikāya*) in the island). In addition, Premadasa appointed one Buddhist nun (*dasa sil mata*), along with the presidents of the ACBC, the Maha Bodhi Society, and the Young Men's Buddhist Associations, three of the most important lay Buddhist organisations in Sri Lanka. With the goal of protecting the Buddhist religion in Sri Lanka, the Supreme Advisory Council has been reorganized three times since its inception, and is appointed and governed by the Ministry of Buddha Sasana.[31] The Concil continued to function in the first few years of the presidency of Kumaranatunga, who has also offered the Council constitutional protection. This deep paradox has not gone unnoticed. One writer, aware of Kumaranatunga's acquiescence with Sinhala-Buddhist fundamentalism, suggests that she seems to be enacting many of the policies of previous governments: 'Sad to say this but attacks [against the press] are beginning to look like those at the onset of the *dharmista* era of 1977 [which began with Jayewardene and was perpetuated by Premadasa]. I appeal (for the sake of credibility and accountability) to the idealist and secular President [Kumaranatunga].'[32]

Yet, as is the case when ethnic governments compete for allegiance from different factions within one ethnic group,[33] concessions will be seized upon by detractors as a sign of weakness. Kumaranatunga's perceived neutral stance in regard to Buddhism, indeed her quasi-European-style secularism, considered a strength by some of the English-speaking élite, is considered a weakness by others, especially some very vocal and powerful Buddhist monks. Criticism of her supposed secular policies resulted, in January 1997, in the resignation of some of the most powerful monks in Sri Lanka from the Supreme Advisory Council. The chairmanship of the Council had been held jointly by the heads of the three monastic fraternities of the island, who themselves had been appointed by Kumaranatunga.[34] Citing Kumaranatunga's failure to address 'ill effects on religion [Buddhism], foreign influence, conversion of Buddhists to other religions, and division of the country [a reference to *dhammadīpa* and to Kumaranatunga's plan for the devolution of power]', the monks resigned. The architect behind the resignation was the Venerable Madihee Pannasiha,[35] who, according to one account, secretly convened the monks of the Council and spoke to them about the 'dangers posed at Sinhala Buddhists' if Kumaranatunga continued to consider devolution a viable option for Sri Lanka.[36] In this critique, the monk recontextualized the *Mahāvaṃsa* view of history to make it relevant to the needs of the day. In arguing against Kumaranatunga's perceived indifference to Buddhism, especially in the light of her capitulation to the 'demands of the minority communities',[37] the Venerable Madihee Pannasiha keeps alive the Sinhala-Buddhist fundamentalist rhetoric of the late nineteenth century. As such, he represents a very influential, yet numerically small, percentage of the Sri Lankan electorate.[38] The 1994 and 1997 election results suggest that the MEP, and other parties espousing Sinhala-Buddhist fundamentalism, are no longer in favour. However, Kumaranatunga's proposal to give protection to a council of Buddhist monks and laity whose job is to advise the government suggests that Buddhism will, in all likelihood, remain the first among equals.

NOTES

1. For instance, Singer (1992, 712).
2. *The Buddhist*, vol. 1, no. 6 (1889). For more on the controversy, see the Introduction to Bartholomeusz and de Silva (1998). The representative (under the British) was invariably Christian. For more on the equation, see Obeyesekere (1979).
3. Quoted in Bond (1988, 55).
4. For more on the characteristics of fundamentalism in general, see Marty and Appleby (1991), particularly 819–21. Also Bartholomeusz and de Silva, *op cit.*

5. There is evidence to suggest that, during the Portuguese period, Sinhala attitudes toward outsiders foreshadowed Sinhala attitudes towards minorities in the British period. For more information see C.R. de Silva (1983, 13–22).

6. I argue this in *Buddhist Fundamentalism* (1998), 167–185.

7. According to Colonel Olcott, the American Buddhist-revivalist and London representative of the 'Sinhalese Buddhists', the Buddhist Defense Committee (comprised of lay and monastic Buddhists) was established in Colombo on 28 February 1884 'to consider the present state of Buddhism in the Island of Ceylon and adopt such measures as may be necessary for obtaining redress for certain grievances'. Quoted from a letter of Colonel Olcott to the Earl of Derby, cited in Somaratna, G.P.V., *Kotahena Riots, 1883*, Nugegoda, Sri Lanka: Deepanee, 1991, 75.

8. *All Ceylon Buddhist Congress: Diamond Jubilee Celebrations (1919–1979)*, Colombo: Metro Printers, 1980, 13.

9. Rahula (1974, 22). The book was originally published as *Bhiksuvage Urumaya* by Svastika Press, Colombo, 1946. At present, I am studying Buddhist just-war thinking in Sri Lanka with a grant from the American Institute of Sri Lankan Studies.

10. *The Betrayal of Buddhism*, Balangoda, Dharmavijaya Press, 1956, i–v.

11. *Ceylon Sessional Papers*, Vol. II (November 1959), 292–6.

12. Immediately after the 1983 riots, in which scores of Tamils were slaughtered, Ariyaratne called for the people of Sri Lanka to unite in a religious and peaceful war against disunity. See 'Sarvodaya leader calls for "Dharma Yuddha"', *The Island*, 10 July 1983. For more, see Bond in Bartholomeusz and de Silva (1998), 36–52.

13. 'Thero attacks LSSP', *Daily News*, 20 January 1958.

14. Though in 1981 a Department of Buddhist Affairs had been established in the Ministry of Cultural Affairs to supervise Buddhist monks, grant financial aid to repair and build temples and oversee Buddhist schools, in 1989 Premadasa strengthened the state's relationship with Buddhism by establishing the Ministry of Buddha Sasana, to be presided over by the President of the country. Yet in June 1997, President Kumaranatunga relieved herself of her duties as Minister of Buddha Sasana. She appointed Lakshman Jayakody as the new Minister, claiming that it was inappropriate for a woman to maintain close contact with the *sangha*, a duty of the Minister. The Department of Buddhist Affairs now falls under the supervision of the Ministry of Buddha Sasana. (Interview with Minister Lakshman Jayakody, Colombo, 11 August 1997.)

15. 'Local Government Polls, 1997, Results', *The Island*, 23 March 1997.

16. 'Ceylon: Text of the Constitution' (1968, 88).

17. Sarvapalli Gopal, 1993, 'Crisis of Secularism in South Asia' *Pravada*, vol. 2, no. 7, 11.

18. For instance, R. Perera, 'Saving Buddhism', *The Island*, 4 August 1994, argues that the spirit of article 9 of the constitution, despite legal protection of Buddhism, is harmony between the faiths, thus invoking the accommodative definition of secularism.

19. Siri Wijaya, 'Is There an Ethnic Problem?' *The Island*, 31 October 1994.

20. See van der Horst (1995) for more on the relationship between Premadasa and Buddhist heroes.

21. In 1997, as the Minister of Constitutional Affairs, G.L. Peiris, promised that the new constitution will foster Buddhism, the English-medium newspapers continued to contain articles on Buddhism and its relationship to the state. For instance, 'GL Outlines Special Status of Buddhism', *The Sunday Times* (Colombo), 29 June 1997; and 'The Special Place of Buddhism', *The Island*, 29 June 1997.

22. 'Opinion Evaluation Committee', *The Island*, 14 October 1994.

23. Gunaseela Vitanage, 'Buddhist–Christian Relations: A Buddhist Response to the "Joint Statement from the Christian Consultation of Sri Lanka"', *The Island*, 20 August 1994. His ideas are repeated in 'Fundamental Right', *The Island*, 17 September 1994. Here again he quotes the constitution's articles on religious freedoms and the safeguarding of Buddhism.

24. *The Island*, 17 September 1994.

25. *The Island*, 17 September 1994.

26. *The Island*, 29 January 1995.

27. *The Island*, 29 January 1995.

28. R. Chula, 'Problems of the Sri Lankan Tamil', *The Island*, 3 September 1994.

29. This idea was also prominent in 1995 during the controversy created by a dance to the Hindu god Shiva performed in the Anglican Cathedral in Colombo. One editorial argued that there is no room for religious divides in Sri Lanka; see 'All Religions Should Unite', *Daily News*, 16 October 1995.

30. K.C.F. Wijeyewickrama, 'Of Logic, Politics, and a Death Wish', *The Island*, 31 October 1994.

31. Interview with the Additional Secretary to the Ministry of Buddha Sasana, Colombo, 11 August 1997.

32. 'Free Media Must be Adversarial', *The Island*, 9 February 1997.

33. Singer (1992, 714), following David Horowitz, *Ethnic Groups in Conflict*, Berkeley, University of California Press, 1985, argues something similar in his discussion of ethnic parties that compete for the allegiance of the same ethnic group.

34. 'Mahinda and Mangala Lock Horns', *The Island*, 12 January 1997.

35. Ven. Madihee Pannasiha was one of the six 'scholar monks' who sat on the committee that produced the Betrayal of Buddhism document (Tambiah 1992, 30, n.1).

36. *The Island*, 12 January 1997.

37. *The Island*, 12 January 1997.

38. Another article, 'Mahanayake [of the Amarapura Nikaya] on Why He Quit Council', *The Island*, 12 January 1997, discusses the views of another monk who resigned, citing the monk's dissatisfaction with Kumaranatunga's failure to protect Buddhism.

BIBLIOGRAPHY

Amunagama, Sarath (1991) 'Buddhaputra and Bhumiputra? Dilemmas of Modern Sinhala Buddhist Monks in Relation to Ethnic and Political Conflict', *Religion* 21, 115–39.

Bartholomeusz, Tessa J. (1998a) 'Buddhist Burghers and Sinhala-Buddhist Fundamentalism', in Bartholomeusz, Tessa and Chandra R. de Silva (ed.) *Buddhist Fundamentalism and Minority Identities in Sri Lanka*. Albany, New York: State University of New York Press.

—— (1998b) 'Buddhist Woman as Self and Other', in Jayawardena, Kumari (ed.) *Daughters of the Soil*. Colombo: Social Scientists' Association (forthcoming).

—— (1991) 'Sri Lankan Women and the Buddhist Revival', *Iris: A Journal about Women*, 12/1 (Fall/Winter), 43–8.

—— (1994) *Women under the Bo Tree: Buddhist Nuns in Sri Lanka*. Cambridge: Cambridge University Press.

Bartholomeusz, Tessa J. and de Silva Chandra R. (1998) 'Introduction', in Bartholomeusz, Tessa and Chandra R. de Silva (ed.) *Buddhist Fundamentalism and Minority*

Identities in Sri Lanka. Albany, NY: State University of New York Press.

The Betrayal of Buddhism. Balangoda: Sri Lanka (1956).

Bond, George (1988) *The Buddhist Revival of Sri Lanka: Religious Tradition, Reinterpretation and Response.* Columbia, SC: University of South Carolina Press.

Bond, George (1996) 'A.T. Ariyaratne and the Sarvodaya Shramadana Movement in Sri Lanka', in Queen, Christopher S. and Sallie B. King (ed.) *Engaged Buddhism: Buddhist Liberation Movements in Asia.* Albany, NY: State University of New York Press.

Ceylon Sessional Papers, Vol. II (1959), 292–6.

'Ceylon: Text of the Constitution' (1968), in Asian–African Legal Consultative Committee, *Constitutions of Asian Countries.* Bombay: N.M. Tripathi Private.

Crimmins, James E (1989) 'Introduction', in Crimmins, James E. (ed.) *Religion, Secularization and Political Thought: Thomas Hobbes to J.S. Mill.* London: Routledge.

de Silva, C.R. (1977) 'Education' in de Silva, K.M. (ed.) *Sri Lanka: A Survey.* Honolulu: University of Hawaii Press.

—— (1983) 'The Historiography of the Portuguese in Sri Lanka: A Survey of the Sinhala Writings', *Samskrti: Cultural Quarterly* (Colombo) 17/4, 13–22.

—— (1998) 'The Plurality of Buddhist Fundamentalism: An Inquiry into Views among Buddhist Monks in Sri Lanka', in Bartholomeusz and de Silva.

De Silva, K.M. and Malalgoda, K. (1977) 'Religion' in de Silva, K.M. (ed.) *Sri Lanka: A Survey.* Honolulu: University of Hawaii Press.

De Silva, K.M. and Wriggins, Howard (1994) *J.R. Jayewardene of Sri Lanka: A Political Biography* Honolulu: University of Hawaii Press.

De Silva, K.M. (1977) 'Historical Survey', in de Silva, K.M. (ed.) *Sri Lanka: A Survey.* Honolulu: University of Hawaii Press.

—— (1993) 'Religion and the State', in de Silva, K.M. (ed.) *Sri Lanka: Problems of Governance.* Kandy: ICES.

—— (1996) 'Coming Full Circle; The Politics of Language in Sri Lanka, 1943–1996', *Ethnic Studies Report* 14/1 (January), 11–49.

Gunawardana, R.A.L.H. (1990) 'The People of the Lion: the Sinhala Identity and Ideology in History and Historiography', in Spencer, Jonathan (ed.) *Sri Lanka: History and the Roots of Conflict.* London: Routledge.

Guruge, Ananda (1991). *Anagarika Dharmapala: Return to Righteousness.* Colombo: Department of Cultural Affairs.

Halpe, Ashley and K.N.O. Dharmadasa (1977) 'Literature and the Arts', in de Silva, K.M. (ed.) *Sri Lanka: A Survey.* Honolulu: University of Hawaii Press.

Jayawardena, Visakha Kumari (1972) *The Rise of the Labor Movement in Ceylon.* North Carolina: Duke University Press.

Kemper, Steven (1991) *The Presence of the Past: Chronicles, Politics and Culture in Sinhala Life.* Ithaca: Cornell University Press.

Manor, James (1989) *The Expedient Utopian: Bandaranaike and Ceylon.* Cambridge: Cambridge University Press.

Marty, Martin E. and Appleby, R. Scott (1991) 'Conclusion: An Interim Report on a Hypothetical Family', in Marty, Martin E. and R. Scott Appleby (ed.) *Fundamentalisms Observed.* Chicago, IL: University of Chicago Press.

Moore, Mick (1990) 'Economic Liberalization versus Political Pluralism in Sri Lanka?' *Modern Asian Studies* 24/2, 341–83.

Nandy, Ashish (1990) 'The Politics of Secularism and the Recovery of Religious Tolerance', in Das, Veena (ed.) *Mirrors of Violence: Communities, Riots and Survivors in South Asia.* Delhi: Oxford University Press.

Obeyesekere, Gananath (1979) 'The Vicissitudes of the Sinhala-Buddhist Identity through Time and Change', in Roberts, Michael (ed.) *Collective Identities, Nationalisms and Protest in Modern Sri Lanka*. Colombo: Marga Institute.

Obeyesekere, Ranjini (1984) 'The Bilingual Intelligentsia: Their Contribution to the Intellectual Life of Sri Lanka in the Twentieth-Century', in Thome, Percy Colin and Ashley Halpe (ed.) *Honouring E.F.C. Ludowyk: Felicitation Essays*. Dehiwala, Sri Lanka: Tisara Prakasakayo.

Phadnis, Urmila (1976) *Religion and Politics in Sri Lanka*. New Delhi: Manohar.

Rahula, Walpola (1974) *The Heritage of the Bhikkhu*. New York: Grove Press.

Rajanayagam, Dagmar-Hellman (1994) 'Tamils and the Meaning of History', in Manogaran, Chelvadurai and Bryan Pfafenberger (ed.) *The Sri Lankan Tamils: Ethnicity and Identity*. Boulder, Col: Westview Press.

Schalk, Peter (1990) 'Articles 9 and 18 of the Constitution as Obstacles to Peace', *Lanka* 5, 280–92.

Seneviratne, H.L. (1989) 'Identity and the Conflation of Past and Present', *Social Analysis* 25, 3–17.

Singer, Marshal R. (1992) 'Sri Lanka's Tamil-Sinhalese Ethnic Conflict: Alternative Solutions', *Asian Survey* 32/8, 712–22.

Spencer, Jonathan (ed.) (1990) *Sri Lanka: History and the Roots of Conflict*. London: Routledge.

Tambiah, S.J. (1986) *Sri Lanka: Ethnic Fratricide and the Dismantling of Democracy*. Chicago, IL: University of Chicago Press.

—— (1992) *Buddhism Betrayed: Religion, Politics, and Violence in Sri Lanka*. Chicago, IL: University of Chicago Press.

Van der Horst, Josine (1995) *Who is He, What is He Doing? Religious Rhetoric and Performances in Sri Lanka during R. Premadasa's Presidency (1989–1993)*. Amsterdam: VU University Press.

Wilson, A. Jeyaratnam (1974) *Politics in Sri Lanka 1947–1973*. London: Macmillan.

—— (1977) 'Politics and Political Development since 1948', in de Silva, K.M. (ed.) *Sri Lanka: A Survey*. Honolulu: University of Hawaii Press.

9
CENTRE AND PERIPHERY: BUDDHISM AND POLITICS IN MODERN THAILAND

DONALD K. SWEARER

INTRODUCTION

Buddhism has been a constant factor in the politics of Thailand, from the formation of the major Thai city-states of Sukhōthai,[1] Ayutthaya, Nakorn Sī Thammarāt and Chiang Mai in the thirteenth and fourteenth centuries until the unified modern nation-state of today. A mutually symbiotic relationship appears to have existed between the classical Thai monarchies and the Buddhist *sangha*, although available historical information from monastic chronicles and archaeological remains undoubtedly omit many details. Royal patrons sponsored the construction of grand monasteries, *cetiyas* (Thai, *jedī*) and colossal Buddha images at Sukhōthai and Ayutthaya. By the early fifteenth century kings sought to enforce religious unity by patronizing the Sinhalese Theravāda Mahāvihāra monastic heritage (Swearer and Premchit 1978, 26–30). Their policies even included the reconsecration of ordination halls and the reordination of monks. A wide variety of extant palm-leaf manuscripts dating from the fifteenth century demonstrate that while Thai kings may have succeeded in promoting a loose religious unity, no monolithic Theravāda orthodoxy of thought and practice existed (Bizot 1988). The political hegemony Thai kings sought to create and enforce through monastic patronage, sectarian favouritism and the creation of ritually legitimated political alliances did not eliminate the the sorts of stresses and strains found in the relationship between the modern Thai nation-state and the Buddhist *sangha*. Stanley J. Tambiah's interpretation of Ayutthaya's galactic cosmological polity tells only that part of the story that fits the model of religiously grounded political legitimation (1976). This study analyses Buddhism and politics in modern Thailand from a dialectical perspective that includes the tensions as well as the mutually symbiotic dimensions of that relationship. The essay focuses on two periods: the era of the formation of modern Thai civil religion from the reign of Rama IV (King Mongkut) up to the reign of Rama VI (King Wajirawut), a period of nearly eighty years from 1851 to 1925, and the four decades beginning with the accession to power of Sarit Thanarat in 1957 to the present, a period marked by anti-communist government policies and the promotion of capital intensive economic development.

Needless to say, this essay does not do justice to the historical development of modern Thailand that forms the backdrop to the complex relationship between Buddhism and the Thai nation-state. However, four factors that distinguish Thailand from its Southeast Asian neighbours deserve special mention: (1) the country was never subject to European colonial rule, leaving intact a relatively unified Thai *sangha* that has been in place from the end of the nineteenth century to the present; (2) the Thai monarchy as a symbol of national unity and supporter of the *sāsana* (Buddhism) has maintained its viability from the late eighteenth century to the present; (3) the country has not been torn asunder by a major war or armed conflict since the establishment of the Chakri Dynasty in the late eighteenth century with its capital at Bangkok; (4) although Thailand has been subject to the trends of the international market economy it has been economically stable and has prospered throughout much of the twentieth century. In addition to these four elements, there are two major recent historical trends of particular relevance. From the end of World War II up until the 1970s, Thai politics has been dominated by its American supported military. The anti-communist regimes that engineered *coup d'états* at will have gradually been replaced by a more democratically constituted, stable government. Rapid urbanization, industrialization and tourism that accelerated during the 1980s and 1990s fostered an economic boom that has increased the gap between the rich and the poor, heightened tensions between the needs of the rural population and the demands of urban expansion, and abetted rapid environmental degradation brought about by unregulated development and corruption. This has resulted in an unprecedented challenge to the Buddhistically grounded values of Thai society. These factors constitute part of the backdrop against which to view the relationship between Buddhism and politics in modern Thailand.

FROM THE TRAIPHŪM TO 'NATION, BUDDHISM AND KING'

Background

King Mongkut (r. 1851–68) and his son, King Chulalongkorn (r. 1868–1910), laid the foundations for the modern Thai nation-state that had profound implications for the nature of Thai Buddhism doctrinally and institutionally, with regard to the *sangha* itself and its relationship to the state. In this section I will examine the complexity of the relationship between Thai Buddhism and the emerging nation-state using four categories: revitalization and reform; accommodation; resistance; and rejection. As background to this analysis, however, it is first neccesary to examine how the classical Thai Buddhist worldview and its transformation during this period relate to the political structures associated with that transformation.

Like its neighbours, Thailand borrowed from India the major elements of its classical world-view. Although from a formal point of view the Thai world-view is identified with Theravāda Buddhism as the dominant religion in the country since the fourteenth century, it represents an amalgam of cosmological ideas and moral values drawn from Brahmanism and indigenous traditions, as well as Buddhism. The Thai Buddhist world-view was systematized by King L'u Tai (Lidaiya Mahādharmarāja I) who, in 1347, came to the throne of Sukhōthai, one of the earliest Thai kingdoms (Andaya 1978,3).

By the middle of the fourteenth century, the kingdom of Sukhōthai had shrunk in size and power since the days when its greatest monarch, Rām Kamheng, held sway over much of present-day Thailand. L'u Tai became king only after overthrowing a usurper to the throne. He then began the task of reconstructing the administrative and political framework, salvaging the alliance structure that had collapsed, and recovering for Sukhōthai some of its lost prestige (Andaya 1978, 4). No doubt this setting of political decline and disruption inspired L'u Tai to compose the *Traibhūmikathā* (Thai: *Traiphūm*) [The Three Worlds of Phra Ru'ang], the first systematic construction of Buddhist cosmology (F.E. Reynolds and M. Reynolds 1981).

Although the treatise accepts the traditional Theravāda view of the five stages of the deteriorization of history, L'u Tai's intention was not to utilize this depressing view of cosmic time to promote religious piety, but rather to affirm the meaningfulness of kammically calculated human lives within a given multitiered universe. As a Buddhist sermon, the *Traiphūm* exhorts its listeners to lead a moral life and by so doing reap the appropriate heavenly rewards. Within its hierarchical framework of various human, heavenly, animal and demonic realms, the text focuses on a central figure, the universal monarch (*cakkavatti*), exemplified by the Buddhist king, Dharmāsokarāja. L'u Tai gained authority and legitimacy by purposely identifying himself with the mythic *cakkavatti* as well as the historical Asoka, who was known for his meritorious works and for easing the material burdens of his people so they could devote more attention to religious matters. That King Rama I (1787–1809), who restored the fortunes of the Thai monarchy with its capital in Bangkok after the Burmese sack of Ayutthaya in 1767, commissioned a new recension of the *Traiphūm* testifies to its longevity and utility as a charter for order and stability at the beginning of Thailand's modern era, also a time of political and social disruption.

The cosmology of the *Traiphūm* and the central place of the kammically valorized *cakkavatti* king was soon to be challenged by European and American missionaries, merchants, government administrators and travellers who came to Bangkok in the mid-nineteenth century. By 1850 Siam, as it then was known, had signed commercial treaties with several Western nations. The Siamese royal élites led by Mongkut, crowned king in 1851, and Jao Phraya Thiphakorawong, his able Minister of Foreign Affairs, proved to be fascinated by Western science and technology and open to its use. Jesse Caswell, an American Presbyterian missionary in Thailand in the early nineteenth century, observed that Mongkut and his followers held to a demythologized Buddhism that included a rejection of 'everything in religion which claims a supernatural origin' (Bradley 1966,39). By the mid-nineteenth century the noise of steam engines and printing presses was heard in the capital. *The Bangkok Recorder* contained articles on astronomy, physics, physiology, chemistry and medicine (Reynolds 1976, 215). In short, among the Siamese élite, especially those sent to England and France to be educated, a pragmatic, scientific empiricism began to develop that challenged the mythologized cosmology of the *Traiphūm*. The new culture of a printed literature reflected this changing world-view. One influential book, the *Pathom-somphōt* [The Buddha's Enlightenment], written in the 1890s by Somdet Phra Ariyawongsākhatayana (Supreme Patriarch Sā), presents a life of the Buddha that greatly reduced the mythological elements found in the Pāli *Nidāna Kathā* (Sā 1922). In 1867, a critique of the *Traiphūm* by Jaophrayā Thiphakorawong entitled *Kitjānukit* [A Book Explaining Various Activities] was published. Many consider that the book reflects Mongkut's own views.

Thiphakorawong's treatise declares that worldly and religious matters are not the same. The foreign minister attempted to demonstrate that nature has its own laws, thereby discounting the *Traiphūm*'s fanciful explanations with others drawn from astronomy, geology and medicine. For example, he theorized that rain falls not because the rain-making deities venture forth or because a great serpent thrashes its tail, but because the winds suck water out of clouds; illness is caused not by the gods punishing evil deeds but by air currents (C. Reynolds 1976, 215). While the explanations were misplaced, they were drawn from the natural sciences rather than from mythology or religion. Buddhism was treated primarily as a system of social ethics realizable through Siamese institutions. Heaven and hell were explained for their moral or pedagogical utility, not as actual places but as enticements to good deeds, and the doctrine of *kamma* was seen primarily as a kind of genetic principle to account for human diversity.

The *Traiphūm* continued to be respected as part of Siam's cultural and religious heritage, but as Craig Reynolds observes, 'an era had really passed; the mold had been broken' (1976, 217). King Chulalongkorn, Rama V (r. 1868–1910), moved even further from the worldview of the *Traiphūm*, character-izing it as an act of the imagination. Even more significantly, he demythologized the *Traiphūm*'s conception of kingship. How could the *cakkavatti* world ruler and the great gem wheel that symbolized his meritorious power (F. E. Reynolds and M. Reynolds 1981, 137–9) be relevant to 'the world of 1885 in which princes and officials would criticize absolute kingship in their petition to Chula-longkorn for a constitutional monarchy?' (C. Reynolds 1976, 217).

Thanissaro Bhikkhu offers another perspective on the abandonment of the *Traiphūm* during the reign of Rama IV.[2] He suggests that the periods of greatest centralization in modern Thai history can be seen as a response to both internal and external threats. In establishing a new dynasty in Bangkok, Rama I's strategies for centralizing the Kingdom included appealing to the *Traiphūm* as the model for a cosmologically grounded, hierarchically structured political and social charter, convening a council in 1788 to unify the *saṅgha* around a newly redacted Pāli canon, and, in 1804, codifying Ayutthayan common law (Wenk 1968, 35–42). Thanissaro proposes that the abandonment of the *Traiphūm* during the reign of Rama IV suggests that the king and his ministers did not feel threatened by outside forces. Subsequently, the *Traiphūm* having been rejected,

Rama V (r.1851–1902) and Rama VI (r. 1910–25) looked to European countries for political models to strengthen the infrastructure of the developing nation-state; and that military governments beginning with Sarit Thanarat (Prime Minister, 1959–63) saw American supported military strength as the key to maintaining the stability of the country in the face of the threat of communism. But the *Traiphūm* was never consigned to oblivion. Since the 1980s the treatise has been exploited by both conservative neo-traditional groups to maintain the status quo of the ruling Thai élites and also by liberal voices urging greater and more rapid democratization. The latter seek to reconstruct the political institutions and cultural products of Sukhōthai to provide participatory, liberal forms of a true Buddhist model of government (Jackson 1991, 210).

The shift from the religiously grounded cosmology of the premodern Thai worldview was paralleled by organizational changes in the Thai state, in particular, the demythologization of kingship and the creation of a more rationalized, national bureaucratic administrative structure that included the *saṅgha*. The traditional Thai political structure has been described as an elaborate, encompassing, persistent structure formally organized on the premise that it existed to serve the king, the source of all authority (Siffin 1966, 25). In theory, the king possessed all legitimate power, a power rooted in a divine, quasi-magical charisma. Although, in Buddhist terms, as *dhammarāja* (righteous ruler) he was to rule according to the universal natural law that governed the cosmos, as *devarāja*, or god-king, he also embodied a semi-divine power. His charismatic omnipotence was symbolized by the procreational potency of his polygamous lifestyle, and perpetuated by such requirements that ordinary people could not gaze upon his face. Twice a year officials were required to swear an oath of allegiance to the king as the Lord of Life (*jao chīwit*).

After the Thais sacked Angkor in the early fifteenth century, the Khmerization of Thai kingship was reflected not only in the quasi-divine status accorded the king, but also the hierarchial organization of Thai society into a structure of ranks and statuses ranging from slaves to the senior princes of the realm. The governmental structure was divided into a centre or headquarters comprising the king, his chief civil and military ministers, four civilian ministries and a department of religious administration. By the seventeenth century the provinces surrounding the centre were grouped into four classes, a structure extensively studied by William Siffin (1966), Fred Riggs (1966) and Stanley J. Tambiah (1976). While the Thai socio-political system was elaborately stratified, it was a relatively loose structure with each administrative entity largely a self-contained universe. Business was conducted for the most part on personal terms. Each administrative unit was 'an informal group consisting of patron and clients, intimately regulated by the legitimate status system and a diffuse set of shared or reciprocal interests' (Siffin 1966, 35).

Mongkut's leadership accelerated changes in the traditional conception of the Thai king as a semi-divine centre of power and authority. He studied geography, physics and chemistry as well as the histories of major Western nations. He opened Thailand to trade with America, Great Britain, France and other European nations. He modernized coinage, expanded the system of water transportation, substituted paid labour for corvée labour on royal public works, enacted laws to improve the status of women and children, took the first steps to eliminate slavery, and sought to improve public health, safety and sanitation. He humanized the office of kingship by allowing common folk to look at the king, made frequent trips outside the palace – even acquiring a steamboat – and brought European advisors into the palace. He also instituted important religious reforms including standardizing monastic practices and Buddhist celebrations, emphasized the study of Buddhist texts in their original Pāli language, and encouraged a more rationalistic approach to interpreting scripture. Do these changes allow us to view Mongkut as a leader who completely transformed the traditional conception of Thai kingship? Riggs contends that Mongkut changed the 'public image of the monarch from that of a divine king apotheosized by the magical and supernatural rites of the Brahman priests, to that of the leading human defender and patron of the Buddhist Church', and one in whose time 'older customs and ceremonies of divine kingship were questioned and were either reinterpreted in Buddhist terms, secularized, or neglected and gradually forgotten' (1966, 99, 101). Tambiah challenges such an interpretation by maintaining that Mongkut's many accomplishments, which included opening up Thailand to the West in an unprecedented way and reforming Thai Buddhism, were added on top of many of the traditional notions of Thai kingship. Mongkut's enlargement of the traditional conception of the monarch coincided with the beginnings of a change in the political effectiveness of the monarch as an initiator of reforms, policy decision maker, and implementor of administrative programmes (Tambiah 1976, 288). But an undue emphasis on Mongkut as a rational reformer must be qualified by the fact that he continued to believe in *devas*, practised astrology, and reported miracles arising from his vows of truth (*sacca-adhiṭṭhāna*).

What Mongkut initiated was further developed by his son, Chulalongkorn. King Chulalongkorn's reign (1851–1902) was marked by the effective integration of Thailand as a modern kingdom. He continued to strengthen the role of the monarch as well as to demythologize the institution of kingship. For example, while he abolished the ancient custom of prostration before royalty, at the same time he centralized and consolidated royal power. He abolished the *phrai* system, a complex organization of master–client relationships through which nobility could control vast resources of labour by replacing its hierarchical structure with a government-regulated system of taxation and military draft, a reformation of old ministries and the modernization of the country's administrative structure (Engle 1957, 18–19).

Chulalongkorn's early reforms included a rationalization of fiscal policy, the development of a national system of communications, transportation, and a programme of surveying and mapping. They laid the foundation for the 1892 edict that changed the basic structure of the government creating twelve ministries with specific functions, each headed by one person. These included ministries for the interior regions of the country, foreign affairs, finance, justice, defence, public works, agriculture and commerce, and religious affairs. Chula-longkorn also created a framework of provincial government to link the outlying regions with the capital. 'The system devised was a simple and logical hierarchy of regional, provincial, and district jurisdictions' (Engle 1957, 69). Below these jurisdictions were the sub-districts and villages. Siffin (1966, 88–9) characterizes this bureaucratic reform as supplanting a simple, stratified, exploitative system existing in principle as the king's domain with a set of purposive, functionally specific, performance-oriented organizations.

Chulalongkorn's reforms served to enhance his own power while at the same time integrating the country, including the Buddhist *sangha*, along modern, rational lines. These changes and the corresponding challenge to the traditional Thai Buddhist worldview carried with them the seeds of the transformation of the absolute monarchy into a constitutional monarchy, an event that occurred in 1932, only twenty-two years after King Chulalongkorn's death. What impact did the political, social and economic changes that occurred from 1851 to 1910 have on Thai Buddhism?

Revitalization and reform

Thai Buddhism played a crucial role in the national reforms instituted during the reigns of Mongkut and Chulalongkorn. It can be argued that Mongkut's tenure as a monk from 1824 until his coronation in 1851 had a direct effect on them. His study of the Pāli scriptures and association with monks from the strict Mon tradition convinced him that Thai Buddhist practice had, in several respects, departed from the authentic Buddhist tradition with the possibility that his own ordination was invalid. He advocated a more rigorous adherence to the study of Pāli, the canonical language of the Theravāda scriptures, and a proficiency in meditation. His efforts at religious reform resulted in improving monastic discipline in an effort to bring it closer to the *vinaya*, and he also demythologized many traditional Thai Buddhist teachings. The group of monks who gathered around Mongkut at Wat Bōwōnniwet called themselves the Thammayut [Pāli: Dhammayuttika], 'those adhering to the doctrine', and formed the nucleus of a new, stricter sect of Thai Buddhism. With its royal origins and connections, the Thammayut sect has played a very influential role in the development of modern Thai Buddhism out of proportion to its size.

It must be pointed out that although Mongkut encouraged a new attitude to Buddhist traditions, he did not impose his views on his immediate court, much less his subjects in general. Thanissaro Bhikkhu suggests that Mongkut was following the example of Rama III, who did not welcome Mongkut's new movement but was gracious enough to tolerate it; furthermore, Mongkut realized that forcing his courtiers to have their sons ordained in the Thammayut sect or trying to force all monks to reordain in his sect would have been counterproductive (Thanissaro 1997). In fact, during his reign the most famous monk Mongkut patronized was Somdet Toh, a Mahānikai monk.

The monastic background to Mongkut's own career and the development of a reformist Buddhist tradition that embodied his ideas and ideals were important in later developments of the Thai *sangha*, especially as they were incorporated and expanded in the policies and programmes instigated by Mongkut's son and successor, Chulalongkorn. Parallel with the implementation of reforms designed to integrate provincial areas politically into the emergent Thai nation-state, King Chulalongkorn also initiated policies to incorporate all Buddhists within the kingdom into a single national organization (Keyes 1971, 555). The principles that established the basis for a national *sangha* were embodied in the Sangha Administration Act of 1902. Prior to that time, regional and local authority and custom dominated monastic practice (Kamala 1997, 18–46).

The more important features of the Sangha Administration Act of 1902 were: (1) the incorporation of all monks into a national structure; (2) the establishment of a hierarchical principle of authority; and (3) the establishment of a national system of clerical education (Keyes 1971, 555). At the time this law was implemented the *sangharāja*, the head of the national Buddhist ecclesiastical organization, was Prince-Patriarch Wajirayān (Pāli: Vajirañāna–varorosa) (1860–1921), the son of Mongkut and brother of Chulalongkorn. Wajirayān traveled to outlying provinces to ensure that the monastic law was being properly obeyed. He established the practice of having monks come to Bangkok for their higher studies, and often appointed central Thai monks to high positions in the provincial ecclesiastical hierarchies that were organized along lines parallel to the national political structure. As *sangharāja*, Wajirayān oversaw the administrative centralization and bureaucratization of Buddhism throughout the country. In addition to his role as administrator, he was an able scholar with many of his books forming the core of a national monastic curriculum (C. Reynolds 1979, xxxiii–1).

As stipulated in the third principle of the 1902 Sangha Admnistration Act, education was a central feature in King Chulalongkorn's programme of national development and integration (Wyatt 1969, 299–375). Because the Thai monastic order was the single most pervasive national institution, a national educational programme through monastic schools figured prominently in Chulalongkorn's plans. Monastic education was also improved by standardizing the monastic curriculum throughout the country and stipulating the content of nine levels of Pāli language study. In addition, two Buddhist academies for higher studies were established in Bangkok, one at Wat Bōwōnniwet for the Thammayut monks and the other at Wat Mahāthāt for the Mahānikai monks. The king's half-brother, Prince Damrong Rajanubhab (1862–1944), appointed Minister of the Interior in 1892, ably assisted Prince-Patriarch Wajirayān in guiding these developments.

It is worth emphasizing that the revitalization of Thai Buddhism in the late nineteenth and early twentieth centuries was initiated as a consequence of royal leaders – Mongkut, Chulalongkorn, Wajirayān and Damrong – who recognized that monks and monasteries constituted an institutional structure and educational network that extended throughout Siam. Twentieth-century Thai

Buddhism was shaped through the creation of a national *saṅgha* organization centred in Bangkok, a national programme of education initially organized through monasteries, a standard curriculum for monks, a national system of approving and rewarding monks through a hierarchy of monastic titles and a regularization of Buddhist rituals for monks and laity. While no one can doubt that the reforms initiated by Mongkut and Wajirayān revitalized Thai Buddhism in the early twentieth century, it is also true that the bureaucratization and centralization of the *saṅgha* and the standardization of Buddhist thought and practice had a deadening effect on mainstream Thai Buddhism over the long term. Some of the most creative voices calling for change in the latter half of the twentieth century are monks and laity on the periphery rather than the centre.

The issue of the impact of the new monastic curriculum on literary creativity within the *saṅgha* is admittedly complex. Wajirayān repeatedly states in his books that he hopes others will make further explorations in the direct study of the Pāli Canon as a source for spiritual guidance, and that the commentaries and the *Visuddhimagga* are to be accepted only when they are in line with the Canon. These attitudes were the basis on which the two major *saṅgha* intellectuals of the twentieth century, Buddhadāsa and Phra Payutto, built their work. In Thanissaro Bhikkhu's opinion Wajirayān's pioneering groundwork, popularizing the notion of advancing knowledge in Buddhism rather than simply elaborating on inherited tradition, was the necessary condition for the later scholarly contributions of Phra Payutto and the innovative doctrinal interpretations of Buddhadāsa (Thanissaro 1997).

Accommodation. Buddhist civil religion and the Thai nation-state

Most Thai monks went along with the principles and regulations of the Sangha Act of 1902. In a sense they had no choice. As Prince-Patriarch Wajirayān observed, monks were required to obey three types of laws: the law of the land, the monastic discipline (*vinaya*), and Thai custom. Furthermore, at least from the Ayutthaya period the king exercised primary authority over the monastic order as its protector and patron. It was the king who nominated the *saṅgharāja*, a custom that continues to this day.

Accommodation meant centralization, regularization, and the development of a complex hierarchical monastic structure. Procedures for conferring ordination, rules regulating the movement of monks from one monastery to another, the method for compiling the annual register of monks, the filing of annual reports from lower ecclesiastical officials to their superiors, provisions for managing the proceeds of monastic lands, approval of plans for monastic buildings, the retirement of aged abbots and the appointment of their successors were all regulated (Keyes 1971, 538). Regional differences in teaching and practice that characterized Thai Buddhism prior to 1902 were gradually reduced or eliminated. Nationwide Buddhist ceremonies such as Visākha Pūja were regularized and new ceremonies, such as Māgha Pūja, were created. Not only were the ritual chants in Pāli regularized, recitations in regional dialects were discouraged. In the 1940s the government even authorized the burning of palm-leaf manuscripts written in the Yüan script of northern Thailand.

The standardization of monastic education undoubtably brought about an overall improvement in the educational level of monks; however, the required curriculum and national monastic examination system controlled from Bangkok eventually served to discourage specialized textual expertise. The informal teaching lineages that had characterized Buddhism in northern and north-eastern Thailand began to disappear, and the routinization of rote learning led to a lack of literary creativity. The decreasing importance of textual study beyond the standard requirements, the gradual development of government schools that replaced schools administered by monasteries, the assumption of other roles once performed by the monk by secular officials, the tendency of monks trained at the two Buddhist universities to leave the *sangha* for secular life and the increasing specialization of the monk as a ritualist rather than a teacher have all undermined the place of the *sangha* in Thai society. Instead of a *sangha* shaped by and reflecting regional custom, it was moulded by initiatives from central government.

Resistance and non-cooperation

Not all monks, however, submitted to the new monastic regulation aimed at minimizing regional religious differences based on language, culture and custom. Two monks, in particular, resisted this change in quite different ways: Khrūbā Sīwijai (1878–1939), a northern Thai monk who rebelled against the government's efforts to control ordination, and Ājān Man (1870–1949), from north-eastern Thailand, who is regarded as the founder of the modern tradition of Thai forest monks. Khrūbā Sīwijai resisted the routinization of Thai Buddhism and its centralization in Bangkok by openly defying the 1902 Sangha Administration Act regulating monastic custom. It might be said that by following the tradition-hallowed monastic practice of living in the forest on the periphery of institutional power Ājān Man chose to follow a policy of non-cooperation. Charles F. Keyes has characterized the difference between the two monks in Weberian terms: Sīwijai's charisma derived from an active involvement in the world as a *nakbun* (Thai), that is, one so endowed with merit that he is able to serve as a means for others to acquire merit, whereas Man's charisma derived from the fact that he spent most of his life pursuing a life of meditation in the forest (Keyes 1981, 261–2). Even though they sought to resist the monastic mainstream, the ideals they represented were eventually compromised. Sīwijai was forced to surrender to the authority of the national ecclesiastical hierarchy, and the tradition of forest monks associated with Man was co-opted by the patronage of the political élite. James L. Taylor refers to the patronage of charismatic forest monks by establishment political and financial élites as a kind of psychological endorsement of the centre of power by the merit of holy men situated in peripheral forests (Taylor 1993, 281). Although in different ways both Khrūbā Sīwijai and Ājān Man were appropriated by establishment Buddhism, their place as charismatic monks who defined themselves over-against the mainstream assured them an unusual prominence both during and well beyond their own lifetimes.

Khrūbā Sīwijai was born in 1878 of poor farming parents from the province of Lamphūn, an area associated with the earliest traditions of Buddhism in northern Thailand (Swearer 1988, 78–81). According to traditional sources, his birth was accompanied by miraculous natural signs. At the onset of his mother's labour, a violent storm broke out and the earth shook. As a youth his special qualities were readily apparent, distinguishing him from other children. At the age of four he set free animals trapped by his father; he loved the tranquillity of his rural life and helped his parents in the fields with a deep feeling of contentment.

Convinced that his family's poor lot was a consequence of bad *kamma* that could be remedied only by serving the Buddha, Sīwijai ordained as a novice at the age of eighteen. He was a diligent student of the *vinaya*, Pāli and northern Thai texts, and apprenticed himself to a noted teacher of insight (*vipassanā*) meditation. Shortly after his higher ordination at the age of twenty-one, the death of the abbot of his home temple (Wat Bān Pāng) left him and a fellow monk in charge of the monastery. Soon thereafter he embarked on an extensive building campaign, recruiting sufficient support to construct a new image hall (*vihāra*), monks' quarters (*kuṭi*) and library on a hill-top outside of the village, providing an ideal setting for monks to study and engage in meditation. Prior to this extensive construction project, Sīwijai sought an auspicious sign, a custom that accompanied many important decisions later in his career. The sign came in the form of a dream in which he saw moonlight radiating through clouds.

Not surprisingly, traditional northern Thai accounts depict Sīwijai as an exemplary Buddhist monk. He lived simply, ate only one meatless meal a day, and refrained from such habit-forming practices as chewing betel and smoking. He was wise, compassionate, steadfastly righteous and, above all, generous. His growing reputation attracted a large following including non-Buddhist tribal peoples–Karen, Hmong, Muser – who brought their children to be ordained as novices under the tutelage of this wise, compassionate monk. Others showered him with gifts, hoping that this merit-making act towards one so virtuous would result in their good fortune. Soon he was thought to be a *bodhisatta* with the power to discern people's thoughts, and it was thought that when he worked in inclement conditions he was protected from rain or the sun (Sanguan Chōtisukarat 1972, 337).

Sīwijai's fame might have remained relatively localized in Lamphūn and Chiang Mai provinces had it not been for his opposition to the growing power and authority of the national *saṅgha* headquartered in Bangkok, and his extensive campaign to build and restore temples and monasteries in northern Thailand. In the pre-modern period the northern region of Thailand comprised several Tai city-states dominated by Chiang Mai. The Tai Yūan of the north with their own language and written script had developed a distinctive cultural and religious tradition enriched by close proximity to Burma (Myanmar). Sīwijai, a product of this northern culture, challenged the efforts of the central government in Bangkok to eliminate the distinctive customs of northern Thai Buddhist practice. In particular he continued to accept novices under his tutelage as their instructor (*upajjhāya*) and to ordain them even though he was not authorized to do so by the governing council of the national *sangha*. He was also accused of disobeying the orders of his ecclesiastical district superior appointed from Bangkok, failing to attend compulsory meetings to instruct monks in the new *sangha* and government regulations, refusing to co-operate with the government census, not rejecting rumours about his miraculous powers, and encouraging separatism within the monastic order (Sanguan Chōtisukarat 1972, 328). He was ordered to defend himself before district ecclesiastical authorities and later before the supreme patriarch in Bangkok. At these hearings he argued that he was not ordaining monks on his own authority but according to the tradition established by the Buddha and followed by the early monastic community. Sīwijai was, in fact, adhering to the *vinaya* which the government was, in effect, superseding by giving the authority of ordination only to monks authorized by the central *sangha* officials in Bangkok.

Throughout this period of conflict Khrūbā Sīwijai repeatedly appealed to the authority of the Buddha, his teachings (*dhamma*), and the ideal monastic community (*ariyasangha*), and also to his own experience. On the night before his first hearing, he dreamt that a large reliquary (*cetiya*) collapsed on tens of thousands of people which only he was able to lift from them. He interpreted the dream as a sign of his special role in righting the *sāsana* (Buddhist tradition). Eventually, a compromise was reached between Sīwijai and the Supreme Patriarch. He was exonerated by the *sangharāja* on the condition that Sīwijai submit to his authority. Had the Supreme Patriarch expelled Sīwijai there can be little doubt that a separatist religious movement would have emerged in northern Thailand.

It may seem odd to characterize Ājān Man, the subject of recent scholarly interest, as a monk who resisted the routinization of the new establishment Buddhism (Keyes 1981, Tambiah 1984, Taylor 1993, Kamala 1997). Man and the tradition of religious practice he established represent a diverse constellation of cultural and religious values and do not fit neatly into a particular model. As a Thammayut monk he can be seen as a continuation of the reformist impulse represented by that tradition, yet he was a forest monk from northeastern Thailand far from the centre of power in Bangkok. Even though as a forest monk he resisted absorption into mainstream Thai Buddhism, scholars have argued that the forest monk tradition of which he is considered the progenitor was gradually incorporated into the 'metacentre of the Thai state' through patronage by the military, political and financial élites (Taylor 1993).

Thanissaro Bhikkhu, an ordained monk in the Thai forest tradition and abbot of a Thammayut monastery, sees the forest tradition as embodying three major components each indebted to the Thammayut reform: *tudong (dhutanga)* practices, strict adherence to the *vinaya*, and meditation (*kamatthāna*)

(Thanissaro 1997). Prior to Ājān Man and his teacher, Ājān Sao Khantisīlo, the tradition of the thirteen *dhutaṅga* or ascetic practices defined in the *Visuddhimagga* were not widely known in Thailand until they were appended to an early Thammayut text, the *Pubbasikkhāvaṇṇana*, written by Phra Amarābhirakkhit (Amaro Koet). It was this appendix that influenced Ājān Sao and differentiated his *tudong* practice and that of Ājān Man from the previous tradition of wandering monks in northeastern Thailand. It is also suggested that Ājān Sao's practice of meditation was inspired by the *Kāyagatāsati Sutta* (*Majjhima Nikāya* 119) newly translated by Thammayut scholars. Thanissaro argues, however, that while the progenitors of the forest tradition were indebted to the Thammayut reforms they did not adopt Wajirayān's rewriting of the *vinaya* or the new ecclesiastical government system but, unlike Khrūbā Sīwijai, they did not openly resist them. Furthermore, some noted forest monks such as Ājān Lī spent several years in Bangkok (Kamala 1997, 184–7). The co-operation of the forest monk tradition with the centre did not mean capitulation, however. The meditation monks (*kammaṭṭhānika*) continued following their *dhutaṅga* practices.

Man Kænkæo was born in 1871 in a remote village in the north-eastern province of Ubon. He was the eldest of nine children of a rice farming family in the poorest region of the country. Ordained a novice at the age of fifteen in the local *wat* (temple-monastery), after two years he left the *sangha* in order to help his father in the rice fields. Unlike most Thai youth who return to lay life, marry and raise a family, Man rejoined the monastic order at the age of twenty-one, taking the monastic name Bhūridatto Bhikkhu. He is best known, however, as Phra Ājān Man, the Venerable Teacher of the Firm Mind.

His unusual decision to seek higher ordination (*upasampadā*; Thai: *buat phra*) foreshadowed an atypical pattern of monastic practice with an intense focus on insight meditation (*vipassanā*). He also embarked on the *dhutaṅga* path of peripatetic asceticism. With the exception of the three-month rains retreat from mid July till mid October, the *dhutaṅga* monk wanders in the forest carrying only a distinctive large umbrella and mosquito net as protection against the elements. He eats only the food placed in his alms-bowl during his morning *piṇḍapata* wandering, will not accept food presented as an offering, and eats only one meal a day (Keyes 1981, 158).

From its beginnings, the Theravāda tradition has had an ambivalent attitude towards *dhutaṅga* practice, in part because wandering forest monks are freed from the customary disciplines of the settled monastic life. In north-eastern Thailand after the turn of the century, *dhutaṅga* practice was further problematized by attempts on the part of the national government to exercise more control over monks and monasteries. Despite the trend towards honouring and rewarding monks who excelled within the routinized structures of the national *sangha*, Man's exemplification of the monastic ideal of moral purity, meditation and single-minded pursuit of *nibbāna* won a devoted following among both monks and laity. Other forest monks adopted a pattern of monastic life modelled after Ājān Man, adhering to a rigorous monastic regimen of extraordinary simplicity combined with meditation. Some, such as Ājān Chā, remained in the Northeast where their followers in recent years have included many Westerners, eventually leading to the establishment of an international centre for Western monks. Others, such as Luang Pū Waen, Luang Pho Sim and Ājān Lee, travelled to other parts of Thailand, thereby establishing the modern forest monk tradition with Ājān Man as its founder. While scholars have been especially interested in how these monks on the periphery have been co-opted by the centre, within his own historical context Ājān Man can be seen as a monk who legitimated his own spiritual independence from the new national civil religion by following the ideal of the *dhutaṅga* tradition and by focusing on meditation as the centre of monastic practice (Man Bhūridatta Thera 1991).

Rejection

The most radical Thai Buddhist response to the developments of modernization in the late nineteenth and early twentieth centuries was an attempt to reject them outright by force. A dramatic example of this development was a millennial movement in north-eastern Thailand between 1899 and 1902. This movement erupted as a consequence of a sudden and radical shift in conceptions of power resulting from the threat of an expansionist French colonialism and from the implementation of provincial reforms instituted by King Chulalongkorn at the end of the nineteenth century (Keyes 1977, 285).

Millennial expectations are based in the Theravāda belief in the future appearance of the *bodhisatta* Metteya (Sanskrit, Maitreya) as a saviour in troubled times, and the Thai Buddhist belief in the *phū mī būn,* a person with a vast reservoir of merit from past lives that can be drawn upon by others to improve the conditions of their lives (Swearer 1993, 154–5). Such persons are regarded as *phū wiset,* extraordinary individuals with miraculous powers. These figures are found in millennial movements in Sri Lanka and Myanmar, as well as in Thailand.

The millennial uprising in north-east Thailand can be seen as a direct result of King Chulalongkorn's efforts to strengthen the central government's control over this area, especially as a counter to the French expansionist threat from Cambodia. The political restructuring of the Northeast rendered the local gentry powerless, putting effective political control into the hands of central Thai commissioners. An increased head tax and other increased financial levies placed such a burden on the north-eastern peasants that they found it difficult to produce enough for their needs. In addition, the harvests of 1890 and 1891 had been extremely poor. Under these conditions some turned to banditry. Others predicted the appearance of a *phū mī būn* who would eliminate the suffering of the peasants. Such persons did appear, the most important being a man from French Laos named Mān who settled in Ubon Province; Lek, a villager who established himself in Mahāsarakham Province; and Thao Buncan, who claimed a following of six thousand men. All three sought to establish a Buddhist kingdom free from domination by the French or the central Thais.

In March 1902 government military forces attacked the *phū mī būn*, killing Thao Buncan. Mān and Lek then led a force of about 2,500 against the government troops, resulting in the death of two of the chief nobles and the capture of the governor of the province. When they returned to Ubon, one of the major towns in the Northeast, they were decisively defeated by government troops resulting in the death or capture of several hundred followers of the *phū mī būn*. The millennialist Buddhist uprising against Bangkok was crushed.

The beginnings of modern Thai civic identity

In 1910, eight years after the *phū mī būn* uprising in the Northeast, Chulalongkorn died. He was succeeded by his son, Wajirawut [Vajiravudh] (r.1881–1925), who had been named crown prince in 1895. David Wyatt (1982, 223) observes that if King Chulalongkorn may be said to have constructed the modern Kingdom of Siam, his two sons, Wajirawut and Prajādipok (r. 1910–25), made it into a modern nation. During the reign of Wajirawut a further transformation of Thai civil religion occurred in which Buddhism began to be overshadowed by the state, thereby setting in motion trends towards a continuing displacement of Buddhism as the core of Thai identity. These trends are in evidence today in the decreasing percentage of young men who ordain temporarily for one rains retreat, the increasing dominance of the monk's role as a ritualist rather than an educator, the consequent decline of the prestige of the *sangha* among the Thai élites, and an increase in the popularity of non-Buddhist cults, in particular the cult of Rama V (Chulalongkorn). The equestrian statue of King Rama V in front of the parliament building in Bangkok has become a major national shrine, and the king's picture now often occupies a place of honour alongside a Buddha image in homes, restaurants, banks and public buildings (Swearer 1995, 103).

Several factors have contributed to these changes, the most important being the growing insinuation of the state into all levels of Thai society, from political administration to education, with the consequence that the *sangha* plays an increasingly peripheral role in the lives of the Thai people, especially the urban élites. During the reign of Wajirawut, the trend towards the construction of a Thai identity rooted more in the symbolism of the nation-state than in Buddhism is suggested by the motto coined by the king, 'nation, religion [Buddhism], king', represented by the tricolour Thai national flag created during his reign. The motto gives priority to an abstract notion of a nation served by Buddhism and guaranteed by the monarchy. In addition to introducing the first national holidays in honour of King Chulalongkorn and the Chakri dynasty (April 6), he promoted a new national identity along modern Western lines. The king introduced surnames, promoted team sports, especially soccer, argued for monogamy in place of the widespread practice of polygamy, and was an ardent supporter of modern education (Wyatt 1982, 118). Wajirawut also sponsored the establishment of pan-Thai organizations outside of the *sangha* to promote national unity. These included the Boy Scouts and the paramilitary

Wild Tiger Corps (*s'ua pā*) 'whose members could come from any segment of Thai society provided they were deemed to be: "good citizens"' (Keyes 1987, 60). The emphasis on the Thai nation as the ground of Thai identity guaranteed by the king and served by Buddhism was made explicit in Wajirawut's reference to the Wild Tiger Corps in his 1911 inauguration speech:

> The aim of this national institution is to instil in the minds of the people of our own race love and loyalty toward the High Authority that controls and maintains with justice and equity the political independence of the nation, devotion to the Fatherland, Nation, and the Holy Religion, and, not the least of all, the preservation of national unity, and the cultivation of mutual friendship. (Wyatt 1982, 225; quoted from *The Souvenir of the Siamese Kingdom Exhibition at Lumbini Park B. E. 2468*, 167).

The emphasis on the Thai nation-state as the ground of Thai identity guaranteed by the monarchy and served by Buddhism has continued unabated to the present. The Village Scouts (Thai: *Luk Su'a Chao Bān*), a government sponsored movement especially active in the politically volatile 1970s to promote national loyalty, has a precedent in Wajirawut's Wild Tiger Corps. The organization was formed in 1971 by the Border Patrol Police with the support of the Ministry of the Interior primarily as a nationwide anti-communist movement (Keyes 1987, 95–6). Furthermore, additional governmental efforts to control the monastic order can be seen in the Sangha Law of 1962, and in the increasing use of the *sangha* to serve the aims of the government through state-sponsored development programmes. New reformist Buddhist movements have arisen on the periphery of mainstream civil religion Buddhism. Several are indebted to a monk from Southern Thailand, Buddhadāsa Bhikkhu. I shall explore these distinctive developments in the following section.

FROM THE SANGHA LAW OF 1962 TO SANTI ASOK

Accommodation. New Forms of Thai Civil Religion

The change of government in Thailand in 1932 from an absolute to a constitutional monarchy was marked by a shift away from the monarchy as the centre of Thai politics. The Thai king did not become an important factor in Thai political life until the 1950s when the current monarch, Bhumibol, became active in public affairs. After the 1932 *coup d'état* led by a relatively small number of civil servants and military who had been educated in England and France, the government was first led by General Phahon Phonphayuhasena, followed by General Phibhun Songkhram from 1938 to 1944. Phibun promoted an authoritarian ultra-Thai nationalism symbolized by the name of the country being changed from Siam to Thailand, and he allied the country with Japan during World War II.

The overthrow of the absolute monarchy led to a redefinition of the relationship between the *sangha* and the state. The 1932 constitution reaffirmed the traditional relationship between the king and Buddhism – 'The King professes the Buddhist Faith and is the Upholder of Religion' – but beyond that statement government leaders formulated no clear-cut policy toward the *sāsana* (Ishii 1986, 100). The Supreme Patriarch responded to the new situation by reaffirming the traditional relationship between *sangha* and government as stipulated in the Sangha Administration Act of 1902. However, another group of younger monks urged a change. In 1935, 2,000 monks from twelve provinces demonstrated in Bangkok to petition Prime Minister Phahon for greater democratization of the *sangha* (Ishii 1986, 101). The eventual result was the Sangha Administration Act of 1941 that broadened the government of the *sangha* by instituting a tripartite separation of powers that included a legislative assembly of up to forty-five members. (See Figure 9.1.)

Although the new *sangha* administrative structure worked well for two decades, it appears to have floundered due to a dispute between Thammayut and Mahānikai monks in which Phra Philmolatham, a Mahānikai monk and abbot of Wat Mahāthāt, was the central figure. Some believe that the case of Phra Phimolatham was a subterfuge exploited by the Sarit Thanarat government to exert even more control over the *sangha*. Others look to intra-*sangha* politics, not only sectarian rivalry between the Thammayut and Mahānikai but internecine conflict within the Mahānikai order itself (Thanissaro 1997).

The Phra Phimolatham case was the *cause célèbre* of the 1960s (Somboon 1982, 57). Born at the turn of the century in Khon Kaen in the north-east, after his ordination in the Mahānikai order Phimolatham quickly established himself as an able scholar and administrator. By 1929 he had passed the penultimate level of Pāli studies and in 1932 was appointed abbot of a royal monastery in Ayutthaya. At two year intervals between 1943 and 1949 he became Ecclesiastical Governor for the central region of the country, the Sangha Minister for Clerical Education, and the abbot of Wat Mahāthāt, the monastery serving as the centre of the Mahānikai order and the Sangha Cabinet (Jackson 1989, 95). He supported the so-called pro-democracy forces within the *sangha* that promoted the 1941 Sangha Administration Act and more than any other monk was associated with its passage. In the 1950s Phra Phimolatham also began to promote the Mahāsī Sayadaw method of insight meditation he had learned in Burma, designed to be taught in local community-based monastery-temples rather than forest retreats (Keyes 1989, 133). Some Thammayut monks saw Phimolatham's programme as an effort to counteract the Thammayut monopoly on meditation in the Northeast. At the same time, his success also served to establish a Phimolatham network throughout the Mahānikai, thereby alarming highly placed monks in the sect's hierarchy. Thus, when Sarit Thanarat assumed the reins of political power, Phra Phimolatham had emerged as one of the most popular, powerful and controversial monks in the country. In addition to attracting a following of young, politically active monks, he had also developed highly placed enemies within the Mahānikai including the powerful abbot of the royal monastery, Wat Benjamabophit.

In 1957, Field Marshall Sarit became the Prime Minister of Thailand in a

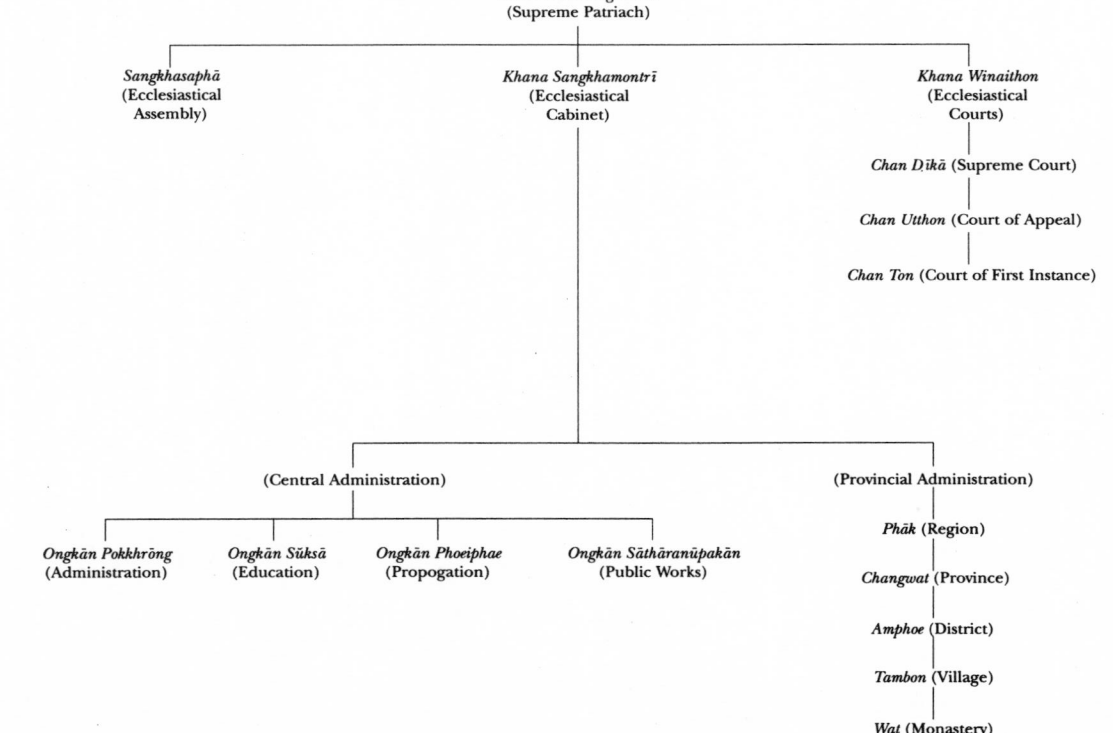

Figure 9.1 *Saṅgha* organization under the Sangha Administration Act of 1941 (from Ishii 1986, 105). (Reproduced here by kind permission of the author.)

bloodless military *coup d'état*. Committed to a programme of rapid economic development, Sarit sought to centralize power in the state administrative organizations, and to strengthen national unity by elevating national values associated with the monarchy and Buddhism (Ishii 1986, 115). Following the death of Supreme Patriarch Krom Luang Wajirayānawong in 1958, what had the appearance of a struggle between the two sects of Thai Buddhism over leadership of the national *sangha*, but was much more complex, became a convenient excuse for Sarit to exercise more control over the *sangha* administration.

At Sarit's request, in 1960 the *sangha* administration dismissed the Sangha Cabinet and appointed a new one without Phra Phimolatham (Mayer 1996, 41). The new cabinet passed a resolution to expel monks who 'expressed opinions that undermined the healthy condition of the religion and that were opposed to government policies' (Somboon 1982, 59). Phra Phimolatham was stripped of his administrative positions and in 1963 was expelled from the monastic order on charges of being a communist. He was eventually exonerated in 1966 and by the mid 1970s had become a symbol for anti-government activitist monks.

With Phra Phimolatham and other pro-democracy monks out of the picture, Sarit was free to enact the Sangha Administration Act of 1962 that eliminated the principle of the separation of powers embodied in the 1941 act. (See Figure 9.2.) The new Act concentrated power in the hands of the *sangharāja* and a Council of Elders (*mahātherasamakhom*), and created a *sangha* authority structure that '[was] intended to make the [*sangha*] an instrument for the promotion of national government policies' (Somboon 1982, 51). In a speech that was to anticipate the strong anti-communist posture of the Sarit government, Foreign Minister Thanat Kōman, acting on behalf of the Prime Minister, asserted that the country prospered under a strong unified authority and that political instability was a result of transplanting 'foreign systems' to Thai soil (Ishii 1986, 116). The Phra Phimolatham case served as a warning to other monks that the government would act without impunity towards anyone 'who might seek to draw on Buddhism to formulate a critical stance toward the existing political system' (Keyes 1989, 133, Somboon 1976, 38–9).

Coinciding with the passage of the new Sangha Adminstration Act, the government instituted two important programmes (Somboon 1976, 1982, 1988). The *thammathūt* (Dhamma Messengers) sought to organize monks for community development projects on the periphery, especially in the Khmerized areas of the north-east and in the far north that, in the eyes of the government, were vulnerable to communist subversion. The *thammathūt* programme was established in 1965 by the Department of Religious Affairs under the Ministry of Education. Schools to train monks were founded in Nong Khai in the north-east, Nakorn Sī Thammarāt in the south, and Chonburi on the eastern sea-board, although the largest centres were in Bangkok at Wat Mahāthāt sponsored by the two monastic universities, and at Wat Phra Sing in Chiang Mai in the north.

The training school in Chonburi was led by Phra Kitthiwuttho, a controversial supporter of right-wing political groups in the mid 1970s. By 1973 over 3,000 monks had graduated from the community development training programmes

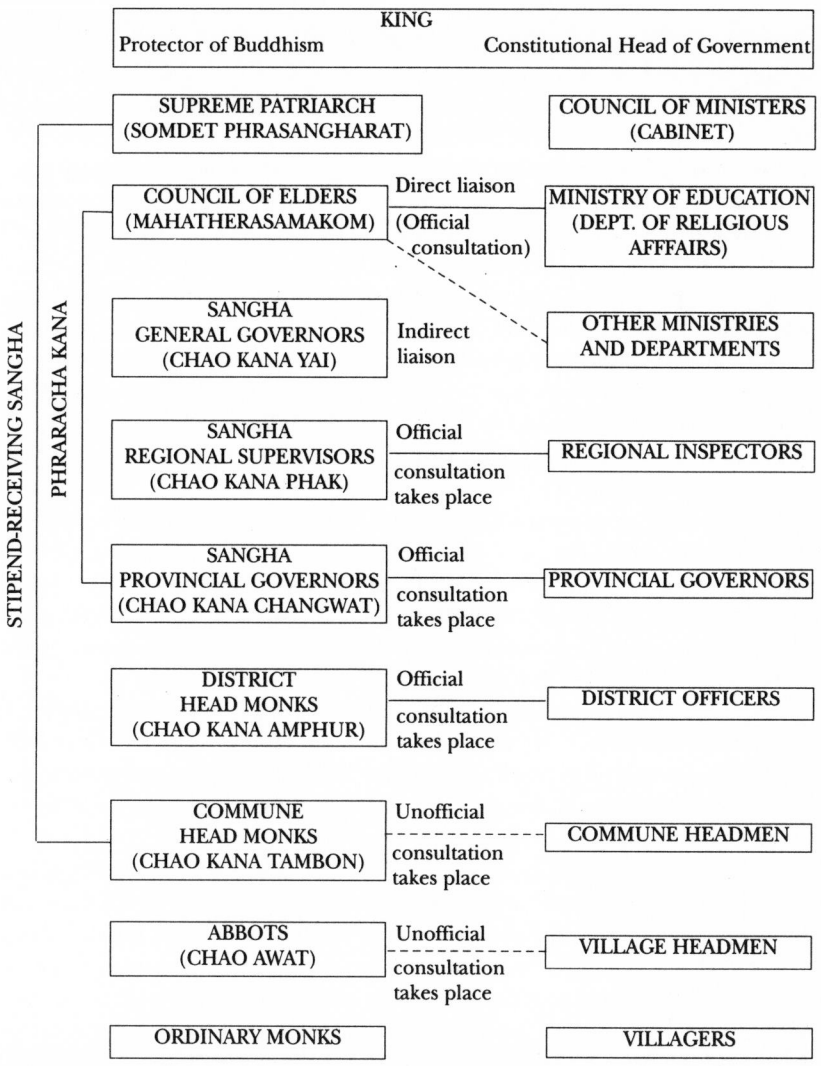

Figure 9.2 Administrative structure of the *Saṅgha* and its relationship to the government (from Somboon 1982, 50). (Reproduced by kind permission of the publisher, Institute of Southeast Asian Studies.)

held at Kitthiwuttho's Cittaphawan College (Swearer 1973, 63). The Cittapha-wan programmes urged monks to instil a work ethic in villagers:

> A life of achievement can only be guaranteed through the good secured from labor. People who don't work are a burden on the world. The Buddha condemned such people as the 'refuse of humanity' because they are parasites on society. . . . Labor is money and money is labor. Money is a master that can produce everything for us. (Somphorn 1972, 72–3).

213

In view of such a philosophy it is not surprising that 'the main impact of the [development] program[s] has been to provide villagers ... with clear evidence that the Sangha approves and supports the economic development efforts of the government' (Keyes 1971, 561).

In the mid 1970s Kitthiwuttho also became a strong supporter of right-wing groups such as the New Force (Nawaphon) that emerged in response to Thailand's 'experiment with democracy' between 1973 and 1976 that ended with a bloody military crackdown on a student demonstration at Thammasat University in Bangkok. In an infamous speech at Cittaphawon College in July 1976, printed under the title 'Killing Communists Is Not Demeritorious', Kitthiwuttho declared that soldiers who kill communists gain more merit for protecting the nation, the religion and the king that demerit from taking life. Citing the Buddha and scripture as authority for his position, he argued that some people are so worthless that to kill them is, in fact, to kill *kilesa* (impurity) (Swearer 1995, 113).

The second major programme launched by the government in the 1960s to recruit *sangha* support for government policies was the *thammacarik* (Dhamma Travellers). Initiated in 1965 by Mr Pradit Disawat, the head of the Tribal Welfare Division of the Department of Public Welfare, the programme is designed to promote the integration of the non-Buddhist hill tribes who live in the northern mountains into the Thai nation-state through the teaching of Buddhism and the ordination of young men as novice monks. Wat Sīsodā, a monastery at the foot of Mount Suthep overlooking the city of Chiang Mai, continues to serve as the headquarters monastery for this programme. Upon receiving their initial education in Chiang Mai, those who remain monks are then sent to Wat Benjamabophit in Bangkok for further study.

A fundamental difference can be seen between the civil religion Buddhism developed by Mongkut and Chulalongkorn and that promoted by the Sarit and subsequent regimes: the former used *sangha* reform to create a nation out of disparate regions; the later used the national *sangha* organization to promote the goals of the national government (Keyes 1971, 559). Through programmes such as the *dhammathūt* and *dhammacarik* the governments of Sarit and Thanom Kittikachorn (1963–73) laid the groundwork for the politicization of the monkhood by involving the *sangha* in programmes whereby monks would, in effect, carry out government policies (Keyes 1981, 33–4). Somboon Suksamran argues the point even more forcefully, contending that these programmes amounted to government manipulation of the *sangha* to the severe detriment of the public regard for the monastic order: 'I disagreed strongly with participation by the monks in rural development programmes directed by the government, as they placed their prestige and position in grave jeopardy by associating themselves with policies which in fact perpetuated underdevelopment' (Somboon 1988, 26). Subsequently, Somboon nuanced his judgement of development monks (Thai: *phra nak patthana*), distinguishing between monks co-opted into government programmes and those innovative movements that have involved monks who have voluntarily organized themselves for development tasks in villages throughout the country: 'Their commitment to development is commitment to liberate the rural population from oppression, exploitation, poverty, and ignorance' (Somboon 1988, 26). In a similar vein, Peter A. Jackson (1989, 60) argues that differences between monks who perceive their primary responsibility to be the state versus those who dedicate themself to working for the common good are at the heart of many conflicts within the *sangha* in the twentieth century.

Subsequently, I shall refer to this latter group of monks actively involved in programmes that address systemic social and economic problems ranging from poverty and environmental degradation to prostitution, drug addiction and AIDS. Here it should be noted that in 1985 the government sought to co-opt activist development monks by associating them with a national programme called *Phændin Tham, Phændin Thong* (Land of Dhamma – Land of Gold), organized through the National Council on Social Welfare. The Council was developed to help co-ordinate governmental agencies, private organizations, religious and educational institutions to promote the spiritual, social and economic well-being of the country. It was explicitly stated that the Council implemented the Land of Dhamma – Land of Gold project in order to support government policies (Somphorn Thephsittā 1985, 11). In a speech on 4 January 1986, inaugurating a Training Center for Development, Prime Minister Prem Tinsulanonda dedicated the Land of Dhamma – Land of Gold project in honour of the King's sixtieth birthday in 1987. Behind the idealistic rhetoric of the Prime Minister's speech was the intent to incorporate monks working independently of government sponsored development initiatives into the project and in so doing promote the government's image as a patron of Buddhist social activism.

One of the most distinctive new forms of Thai Buddhist civil religion is the Thammakāi (Pāli: *dhammakāya*) movement. Headquartered at Wat Thammakāi located on a thousand acres in Prathum Thani near Bangkok, the movement owes its initial inspiration to the Venerable Monkhon Thepmuni (Luang Phọ Sot), the abbot of Wat Paknām in Thonburi. Luang Phọ Sot taught a distinctive form of visualization meditation whose aim was to internalize the Buddha in the form of the *dhammakāya* (dhamma-body) within the meditator's mind and body. Although this method differs considerably from traditional Theravāda insight meditation (*vipassanā*), it attracted a wide following that included two college graduates from Kasetsart University who subsequently ordained as monks in the early 1970s and founded Wat Thammakāi.

The movement has developed several forms of teaching and practice at odds with mainstream Thai Buddhism including encouraging lifetime ordination. Although the movement was originally independent, it quickly ingratiated itself with the Mahānikai ecclesiastical hierarchy, including sponsoring mass ordinations at Wat Benjamabophit and donating some of its surplus funds to the Mahānikai *sangha* hierarchy. Its leaders, Phra Thammajayō and Phra Thattajīwo, were educated in marketing and have used their skills in business administration to promote their network in Thailand and abroad. Its critics point out that like the new religious movements in Japan, Wat Thammakāi is run like a modern business.

Prathum Thani has become a national religious centre with tens of thousands of devotees making pilgrimage to Wat Thammakāi during Visākha Pūja and other major religious holidays. The movement is noted for its national *dhamma* exams conducted through the public schools and its domination of university Buddhist Student Associations. Wat Thammakāi has been so successful in organizing itself nationally through many diverse networks, especially its meditation centres (Thai: *samnak vipassanā*), that the movement can be likened to the model of the primordial galactic polity of civil religion in Thailand's premodern era (Tambiah 1976, 102–31; Swearer 1991, 662–7). The movement has received strong support from the royal family and major military figures including General Arthit Kamlengek, Commander-in-Chief of the Army from 1983 to 1985, and former General Chavalit, the Prime Minister until his resignation in November 1997. It has been reported that Phra Thammajayō, the chief abbot of Wat Thammakāi, has personally instructed the Crown Prince, Vajiralongkorn, heir to the throne.

Revitalization and reform

In the late nineteenth century religious reform was initiated by King Mongkut, who had been a monk for twenty-five years before ascending the throne. He promoted changes in monastic discipline and practice that led to the creation of the Thammayut sect and routinized the public expression of Buddhism nationwide by creating what can be called a 'book of common worship'. This tradition was continued by Prince-Patriarch Wajirayān who, as the head of a national *saṅgha* organization, standardized a nationwide religious curriculum for both monks and laity. In effect, the government, through the Department of Religious Affairs of the Ministry of Education, has come to control religious knowledge, namely what is taught about Buddhism in both monastery and government schools.

The impulse for religious revitalization and reform subsequent to the initiatives by Mongkut and Wajirayān has come in part, but not exclusively, from monks outside of the modern Thai civil religion that they created. One of the most influential of these reformers has been Buddhadāsa Bhikkhu [Phra Thepwisutthimethī (Ngū'am)]. He represents the integration of two major trends: the tradition of Buddhist modernist rationalism begun by Mongkut, and a distinctive forest tradition with a strong emphasis on teaching (*ganthadhura*) in contrast to the tradition of forest monks in north-eastern Thailand founded by Ājān Man.

Buddhadāsa's interpretation of the *dhamma* has found a large following among urban élites, while also providing an ideological base for Buddhist social activists on the periphery – both monks and laity – who are critical of the establishment and the Buddhist civil religion identified with it. This was not always the case, however. Buddhadāsa's biting criticisms of mainstream Buddhism and his innovative interpretations of the *dhamma* distressed some political and religious leaders. However, he was protected from Phra Phimolatham's fate because he chose to live and teach far from the centre of power in Bangkok and absented himself from the power struggles within the Thai *sangha*, and also because of his increasingly broad, non-politicized popularity.

Buddhadāsa began his monastic career in a conventional manner, but soon opted out of the hierarchically structured national *sangha* system of education, exams, advancement and titles. Born in 1906 in Chaiya, southern Thailand, he was ordained a monk in 1927. In 1928, when he went to Bangkok for further studies, he found the city noisy and dirty and the monastic lifestyle not to his liking. He returned to his rural home monastery where he passed the third and final level of Dhamma studies. In 1930 he resumed his studies at Wat Pathum Kongkhā in Bangkok but found it no more tolerable than before. After passing the third level of Pāli studies while in Bangkok, he returned once again to Chaiya where he first occupied an abandoned monastery and then later founded a forest monastery on the outskirts of the town (Santikaro 1996, 148–153). Although Buddhadāsa occasionally travelled to other parts of Thailand to lecture and made one trip outside the country to visit Buddhist sites in India, he spent most of his monastic career at his monastery in Chaiya where he taught and pursued the monk's path of study and meditation. Buddhadāsa called his forest monastery Wat Suan Mokkhabālārāma, the Garden of Empowering Liberation. As a centre of study and practice rather than ritual observance, it annually attracts thousands of students and visitors from all parts of Thailand and the world. Buddhadāsa's death on 8 July 1993, was an occasion for national mourning.

Throughout his long career, Buddhadāsa adopted a critical stance toward religious, social and political structures. In doing so he applied the normative teachings of Theravāda Buddhism–non-attachment, not-self (*anattā*), emptiness (*suññatā*), dependent co-arising (*paṭiccasamppāda*) and *nibbāna*–to show people how to live in the world. Most Thais, observes Buddhadāsa, believe that the highest principles of Buddhism demand a separation from the world. Such, however, is not the case. The principles of *nibbāna* are for everyone because the state of non-attachment is our original, true nature and what we strive to rediscover in the midst of our present state of stress and dis-ease (*dukkha*): 'To be non-attached means to be in our true, original condition – free, at peace, quiet, non-suffering, totally aware' (Buddhadāsa Bhikkhu 1975, 13). Buddhadāsa contends that *nibbāna* in the above sense is not solely a monastic pursuit but a goal for everyone. After all, those who live and work in the world experience more stress than the forest monk: 'Those who are are hot and bothered need to cool off. For this reason the Buddha intended the teaching about emptiness (*suññatā*) as the basis for action on the part of ordinary people' (Buddhadāsa Bhikkhu 1975, 14–15).

As Buddhadāsa transforms the teachings of not-self, emptiness and *nibbāna* into ethical principles, so he sees dependent co-arising (*paṭiccasamuppāda*) to be not only an explanation of the origin and cessation of suffering but also as a universal principle of conditionality that applies to all aspects of our lives, including politics. Politics in the true sense, suggests Buddhadāsa, is a spiritual or dhammic socialism, namely, a state where individuals act not out of self-interest but out of regard for the common good. A spiritual socialism is based on the principle of interdependence. For example, policy matters in one area cannot be isolated from policies in another. Take the case of population growth. In Buddhadāsa's view, the increasingly critical problem of the exploding world population must be approached not in isolation but in relationship to resource use, production and distribution. If such factors were taken into consideration, the earth might be able to accommodate a larger population but this would require promoting less competitive and acquisitive lifestyles and a more equitable distribution of the world's resources (Buddhadāsa Bhikkhu 1976, 16).

Buddhadāsa's influence has extended from Sanyā Thammasak, a highly respected former chief justice, to ordinary laypersons in towns and villages. His impact has remained especially strong among university students, professional élites and social activist monks and laity. Monasteries found throughout the country, such as Wat Umong in Chiang Mai, promote his teachings, and noted Buddhist lay men and women such as Magsaysay Award winner Dr. Prawet Wasī, and Buddhist feminist and university professor Dr. Chatsumarn Kabilsingh, publicly acknowledge their indebtedness to Buddhadāsa's teachings and example. Even those who disagree with Buddhadāsa's interpretations of the *dhamma*, such as scholar-monk Phra Payutto, recognize his unique contribution in bringing seminal Buddhist concepts to bear on contemporary social, economic and environmental problems.[3] Among those who seek to put the principles of Buddhadāsa's teachings into practice is the lay Buddhist social activist Sulak Sivaraksa.

Resistance and protest

Since the 1970s many Buddhist groups have emerged on the periphery of the mainstream to challenge the development policies of the central government and the increasingly secular, materialist ethos of Thai society. Their leaders and the movements associated with them have been interpreted from several different perspectives: urbanization (Jackson 1989, 158–98), Weberian 'practical rationalism' (Keyes 1989, 133–42), individualistic cults (Taylor 1990, 135–54), fundamentalistic movements (Swearer 1991, 652–90), reformism (Swearer 1996, 195–237), and dissident sectarianism (Heikkilä-Horn 1997, 109–43). The groups differ, but the three included here as representative of resistance to government development policies and establishment Thai civil religion attack the increasing disparity between the rich and the poor, the destruction of the natural environment under the pressure of urbanization and industrialization, the erosion of cultural, moral and religious values, and the government's mixed record on social justice and human rights issues. The three groups are: organizations founded by Sulak Sivaraksa, which include the Santi Prachā Dhamma Institute [Peace, Democratic Participation and Justice] and the International Network of Engaged Buddhists; activist monks engaged in development (Thai: *phra nakpatthana*) and forest conservation (Thai: *phra nak anurak pā*) many of whom are affiliated with Sekhiya Dhamma [Dhamma for Training]; and the Santi Asok movement. Each group is directly indebted to the teaching and example of Buddhadāsa Bhikkhu.

The one person justifiably singled out as the progenitor of contemporary Thai Buddhist social activism is the controversial Buddhist layman Sulak Sivaraksa. He began his career as educator, moral critic, intellectual gadfly and Buddhist social activist in 1961 after graduating from St David's University College, Lampeter, Wales and the study of law in England. He has been involved in the founding and sponsorship of numerous non-governmental organizations (NGOs) in Thailand including the Coordinating Group for Religion and Society (1976), an ecumenical Buddhist and Christian human rights organization; the Asian Cultural Form on Development (1977) dedicated to the uplift of the rural and urban poor; the Thai Inter-Religious Commission for Development (1978) which co-ordinates work among individuals, groups and agencies dealing with religion and development; and the Santi Prachā Dhamma Institute (1988), whose main objectives are to deepen the knowledge of non-violence, democracy and social justice, to apply this knowledge to current situations in Thai society and to develop the human resources to realize these principles. Other organizations Sulak has founded include the Wongsanit Ashram, a meditation-study centre with the purpose of integrating personal and social transformation, and Sekhiya Dhamma, a *saṅgha* of development and conservationist monks.

Reflecting on his reasons for founding the Komol Keemthong Foundation in 1971, an agency that has spawned the Foundation for Children, the Folk Doctor Foundation, and the Coordinating Group for Religion and Society (Thitima 1994, 23) that has underwritten many of Sulak's publications, Sulak comments: 'Our main objective was to promote idealism among the young so that they would dedicate themselves to work for the people. We tried to revive Buddhist values ... We [also] felt that the monkhood could play a role again through education and public health' (Sulak 1985, 316).

Sulak has also been the inspiration behind the International Network of Engaged Buddhist founded in 1989, a worldwide organization of Buddhist social activists that holds annual meetings, workshops and peace walks in Thailand. His most recent international project, based in Thailand and begun in 1995, is the Spirit in Education Movement. This organization is committed to offering a 'spiritually based, ecologically sound, holistic alternative to mainstream education with its narrow unconnected fields' (SEM 1996/1997).

Sulak has been unstinting in his support of human rights and social justice issues in Thailand, and unrelenting in his criticism of government development policies and consumerist social values (Sulak 1992). He observes:

> The great department stores or shopping complexes have now replaced our Wats which used to be our schools, museums, art galleries, recreation centres and cultural centres as well as our hospitals and spiritual theaters. The rich have become immensely rich, while the poor remain poor or even become much poorer ... Not

only our traditional culture, but our natural environment, too, is in crisis. (Sulak 1989, 5)

Sulak's outspoken criticism of the Thai government has brought reprisals. In 1984 he was arrested but released after four months in prison. In September 1991 the military government, stung by his attacks, again issued a warrant for his arrest. Fearing for his life, Sulak lived in exile for a year, lecturing in Europe, the United States and Japan. In March 1995 he was cleared of all charges against him.

Althtough Sulak lacks the international visibility of the Dalai Lama or the Vietnamese monk Thích Nhất Hạnh, he enjoys a worldwide reputation as a Buddhist peace activist. In January 1994 he was nominated by the American Friends Service Committee for the Nobel Peace Prize and in 1995 he was given the Right Livelihood Award by the Swedish government as an 'alternative Nobel' (Sulak 1995, 44–47). Widespread international support for Sulak contributed to his exoneration by the Thai government in 1995.

In recent years Thai Buddhist social activists, including Sulak, have fought against both government and private efforts to exploit the natural environment solely for profit. The destruction of the northern forests, in particular, has led to severe environment degradation including the destruction of watersheds, flooding, and the widespread erosion of arable land. Buddhist monks, in particular, have played an important role in the protection and conservation of community forests, a natural resource crucial to local village life, by defending them from encroachment by outside commercial interests and educating villagers in better conservation methods. Another strategy employed by monks is to 'ordain' trees by wrapping monks' saffron robes around them.

In 1987 Phra Khru Man Nāthīpitak, abbot of Wat Bodharama in the northern province of Nān, pleaded with a local logging company not to clear-cut the last stand of woods in his area. When his personal request fell on deaf ears, he developed the idea of tree ordination and with the help of several NGOs successfully put a halt to the logging (Pipob Udomittipong 1995, 40). The idea caught on. In 1989 Phra Prachak Kuttajitto began ordaining trees in the Dong Yai forest in Buriram Province, north-eastern Thailand. In 1994 he was charged with forest trespass and tree poaching. After further government harrassment he was forced to disrobe. A similar fate befell Ājān Pongsak Techathamanō. In the early 1980s he began working with villagers in the Mae Soy valley of Chiang Mai Province to help them protect their natural environment against further destruction both from their own lack of knowledge and from outside commercial interests. He advised the villagers to seek permission from the Royal Forestry Department to declare the forest area of the Mae Soy valley as a Buddhist Park in order to protect both trees and animals. He also worked to change the attitude of the villagers towards the forest by convincing them that environmental problems have a spiritual as well as a material dimension; that morality was not merely a matter of obeying the Buddhist precepts but also of striving for a balance between the human and natural environments (Swearer 1995, 127). In

1993, Ājān's Pongsak's work was interrupted when he was charged with a *pārājika* violation of the monastic code (*vinaya*) and he was forced to disrobe. Pongsak, however, continues his efforts as a white-robed *anagārika* living in a forest *ashram* that overlooks the Mae Soy valley.

Other monks have been spared such harsh government treatment. Phra Khru Pitak Nanthakun began campaigning for forest preservation among villagers in his home village of Kew Muang, Nān Province, in 1975 when he was a novice monk. His efforts at education eventually bore fruit. Teak and other trees were planted in degraded areas to preserve watersheds. His activities expanded to include the construction of roads and reservoirs, the initiation of local co-operatives and the introduction of more appropriate alternatives to environmentally destructive cash crops and logging (Pibop 1995, 41). Luang Phọ Nān, abbot of Wat Samakī, Surin Province, in north-eastern Thailand, has spent the last forty years working to alleviate poverty among the people of north-eastern Thailand by helping them to preserve local forest habitat and to promote alternative approaches to community development (Pithaya 1995). In 1987 he became head of a network of development monks in Surin Province known as the Saha Dhamma Group. They have been successful in promoting village self-reliance through rice co-operatives, community stores with low-cost food, credit unions that provide low interest loans, integrated agriculture and animal husbandry (Pithaya 1995, 39).

The most ambitious organization of conservation and development monks is the Sekhiya Dhamma Sangha. The group was formed in 1989 and currently lists 700 on its membership list with 60 to 70 monks constituting the core of the leadership. The group's annual meeting and bi-monthly publication is facili-tated by the Thai Inter-Religious Commission for Development. Its main objectives are to co-ordinate the work of monks involved in development, to provide a network of communication and moral support, and to conduct training seminars and workshops. Projects range from support for a nunnery school in Rachaburi that provides free education and accommodation for poor girls (Pibop 1994, 22) to a 'dhamma walk' in 1996 around Songkhla Lake in southern Thailand to protest against the destruction of the ecosystem by commercial interests (Mayer 1996, 61). Admittedly, the efforts of Sekhiya Dhamma monks to teach alternatives to the personal, social and natural destruction that consumerism and economic exploitation bring to rural areas is an uphill battle. As the work of Luang Phọ Nān, Phra Khru Pitak and other activist monks illustrate, the economic and spiritual sides of development are difficult to keep in balance (Pithaya 1995, 40–44).

Santi Asok, founded by Phra Bodhiraksa in 1970, has emerged as the most tightly knit sectarian protest movement in the diverse spectrum of Buddhist groups on the periphery of the Thai political and religious mainstream. Bodhi-raksa became a monk after a career as an entertainer. At the age of thirty-six at the peak of his career he changed his life abruptly by resigning from his job and giving away most of his possessions, and after a conversion experience he decided to become a monk: 'Suddenly a brilliant flash occurred within me – a brightness, openness, and detachment that could not be explained in human terms. I knew only that my life opened before me and that the whole world seemed to be revealed' (Bodhiraksa 1982, 186).

Bodhiraksa was first ordained a Thammayut monk in 1970 and was later reordained into the Mahānikāi order after his Thammayut preceptor objected to his independent ways, which included establishing a centre near Nakorn Pathom called Asoka's Land (Thai: Dan Asok). The Supreme Sangha Council ordered Bodhiraksa to stop his activities at Dan Asok but he refused, and on 6 August 1975 he severed all ties with the national *sangha* organization (Swearer 1991, 670). Bodhiraksa then proceeded to found other centres for the 'People of Asok': Santi Asok in Bangkok, Sri Asok in Sisaket, Sali Asok in Nakorn Sawan and Pathom Asok in Nakorn Pathom. The movement grew rapidly, attracting both rural and urban middle class followers. In 1984, its core membership probably numbered more than 10,000, although the number of people marginally involved may have reached 100,000. It quickly gained national political visibility owing in part to former Major General Chamlong Srimuang's election as the governor of Bangkok and later as a member of parliament on the Phalang Dhamma (Power of Dhamma) ticket, a political party associated with Santi Asok. Chamlong maintained a cottage at Pathom Asok and was a leader in Kongtap Tham Munniti (Dhamma Army Foundation), a Santi Asok organization. Bodhiraksa's independence of the national *sangha*, his claim to high spiritual attainment (Thai: *phra ariya*) that invested him with special power both to ordain monks and to interpret the *dhamma*, the distinctive practices of the People of Asok communities that included a regimen of one vegetarian meal a day and a special ordained status for women (*sikkhamāt*), the movement's heterodox iconoclasm, Bodhiraksa's continuous and outspoken criticism of establishment Buddhism and the immorality in Thai society, and the possibility that the movement might gain political power through the Phalang Dhamma party proved to be a greater threat than either the political or the religious authorities could sanction.

Attacks on Santi Asoka came from many sides. Liberal Buddhist reformers criticized the movement for its excessive sectarianism and moralistic authoritarianism. In an interview on 15 February 1988, later published in booklet form, Phra Prayutto voiced the major criticisms held by ecclesiastic authorities, in particular, that Bodhiraksa had not only violated Thai ecclesiastical law but had placed himself above the *vinaya* (Payutto 1989). On 2 September 1988, the Ministry of Education ordered Santi Asok to submit to the authority of the Supreme Sangha Council, to constitute itself as a *wat* and abide by the regulations of the Sangha Administration Act of 1962, and to refrain from excessive criticism of the national *sangha* (Swearer 1991, 676). A meeting of 151 ecclesiastical governors on 22 November 1988 passed a resolution to instruct the Supreme Sangha Council to defrock Bodhiraksa. The government, fearing a protest reaction that would benefit the political fortunes of Chamlong Srimuang and the Phalang Dharma Party, tried unsuccessfully to work out a compromise. Finally, on 9 May 1989, a government decree expelling Bodhiraksa from the monastic order was delivered by the secretary of the Ministry of Education to Santi Asok headquarters. The decree contained seven charges, the most serious being that Bodhiraksa had broken the Sangha Administration Act of 1962 by ordaining sixty monks and twenty nuns (*sikkhamāts*) on his own authority (a charge similar to that brought against Khrubā Sīwijai) and that he had broken the *vinaya* rule forbidding claims to supranormal spiritual attainment. When Bodhiraksa refused to comply with the decree he was arrested. Two days later he was released on bail owing to government apprehension of demonstrations by his supporters. Bodhiraksa's case was deliberated upon for six years. Finally in December 1995, the court ruled that he was guilty as charged (Heikkilä-Horn 1997, 72). Bodhiraksa still leads a monastic lifestyle even though he is not officially recognized as a monk under *sangha* law. He divides his time between two Asok centres, Santi Asok and Pathom Asok, lives very simply in a small lodging (*kuti*) at each centre and generally preaches every morning at 4.00 a.m. when he is in residence (Heikkilä-Horn 1997, 45).

The future of Santi Asok is uncertain. It has been bent but not broken. Its largest centre is Sri Asok in Sisaket Province. The site contains fifty houses and the largest Asok school with an enrollment of approximately eighty students (Heikkilä-Horn 1997, 56). Like other contemporary Asok centres, the primary activities are agricultural – vegetable gardens, rice fields, mushroom culture – although it also maintains a tofu factory, a co-operative handicraft store and several workshops for the production of agricultural tools. It appears that Santi Asok will continue primarily as an agriculturally-based utopian community that continues to resist and protest against the establishment mainstream.

POSTSCRIPT. THAI BUDDHISM AND THE STATE IN THE TWENTY-FIRST CENTURY

During the first half of the twentieth century the state played a major role in defining and revitalizing modern Thai Buddhism. It created a vital, powerful centre that formed a national *sangha* inclusive of both the Mahānikai and Thammayut sects headquartered in Bangkok and organized nationwide along lines that paralleled the state. Throughout all regions of the country a relatively uniform system of monastic education and ritual practice gradually took shape. The distinctive local and regional traditions of teaching and practice that had characterized the time prior to Rama V were either eroded or disappeared. However, it would be erroneous to conclude that after 1910 Thai Buddhism became monolithic. Variations continued to exist. As we have seen, some monks on the periphery resisted the hegemonic power of state Buddhism centred in Bangkok, but, as with Khrūbā Sīwijai, accommodations were eventually worked out. Although the reformist Thammayut sect's promotion of meditation appears to have inspired the distinctive tradition of forest monks in north-eastern Thailand, the new Buddhism's standarization of curriculum and exams, and its elaborate hierarchy of ranks, were superimposed on local traditions.

From the era of King Mongkut to the present it might be said that the attitude of the government towards Buddhism encompassed four phases: the purification and revitalization of the *sāsana*; the creation of a unified and uniform national *saṅgha* for the promotion of national integration; the development of a Buddhist civil religion linked to the concept of the nation-state; and the exploitation of the *saṅgha* to promote specific political goals. These four phases can be correlated with: Mongkut's creation of the reformed Thammayut order; Chulalongkorn's support of the first National Sangha Administration Act; Wajirawut's adoption of the abstract notion of 'nation' (*chāt*) to complement Buddhism and kingship, the traditional foci of Thai loyalty and identity (F.E. Reynolds 1978, 135–6); and the *thammathūt* and *thammacarik* programmes promoted by the Sarit regime.

What will the twenty-first century hold for the relationship between Buddhism and the Thai state? The four phases mentioned above suggest that the nation-state has not only played an increasingly dominant role in the relationship, but that during the last half of the twentieth century political developments have contributed to the erosion of the place of Buddhism in Thai society relative to the state. As a case in point, it would be interesting to compare the place of the civil service in Thai society with the monkhood.

I have suggested in this essay that the Buddhist movements emergent in Thailand since World War II might be understood as responses to the gradual displacement of Buddhism as the core of Thai cultural and social identity. Although Wat Thammakāi in Prathum Thani, Buddhadāsa's Wat Suan Mokkha-balārāma in Chaiya, Sulak Sivaraksa's NGOs and Sri Asok in Sisaket differ profoundly in many respects, each can be seen as an attempt to revitalize Buddhism as the foundation of Thai personal, cultural and social identity. From this perspective the solutions they propose might be characterized as follows: the Thammakāi movement's project to restore a modernized version of a Buddhist civil religion built around a national shrine; Buddhadāsa's utopian vision of an egalitarian dhammic community governed by wisdom and compassion; Sulak Sivaraksa's inclusive, pluralistic society built on justice and human rights; and the agrarian, utopian communitas of Santi Asok.

With the exception of Wat Thammakāi, many of the voices of revitalization and reform, resistance and protest are being heard from the political periphery rather than the centre. Although the government has co-opted some of these groups, as in the Land of Dhamma – Land of Gold project, the power of others stems precisely from their relative independence from the centre: monks in the Thammayut lineage of Ājān Man's forest tradition, Buddhadāsa's doctrinal creativity outside of the *saṅgha*'s educational structures, the Sekhiya Dhamma monks organizing villagers to save and conserve a community forest, the Spirit in Education programmes in alternative education.

Buddhism originated in India as a religion on the periphery of the political and religious mainstream although throughout its history it has sought to negotiate a balance between these two poles. In the twenty-first century, the promise of the *sāsana* in Thailand appears to lie in the creative tension between new movements on the periphery and the civil religion of the centre.

NOTES

1. Transliteration from Thai follows the Library of Congress with some modifications. In particular, 'čh' is changed to 'j', e.g. Jao rather than Čhao. In most cases proper names also follow Thai pronunciation rather than the Pāli spelling, e.g. Mahāthāt rather than Mahādhātu.

2. Personal communication, 23 December, 1997. I am grateful to Thanissaro Bhikkhu (Geoff DeGraff), abbot of the Metta Forest Monastery, Valley Center, California, for his critical reading of this essay. I have incorporated several of his suggestions into the text. Although Thanissaro favors a historical narrative approach to *sangha*–state relations in modern Thailand over a systematic model because it provides a more nuanced, historically accurate picture, he suggests that a tripartite centre–periphery paradigm adapted from the narratives of the first three Buddhist councils could be applied to Thailand. He sees the First Council as a balance between the royal sponsor (King Ajatasattu) and the *sangha* and among different *sangha* constitutents. Although according to the texts the council achieved a common standard for *dhamma* and *vinaya*, it did not try to impose it on those who did not participate. The centre is strong. The periphery is independent but co-operative. They coexist in peace. The Second Council can be seen as a case of the periphery straightening out the corrupt centre. The monks in Vesali abused their power, the abused monks gathered support from the forest dwellers, and the dominant consensus managed to convince the royal sponsor of the conference of the rightness of their view. The Third Council reverses the dynamic. It is a case of the centre, King Asoka and the members of the convening council, establishing an orthodoxy in the face of a problematic pluralism. Applying this paradigm to Theravāda history in Thailand, Thanissaro proposes that in times of crisis, models two and three come to the forefront, yet in subtle ways that reflect solutions grounded in the relativity of Thai custom rather than rigid, codified laws. Using a musical analogy, he suggests that *sangha*–state relationships in Thailand are more analogous to the improvisation of a Thai musical performance (*phin phāt*), rather than to the formal notation of classical Western music.

3. Phra Payutto (Dhammapiṭaka), the most highly regarded scholar-monk in the Thai *sangha*, has produced an important body of scholarly work including two important Pāli dictionaries. He made a major contribution to the new Thai edition of the Pāli canon and the Mahidol University CD-ROM Pāli canon. Although he has held administrative posts in the *sangha*, serving as the Deputy Secretary-General of Mahāchulalongkorn Buddhist University and the abbot of Wat Phra Phīrain in Bangkok, he has devoted most of his monastic life to scholarly work. His monastic career has been less independent and idiosyncratic than Buddhadāsa's but, unlike Wajirayān he has not been as centrally involved in the national *sangha* as an ecclesiastical institution.

BIBLIOGRAPHY

Andaya, Barbara Watson (1978) 'Statecraft in the Reign of Lü Tai of Sukhodaya (*c.* 1347–1374)', in *Buddhism and Legitimation of Power in Thailand, Burma, and Laos,* Smith, Bardwell L. (ed.). Chambersburg, PA: Anima Books, 2–19.

Bizot, François (1988) *Les Traditions de la Pabbajjā en Asie du Sud-Est: Recherches sur le Bouddhisme Khmer, iv.* Philologisch-Historische Klasse Dritte Folge, no. 160. Göttingen: Vandhenhoeck & Ruprecht.

Bodhiraksa, Phra (1982) *Sacca Haeng Chīwit* [The Truth of My Life]. Bangkok: Dhammasanti.

Bradley, William L. (1966). 'Prince Mongkut and Jesse Caswell', *Journal of the Siam Society* 54 2 (January), 29–41.

Buddhadāsa Bhikkhu (1975) *Kan Tham Ngan Duai Jit Wāng* [Acting Without Attachment On Behalf of Society]. Bangkok: Society For the Propagation of Buddhism.

——(1976) *Sangamaniyama Chanit Tī Chuai Lōk Dai* [The Kind of Socialism That Can Help the World]. Bangkok: Sublime Life Mission.

Engle, David M. (1957) *Law and Kingship in Thailand During the Reign of King Chulalongkorn.* Michigan Papers on South and Southeast Asia, no. 9. Ann Arbor: University of Michigan.

Heikkilä-Horn, Marja-Leena (1997) *Buddhism With Open Eyes: Belief and Practice of Santi Asok.* Bangkok: Fah Apai.

Ishii, Yoneo (1986) *Sangha, State, and Society: Thai Buddhism in History.* Honolulu: University of Hawaii Press.

Jackson, Peter A. (1989) *Buddhism, Legitimation, and Conflict; The Political Functions of Urban Thai Buddhism.* Singapore: Institute of Southeast Asian Studies.

——(1991) 'Thai-Buddhist Identity: Debates on the Traiphuum Phra Ruang', in *The Ram Khamhaeng Controversy: Collected Papers,* Chamberlain, James R. (ed.). Bangkok: The Siam Society, 191–226.

Kamala Tiyavanich (1997) *Forest Recollections: Wandering Monks in Twentieth-Century Thailand.* Honolulu: University of Hawaii Press.

Keyes, Charles F. (1971) 'Buddhism and National Integration in Thailand', *Journal of Asian Studies* 30, 3 (May); 551–67.

——(1977) 'Millennialism, Theravada Buddhism, and Thai Society', *Journal of Asian Studies,* 36 2 (February); 283–302.

——(1981) 'The Death of Two Buddhist Saints in Thailand', Williams, Michael (ed.) *Charisma and Sacred Biography* (Journal of the American Academy of Religion Thematic Series) 48, 3 & 4; 149–80.

——(1987) *Thailand: Buddhist Kingdom as Modern Nation-State.* Boulder and London: Westview Press.

——(1989) 'Buddhist Politics and Their Revolutionary Origins in Thailand', *International Political Science Review* 10/1 (February), 121–42.

Mayer, Theodore (1996) 'Thailand's New Buddhist Movements in Historical and Political Context', In *Loggers, Monks, Students: Four Essays on Thailand,* Husaker, Bryan *et al.,* (ed.) DeKalb, IL: Center for Southeast Asian Studies, Northern Illinois University, 33–66.

Mun (Man) Bhūridatta Thera, Phra Ajaan (1991) *A Heart Released: The Teachings of Phra Ajaan Mun Bhūridatta Thera.* Selangor, Malaysia: W.A.V.E.

Payutto, Phra (1988) *Karanī Santiasok* [The Case of Santi Asok]. Bangkok: Buddhadhamma Foundation.

Pibop Udomittipong (1995) 'Buddhist Natural Conservation in Thailand', *Seeds of Peace* 11/1 (Jan.–Apr. 1995), 39–42.

Pithaya Wongkun (1995) *Luang Pho Nan: Building Peace* trans. Joshua J. Prokopy. Spirit In Education Movement, Occasional Paper III. Bangkok: Thai Inter-Religious Commission for Development and Santi Pracha Dhamma Institute.

Reynolds, Craig J. (1976) 'Buddhist Cosmography in Thai History, with Special Reference to Nineteenth Century Cultural Change', *Journal of Asian Studies* 25/2 (February), 203–20.

Reynolds, Frank E. (1978) 'Legitimation and Rebellion: Thailand's Civic Religion and the Student Uprising of October, 1973', in Bardwell L. Smith (ed.) *Buddhism and Legitimation of Power in Thailand, Burma, and Laos*, 134–46.

Reynolds, Frank E. and Mani Reynolds (1981) *The Three Worlds of King Ruang*. Berkeley CA: Asian Humanities Press.

Riggs, Fred W. (1966) *Thailand. The Modernization of a Bureaucratic Polity*. Honolulu: East–West Center Press.

Sā Putasathewa (1922) *Nangsū' Thet Pathomsomphōt* [A sermon version the Buddha's enlightenment]. Bangkok: Sōphan-phiphantthanāchon.

Sanguan Chōtisukarat (1972) *Khon Dī Mu'ang Nū'a* [The good people of northern Thailand]. Bangkok: Odian Store.

Santikaro Bhikkhu (1996) 'Buddhadasa Bhikkhu: Life and Society through the Natural Eyes of Voidness' in Queen, Christopher S. and King, Sallie B. (eds.) *Engaged Buddhism: Buddhist Liberation Movements in Asia*, Albany, NY: State University of New York Press, 147–193.

Siffin, William J. (1966) *The Thai Bureaucracy. Institutional Change Development*. Honolulu: East-West Center Press.

Somboon Suksamran (1976) *Political Buddhism in Southeast Asia*. New York: St Martin's Press.

——(1982) *Buddhism and Politics in Thailand: A Study of Socio-Political Change and Political Activism of the Thai Sangha*. Singapore: Institute of Southeast Asian Studies.

——(1988) 'A Buddhist Approach to Development: The Case of "Development Monks in Thailand",' in Lim Teck Ghee (ed.) *Reflections on Development in Southeast Asia*, 26–48. Singapore: Institute of Southeast Asian Studies.

——(1993) *Buddhism and Political Legitimacy*. Bangkok: Chulalongkorn University.

Somphorn Phechāwut (1972) 'Lak Khamson Khong Phutasāsanā Kap Kān Phatthana Thong Thin.' [The teachings of Buddhism regarding community development]', *Chofā* [The publication of Kitthiwuttho's foundation] 7/(October), 70–80.

Somphorn Thephsitthā (1985) *Udomkān Phaendin Tham-Phaendin Thong* [The ideals of Land of Dhamma–Land of Gold]. Bangkok: National Council on Social Welfare.

'Spirit in Education Movement' (1996/1997), Prospectus.

Sulak Sivaraksa (1985) 'The Growth of the Voluntary Sector in Siam', in Sulak Sivaraksa, *Siamese Resurgence*. Bangkok: Asian Cultural Forum on Development, 312–26.

——(1989) *Crisis of Siamese Identity*. Occasional Paper. Bangkok: Santi Pracha Dhamma Institute.

——(1992) *Seeds of Peace*. Berkeley, CA: Parallax Press.

——(1995) 'Acceptance Speech for Right Livelihood Award', *Seeds of Peace* 12/(Jan.–Apr.) 44–7.

Swearer, Donald K. (1973) 'Community Development and Thai Buddhism. The Dynamics of Tradition and Change', in *Visakha Puja 2516*. Bangkok: Buddhist Association of Thailand, 59–67.

——(1988) 'The Monk As Prophet and Priest', in Gaeffke, Peter and Utz David A. (eds.) *The Countries of South Asia: Boundaries, Extensions, and Interrelations.* Philadelphia: Department of South Asia Regional Studies, 71–90.

——(1991) 'Fundamentalistic Movements in Theravada Buddhism', in Marty, Martin E and Appleby, R. Scott (eds.) *Fundamentalisms Observed.* Chicago and London: University of Chicago Press, 628–90.

——(1993) 'Buddhist Eschatology, Millenialism, and Revitalization Movements', in Sulak Sivaraksa (ed.) *Buddhist Perceptions of Desirable Societies in the Future.* Bangkok: Thai Inter-Religious Commission for Development, 148–166.

——(1995) *The Buddhist World of Southeast Asia.* Albany, NY: State University of New York Press.

——(1996) 'Sulak Sivaraksa's Vision for Renewing Society', in Christopher Queen and Sallie King (eds) *Engaged Buddhism: Buddhist Liberation Movements in Asia.* Albany: State University of New York Press, 195–237.

Swearer, Donald K. and Sommai Premchit (1978) 'The Relationship Between the Religious and Political Orders in Northern Thailand (14th–16th Centuries)', in Bardwell L. Smith (ed.) *Religion and the Legitimation of Power in Thailand, Laos, and Burma.* Chambersburg, PA: Anima Books, 34–51.

Tambiah, Stanley J. (1976) *World Conqueror and World Renouncer. A Study of Buddhism and Polity in Thailand Against a Historical Background.* Cambridge: Cambridge University Press.

——(1984) *The Buddhist Saints of the Forest and the Cult of Amulets: A Study in Charisma, Hagiography, Sectarianism, and Millenial Buddhism.* Cambridge: Cambridge University Press.

Thanissaro Bhikkhu (1997) Personal comunication, 23 December.

Taylor, J.L. (1990) 'New Buddhist Movement in Thailand: An "Individualistic Revolution", Reform and Political Dissonance.' *Journal of Southeast Asian Studies* 31/1 (March), 135–54.

——(1993) *Forest Monks and the Nation-State: An Anthropological and Historical Study in Northeastern Thailand.* Singapore: Institute of Southeast Asian Studies.

Thitma Khuntiranan (1994) 'The Komol Keemthong Foundation', *Seeds of Peace* 10/3 (Sept.–Dec. 2537), 23–4.

Vajirañāṇavarorasa, Prince (1979) *Autobiography: The Life of Prince-Patriarch Vajirañāṇa of Siam,* trans. and ed. Craig J. Reynolds. Athens: Ohio University Press.

Wenk, Klaus (1968) *The Restoration of Thailand Under Rama I, 1782–1809,* trans. Greeley Stahl. Association for Asian Studies: Monographs and Papers, no. 24. Tucson, Ariz.: University of Arizona Press.

Wyatt, David, K. (1969) *The Politics of Reform in Thailand: Education in the Reign of King Chulalongkorn.* New Haven and London: Yale University Press.

——(1982) *Thailand: A Short History.* New Haven and London: Yale University Press.

10
RENEWAL AND RESISTANCE: TIBETAN BUDDHISM IN THE MODERN ERA

RONALD D. SCHWARTZ

INTRODUCTION: THE DEVELOPMENT OF BUDDHISM IN TIBET

Buddhism was brought to Tibet in the seventh century, following the consolidation of a Tibetan empire under the king Srong-brtsan-sgam-po. It became the official religion of Tibet in the second half of the eighth century during the reign of Khri-Srong-lde-brtsan (Stein 1972, 65–8). The collapse of the Tibetan monarchy in the middle of the ninth century precluded the further development of a centralized state ruled by a Buddhist king. A period of civil war followed in which the old aristocratic families attempted to carve up portions of the kingdom for themselves.[1] Thus, throughout most of Tibetan history the monasteries were never subjugated by a strong centralized power. Religious leadership in Tibet was much more free-floating and charismatic in its origins, based on the personal qualities of particular teachers or lamas.[2] Important monasteries exercised considerable political power in their regions. Individual lamas, and the religious establishments that they founded and headed, vied for power and were principal players in the political arena, seeking alliances with both internal and external forces.

The development of the institution of the reincarnated lama, who is tutored as a child to assume control over a religious establishment (his *bla-brang*), formalizes this dependence on personal charisma in Tibetan Buddhism. This method of succession for lamas first appears within the *bKa'-rgyud-pa* order during the thirteenth and fourteenth centuries as an alternative to the hereditary lineage of the *Sa-skya-pa* (Samuel 1993, 494). During the fourteenth and fifteenth centuries it spread to other religious orders. Clerical Buddhism in Tibet has come to be organized around these exceptional teachers, who are also the bearers of the tantric tradition, and who combine spiritual and political leadership as heads of powerful *bla-brang*.

Tibet poses something of a special case in terms of the traditional paradigm for Buddhist kingship. The lama as head of state originates with the relationship between the Mongol emperor Kublai Khan and the *Sa-skya* lama. A centralized Tibetan state only emerged again with the ascendancy of the *dGe-lugs-pa* sect under the 5th Dalai Lama in the seventeenth century, installed by Gushri Khan, a Mongol ally of the *dGe-lugs-pa* (Shakabpa 1967, 100–24). During the eighteenth century the Manchu government of China militarily intervened several times in response to internal disorder and external threats, but effective Chinese influence over the Lhasa government through its commissioners (*ambans*) diminished over the course of the nineteenth century. Because the 9th to 12th Dalai Lamas all died young, administration was largely in the hands of one or another regent, reincarnated lamas allied with monastic factions within the great *dGe-lugs-pa* monasteries (Shakabpa 1967, 140–91; Goldstein 1989, 44).

Tibetan political theory describes the relationship between the Dalai Lama, as the temporal and spiritual ruler of Tibet, and the Manchu emperors of China in terms of the roles of lama and patron (*mchod-yon*) rather than as political subordination (Shakabpa 1967, 71; Goldstein 1989, 44). The traditional formula for the Tibetan polity under the Dalai Lamas was 'religion and politics combined' (*chos-srid-gnyis-ldan*). This formula was epitomized by the Dalai Lama himself, who combined in his person both functions. In turn, the government of the Dalai Lama was both the most powerful patron of religion, protecting the interests of the monasteries under its jurisdiction, and, at the same time, was headed by the highest religious figure, the Dalai Lama (Schwartz 1994, 89; Goldstein 1989, 2).

The government headed by the Dalai Lama, however, never extended to all Tibetan-inhabited areas, nor did it succeed in suppressing other sects of Tibetan Buddhism.[3] Loyalty to local lamas and local powers remained foremost for Tibetans. The means of force at the disposal of the Lhasa regime were limited, and thus the autonomy and functioning of the Tibetan state depended on maintaining a precarious balance between external powers and competing internal interests (Norbu 1985).

THE TIBETAN STATE AND THE MONASTERIES IN THE TWENTIETH CENTURY

The balance was upset when, largely out of fear of Russian influence in Tibet, the British mounted an invasion in 1904, withdrawing only after extracting diplomatic and commercial concessions from the Lhasa government (Richardson 1962, 73–97). Before the British mission reached Lhasa the 13th Dalai Lama fled to Mongolia, where he unsuccessfully sought to enlist the aid of the Russians. The Chinese responded by stripping the Dalai Lama of his temporal power and in response to the British incursion attempted for the first time to bring all of Tibet under direct control. An army was sent to pacify the autonomous principalities of eastern Tibet, incorporating them for purposes of administration and taxation into the Chinese province of Sichuan. The Dalai Lama was allowed to return to Lhasa in 1909, but fled again after only a few months, this time to British India, as the Chinese army continued on to enter and occupy Lhasa. The Chinese government now responded by stripping the 13th Dalai Lama of his religious titles as well as his temporal power and declared that a search for a new incarnation was to be initiated (Goldstein 1989, 45–58).

Following the collapse of the Manchu dynasty and the establishment of the Chinese Republic in 1912, a successful armed rebellion was organized by the Dalai Lama from exile, resulting in the expulsion of all Chinese troops from territory under the jurisdiction of the Lhasa government. Uprisings against the Chinese also took place in eastern Tibetan areas. The 13th Dalai Lama returned to Lhasa in January 1913. He refused an offer by the Nationalist Chinese government to restore his rank and titles, declaring that henceforth he would rule Tibet without titles and dispensations from the Chinese government – effectively a declaration of Tibetan independence (Shakabpa 1967, 238–48; Goldstein 1989, 59–62).

During his three years in British India the 13th Dalai Lama was exposed to modern political ideas and saw the importance of an efficient bureaucracy and a modern army. Nevertheless, he faced enormous obstacles in reforming and modernizing Tibet. Attempts to raise taxes on monastic and aristocratic estates to finance an expansion of the Tibetan army met with immediate opposition.[4] The *dGe-lugs-pa* monastic establishment in particular feared not only the loss of revenues, but the potential challenge to the monopoly on force represented by the mass of monks at their disposal. They also feared that Western ideas and advancing secularism would undermine the commitment of the Tibetan state to support religion.

Unlike in *Theravādin* countries, where only a small minority of the population become monks and nuns, Tibetan monasteries before 1959 recruited on a mass basis.[5] Monks were placed in monasteries by their families at seven or eight years of age, sometimes against their will, for a variety of economic as well as religious reasons – to fulfil corvée tax obligations, to reduce the economic burden at home, to gain access to monastic resources, or to enhance the prestige of the family. Only a small minority actively pursued a life of scholarship or meditation. The three major *dGe-lugs-pa* monasteries around Lhasa – Drepung ('Bras-spungs) with some 10,000 monks in 1951, Sera (Se-rwa) with 7,000, and Ganden (dGa'-ldan) with 5,000 – constituted a powerful army in their own right, and were not above challenging the central government if they felt that their interests were threatened.

In 1921, during the reign of the 13th Dalai Lama, several thousand monks of Loseling (bLo-gsal-gling) college in Drepung marched to the Norbulingka (Nor-bu-gling-kha) and vandalized the Dalai Lama's gardens, demanding to see the Dalai Lama, in a dispute over ownership of a monastic estate (Goldstein 1989, 496–506). Relations between Loseling and the government had been strained since 1912, when Drepung had supported the Chinese and sheltered the fleeing Chinese Amban at a time when, following the collapse of Manchu rule, the Dalai Lama and the government were attempting to drive the Chinese from Lhasa. In the end Loseling was forced to capitulate and surrender its leaders after the monastery was surrounded by government troops (Goldstein 1989, 104–8).

By 1924, fearing a threat to his own power, the 13th Dalai Lama abandoned efforts to modernize Tibet. The officers responsible for building up the army were dismissed and the English school at Gyantse, opened in 1923, was closed.[6] After the death of the 13th Dalai Lama in 1933 Tibet entered a period of isolation and political infighting during which the conservative monastic establishment presented a formidable obstacle to any opening to the modern world. The 14th Dalai Lama was identified at the age of two in 1937, but Tibet was ruled until 1950 by two regents. Reting (Rwa-sgreng), the first regent, resigned in 1941 at the time of the young Dalai Lama's ordination as a novice (*dge-tshul*). His continuing intrigues to regain the regency from Taktra (sTag-brag), his successor, divided Tibetan society, pitted the monasteries against each other, and culminated in 1947 in the open armed rebellion of the monks of Sera Che (Sera-byes – one of the two colleges in Sera), who supported Reting against the Tibetan government. Some 200–300 monks died in the battle to retake the monastery (Goldstein 1989: 464–520).

Reting died in prison in 1947, apparently poisoned, after his arrest on charges of conspiring to assassinate Taktra. He had been accused of requesting military assistance from the Nationalist Chinese government of Chiang Kai-shek and of offering to give away Tibetan territory and accept Chinese overlordship in return. Throughout this period elements of the monastic community continued to see the Chinese as allies and sought their help in advancing their own political and economic interests. The political independence of Tibet held little value for the monks. On the other hand, many of the monks came from areas of Khams and A-mdo that were under Chinese jurisdiction. Thus they were inclined to seek Chinese protection when in trouble. The Chinese cultivated relationships with these elements of the monastic leadership, portraying themselves as patrons and protectors of religion.

RELIGION IN TIBET UNDER COMMUNIST RULE

The Tibetan government, and the institutions of Tibetan society, were ill prepared to resist the Chinese invasion. The Chinese People's Liberation Army entered Lhasa in 1951, following the signing of the Seventeen-Point Agreement between representatives of the Tibetan government and the new communist government in Beijing. The agreement offered assurances that the traditional political and economic system in Tibet would be allowed to continue for some time in return for acceptance of Chinese sovereignty over Tibet. However, eastern Tibetan areas in Khams and A-mdo that came under direct Chinese administration were not covered by the agreement, and thus the Tibetan population in these areas was not exempted from the socialist reforms under way in China, which included attacks on religion and the destruction of monasteries. Monasteries in these eastern Tibetan areas quickly became centres of resistance to the Chinese. The fear of similar measures being introduced in central Tibet, combined with a flood of refugees from the east, in turn precipitated attacks on Chinese troops by a growing guerilla army. The uprising in 1959 against the Chinese presence in central Tibet involved many hundreds of monks, who took up arms to protect the Dalai Lama as he fled to India along with some 80,000 Tibetans. A draconian suppression of religion marks Chinese policy from this point onward until the relaxation of religious policy in the 1980s.

During the first few years following the uprising most of the monks and nuns were sent home and the monasteries and nunneries closed. Monks and nuns were denounced as 'counter-revolutionaries' and targeted in 'struggle sessions'. The entire institutional framework of Buddhism in Tibet was forcibly dismantled. The inauguration of the Cultural Revolution in Tibet in 1966 marked the beginning of a complete assault on Tibetan society and culture. Under the banner of destroying the 'four olds' (old ideology, old culture, old customs, old habits), Tibetans were punished for deviating even slightly from the new proletarian culture exemplified by the Red Guards (many thousands of whom were young Chinese who had come to Tibet to launch the campaign). Any display of religion was prohibited, the remaining monasteries were torn down, and all religious objects confiscated or destroyed.[7] The new round of 'struggle sessions' and political education aimed to eradicate every vestige of Tibetan culture and identity, targeting not just former 'class enemies' and 'reactionaries', but virtually anyone. The practice of religion for both lay and clergy alike survived only in memory.

The renewed practise of Buddhism did not begin until the end of the Cultural Revolution and the implementation of Deng Xiaoping's reform policies in Tibet after 1979. Individual religious practices – burning incense, reciting prayers and performing rituals, building altars – reappeared spontaneously as people discovered that they were no longer forbidden. Throughout Tibet there has been an enormous amount of spontaneous rebuilding and repopulating of monasteries and nunneries. In remote areas this often went on without government interference. The break-up of the communes in the 1980s, and the division of the land among individual families under the 'household responsibility system', has meant that Tibetan families have been able to take their agricultural surplus and use it to support the monasteries.[8] In Tibet before 1959 the large monasteries received income from extensive estate holdings, as well as endowment funds, government grants and donations. Lay support for the monasteries following the reconstruction during the 1980s has been entirely voluntary, consisting of donations to temples, money and food to sponsor ceremonies, or contributions to individual monks.

The traditional organization of the monasteries, however, has not been restored. The large monasteries in Tibet had an elaborate system of administration and self-government. Monasteries such as Sera, Drepung and Ganden were made up of independent colleges (*grwa-tshang*), each headed by an abbot (*khan-po*). Abbots were appointed for a fixed term of six years by the Dalai Lama. Other officials selected by the college were responsible for maintaining discipline within the college, administering the college's finances and overseeing the curriculum. The colleges in turn consisted of a number of residential units (*khang-mtshan*) in which monks enrolled, generally on the basis of their region of origin. These, too, had their own economic resources and internal administration.

This self-governing monastic organization has been supplanted in the rebuilt monasteries in Tibet by the Democratic Management Committees established by the Religious Affairs Bureau of the Chinese government. The selection of members of these committees has become a continuing source of friction between the monks and the Chinese administration – as has the allocation and control of economic resources. The structure of colleges has been abolished. The young monks are aware of the former system, and the colleges and residences retain their former names, but the monks at the large monasteries are amalgamated into one unit. An abbot is selected for the entire monastery, but he has no administrative power. Instead, important decisions are made by the Democratic Management Committee, which in turn is supervised by the Communist Party apparatus and the Public Security Bureau.[9]

THE INDEPENDENCE MOVEMENT AND TIBETAN BUDDHISM IN EXILE

The notion of a political movement for Tibetan independence that incorporates both modern political ideas of freedom and human rights along with the central values of Buddhism is largely the creation of the present Dalai Lama. A guest of Nehru, and surrounded by the political environment of democratic India, with its own legacy of colonial rule and an independence movement, the Dalai Lama early on came to see the struggle for Tibetan independence in a similar light. He was profoundly influenced by Gandhi, who had emphasized non-violence, and thus linked political activism to spiritual values consonant with Buddhism. A draft Tibetan constitution was prepared by the government-in-exile in 1963. Here, for the first time, a framework for an independent democratic Tibetan state is portrayed as consistent with the values of Buddhism.[10]

The Dalai Lama has on a number of occasions suggested that he should in fact remove himself from a direct political role in the Tibetan government, turning over the exercise of power to democratically elected representatives. Efforts have been made to democratize the administration of the government-in-exile, particularly since 1991, when members of the Dalai Lama's cabinet (the *bka'-shag*) were first elected by the parliament-in-exile. Nevertheless, the principal impetus for these changes has come from the Dalai Lama himself, who regularly scolds Tibetans for refusing to participate actively in the democratic process. But the authority of the Dalai Lama, who is regarded by Tibetans as an emanation of Avalokiteśvara, the Buddha of compassion and the patron deity of Tibet, is based in religion. Thus, many Tibetans in exile perceive democracy as a 'gift' bestowed by the Dalai Lama on his subjects rather than their right as citizens, and find it difficult to imagine a Tibetan government without the Dalai Lama as its head.

Since the 1960s a distinctive modern political culture has evolved among the exile community. The educational system instituted by the exile government for Tibetan refugee children in India has exposed a new generation of Tibetans to modern ideas, including ideas of political democracy, while retaining the Dalai Lama as a unifying symbol.[11] The elements of this political culture are overtly nationalistic. It includes the symbols of the modern nation-state – a flag, a national anthem and commemorative events (most important being the 10 March commemoration of the 1959 uprising, which has become the Tibetan national day). This is very much an 'invented' national tradition, the symbols themselves (e.g. the flag) going back no further than a few decades and reflecting the attempt of Tibet to establish its position as a modern nation-state within the twentieth century.

Buddhist institutions in exile throughout most of their history have not been centres of political activism, seeing their primary role as the preservation of monastic traditions. The traditional 'three seats' – the monasteries of Ganden, Sera and Drepung – were all re-established in south India, with as much of the internal structure as possible. Likewise, the system of reincarnate lamas was maintained, and efforts were made to find incarnations (*yang-srid*) from among the children born into the refugee community. The government-in-exile has been obliged to represent itself as the patron of all of the sects of Tibetan Buddhism – *bKa'-rgyud-pa, Sa-skya-pa, rNying-ma-pa*, and the indigenous *Bon* religion, as well as the *dGe-lugs-pa* religious establishment, which no longer has an exclusive claim on the support of the Tibetan government. These other sects were especially prevalent in areas outside the jurisdiction of the Lhasa government, in Khams and A-mdo, from where many refugees come. Thus, seats in the Assembly of People's Deputies, the elected body of the exile government, are reserved for representatives of each of the five sects of Tibetan Buddhism and the three regions of Tibet.

Different centres of monastic power and prestige have flourished in exile, serving not only a Tibetan constituency, but increasingly proselytizing to a non-Tibetan population as well, with individual lama-entrepreneurs building Dharma centres in Western countries (as well as East Asian countries like Taiwan and Singapore). Throughout the 1970s and into the 1980s this Western Buddhist mission was largely non-political, focusing on the universality of Buddhist teaching and practices rather than on the particular national situation of Tibetans. On this basis, diaspora Tibetans have managed to portray themselves to Western sponsors and benefactors as a deeply religious people with a spiritual gift for the whole world, as a non-violent people, and as hapless victims of oppression deserving aid and support.[12]

A transnational political movement specifically focused on the political situation inside of Tibet, with Tibetan independence as its goal, has only emerged since the outbreak of renewed protest inside of Tibet in 1987. Demonstrations by monks and nuns in the streets of Lhasa fostered a new image of committed, politically active Buddhism. Western tourists who have travelled to Tibet in turn found a new basis for relationships with Tibetans (Schwartz 1991). This activist picture of Tibetan Buddhism, with young monks and nuns braving arrest, imprisonment and death for the peaceful expression of their beliefs has been specifically emphasized by such Western-based advocacy organizations as the International Campaign for Tibet and Students for a Free Tibet. The award of the Nobel Peace Prize to the Dalai Lama in 1989, which was a way of acknowledging renewed protest inside Tibet, has done much to enlarge the political dimension of Tibetanness.

In general terms, however, the Tibet movement in the West has relied on an image of Tibet as an 'endangered global spiritual resource' (McLagan 1997). Tibetan culture has been defined primarily in spiritual terms, and monks in particular have been portrayed as the exemplars of that culture. The Year of Tibet in 1995, which prominently featured performances of ritual art and music by Tibetan monks, used this 'culture strategy' as a way of recruiting Westerners to the Tibet movement. Aspects of Tibetan Buddhist culture are idealized and exaggerated, separated from an often highly secretive original context, and made accessible to a mass audience. In this way the Tibet movement draws on widespread New Age spirituality and prevailing orientalist expectations of Tibet as a kind of Shangri-la in promoting the Tibetan cause.[13]

RELIGION AND THE RENEWAL OF PROTEST IN TIBET

The most recent wave of protest against Chinese rule in Tibet began in the autumn of 1987 with three demonstrations in the centre of Lhasa, the Tibetan capital, led by monks from the nearby monasteries of Drepung and Sera. Almost all of the demonstrations that have taken place in Lhasa since 1987 have had the same form. Small groups of monks and nuns assemble near the Barkhor (Barskor), the circular lane in the centre of the old part of Lhasa, then march around the Barkhor circumambulating the Jokhang (Jo-khang) temple, carrying the Tibetan flag as they shout independence slogans. After completing a circuit or two of the Barkhor, the protesting monks and nuns are sometimes joined by ordinary Tibetans who fall in behind. This continues until the demonstration is halted by the arrival of security forces.

In choosing the Barkhor as the site for protest in the first demonstration on 27 September, the Drepung monks were able to mobilize and build on the familiar meaning of *bskor-ba*, the circumambulation of holy places (Ekvall 1964, 235; Schwartz 1994, 26–9). By combining *bskor-ba* with symbols of Tibetan nationhood – the Dalai Lama, the flag – the Drepung monks forged a link between the powerful motivation that underlies religious ritual and the national consciousness that divides Tibetans from Chinese. At the same time, the symbolic centre of Tibetan protest since 1987 has been the Jokhang temple. The Jokhang was damaged during the Cultural Revolution and remained closed until 1979, but it has now been restored and continues to function as a religious centre for Tibetans with its own monastic staff. It remains the most important place of pilgrimage for Tibetans and it continues to evoke a multi-layered symbolism of Tibetan nationhood and political identity that stretches back to the time of Srong-brtsan-sgam-po and the ancient kings.[14]

As protest has continued inside Tibet virtually every religious act has assumed political significance. The Chinese administration has been forced to impose ever tighter restrictions on religious observances. Events in October 1989, at a time when martial law was in force in Lhasa and overt political demonstrations were impossible, illustrate the dilemma faced by the authorities. Residents poured into the Barkhor to celebrate the award of the Nobel Peace Prize to the Dalai Lama by performing *bskor-ba*, burning immense quantities of *bsangs* (juniper branches) in incense burners along the Barkhor circuit and throwing handfuls of *rtsam-pa* (roasted barley flour) into the air (*lha-rgyal* – a symbolic gesture associated with the Dalai Lama). A large crowd proceeded to the Norbulingka, the Dalai Lama's summer palace, leaving *kha-btags* (ceremonial scarves) at the entrance.

At first the authorities took no notice of the celebration, since it fell within the bounds of traditional religious practice and the crowd did not display a Tibetan flag or chant independence slogans. But after several days, meetings were organized in government departments to denounce the award of the Peace Prize to the Dalai Lama and security forces were instructed to begin arresting people throwing *rtsam-pa*, whose activities were henceforth to be treated as 'counter-revolutionary'. Likewise burning incense around the Barkhor was banned and public religious observances in monasteries were forbidden without official permission.

To the extent that the Chinese government has attempted to take over the role of legitimate patron of religion, usurping the traditional role of the pre-1959 Tibetan government, it has been drawn into the logic of Tibetan religious politics. This was graphically illustrated by events during the *smon-lam chen-mo* (Great Prayer Festival) in March 1988. The festival had been held in 1986 for the first time since the 1959 uprising and was thus an important marker of the new policy of religious toleration. The monks of Ganden, Drepung and Sera had collectively decided to boycott the festival in 1988 to protest against the continuing imprisonment of demonstrators from the previous fall.[15] Eventually fifty-nine arrested monks were released, largely because of the intercession of the Panchen Lama, and in the end about half of the monks were persuaded to participate.

Protest broke out on 5 March when monks assembled for the close of the festival stood up and challenged the local Party officials, demanding the release of their comrades who remained imprisoned. After completing three circuits of the Barkhor they retreated into the sanctuary of the Jokhang, closing the heavy wooden doors of the temple behind them. Eventually, Chinese troops forced open the doors and stormed the temple, beating and arresting the monks inside. But the Party officials, trapped for two hours in an office in the Jokhang, were publicly humiliated.

The *smon-lam chen-mo* in fact has a special significance among Tibetan religious festivals. Instituted by Tsong-kha-pa in the fifteenth century, the festival rededicates Tibetan society each year to the supremacy of Buddhism (Tucci 1980, 149–53). During *smon-lam* the political roles of the secular authorities and the monasteries are reversed. In pre-1959 Tibet the administration of Lhasa was turned over to the monastic officials of Drepung (the *zhal-ngo*), who traditionally police the festival. The ceremonial attendance of state officials likewise signified their submission to the authority of religion and their acceptance of the role of custodians of religion. Whether the Chinese government was fully aware of the symbolism of the festival for Tibetans is impossible to know. But the meaning of the action by the monks was clear to Tibetans, for whom it signified the denial of religious legitimacy to the Chinese state.

PROTEST BY MONKS AND NUNS

The first demonstrations in 1987–8 were initiated by monks from the large *dGe-lugs-pa* monasteries near Lhasa whose allegiance is to the Dalai Lama. Protest has spread as dissident monks have communicated with affiliated monasteries and nunneries in nearby areas of central Tibet. Protest has also spread to monasteries and nunneries belonging to the other schools of Tibetan Buddhism, as well as to monasteries and nunneries in more remote rural areas. A detailed compilation of Tibetans known to have been detained for political offences during the period 1987–95 identifies 1,276 prisoners by name, of whom 610 remained in detention. Two-thirds of those detained have been monks and nuns. Almost one third of the detained are women, of whom 80 per cent are nuns. The most striking fact, however, is the age of the prisoners: 83 per cent are under thirty years of age, a third are between the ages of eighteen and twenty-one, and more than 7 per cent are between eleven and seventeen (*Cutting Off the Serpent's Head* 1996, 92–5).

Most of the young monks and nuns in Tibet come from rural backgrounds and have received very little formal education. For many of them the monasteries offer the only opportunity to receive a Tibetan education. Sometimes, entering small monasteries near their villages while still in their early teens, they discover that they are unable to pursue an education for lack of qualified teachers. This in turn drives them to the larger monasteries around Lhasa. Officially a quota exists for the number of monks allowed to reside at the large monasteries. This has resulted in the growth of a population of monks who reside there illegally and live under constant threat of expulsion – so-called 'unlisted' monks (*them-tho med-pa*) – who are not allowed to take part in prayer sessions or in the organized debates which are the focus of the educational curriculum in the monasteries.

Quotas and other regulations, such as restrictions on age limits for monks, are selectively applied in response to periodic demands by the Chinese government for greater vigilance and political control over the monasteries. After the 1987 demonstrations there was a freeze on new admissions to the large monasteries around Lhasa. Since 1989 there have been several rounds of expulsions from monasteries and nunneries for refusing to comply with political demands.[16] Political work teams (*las-don ru-khag,* Chinese: *gongzuo dui*) have become a permanent feature of monastic life, taking up residence in the monasteries for weeks or months at a time as they carry out investigations, identify potential dissidents and hold political meetings. The meetings frequently provoke a confrontation, as the monks and nuns use the opportunity to resist and frustrate the political workers, arguing points and refusing to submit to their demands. Sometimes this has led to violent incidents where the political workers are attacked by the monks and local villagers.[17]

As the number of incidents of protest by monks and nuns in the countryside increased in the period since 1990, the exercise of political control over the monasteries has become stricter and work teams have been sent to many more monasteries than ever before, regardless of their political record. Continuing political interference in the life of the monasteries and periodic expulsions have forced thousands of young monks and nuns to flee to India during the 1990s, where they have been accepted into monasteries and nunneries and now constitute the majority of the young clerical population in exile.

THE ROLE OF NUNS IN PROTEST

Protest by nuns began shortly after the first demonstrations by monks. There were several demonstrations by nuns from nunneries near Lhasa in the spring of 1988. From 1988 onwards, monks and nuns co-ordinated their protest activity and maintained clandestine lines of communication. By the end of 1988 they were appearing together, marching side by side in demonstrations. Despite facing harsh treatment following arrest, nuns have continued to protest through the period of martial law up to the present. Nuns frequently have staged small demonstrations in the Barkhor where arrest is a certainty. Though nuns comprise perhaps 3 or 4 per cent of the present monastic population they represent some 23 per cent of the total number of Tibetans detained since 1987 (*Cutting Off the Serpent's Head* 1996, 92).

There is little or no precedent for organized political activity by nuns within Tibetan society before 1959. Nunneries did not command the same economic and political power as the monasteries, nor were they supported by subsidies from the government or grants of estates. Traditionally nuns have occupied a lower status than monks in Tibetan society. A tradition of full religious ordination for nuns does not exist in Tibet and thus nuns are only able to receive the ordination of novices (*dge-tshul*).[18] Most nuns did not have an opportunity for philosophical studies and were limited to elementary practices such as performing rituals and reciting prayers. In general, Buddhist norms demand that nuns defer to monks, and traditional Tibetan stereotypes of nuns diminish their status by doubting their commitment and discipline (Havnevik 1990, 141–78).

These prejudices reflected the relative powerlessness of nuns in traditional Tibetan society. However, under current conditions in Tibet the economic situation, background and motivation of nuns and monks are very similar. In both cases the choice requires strong motivation and family support. The lack of support from the government puts monks and nuns in a roughly comparable position, whereas in pre-1959 Tibet monks had a considerable political and economic advantage. Both enter monastic life in their teens or early twenties; for both the choice of a religious career appears to be part of a religious revival felt especially by the young. Both young monks and young nuns come from predominantly rural backgrounds.

Monks and nuns stress the same themes in describing the strength of their commitment to a religious career: the importance of keeping their vows, their sense of responsibility for rebuilding Buddhism, and a willingness to sacrifice their lives for Tibetan independence. Through political protest nuns are thus in a position to change Tibetans' perceptions of their status and gain respect (Havnevik 1994).

THE RELIGIOUS MOTIVATION FOR POLITICAL PROTEST

A view frequently expressed by young monks and nuns is that sacrificing one's life for Tibetan independence is consistent with their vows. It is also said by monks and lay people alike that, because monks have taken vows of celibacy and therefore have no families of their own, they are more able than lay people to sacrifice their lives for Tibetan independence. In religious terms, however, perhaps the most important justification given for dying for independence is the belief that it guarantees rebirth in the next life as a human being. According to Buddhist doctrine, one can only work effectively towards the ultimate goal of Buddhahood through a human rebirth. This is a primary incentive for taking the monastic vows, since faithfully keeping one's vows as a monk is also believed to guarantee rebirth as a human being. Keeping one's vows as a monk and dying for independence thus are linked to the same religious motivation.

In Buddhist societies the laity offer support to the monks, who just by the act of receiving confer spiritual benefits. The same logic of merit-making applies to families staffing monasteries with their own children. From the monks' side, they are expected to respect and keep their vows (*sdom-pa*). It is their vows which qualify monks to receive offerings from the lay community and endorse giving as religious merit-making. The vow of celibacy in particular epitomizes the spiritual qualifications of the monks. Young monks and nuns have a strong sense of their role as bearers and preservers of a tradition. To become a monk or a nun under present conditions requires strong motivation, financial support and sacrifice by the family, and persistence in overcoming administrative obstacles. Young monks and nuns today are in no sense following customary careers. The choice of a monastic career is an exceptional decision, supported by the community, but lacking the institutional security of pre-1959 Tibet.

Tibetans perceive restrictions on religious practice and government control over the monasteries as directly interfering with the traditional relationship between the monastic community and the laity. Taking the vows of a monk is a religious status validated by Buddhist tradition; monks may be disciplined or lose their monastic status and be disrobed only for breaking those vows. Monks frequently express the view that the discipline and expulsion of monks is the responsibility of the assembly and its elected leaders, not the Democratic Management Committees and the Chinese administration, who have no place interfering in the traditional procedures and rules of the Buddhist *sangha.*

At the same time, the monks regard their vows as authorizing them to act politically. Here they claim to be acting in the general interests of the community and appeal to universalistic values (e.g. freedom, independence, human rights). The equation that they draw between religiously motivated action and political action is a product of the current situation of Buddhism, where following two decades of systematic destruction, Buddhism has been reduced to its starkest and simplest terms. In the absence of the specialized ritual services that monks traditionally performed in Tibetan society, the ethical features of Buddhism have assumed a special prominence. The conception of Buddhist practice in Tibet has thus come to resemble in some ways Theravādin conceptions of Buddhist practice.

THE POLITICAL IDEAS OF THE MONKS

Posters and pamphlets produced by young monks since the outbreak of protest in 1987 reveal how changed their thinking is from that of the monks of the past. In pre-1959 Tibet the monasteries were generally hostile towards Western ideas and influences, perceiving a threat to the centrality of religion in society. Now the continuing flow of information from the outside world provides Tibetans with an alternative point of reference and an alternative vocabulary to that of the Chinese, who regularly attack Western political ideas. The articulation of Tibetan independence as a political ideology is a response to the conditions of Chinese communist rule in Tibet, which has attempted to validate the reorganization of Tibetan society along Chinese lines through communist ideology. The monks and nuns do not see any contradiction between their own national and cultural aspirations and political modernization. Thus they have been able to utilize ideas of democracy and human rights to endorse demands for independence. They describe their protests not just as a struggle for independence, but as a fight for human rights ('*gro-ba-mi'i thob-thang*). Closely associated with human rights in Tibetan thinking is the idea of 'truth' (*bden-pa*) – which in Tibetan also conveys the meaning of 'justice'. Tibetans speak of the 'truth' (or 'justice') of their cause, their 'true rights' [*bden-pa'i thob-thang*] and their 'true history' [*bden-pa'i lo-rgyus*].

Perhaps the most detailed statement of the political ideas of the young monks to come out of Tibet since the current wave of protest began in 1987 is 'The

Meaning of the Precious Democratic Constitution of Tibet', a manifesto for an independent democratic Tibet produced by a group of Drepung monks in the summer of 1988.[19] The monks who composed this manifesto had all taken part in the first demonstration in the Barkhor on 27 September 1987. They began publishing leaflets following their release from prison in January 1988. From the outset the group described its aims as political education. From rural backgrounds themselves, the Drepung group intended their manifesto, which is a commentary on the 1963 *Constitution of Tibet* prepared by the Dalai Lama's government-in-exile, to be taken back to villages to counter Party propaganda and to educate villagers about the meaning of democracy. Much of it specifically counters claims made by Party workers in political meetings that the Chinese have brought progress and democracy to Tibet.

The most striking feature of the Drepung manifesto is the absence of an appeal to religious orthodoxy. Buddhism is characterized in general terms as a set of moral principles compatible with democracy and human rights. Also from Buddhism comes a commitment to non-violence and respect for the integrity of the individual. The Drepung manifesto speaks of 'democracy embodying religious and secular principles' (*chos-srid gnyis-ldan gyi dmang-gtso*), but this is intended to establish that Buddhism rather than communism 'accords with the general practice of the contemporary world' (*deng-dus 'dzam-gling spyi-srol dang mthun-pa*). As the monks see it, the Chinese political system is antithetical to both religion and democracy; thus they focus on the political rights and freedoms that they understand to be characteristic of contemporary democratic societies.

The influence of the Dalai Lama is certainly responsible for the development of a socially progressive and undogmatic understanding of Buddhism. Equally important, however, the manifesto represents a response on the part of the monks to the ongoing efforts at political re-education mounted by the work teams sent to the monasteries. Monks are accused in political meetings of wanting to restore feudalism, and characterizations of pre-1959 Tibet as 'feudal' are used to justify 'liberation' and Chinese rule. Significantly, the Drepung manifesto excludes any special political role for the monks and monasteries in an independent democratic Tibet. The undesirability of the 'old society' (*spyi-tshogs rnying-pa*) is a point that the monks willingly concede. The terminology that they use to describe the old society is the same terminology as that used by the Party cadres; however they understand an independent democratic Tibet to be a complete break, socially and politically, with the past:

> Having completely eradicated the practices of the old society with all its faults, the future Tibet will not resemble our former condition and be a restoration of serfdom [*shing-bran gyi lam-lugs*] or be like the so-called old system of rule by a succession of feudal masters or monastic estates [*bkas-bkod-brgyud-'dzin-pa*].

The Drepung monks are prepared to borrow terminology from the communist lexicon, which they have acquired in the course of a Marxist-oriented Chinese education. Over the years the Chinese media have regularly celebrated struggles for 'national liberation' and drawn attention to colonialism and imperialism. The monks are thus in a position to apply this vocabulary to their own situation – referring to Chinese rule as 'imperialism' (*btsan-rgyal-ring-lugs*) and describing the Chinese themselves as 'reactionaries' (*log-spyod-pa*) for standing in the way of social progress. Terms like 'the broad masses' (*rgya-che'i mi-dmangs*) and the term for 'democracy' itself (*dmangs-gtso*) were introduced into the Tibetan language to translate Chinese communist material. Here they are used to validate an independent democratic Tibet. Thus, outlining the conditions necessary for a 'people's government' (*mi-mang gi gzhung*), the term 'people' is explained as referring to the 'broad masses', and democracy is defined as 'a popular system which fundamentally accords with the needs, wishes, and choices of the broad masses'. Chinese rule in Tibet is understood to be undemocratic and unrepresentative.

THE EVOLUTION OF CHINESE RELIGIOUS POLICY IN THE 1990s

Article 36 of China's 1982 constitution guarantees the right to engage in 'normal religious activities'. (*Constitution of the People's Republic of China* 1983, 32). Nevertheless, the state assumes broad powers to oversee and regulate the practise of religion, managing the affairs of the monasteries through its apparatus of Democratic Management Committees, the Religious Affairs Department and the United Front Work Department of the Communist Party. Toleration of religion remains an expedient and Party members are expected to be atheists. Particularly where religion is entangled with ethnicity, the aim of religious policy is to avoid alienating the 'religious masses', while steering religion in socially constructive directions. The officially stated aim of religious policy is to train a 'younger generation of patriotic religious personnel' who 'fervently love their homeland and support the Party's leadership and the socialist system'.[20]

The principal fear of the Chinese leadership has been that religion will become a vehicle for nationalist aspirations. During the 1980s, when reformers in the Party held sway, the argument was made that a relaxation of religious policy, enabling Tibetans to rebuild their religious institutions, would contribute to social stability and win their loyalty to the Chinese state. The 10th Panchen Lama, before his death in 1989, persistently advocated leniency in dealing with monks and nuns arrested for demonstrating, believing that the crackdown called for by Party hardliners would further alienate religious Tibetans. Throughout the 1980s reformers within the government in Tibet argued that the 'special characteristics' of Tibet, its unique culture and religion, had to be taken into account.

Despite continuing demonstrations and protest, attempts to limit and direct the growth of religion in Tibet were sporadic and only partly implemented during the 1980s. Religious policy underwent a dramatic shift following the Third National Forum on Work in Tibet, held in Beijing in July 1994.[21] The latitude that had crept into the interpretation of Party guidelines on religion by local Tibetan cadres was branded as unacceptable and they were now held accountable for the forceful implementation of those guidelines.

The target of the new policy is the pro-independence movement, which is now clearly identified with the resurgence of Buddhism. In the weeks following the Third Forum work teams were sent out to monasteries to inform the clergy of the new requirements, which included political vetting of monks sitting on the Democratic Management Committees, the enforcing of a ban on new construction of religious buildings, the enforcing of existing limits on the numbers of monks and nuns that had been ignored in previous years, and the exacting of a declaration of loyalty to the Communist Party and the Chinese motherland from monks and nuns. Teams were sent out again three months later to determine if the requirements had been met. It seems that a number of demonstrations in late 1994 and 1995 were a response to the new demands of the work teams (*Cutting Off the Serpent's Head* 1996, 29).

While religion has been tolerated under the post-reform policies as a matter of personal belief and as a concession to ethnic minorities, an emphasis has been placed in the 1990s on tailoring religious belief to suit the requirements of a modernizing society. Thus a propaganda guide for Party cadres issued in 1990 instructs them to 'propagate and popularize the knowledge of science and opposition to feudal customs' and advocates a 'humanist Buddhism' which will reorient 'the masses of religious people and the monks' toward the reality of the present time, 'add new content to doctrines', and 'make new explanations for the development of the cause of socialist construction'.[22] At the same time religion is characterized as wasteful of resources that might otherwise be productively utilized – an argument used to justify restrictions on building and staffing of monasteries.

By 1994, following the Third Forum, it is clear that the Party leadership was prepared for a direct assault on the doctrinal basis of Tibetan Buddhism. The published guidelines for cadres that were distributed following the meeting demand that 'religious tenets and practices which do not comply with a socialist society should be changed'.[23] The Party leadership had decided that reverence for the Dalai Lama as head of Tibetan Buddhism is the root cause of continuing protest against Chinese rule in Tibet. In effect they demanded a Tibetan Buddhism without the Dalai Lama:

> The purposes of religion is to deliver all living creatures in a peaceful manner. Now that Dalai and his clique have violated the religious doctrine and even spread rumours to fool and incite one people against the other, in what way can he be regarded as a spiritual leader? (*Cutting Off the Serpent's Head* 1996, 33)

An effort to suppress the display and distribution of photographs of the Dalai Lama was launched in mid 1994. A ban was imposed on the display of Dalai Lama photographs by workers in government offices, including semi-official enterprises such as tourist agencies and taxi companies. Photographs for sale in city markets were confiscated by the police (*A Season To Purge* 1996, 56). In the fall of 1994 a ban on the possession or display of all religious symbols that had previously only applied to Party members was extended to include all government workers and their families, who were required to allow their homes to be searched for altars, religious pictures and other religious paraphernalia (*Cutting Off the Serpent's Head* 1996, 37–8).

The campaign against the Dalai Lama intensified in the spring of 1996. In April police began visiting hotels and restaurants in Lhasa ordering pictures to be removed (*TIN News Update*, 29 April 1996). An article on 5 April in the *Tibet Daily* called for the removal of pictures of the Dalai Lama from monasteries and nunneries as well on the grounds that they were now to be considered 'reactionary material' and that 'the Dalai Lama is no longer a religious leader who can bring happiness to the masses, but a guilty person of the motherland and the people'.[24] A work team sent to Ganden on 7 May to implement the ban on photographs of the Dalai Lama was attacked by monks. In the unrest that followed three monks were shot, at least forty monks were arrested, and Ganden along with several other monasteries was closed (*TIN News Update*, 17 May 1996). Further clashes were reported a week later in which as many as eighty monks and nuns from monasteries and nunneries in the Lhasa area were severely beaten by police as they resisted attempts to remove pictures of the Dalai Lama from shrines (*TIN News Update*, 18 May 1996).

THE CONTROVERSY OVER THE SELECTION OF THE PANCHEN LAMA

The dilemma facing Chinese religious policy in Tibet is illustrated by the controversy over the selection of the reincarnation of the 10th Panchen Lama, who died in 1989. The Chinese government has sought to achieve political control in Tibet through a compliant religious establishment. It has been forced, however, to intervene directly in religious matters in order to shape Tibetan Buddhism to suit its political requirements. The events surrounding the selection of the Panchen Lama demonstrate how much Chinese policy has hardened since the Third Forum, alienating virtually the entire religious community, including figures whose loyalty the Chinese government has relied on in the past.

During the first decades of Chinese rule the question of recognizing new incarnate lamas did not arise. Existing lamas, however, were accorded status and offered positions in the new Chinese administration if they were prepared to co-operate in implementing Chinese rule. By the late 1980s the selection of incarnate lamas appears to have been tolerated unofficially by local authorities. Regulations for the discovery of incarnations were publicized in the early 1990s, requiring that the incarnations be found within Chinese territory and that only lamas living within China take part in the selection. In 1991 a reincarnate lama was enthroned in A-mdo in the presence of local officials with the blessing of the government. Then in 1992 an eight-year-old boy was approved by the central government as the seventeenth Karmapa, head of a branch of the *bKa'-rgyud-pa* sect, historical rivals of the *dGe-lugs-pa*. The boy was located inside Tibet by senior monks from his monastery in Sikkim. The Dalai Lama confirmed the selection and the boy took up residence at mTshur-phu, his principal monastery in Tibet, without provoking conflict with the Chinese government (Schwartz 1994, 211).

The search for the incarnation of the Panchen Lama was authorized by the State Council shortly after his death in 1989. The decree stipulated that the final approval of the selection would be made by the State Council, but the religious procedures would follow Buddhist tradition (Schwartz 1994, 152). A search team composed of monks and officials of Tashilhunpo (bKra-shis-lhun-po), the Panchen Lama's monastery, was to be formed and would employ dreams, divinations and signs to identify the candidates. But authority over the selection of the Panchen Lama is for the Chinese government ultimately a question of sovereignty – a continuation of the practice where religious figures have, since imperial times, received their titles and exercised power as a dispensation of the Chinese state. On the other hand, Tibetan religious tradition demands that the choice of a new Panchen Lama be confirmed by the Dalai Lama. Without this Tibetans will not accept the validity of the choice.

Initially, the stance of the Chinese government was conciliatory. On the urging of the monastic officials overseeing the search, an effort was made to involve the Dalai Lama in the selection. In July 1993 Chadrel Rinpoche, the abbot of Tashilhunpo and head of the search team, was allowed by Beijing to send a letter to the Dalai Lama requesting his aid in the selection process. Chadrel Rinpoche maintained further informal contact with the Dalai Lama and in early 1995 asked him to confirm the selection of one of the candidates, Gendun Chökyi Nyima (Gen-dun-chos-kyi-nyi-ma), as the true incarnation.[25]

By the spring of 1995 a fundamental shift had taken place in the Chinese attitude. Whatever tacit understanding had been reached with the Dalai Lama had broken down and his participation in the selection was no longer deemed necessary. Chadrel Rinpoche was asked to submit the names of several candidates for a final drawing from a ceremonial golden urn, a system of selection imposed on the Tibetan government by the Qianlong Emperor in 1792, but not used in the selection of the last Panchen Lama or either of the last two Dalai Lamas.[26] The use of the lottery, an artefact of Manchu imperial power, signified for the Chinese government not just supremacy in deciding matters of religion but the exercise of sovereignty. The preoccupation with using the selection of the Panchen Lama to demonstrate Chinese sovereignty over Tibet meant risking a choice that had not been confirmed by the Dalai Lama, and therefore lacked legitimacy in the eyes of Tibetans.

In a move to pre-empt any bid by the Chinese government to install another child, the Dalai Lama announced on 14 May the discovery of the new Panchen Lama, confirming the choice made by Chadrel Rinpoche and the Tashilhunpo search committee. The reaction of the Chinese government was swift. Chadrel Rinpoche and his assistant were arrested and accused of conspiring with the Dalai Lama.[27] The boy, Gendun Chökyi Nyima, and his family were also taken into custody. Within three days a work team was sent to Tashilhunpo monastery to hold political education sessions in order to get the monks to accept the use of the golden urn lottery and to denounce Chadrel Rinpoche. After two months of increasingly confrontational meetings, along with repeated interrogation of individual monks, the People's Armed Police entered the monastery and arrested thirty-two dissident monks (*Cutting Off the Serpent's Head*, 1996, 52–4).

A meeting in Beijing of Tibetan religious leaders was convened by the central Party leadership on 4 November There they were required to accede to the selection of an incarnation by lot from a list that specifically did not include the child already recognized by the Dalai Lama. They were also required to declare that Gendun Chökyi Nyima was not the true incarnation. In an elaborate ceremony held behind locked doors inside the Jokhang temple the final lottery was conducted on 29 November. Denouncing the boy confirmed by the Dalai Lama and accepting the boy selected through the lottery has since become a measure of political loyalty for Tibetan religious leaders and the monastic community in general.

CONCLUSION: THE FUTURE FOR RELIGION IN TIBET

Chinese religious policy in the late 1990s has shifted from attempting to co-opt the religious leadership to outright confrontation. As the controversy over the selection of the Panchen Lama demonstrates, political considerations – including the intensified battle against the influence of the Dalai Lama – have taken precedence over concern for a religious hierarchy that might command some legitimacy in the eyes of the monastic community and lay Tibetans. The Democratic Management Committees of the monasteries have been subjected to increasing demands to demonstrate their loyalty; leaders who are found to be politically unreliable are replaced. Thus, what remains of the religious leadership in Tibet is weakened and divided. At the same time, the Chinese government has not succeeded in generating loyalty among the mass of young monks and nuns. They remain fervently loyal to the Dalai Lama and resist government demands and restrictions, repeatedly braving expulsion and arrest. The lack of a functioning religious hierarchy generates precisely the conditions for continuing political activism.[28]

Developments in Tibet must also be seen in the context of growing restrictions on religious practice throughout China. New legislation introduced on the national and local levels since 1994 requires the registration of temples, monasteries, mosques and churches, and attempts to regulate the kinds of religious activities that take place. There is a renewed focus on the threat posed by religion to 'social stability', and, in particular, to 'national unity', and a renewed emphasis on the need for 'patriotism', particularly among ethnic groups for whom religion is part of national identity. Of special concern are links to outside religious figures and organizations.[29]

A long-standing concern of Chinese religious policy has been to suppress so-called 'feudal and superstitious activities' – heterodox and non-institutionalized forms of religious practice that defy regulation by the state (*Constitution of the People's Republic of China* 1983, 32). The Criminal Law of China specifically prohibits 'utilizing feudal superstitious beliefs' to carry out 'counter-revolutionary activities' (*Criminal Law and Criminal Procedures of the People's Republic of China* 1984, 37). These China-wide stipulations are aimed at such diverse local practices as fortune-telling, sorcery, folk healing and exorcism, as well as secret societies and underground churches. Popular cults based on spirit-possession and divination, which have the potential for mass mobilization and can easily assume volatile political forms, also have a basis in Tibetan religion.[30]

The extensive rebuilding of monastic institutions during the 1980s eclipsed this aspect of popular religion, and thus it has not been conspicuous in current protest led by young monks and nuns. Under other conditions, however, these elements may come to the fore, producing a religious revival along millenarian lines, where religious longing becomes a substitute for political power. The increasing scale of restrictions on state-sanctioned monastic Buddhism may lead to a resurgence of heterodox forms of popular religion. Likewise, the increasing marginalization of the rural Tibetan population with urban economic development and the influx of Chinese migrants, which has already generated widespread rural protest, may also create conditions favouring millenarianism.

In coming years Chinese policy in Tibet promises to be less and less accommodating to Tibetan religion. Economic and immigration policies in the 1990s stress the rapid integration of Tibet into the Chinese market economy. Sensitivity to the so-called 'special characteristics' of Tibet – its language, culture and religion – is no longer a priority. Current policy favours rapid assimilation; thus, programmes to promote the use of the Tibetan language in government and education and develop Tibetan cultural institutions have largely been abandoned. The principal justification for this policy is that it will overcome 'backwardness' and accelerate modernization, but these shifts in central government policy occur against a backdrop of political instability where security concerns are paramount. Hence, all expressions of national identity – which includes religion – are viewed with suspicion insofar as they potentially threaten the security of Chinese rule in Tibet.

NOTES

1. Wylie (1963) refers to this period, which lasted until the establishment of Mongol overlordship in the thirteenth century, as the 'local hegemonic period'. The *Sa-skya* lamas nominally ruled all of Tibet as representatives of the invading Mongols, but Tibet reverted back to a pattern of regional conflict and dynastic rivalry after the collapse of *Sa-skya* and Mongol rule in the middle of the fourteenth century (Samuel 1993, 500–1).
2. Samuel (1993, 29–30) suggests that the *sangha* in Tibet was never 'domesticated', as

it was in Southeast Asia, and that Tibetan forms of Buddhism resemble the 'millennial Buddhism' of the Thai and Burmese forest monks – with the difference that this kind of 'undomesticated' Buddhism has come to constitute the established political order in Tibet, rather than being a constant threat to the power of the state.

3. In A-mdo in the north-east nomadic pastoralists were organized into tribes and not subject to any political authority, though they formed alliances with monasteries for economic as well as religious reasons. In the eastern Tibetan areas of Khams there were a variety of large and small polities, some ruled by hereditary princes, some by hereditary lamas or by reincarnate lamas, and some by officials appointed by Lhasa (Samuel 1993, 73–98). Control over these indigenous states shifted back and forth between Tibet and China throughout the nineteenth and into the twentieth century, while local powers resisted the encroachments of both governments. The largest of these states, sDe-dge, was a center for the *rigs-med* movement in the nineteenth century, an ecumenical synthesis of Buddhist traditions that contrasted with the clerical orthodoxy of the *dGe-lugs-pa* (Samuel 1993, 533–43).

4. In 1923 the ninth Panchen Lama fled to China rather than submit to the increased taxes demanded by the Dalai Lama's government. He sought to enlist the aid of the Nationalist Chinese government in restoring the autonomy of his monastery, Tashilhunpo, and re-establishing its exclusive jurisdiction over those areas of Tibet under its control (Goldstein 1989, 110–20).

5. Though a figure of some 25 per cent is often cited for the proportion of the male population who were celibate monks in Tibet, Samuel (1993, 578–82) reviews the available evidence and concludes that the likely figure is around 10–12 per cent in the centralized agricultural areas.

6. An attempt was made to open another English school in Lhasa in 1944, but it was closed after just five months because of opposition from the *dGe-lugs-pa* monasteries around Lhasa. The monks feared that an English-educated élite would no longer patronize Buddhism and threatened to close the school by force if the government did not reconsider (Goldstein 1989, 423–5).

7. Though much of the turmoil of the Cultural Revolution was uncontrolled mob violence, the destruction of the monasteries was carefully orchestrated. First, precious stones, gold and silver were catalogued and removed, then teams of Red Guards orchestrated the razing of the buildings by villagers. Bricks and wood were carted off for re-use; scriptures were burned in bonfires. Norbu (1997, 269–74) offers an account of the destruction of monasteries and nunneries in *Sa-skya*. See also Avedon (1984, 358–9).

8. Party Secretary Hu Yaobang's six-point reform policy for Tibet, announced after his fact-finding mission in 1980, sought to undo the damage done by the Cultural Revolution. It allowed the rebuilding of religious institutions and called for an exemption from taxes and compulsory quotas for farmers. These exemptions were soon supplanted by 'voluntary' sales to the state; nevertheless, with control over the disposal of their surplus, families have been able to rebuild and restaff local monasteries on a scale unanticipated by the government (Schwartz 1994, 16).

9. For a description of the Democratic Management Committees and the administration of the monasteries see Schwartz (1994, 59–63); also *Forbidden Freedoms* (1990, 24–30).

10. The Dalai Lama had indicated his admiration for Gandhi and Nehru as early as 1956 during his first visit to India (Gyatso 1962). Work on a draft *Constitution of Tibet* (1963) began shortly after his arrival in exile in 1959. He described the new 'liberal and

democratic constitution of Tibet' as 'based on the principles of the Lord Buddha and the Universal Declaration of Human Rights' (Gyatso 1962: 231).

11. Margaret Nowak describes the inculcation of values within the refugee education system and shows how the symbol of the Dalai Lama enables young Tibetans to 'interpret the lessons of contemporary, alien, social experience in the light of the traditionally ambiguous and therefore flexible ideology of *chos-srid zung-'brel*, "religion and politics combined"' (Nowak 1984, 157).

12. Klieger (1992) has examined how Tibetans have cultivated Westerners as *spyin-bdag*, patrons of religion, and have extended the meaning of the traditional relationship to include ordinary non-clerical Tibetans, who are also worthy of sponsorship on the basis of embodying Tibetan culture and values.

13. See Lopez (1994). McLagan (1997) examines in detail the events of the Year of Tibet in New York City and the self-conscious use of a 'culture strategy' by activists to recruit American support for the Tibet movement.

14. Dreyfus (1994) discusses the sources of Tibetan 'proto-nationalism' in the constructed memory of Strong-brtsan-sgam-po and his association with the Jokhang. Later centuries also identified the king as an incarnation of Avalokiteśvara (as are the Dalai Lamas), and Tibet is regarded as a country whose people have a special collective relationship with this deity.

15. The threat of boycotting *smon-lam* in defence of monastic prerogatives is not without precedent in Tibetan history. In 1944 the monks of Sera Che threatened a boycott rather than turn over a group of monks accused of murdering a district commissioner in 'Phan-po. This dispute was part of the internecine political struggle between Reting and Taktra that culminated in armed conflict in 1947 (Goldstein 1989, 437–40).

16. Some 200 monks and nuns were expelled from monasteries near Lhasa in 1989–90, during a China-wide 'Screening and Investigation' campaign following the Tiananmen Square incident. Many of these were unlisted monks as well or monks and nuns who had been arrested for political protest. (*Defying the Dragon*, 1991, 18–19). Another round of expulsions occurred in the autumn of 1994, in response to a renewed attack on religion launched after the Third National Forum on Work in Tibet, held in Beijing in July 1994 (*Cutting Off the Serpent's Head*, 1996, 29).

17. See Schwartz (1994, 118–20) for an account of one incident that occurred in March 1988 at Ra-stod monastery near Lhasa. There are an increasing number of reports of unrest involving rural communities and monasteries from 1992 onwards (*Cutting Off the Serpent's Head*, 1996, 26–7, 94–5).

18. Full ordination for nuns in the *Mahāyāna* tradition continues in some Chinese communities, including Hong Kong, where it is claimed that one such lineage of fully ordained nuns has survived. Whatever the historical reasons, Tibetan women seeking clerical status are at a distinct disadvantage. Some young exile nuns have gone to Hong Kong for ordination.

19. Several hundred copies of this 11-page pamphlet were printed using wood blocks. The group printed and distributed several documents before being arrested in 1989. A translation of the document is in Schwartz (1994, 232–4). The thirty-year-old leader of the group, Ngawang Phulchung, was convicted along with ten other monks for 'spreading counter-revolutionary propaganda' and received a nineteen-year sentence at a mass sentencing rally. The monks were described as the 'scum of the religious circles' who had 'betrayed the religious doctrines and canons of Buddhism by their actions' (Schwartz 1994, 125).

20. MacInnis (1989, 19–20). The authoritative statement on Chinese religious policy is

'The Basic Viewpoint and Policy on the Religious Question during Our Country's Socialist Period', promulgated in 1982. Usually referred to as 'Document 19', it is reprinted in MacInnis (1989, 8–26).

21. A detailed analysis of the policies instituted during the Third National Forum on Work in Tibet is found in *Cutting Off the Serpent's Head* (1996).

22. From chapter 5 of 'Propaganda Speeches on Strengthening National Solidarity and Preserving the Unification of the Motherland', by the Propaganda Committee of the Ganze Prefectural Committee of the Communist Party of China, February 1990, translated from Chinese and reprinted in *Defying the Dragon* (1991, 112).

23. From *A Golden Bridge Leading into a New Era*, cited in *Cutting off the Serpent's Head* (1996, 28).

24. The 5 April 1996, edition of *Xizang Ribao* cites a 'Circular on Seizing and Confiscating Reactionary Propaganda Materials and Stepping Up Anti-Infiltrative Work in Religious Centres' (*TIN News Update*, 29 April 1996). It is unusual for directives for cadres to be openly published.

25. For an account of co-ordination between Chadrel Rinpoche and the Dalai Lama between 1993 and 1995 see Goldstein (1997, 102–8); see also *Cutting Off the Serpent's Head* (1996, 52).

26. The tenth Panchen Lama was located in Qinghai province by monks of Tashilhunpo monastery in 1941. He was formally recognized by the National government and enthroned at sKu-'bum monastery in 1949 without recourse to the golden urn lottery. His acceptance by the Tibetan government was a precondition of completing the Seventeen-point Agreement in 1951. The requirements of religious tradition were satisfied when the Dalai Lama conducted his own ritual divination (Goldstein 1989, 762–3).

27. Chadrel Rinpoche was sentenced to six years in prison on 21 April 1997, for crimes of 'splitting the country' and for leaking 'state secrets' – a reference to providing the Dalai Lama in December 1994 with the names of candidates assembled by the search committee, including their choice for the true incarnation, Gendun Chöskyi Nyima (*TIN News Update*, 9 May 1997).

28. This is not unlike the situation Tambiah describes for Burma during and after British colonial rule where a 'vacillating and destructive religious policy' led to an 'atrophy of any hierarchical authority exercising control over the monks and monasteries' and contributed to 'the politicization of monks and their engagement in militant, anticolonial, nationalist politics' (Tambiah 1976, 461–2).

29. See the report *Religious Repression in China* (1996) from Amnesty International for a summary of the new regulations and an account of recent crackdowns on religious activities in China.

30. Schwartz (1994, 227–9) discusses one popular movement organized around spirit-possession and magical practices with millenarian overtones that occurred in a nomadic area in the early 1980s. The movement, which was suppressed by the authorities as 'reactionary feudal superstition', centered on the legendary warrior-hero King Ge-sar of gLing, and called on the deities to protect the virtuous and overcome demonic forces of evil, identified with the Chinese. Internal Chinese documents refer to other similar outbreaks and recognize the phenomenon as a threat. There have been a number of reports of spirit-possession from Tibet in recent years.

BIBLIOGRAPHY

Avedon, John, F. (1984) *In Exile From the Land of Snows.* New York: Alfred A. Knopf.

[The] *Constitution of the People's Republic of China* (1983) Beijing: Foreign Language Press.

[The] *Constitution of Tibet* (1963) New Delhi: Bureau of His Holiness the Dalai Lama.

Criminal Law and Criminal Procedures of the People's Republic of China (1984) Beijing: Foreign Language Press.

Cutting Off the Serpent's Head: Tightening Control in Tibet, 1994–1995 [March] (1996) Tibet Information Network and Human Rights Watch. New York: Human Rights Watch.

Defying the Dragon: China and Human Rights in Tibet [March] (1991) LAWASIA and Tibet Information Network. London: Tibet Information Network.

Dreyfus, Georges (1994) 'Proto-Nationalism in Tibet', in Kvaerne, Per (ed.) *Tibetan Studies: Proceedings of the 6th Seminar of the International Association of Tibetan Studies* 1, 205–18. Oslo: Institute for Comparative Research in Human Culture.

Ekvall, Robert B. (1964) *Religious Observances in Tibet.* Chicago, IL: University of Chicago Press.

Forbidden Freedoms: Beijing's Control of Religion in Tibet. [September] (1990) International Campaign for Tibet. Washington: International Campaign for Tibet.

Gyatso, Tenzin (The Fourteenth Dalai Lama) (1962) *My Land and My People.* New York: McGraw-Hill.

Goldstein, Melvyn C. (1989) *A History of Modern Tibet, 1913–1951.* Berkeley, CA: University of California Press.

—— (1997) *The Snow Lion and the Dragon: China, Tibet and the Dalai Lama.* Berkeley; University of California Press.

Havnevik, Hanna (1990) *Tibetan Buddhist Nuns.* Oslo: Universitetsforlaget.

Havnevik, Hanna (1994) 'The Role of Nuns in Contemporary Protest', in Barnett, Robert and Akiner, Shirin (eds) *Resistance and Reform in Tibet.* London: Hurst, 259–66.

Klieger, P. Christiaan (1992) *Tibetan Nationalism: The Role of Patronage in the Accomplishment of a National Identity.* Berkeley, CA: Folklore Institute.

Lopez, Donald S. (1994) 'New Age Orientalism: The Case of Tibet', *Tibetan Review*, May, 16–20.

MacInnis, Donald E. (1989) *Religion in China Today: Policy and Practice.* Maryknoll, New York: Orbis Books.

McLagan, Margaret J. (1997) 'Mystical Visions in Manhattan: Deploying Culture in the Year of Tibet', in Korom, Frank J. (ed.) *Tibetan Culture in the Diaspora.* Vienna: Austrian Academy of Sciences.

Norbu, Dawa (1985) 'An Analysis of Sino–Tibetan Relationships, 1245–1911: Imperial Power, Non-Coercive Regime, and Military Dependency', in Aziz, Barbara Nimri and Kapstein, Matthew (eds) *Soundings in Tibetan Civilization.* New Delhi: Manohar Publications, 176–195.

Norbu, Dawa (1997) *Tibet: The Road Ahead.* New Delhi: HarperCollins.

Nowak, Margaret (1984) *Tibetan Refugees: Youth and the New Generation of Meaning.* New Brunswick, NJ: Rutgers University Press.

Religious Repression in China. [July] (1996) London: Amnesty International.

Richardson, H.E. (1962) *A Short History of Tibet.* New York: E.P. Dutton.

Samuel, Geoffrey (1993) *Civilized Shamans.* Washington, DC: Smithsonian Institution Press.

Schwartz, Ronald D. (1991) 'Travelers Under Fire: Tourists in the Tibetan Uprising',

Annals of Tourism Research 18/4, 588–604.

Schwartz, Ronald D. (1994) *Circle of Protest: Political Ritual in the Tibetan Uprising.* New York: Columbia University Press.

Shakabpa, Tsepon W.D. (1967) *Tibet: A Political History.* New Haven, CT: Yale University Press.

[A] *Season to Purge: Religious Repression in Tibet.* [April] (1996) International Campaign for Tibet. Washington: International Campaign for Tibet.

Stein, R.A. (1972) *Tibetan Civilization.* Stanford, CA: Stanford University Press.

Tambiah, S.J. (1976) *World Conqueror and World Renouncer.* Cambridge: Cambridge University Press.

TIN News Update. 29 April (1996); 'Dalai Lama Photographs Banned from Monasteries – Dalai Lama "no longer a religious leader"'. London: Tibet Information Network.

TIN News Update. 17 May (1996) 'Lhasa Monasteries Closed after Monk Shot, 40 Detained'. London: Tibet Information Network.

TIN News Update (1996) 'Second Serious Incident in Lhasa Area: 30 Nuns and up to 50 Others "Severely Beaten"', 18 May. London: Tibet Information Network.

TIN News Update (1997) 'Senior Lama Sentenced in Panchen Lama Search Dispute', 9 May. London: Tibet Information Network.

Tucci, Giuseppe (1980) *The Religions of Tibet.* London: Routledge & Kegan Paul.

Wylie, Turrel V. (1963) 'Mar.pa's Tower: Notes on Local Hegemons in Tibet', *History of Religions* 3, 278–91.

11

THE QUEST FOR ENLIGHTENMENT AND CULTURAL IDENTITY: BUDDHISM IN CONTEMPORARY VIETNAM

THIÊN DÔ

INTRODUCTION

Buddhism in Vietnam is predominantly Mahāyāna in character, containing widespread and varied popular components, not dissimilar to those found in other East Asian countries. As Vietnamese history over the last one hundred years or so has been marked by the tragic consequences of colonialism preceded by civil wars and territorial expansion, Buddhism has inevitably been situated and shaped by those major upheavals. Yet it has also endured, and renewed itself with no uncertain vigour, after centuries of decline. Given its large scale popular support and connection with national identity, this chapter seeks to question the perception of a 'decline' or 'decay' of the 'Buddhist religion in Vietnam' in the nineteenth century and earlier.[1] Also to be re-examined is what has been claimed as the Buddhist contribution to radical change in Vietnamese consciousness since the 1930s, a time of tension, tragedy and contrast at the intersection of modernization and nationalism, politics and culture.

Seeing that historical records tend to inform us more about court and élite politics than anything else, attempts at an alternative perspective on Buddhism in Vietnam will need to tackle established views concerning its decline and revival. Moreover, élite descriptions imply particular frameworks of national or cultural identity.[2] The view is made more complicated by the apparent homogeneity of the elements of *Tam Giáo* (the three religions: Buddhism, Confucianism, Daoism), underlined by Chinese discourse from the fourteenth century up to the present.[3] Alongside considerations of the role of Buddhism in the independence struggle, any history of Vietnamese Buddhism also needs to account for issues closer to its daily manifestations at grass-roots level. I suggest we may look at these issues as they weave around the ethos and practice of self-cultivation, which have hitherto been given scant recognition by historians.

To many Vietnamese who claim to be Buddhists, the project of perfectibility is also imbued in one way or another with supernaturalism. It is important to recognize that through this trope of self-cultivation, Vietnamese Buddhism and other popular religions derive their similar psycho-social configurations through the putative interaction between the spirit realm and the world of the living. In the context of the production and transformation of local practices, this means that self-cultivation not only offers rich potential for cultural adaptation, it also serves as an incubator of social change. Our understanding of the recent evolution of Buddhism can only benefit more from this wider perspective. Before we proceed further, let us turn to a general sketch for the various forms of Buddhism in Vietnam.

TYPOLOGY

At the risk of oversimplification, the different schools of Buddhism can be grouped in three strands which parallel the most commonly seen iconic display on the main altars of Buddhist temples. One of these triadic arrangements, called the 'Three-generation Buddhas' (*Phật Tam Thế*), has Śākyamuni in front of Amitābha (*Phật Di Đà*) and behind Maitreya or, in some temples, behind the infant Siddhārtha. In the first group, both the Zen and Theravāda schools with self-development through meditation as their principal focus regard Śākyamuni as a chief symbol, while the Pure Land or Amidist groups, who hold that salvation comes from outside oneself, focus on Amitābha. This leaves the final group, comprising Tantric schools, popular millenarian groups such as the *Hòa Hảo* and perhaps the *Cao Đài* (who originally called themselves 'Renovated Buddhists'), having a common devotion to Maitreya Buddha who symbolizes their more apocalyptic character. The three strands could therefore be said to represent three possibilities of human transformation.

Another commonly seen arrangement also involves Amitābha Buddha, but with two female emanations of Avalokiteśvara Bodhisattva, popularly known as *Phật Bà Quan Âm* (Ch. Guanyin). This representation touches on the feminine aspect of Vietnamese religion, which has its roots in images of motherhood, gentle compassion and sacrifice, converging in the cult of goddesses and fertility linked to an agrarian past. Mainly found in smaller temples, this trinity bespeaks an ensemble less easy to differentiate into discrete strands. The *Cao Đài*, who engage in spirit writing, together with other small groups similarly informed by the *Minh Su'* (Luminous Master) school of southern Chinese *émigrés*, would belong here.[4] The above structure does not say much about the development of a many-faceted Buddhism of Vietnam over the last hundred years or so, but will serve as adequate framework for our purposes. To appreciate its changes in contour and composition, it pays to look at some historical contexts.

DECLINE

The evolution of Buddhism in Vietnam from the late nineteenth century, has often been summarized in terms of a revitalization following at least four centuries of decline caused by the state's adoption of Confucianism as its central ideology (Mai Thọ Truyền 1962; Nguyễn Văn Huyên 1944; Nguyễn Tài Thu' *et al.* 1992; Thích Mật Thể 1960; Trần Văn Giáp 1968). However, this interpretation privileges politics as central to the diffusion of religions[5] thereby understating the Southeast Asia-wide patterns of localization as reflected in the Buddhism of Vietnam. Such understatement in turn reflects the dominant view of neo-Confucianist literati in defining orthodoxy or authenticity.

Most direct observation of the condition of temples and clergy saw little variation from the 1920s (Coulet 1929) to the 1950s (Phạm Gia Tuân 1954). However, in a thorough-going survey of the whole of the Vietnamese temple (*chùa*) constituency, Phan Kế Bính, writing in the 1930s, assigned considerable significance to the northern Vietnamese *chùa*, by drawing attention to the role of the women who formed *hội chu' bà*, or the Senior Women's Association in this region. These were women past child-bearing age or widows, under the leadership of their most senior and respected member, all committed to a Buddhist way of life and to the service of the temple, where no monks or nuns were in charge. Phan Kế Bính maintains that this system existed in symmetrical relation to the male-dominated structure of Daoist-Confucian style village communal houses (*đình*).[6] While such a symmetry may have been absent in the South where temples there normally housed both monks and nuns, the situation is all the more remarkable for the close intimacy women in the country and small towns had with the local *chùa*, an intimacy that must have antagonized the priestly regime of the time. A guidebook to 'Buddhist practice' published in Gò Công in 1929, for instance, condemned other kinds of lax behaviour at temples, for example chewing betel, and bringing in small children without keeping them quiet (Trần Quang Văn, 1929).

To seasoned observers like Father Cadière (1953), early twentieth-century Buddhism, particularly given its deep plebeian roots, merged into a veritable jungle of Vietnamese religions. It appears that 'Buddhism' in Vietnam may as well have not existed, for, as Cadière states, 'nine-tenths of the Vietnamese in Annam, and rather fewer in Tonkin where numerous pagodas attract devotees, live and die without performing the most trivial religious observance inspired by the Buddhist religion'. Others argued that the strength of Buddhism depended not so much on ritual patterns, but on the direct attention the ruling élite gave to architectural sites and doctrinal purity. From this prospective as well, Vietnamese Buddhism seemed to be in decline.

Even before the time that central support for Buddhist temples began to reduce, scholars have highlighted signs of decline in Buddhism. In the late 1200s and early 1300s, the Trần kings Nhân Tông and Anh Tông entertained a strangely named monk, Du-chi Ba Lâm, for two years in the palace. Writing about this period, Venerable Thích Mật Thể (1960, 166–7),[7] an important reform activist and author of one of the few modern histories of Buddhism in Vietnam, suggests the royal guest was a Tibetan, in possession of heterodox Tantric knowledge. The puzzling aspect of this affair is that the two kings are considered as the founding and second patriarch respectively of the *Trúc Lâm* school, the only known Vietnamese-bred Zen 'lineage'. Yet Mật Thể condemns whatever influence this foreign monk had on the monarchs and concludes:

In brief: Buddhism in Vietnam towards the end of the Trần dynasty [was such that] monks had no qualms in inviting heads of other outside [heterodox] sects and sundry spirits to share the temples with Śākyamuni Buddha. With Buddhism retreating to concede room to other religions, is it any surprise that [literati such as] Trương Hán Siêu, Nguyễn Trung Ngạn later publicly attacked Buddhism?

The royal relationship with the *sangha* is known to have been the source of sustained attack from court *literati* in the Trần era. Mật Thể also finds that the criticism these neo-Confucian literati meted out to Buddhist monks in the late fourteenth century was generally aimed at the Buddhists' supposed incompetence:

> The strangest thing is in the fifth Xu'o'ng Phù year of King Phế Đế (1381), the court ordered Zen Master Đại Thân to lead all the monks and recluse ascetics in the villages to fight against the Cham invaders.
> It must be said that at that time the country's resources were low and the *sangha* had become a bunch of good-for-nothing's, a thorn in the eye of Confucian officials, that was why they sent [Master Đại Thân] to war.

In the fifteenth century the neo-Confucian ideology prevailed, with King Lê Thái Tôn continuing the practice of the previous Trân dynasty and holding examinations held for those who wanted to become monks. However, the fact that the king had the queen mother's statue cast with a Zen master ritually putting the final eye on it proved, for Mật Thể, that 'monks had become sorcerers'. Similarly, during the drought of 1434, the Buddha statue at Pháp Vân temple was transported to the palace where chanting rituals were performed by monks. This was repeated in the drought of 1449 when the Rites Ministry was ordered to pray for rain at a Buddhist temple, where the queen officiated. This was tantamount to 'turning Buddha into a protector spirit in the Vietnamese folk belief system' (Thích Mật Thể 1960, 166–74). In other words, the statue at Pháp Vân temple, which had the form of a black goddess, represented a localized Buddhism powerful enough to engage royal support, but this counts for little in Mật Thể's eyes. These instances and similar partial views of the subsequent centuries, as we shall see below, show that interpretations of Buddhism's decadence are clearly biased towards élitist Zen fundamentalism and the neo-Confucian supremacy of the court.

In 1798, as he was consolidating his power in the most southerly region of Gia Định, Nguyễn Ánh (later Emperor Gia Long) reportedly wanted to execute a senior Buddhist monk who broke the law. He also planned to have abbots, Daoist priests and spirit mediums registered, exempting only those aged over 50 from corvée labour. Officials pleaded against the death penalty and pointed out the monk's reputation as a 'true self-cultivator'. In the end, however, the anti-Buddhist stance of the neo-Confucians in the Nguyễn Lord's retinue prevailed.[8] The Nguyễn Gazette does not reveal the alleged crime and fate of this monk, but only records that Nguyễn Ánh went ahead with the installation of the anti-Buddhist measures (Tạ Chí Đại Tru'ò'ng 1973, 306).

If this incidence demonstrates the ascendancy of the neo-Confucian faction, it also indicates the depth of respect commanded by the Buddhist *sangha* and the considerable popularity of Buddhism during that time, at least in the newly settled southern region. Moreover, under Nguyễn rule, Buddhist temples continued to secure attention by élite and ruling groups. The nineteenth century in particular was marked by monarchic attention to cultural sites in Đãng Trong (ie. the southern region), a fact which points to some vitality in orthodox Buddhist institutions and not a general decline in the religion.[9]

Recently, the Hán Nôm Research Institute in Hanoi published a compilation which covers geographical, historical and literary notes and commentaries, in prose and in poetry, concerning 1,064 culturally significant sacred places of worship known to have been established from the sixth century up to 1900.[10] The places listed were obviously considered important as pilgrimage sites which fell into the ruling élite's sphere of power and authority. However, if we attempt to assess the state of health of Buddhism in the nineteenth century from the information presented in the above compilation, what can we see?[11]

Of the 377 Buddhist temples listed, with the oldest among them built in the third century AD, at least 228 or 60 per cent are mentioned in nineteenth-century official literature. Of these 228 temples, 98 (or 25 per cent) received direct attention from both the ruling élite of the Nguyễn dynasty (1802–1956) and others (e.g. resident abbots and locals), with two-thirds receiving attention from the ruling élite. By direct attention, I mean they may have been built anew, repaired, refurbished, or have been provided with a building converted from a different type of temple, or given crown land to supplement income, or a new name plaque, ornaments, and furniture as a sign of royal recognition. While this may not be total support, it does not really indicate a state of decline in Buddhist practice and belief, as commonly suggested by the majority of contemporary writings. Certainly, orthodox or text-based institutions may have dwindled but ritual and sumptuary edifices retained the support of ruling élites and local devotees. The term 'decline of Buddhism' should therefore read only as 'ascendancy of neo-Confucianist court officials in political and ideological spheres' and their privileging of a Zen fundamentalism as part of their central-izing strategy.[12] None of this evidence can be legitimately used to deny the cultural vitality of Buddhism as a multi-faceted religion, having deep roots, particularly in the rural areas.

Scholars' recent views on the status of Buddhism are coloured by their recognition of varying historical contexts. In contrast to Thích Mật Thể (1960, 215–16), who tends to focus on the ruinous state of temples and the dispersal of clergy after the Nguyễn–Tây So'n war (1771–1802), recent studies do not paint as black a picture of the nineteenth century.[13] Under the Nguyễn, the *sangha* was still a major force. Up to thirty monks resided in each large temple, with five or six in smaller establishments. Through regular organized competitive exams (fifty inspectors from the Ministry of Rites were appointed for this task), the state took over control of the monastic population. Many pagodas and towers were repaired or rebuilt, especially in the South where new temples were built with architectural features borrowed from other Southeast Asian countries (Mĩnh Chi *et al.* 1993, 187–93).

However, the present nuanced view of Buddhism is not sufficient to offset the commonplace acceptance of general decline. The privileging of a text-based religion with its countrywide clerical hierarchy in tandem with a relative disregard for local diversification, has also fuelled the drive for reform since the 1920s. Indeed the perception of decadence can be partly understood as a consequence of the failure of the Nguyễn to unite the kingdom and strengthen it against the advance of French colonialism towards the latter half of the nineteenth century. Whatever the explanation, the conclusions based on a decadent Buddhism over the centuries lie totally within the horizon of surprisingly resilient élite perspectives.

REFORM AND REVITALIZATION

It is possible to regard local Buddhist-led uprisings against French occupation as an index of the significance of Buddhism in popular resistance. In the South, the arrest of the *Bũ'u So'n Kỳ Hu'o'ng* (BSKH) sect's founder in 1849 reflected the courts' disapproval of lay Buddhist movements. It could not, however, stop the growth of this rural-based Buddhist group. In the 1860s armed struggle against French rule by patriots was led by Trân Văn Thành, who joined the BSKH sect in 1847, and by Võ Trú' Phu'o'ng in the North during the 1890s.[14] But this view can only be partial. In the former case at least, resistance was motivated by both patriotism and local determination to lead a Buddhist way of life. This double perspective must be taken into account when considering evidence for the persecution of BSKH groups which predates the French conquest (Ho Tai, 1983, p.11). The anti-colonial image, therefore, must be tempered by evidence of local resistance to various forms of court control since pre-colonial days. However, this should not lead us to assume that those who expressed their world-view in religious terms were necessarily seditious any more than the state was fundamentally anti-Buddhist.[15]

For many settlers in the South of Vietnam, a Buddhist ethos gave meaning and direction in the ordering of their everyday life. An emphasis on self-cultivation underlined their attitude towards adaptation to the new social and natural environment. Their desire for a peaceful existence should be viewed in terms of this personal orientation towards the project of self-cultivation rather than as a social protest against the central power's stipulations and ideologies. Today, members of an offshoot of the BSKH, the *Tú' Ân Hiêu Nghĩa* (Four Favours, Filial Piety and Righteousness) group, founded in 1878, still regard the torchings of their village several times in the 1870s and 1880s by the French as having represented 'perilous challenges' not exclusively to their patriotism, but to their faith in the *dharma* (Hà Tân Dân, 1974).[16] The BSKH model of self-cultivation, which is unmediated by the monastic pattern, also finds continuity with the *Tịnh Độ Cu' Sĩ Phật Hội* (Householder Pure Land Buddhist Association) today. Their claim to be non-political is demonstrated by a strict focus on charity, and for this reason they have a transparency quite unlike that of the other groups, whose chief motive was to evade colonial harassment.[17]

Local innovations entail an amalgam of motifs appropriated from both the dominant ideology and the matrix of traditional beliefs. Thus we recognize among the Four Favours (*Tú' Ân Hiêu Nghĩa*) millenarian Buddhists the preservation of Confucian values expressed in honouring the 'parents' and monarch's favours', besides those of the triple gem (Buddha, *dharma* and *sangha*) and concern for 'all sentient beings' (Tạ Chí Đại Tru'ò'ng 1989, 347).[18] While the countryside looked to cosmic change as the precondition for return to an ideal, just, and compassionate world as featured in their prophets' discourse, the urban centres faced challenges of modern technology and ideology on the one hand, and a confused sense of identity on the other. This difference is necessary, though not sufficient, to explain the subsequent distancing of the urban educated *sangha* from rural millenarians.

As each strand of Buddhism moved along its different promulgative path, the revitalization period, which began in earnest in the 1930s, may be regarded as having two main components. The first was a 'reverse Orientalism' combined with the stimuli provided by modernization and nationalism. Reverse Orientalism took place following the initial interest of Western scholars in Hindu and Buddhist doctrine at the turn of the nineteenth century. Once disseminated worldwide, this interest aroused a revivalist response from the Asian countries themselves. The phenomenon is symbolized by the formation of the Maha Bodhi Society in Colombo, the Theosophical Society being one of the main organizations to give impetus to religious studies in various Asian countries (Clarke 1997, 87–92). Books on Buddhist philosophy and 'sacred texts', as well as writings on other occult or supernatural topics, such as de Kardec's on spiritism, reached many modern educated readers early in the twentieth century and print technology made it possible for a large readership to access scriptures, commentaries and translations of writings on Buddhism, as well as material on their world religions and religious issues. Chinese reformist literature such as Daixu's writings also reached Vietnam and exerted a strong influence on Buddhist scholars.[19] The second component concerns the leadership vacuum in the anti-colonial struggle. In effect, the French anti-insurgency agenda fostered the formation of a national Buddhist leadership. Traditional people, in the rural areas as well as the modern educated élite, looked to Buddhism as a major player in the struggle against colonialism in Vietnam, particularly after the Confucian literati failed to provide effective leadership. Taking advantage, as Keyes remarks (1977), of a French design to encourage a Buddhist renewal on rational principles, a large number of Buddhists managed to recreate a new national religious identity.

This twofold characterization, however, glosses over contributions at the grass-roots level. Much of this 'marginalized' Buddhism blends what I call 'Confucianist Daoism' with hybridizations of diverse inter-ethnic contacts, notably with Chinese groups that migrated from south-eastern China since the seventeenth century. The marginalization of such hybrid groups is consistent with the politics of centrality of the power élites and literati. In particular, the privileging of Zen/Mahāyāna doctrine over others is the result of an impetus by the new literati, i.e. scholars with both a classical and a modern education who regarded textual neglect as a symptom of total disarray and decline. We must turn, therefore, to the oral tradition to find out more about the role of virtuoso practitioners of esoteric arts such as Daoist Zen meditation and magic. Certainly they were very much the promoters of another hybridization of the three religions with a strong Buddhist ingredient. Such figures were known to have received training in Laos, Thailand or Cambodia under local teachers, but often, as was the case with Nguyễn Thuần Hậu before the 1950s, and the 'Coconut Monk' in the 1960s, they seem to have been instructed by Chinese teachers of meditation whom they met in the mountains of Chau Doc or in Cambodia's Kampot area.[20]

PATRIOTISM AND NATIONAL CONSOLIDATION

A lack of scriptural knowledge accounted for a decline in classical learning in the early twentieth century and was considered a sign of decline for Buddhism. A few scholarly monks, aided greatly by modern print technology, were dedicated to the dissemination of explicatory texts on Buddhist philosophy and the translation of Buddhist scriptures while calling for a countrywide reform of the *sangha* in terms of education and training. There was no clear agenda, but the idea of progress towards national unification, inspired by contemporary Chinese reforms led by the monk Daixu, seems to have been a motivating factor. The first moves were spearheaded by Reverend Khánh Hòa of Bến Tre province in the South when, in 1923, he founded the 'Hội Lục Hòa Liên Hiệp' (Association of Alliance for the Six Harmonies), attracting many monks and village notables. During the following four years Khánh Hòa travelled the country earnestly looking for like-minded monks in order to establish a national association, but without any great success. He also sent his chief disciple, Thiện Chiếu, to the North in another effort, also unsuccessful, to work towards a national organization.

In 1930, with the approval of the colonial authorities, the Southern Association for Buddhist Studies was formed and led by Khánh Hòa with a combined membership of monks and modern educated lay Buddhists. In 1932 the Central Vietnam Buddhist Studies Association was established in Hué, with a northern outpost in Hanoi following in 1934. However, such a centralized Buddhist body had a large popular base to win over. Looking back on this period, Đoàn Trung Còn, a noted Buddhist scholar and founder of a group dedicated to the veneration of Amitābha Buddha, had an ambivalent attitude towards the local scene. Writing in 1930, he was critical of the fee-earning and secularized roles the Buddhist monks took up, but did not fail to recognize the deep penetration of Buddhism through all social strata:

> Nowadays, because the learned are few, hardly anyone knows the difference between the schools (which are similar to those in China). The *sangha* is also in a similar condition. People lumped the schools together, as a result everyone normally keep five or ten precepts and pray to Amida Buddha.
>
> Those who have been initiated into the teachings still observe beliefs in ghosts and spirits. And they also respect those Daoists who train in talismanic magic and in ways of inviting the souls of the dead. Therefore they often make offerings and pray to spirits so that the latter either won't disturb them or will protect them. They enjoy this more than studying Buddhist scriptures and find that worshipping Buddha and cultivating themselves according to the Dharma is slower in bringing results compared to the spirits! ... In the old days, monks were not those who attend to funerals, and get paid for reciting *sūtras*. Today, no matter what occasion, not many monks refuse an invitation to private ceremonies. Those who are living apart from the world are few. Most monks are married with children, mixing with ordinary people in the markets and villages ... These monks give all sorts of services, sometimes using talismans and *mantras*, even calling on the supernaturals. (Đoàn Trung Còn 1950, 82–3)

These comments reflect the western-educated Buddhist scholars' attitude towards modernity and their overriding desire to unite all Buddhists. However, the above remarks could be read differently. By reversing the perspective we can detect a 'popular' Buddhism unadorned by emphasis on scriptural scholarship and closer to the daily concerns of many. As Đoàn Trung Còn observes later in the same essay (1950, 84–5):

> There is an excellent thing which happens, that is the wonderful way Buddhism has permeated the stratum of ignorant people. ... Foreigners who come to our country are surprised to find in a big country stretching thousands of kilometers from north to south, for a thousand years a religion with no patron but which keeps on going in strength. Many times the Confucians make life difficult, the state is indifferent, there is no leadership, but there are no less followers than former time.
>
> ... There are abbots who are popular with adherents, and are regarded by the public as a kind father figure. Generous offerings are brought to them, and they are respected as a Teacher. I have witnessed adherents who visit a temple, seek the abbot out and prostrate in front of him as if they are paying respects to Buddha. And if the abbot happens to pass away, followers from districts and provinces will gather (at the temple). They cry and mourn as if it was their own father. The funeral may be bigger and more solemn than one reserved for the head of a nation.

In his speech of 17 March 1935 at Quán Sú' pagoda, Hanoi, Trần Trọng Kim, a scholar, high level official in the colonial government, and lay intellectual mentor of the Northern Buddhist Association, also equated popular practice with a loss of the deeper meaning of the religion (Trần Trọng Kim 1935, 14):

> To be frank, today when people refer to Buddhism, most would think it is only practiced on the middle and first day of each lunar month when they go to the temple

to honour the Buddha, besides that no-one knows what the origin [of Buddhism] is, how deep the teachings can be, even those who daily pray, holding the rosaries in their hand but their action is all contrary to Buddhism. That is only the custom of our people, who follow habitual pattern without a thought for the meaning of the action. That is a thing we should be concerned with changing.

Nguyễn Lang (1994, 182–3) sees in Trần Trọng Kim's ideas of reform a fourfold modality:

We see in that simple statement [of Trần Trọng Kim] the objectives of *reforming* ('To restore the brilliant clarity of a religion made obscure,') of *making it relevant to the present situation* ('appropriate to the needs of the world,') *so that it can have an active cultural role* ('for followers to know well their religion and to behave and live accordingly') and *create a spiritual focus and direction for the people* ('rather than hanging on to a materialistic, shallow and narrow mind . . . like a boat drifting in the current without anywhere for landing.').

Trần Trọng Kim and other learned Buddhists like Đoàn Trung Còn were not the only figures concerned with such issues. As McHale points out, we should also turn our attention to the printed literature of the 1920s and 30s that was allowed by the French to appear under the rubric of religion (McHale 1993, 22; Marr 1979, 313–39; Marr 1981, 41–52, 303). By 1945, about 1,200 titles had been published in this category, with Pure Land Buddhism representing an important proportion of the whole. Nguyễn Kim Muôn's group was a good example of innovative practice in the South based on Pure Land Buddhist principles. The School's pursuit of self-enlightenment entailed Daoist-like meditation techniques, although popular belief in spirits was not abandoned.[21] The *Tịnh Độ Cư' Sĩ* formation was another example of Pure Land adaptation. Finally, the *Cao Đài* attracted a large female following in the 1930s. It is worth noting that *Phụ Nữ' Tân Văn* (Women's News), a prominent women's weekly magazine at the time, raised the issue of the collective power of women who joined self-cultivation groups and called for legal measures to protect them from all kinds of exploitation.[22] Around this time, householder self-cultivation, also in the Pure Land tradition, was advocated by a number of urban single women. These women seem to have sought an escape route from male exploitation as well as from the constraints imposed by colonization on traditional gender structure. They endeavoured to achieve solidarity and a new social space although they were not simply concerned with escape from a vulnerability determined by their socio-economic status.

A number of magazines appeared with writings in *quốc ngữ'*, i.e., romanized script, by learned monks. *Tù' Bi Âm* (Sound of Compassion) in the South, *Viên Âm* (True and Perfect Sound) in the Centre and *Đuốc Tuệ* (Torch of the Mind) in the North were the respective publications of their respective regional Buddhist Associations. In such periodicals, the idea of Buddhist reformation was mooted. One writer suggested there were three reasons for reformation: (1) the pride of a people; (2) the thirst for an ideal to live up to; and (3) the world economic crisis.[23] Indeed, as Ho Tai (1983) points out, three further factors operating in the 1930s were floods, the Depression and the threat of war. These external conditions no doubt heightened the sense of crisis.

Thanks to print technology, the writings of well-known literati were widely broadcast and Buddhism began to enjoy the attention the country's intelligentsia. If Phan Khôi, a journalist well-respected for his patriotic ideas, showed irritation with the inactivity displayed by the *sangha*, this was probably because he expected more than the reform of traditional education, wanting to see a fuller development of socially engaged Buddhism.[24] Huỳnh Thúc Kháng, another prominent patriot, helped *Viên Âm* to contribute to the raising of consciousness so that it could be counted among those who 'bring cure for the country's illness.' If the reform agenda was not clear, the urgent need for reform was. The *Viên Âm* magazine, in 1934 outlined four main reasons for this:

1. There is a crisis in traditional Confucian values with the old culture in a ruinous state.
2. Buddhism can lay a new foundation most appropriate to Vietnamese national identity.
3. Buddhism is compatible with science and can steer science away from wrongful usage.
4. Shorn of complicated rituals, a reformed Buddhism will better serve the generations who prefer a rational and scientific approach to knowledge.[25]

Although the initiator of this galvanizing effort, the southern Association was unable to achieve a great deal. The reason given by Nguyễn Lang (1994) for this was that its vice-president, Trần Nguyên Chấn, was a colonial official who seemed to use the Association to further his personal influence, thus clashing with the other executive members. The first schism in the southern Buddhist Association, a consequence of his domineering ways, it led to the establishment of two more associations: *Lưỡng Xuyên Phật Học Hội* (The Two-River Buddhist Studies Association) in Trà Vinh province in 1934 and *Hội Phật Học Kiêm Tế* (The Studies-cum-Welfare Action Association) of Rạch Giá (now Kiên Giang) in 1937.[26] The latter was organized by Venerable Trí Thiền, a friend of Thiện Chiêu. The situation was not static, and new alliances were sought. The *Lưỡng Xuyên* group tried to merge, in vain, with the *Tịnh Độ Cư' Sĩ*, while the *Kiêm Tế* group was eventually disbanded following the imprisonment of most of its leading members.[27]

The slow response to reform also caused frustration for activists like Thiện Chiêu. In his case, it forced him to abandon Buddhism altogether to join the Communists. Thiện Chiêu was one of the more erudite and energetic of the young monks who, as has already been mentioned, had engineered the formation of the first Association. Another reason for the lack of progress, according to Thích Mật Thể, was that, even though much of the promotional material was in *quốc ngữ*, the bulk of the texts were still in Han Chinese. The task of translation was monumental, especially in the case of the *sutras*, where specialist knowledge was called for. An innovative approach was undertaken in the 1930s and '40s, and between 500 and 1,000 different Buddhist texts were printed, many of which were second or partial editions (McHale 1993, 22). The printing and circulation of these texts, often under 50 pages each and given away free, were paid for by devout women who hoped to gain religious merit in consequence.

Of these texts, Pure Land booklets were among the most frequently printed, reflecting the popularity of this school (McHale 1993, 24). In short, the printed literature of the 1920s and '30s offered a rich variety of work, approved by the colonial censors, including studies of and commentaries on Buddhism ranging from translations to essays. These particular genres reveal a widespread interest in self-cultivation, which was discussed as a new response to modern materialistic challenges, and the economic crisis of the 1930s. Meanwhile, the BSKH movement also had its own circulation of teachings, including hand-copied school exercise books and, by the 1960s, printed oracular verse books recording the utterances of the Buddha Master of the Western Peace and his successors down to Huỳnh Phú Sổ, founder of the *Hòa Hảo* movement.[28]

It has been claimed that printing and translation transformed the Vietnamese approach to Buddhist texts. Emphasis moved from the oral-performative to the meaning content of written words, transposing the spoken form to a more 'scriptural' mode. However, it may be an exaggeration to claim, as McHale does, that this change signalled a revolution in Vietnamese religious consciousness. One of the reasons is that the oral mode still remained a preference for the largely rural populace. The existence, up to 1975, of over a thousand 'reading towers', many equipped with microphones and loudspeakers, in the Hòa Hảo villages are proof of this preference. Indeed, orally communicated traditional modes and meanings still remain powerful influences for the suburban and rural populations. But a shift of consciousness towards a sense of 'imagined community' took roots in various groups and movements in the urban areas.

By the mid 1930s, the *Tịnh Độ Cư' Sĩ* (Householder Pure Land) group formed an Association with the approval of the colonial authorities. Its publication activity, starting in 1937, often revealed strident radical socialist/leftist voices. The *Tịnh Độ Cư' Sĩ's* success, however, should be measured largely by reference to its welfare services, especially the giving of free traditional medicine to the poor.[29] Coming from the lower echelon of classically trained literati, the *Tịnh Độ Cư' Sĩ* leadership attracted a large membership among southern folk Buddhists, whether rural or from the outer urban areas.

'Imported' from Cambodia, Vietnamese Theravāda Buddhism saw its first temple built in Thủ, Đú'c, north of Saigon, in 1938. Its Pāli name was given by the Head of the Cambodian *saṅgha*, who presided at its inauguration in 1939. Towards 1943, another important Theravāda group was formed by Venerable Minh Đăng Quang in Mỹ Tho province. An itinerant mendicant practice was to be its distinctive feature (Trần Hồng Liên 1995, 102–3). The members of this group called themselves *Du Tăng Khất Sĩ* (Itinerant Mendicant Sangha), and their founder's teachings, as well as versified commentaries by his chief disciple, the nun (*bhikkhuni*) Huỳnh Liên, were conceived as texts to be read aloud, with emphasis on their lyrical quality.

In addition to these large popular groups, there was a 'frontier intelligentsia' made up of a spectrum of individuals who, as healers and teachers, played a prominent role in the construction of southern identity. Both within the BSKH movement and outside, oral literature provided ample evidence of the creative blending of traditions under the rubric of Buddhism. McHale has rightly pointed out that in this shift of consciousness, Pure Land played an important role. Pure Land utopianism combined with the millenarian currents of the nineteenth century had already surfaced in the BSKH movement as a response to the cultural crisis of its time. Thus, notions of paradise combined with a nineteenth-century millenarian cosmology are a decisive factor in the BSKH's outlook. The dual-practice model was also taken up by *Hòa Hảo* which mixed Confucian 'humanity' with Buddhist self-cultivation derived from Zen and Pure Land Sources. Another example is found in the group established by the French educated account Nguyễn Kim Muôn, which combined Daoist meditation with devotive to Amitabha. As we have already noted, the French-educated accountant Nguyễn Kim Muôn also founded a group which combined Daoist meditation with devotion to Amitābha Buddha. In response to the challenges of modernity and colonialism, the self-cultivation matrix present in the three teachings of Confucianism, Daoism and Buddhism was a ready choice for those who eschewed a violent revolutionary path. And in a more affirmative tone, Pure Land offered a resolution of the tension between this worldly engagement and other-worldly detachment.

The 'imagined community' was not engendered through the print media alone. Other public manifestations in the form of the celebrating of Vesak, processions, and meetings began to appear from 1935, when electronically amplified public address systems were used for the first time. News of these gatherings of thousands of people were reported in newspapers such as *Tràng An*, Nguyễn Lang (1994, 33–5) notes that this 'method of public display of the people's power is applied many times afterwards by the Buddhist Associations of the three regions [northern, central and southern Vietnam]'. This is why, in the decades that followed, growing numbers of Buddhists engaged in national political activity in an effort to make their religion more relevant to contemporary challenges.

In the years up to 1945, the Associations could not claim to have achieved dramatic change. A number of monks had been trained, but 'did not count for much', as Nguyễn Lang notes, and the number of nuns was even more insignificant at less than 500 in the whole country. As for publications, most did not last more than two years. The expression of radical views on the urgency of social revolution led to their closure by order of the colonial censors. Nevertheless, the Buddhist intellectual contribution to an alternative direction for the country is undeniable for the medium of print provided a practical space for differing voices expressing the fervent wishes and hopes of a large section of Vietnamese society at the time. It is in this context that we can better appreciate the powerful and poignant symbolism of Thích Quảng Đú'c's self-immolation by fire, while seated in a meditative posture, in 1963. In that shocking sacrificial symbol thoughts and feelings converged, which led many urban Buddhists to an intensely passionate commitment to Buddhism as a way out of national and international conflicts.

MARXIST AND BUDDHIST CRITIQUES

Parallel with the debates in the 1930s on the question 'What to do with colonialism and modernity?', some Buddhists pursued other more traditional religio-philosophical questions, which included such matters as (1) should Buddhists be involved in politics or remain non-political?; (2) is Buddhism theistic or atheistic?; (3) does man have a soul?; (4) where is the Pure Land of Bliss (*Sukhāvati*)?; and (5) what is being?

On the one hand, Buddhism was being credited with supplanting Confucianism through the support of scholars allied to the nationalist cause (Nguyễn Tài Thu' *et al.* 1992, 396–420). On the other, some criticized the Buddhism of the 1930s as 'stuffed with French notions'. Đào Duy Anh, who had been educated in both modern and classical systems, is a good example of the latter. Others like the radical marxist critic Nguyễn An Ninh, a leading southern anti-colonialist figure, saw Buddhism decaying in two ways. First, the masses, through ignorance, had gradually converted Buddhism into a religion filled with superstition, – the exact opposite of the Buddha's teachings. Secondly, monks had debased Buddhism by requesting money for prayers, amulets and incantations, all of which served to enhance their material fortunes.[30] For Nguyễn An Ninh, 'Nirvana and Paradise are both created by the imagination of man, they are strange shadows falling into this real world through the mind of man' (Nguyễn Tài Thu' *et al.* 1992, 426). 'The Buddhist revival today', he added, 'devotes all its attention to keeping the Old Order from falling to pieces.'

Theoretical arguments against Buddhism came in other forms. Although Thích Mật Thể, as already mentioned, maintains that Thiện Chiếu's frustration was about the slowness of change, Thiện Chiếu's publicly stated reasons were different. It was the apparent limitations or restrictions within Buddhism itself that forced him to leave the fold.[31] He wrote that it was historical necessity, and the natural development of his awareness, that led to his outgrowing of Buddhist philosophy. No one can get rid of ambitions and interests and enter *nirvāṇa*, he contends, 'not even Daixu and Japanese Vo Dang Tau Quan (= Sōen Shaku) who proved this by arguing heatedly in Paris as to who first brought Buddhism to Europe!' He also believed that Buddhism was unable to save sentient beings from hunger and misery. 'The theory of no-self of Buddhism, no matter how powerful and effective, cannot do anything good in the elimination of heavenly authority and superstition which are the ramparts protecting the current [French colonial] regime' (Nguyễn Tài Thu' *et al.* 1992, 424–5). The Marxist Hải Triều also held the view that Buddhists make a basic mistake in annihilating desire, a factor that is actually fundamental to life (Nguyễn Tài Thư' *et al.* 1992, 422). To ignore the real life of the people is tantamount to putting oneself to death. In summary, these Hanoi-based authors agreed that Buddhism was incapable of playing a leading role in national and social liberation. However, the critics of the 1930s (and also some contemporary authors) misinterpreted the Buddhist context, for Buddhist reform managed to bring about changes in public consciousness which led to a reacquisition of its national role in later decades. (McHale 1993; Keyes 1977, 198).

ACTIVISM AND POLITICS

Referring to earlier 'non-political' positions, Nguyễn Lang recognizes two trends within Vietnamese Buddhism. The first embraces those who claim non-involvement as a self-defence strategy, in the context of colonial oppression. While these groups wanted their organizations to be left alone to grow in peace, they did not oppose the militant revolutionary cause taken up by others. The second is represented by those with interests vested in the status quo who categorically opposed any political involvement and who constituted a conservative right-wing faction. It is this grouping that has usually been blamed for the lack of progress of reform (Nguyễn Lang 1994, 245).

Claims to 'non-political' status, however, can cover a wide range of meaning. For instances the historian Nguyễn Văn Hầu, himself an Hòa Hảo adherent, claims that in the 1960s the BHSK and Hòa Hảo were not political groups, nor revolutionary parties under the guise of religion even though they had clearly engaged in military and diplomatic activity since the 1940s. He argues that a sense of indebtedness towards one's country is but one of many religious precepts, and that patriotic fighters in the BSKH and Hòa Hảo movements were few in comparison to numerous adepts who concentrated on spreading the Buddha's teachings.[32]

Tịnh Độ Cu' Sĩ's leftist views were expressed in the magazine *Pháp Âm* (Dharma Sound), which first saw the light of day in 1937, one year after the *Tịnh Độ Cu' Sĩ* established its headquarters at a temple in Cholon. Led by modern-educated members such as Trần Huỳnh, who had contributed to the Lu'õ'ng Xuyên Association's journal, *Duy Tâm* (Idealism), *Pháp Âm* challenged readers to start a social revolution through Buddhism. *Pháp Âm* authors were impatient with the slow progress made by Buddhist reform, especially in the national co-ordination of Associations. Their calls were often strident and radical and the publication was closed after sixteen issues. Nevertheless, the Association always firmly adhered to their categorical claim to be non-political in practice and have survived three regime changes, not least because they have pursued a non-violent path.[33]

In tandem with the popularization of modern ascetism stimulated by the arrival of mass printing, a new type of religious adept, the ông Đạo (Daoist), also gained prestige through the manifestation of healing powers and other non-ordinary abilities. Such figures practised an individualistic and innovative Daoist Buddhism, becoming the focus of popular hagiography in the vernacular South. The development in popular religion in the south then, was influenced by the emergence of the Daoists, and by massive peasant millenarian movements, both engaged in the discourse and practice of self-cultivation.

In 1937, Nguyễn Hiến Lê, then a trained land surveyor, passed through Đồng Tháp Mu'òi and encountered this totally southern phenomenon. The presence of Daoists and a devout atmosphere of popular Buddhism that pervaded the Mekong Delta region were unlike anything he had experienced in the North. Although he dismissed much of what he saw then as charlatanism, he could not help being impressed by the prestige this 'frontier intelligentsia' enjoyed. Oral accounts abound in Huỳnh Minh's series on the southern provinces in the 1960s and 1970s.[34] The presence of Daoists continued through the 1960s, when Hickey (1964) studied a village in Tân An province.

As healers and teachers, the Daoists embodied the innovative spirit of new settlers both in their exemplary manner of overcoming obstacles to human adaptation to a new environment and through their idiosyncratic behaviour. The lore of supernatural power, in which motifs from Buddhist meditation blended charisma and thaumaturgy, with an occasional claim to kingship, gave the Daoists an undeniable aura of mysticism. While many of these Daoists did not claim to carry the Buddhist torch, their role in promoting a model of self-cultivation also conducive to the growth of mass Buddhist movements in Southern Vietnam has been grossly underestimated.

1945, the year in which World War II ended, was a momentous year for the Vietnamese. The Buddhists, like most other groups, joined the Communist-led Revolution. The final issue of the journal of the Northern Buddhist Association, *Đuốc Tuệ* on 15 August 1945 carried on its back page the following appeal (Nguyễn Lang 1994, 207):

> Support the People's Government
> Hurry and join the Liberation Army of Vietnam!
> Resist all foreign invasions!
> Vietnam is completely independent!
> Prepare to welcome the Provisionary Government and the Liberation Army who will
> return soon!
> Read *Cú'u Quốc* (Rescue the Country), organ of the Viet Minh Front!

Other Buddhist publications in the Centre and the South followed suit and effectively closed down. Suspension of the revitalization drive was accepted as necessary by most Buddhists, who now decided that participation in national affairs was the major imperative. The Buddhist Youth movement, growing since 1942, now joined forces with younger monks and lay members in taking to the streets and organizing mass demonstrations, meetings and literacy classes and promoting the Revolution. However, these new revolutionaries, after two to three years' involvement, encountered an inner crisis as the ruthlessness of the power struggles between component groups within the movement started to clash with their idealism.[35]

Thus the 1940s saw a more dramatic blurring of the boundary between politics and religion. The presence of the Japanese from 1941 shielded the Hòa Hảo leader Huỳnh Phú Sổ from French harassment. The Japanese were also instrumental in militarizing the Hòa Hảo, which gave Sổ cause to join the secular National Restoration League (Ho Tai 1983, 125). However, the orthodox *sangha* refused to deal with him when, in 1945 he tried to establish a United Vietnamese Buddhist Association. The monks also seemed unaffected, on the whole, by Japanese overtures, despite various contacts made between Japanese and Vietnamese monks (Marr 1995, 81).

Throughout the period the French were relentless in creating animosities between the religious groups and the Viet Minh (Marr, 1987). It was during a meeting with Viet Minh leaders to negotiate the cessation of fighting that Sổ was killed. Soon after Sổ's death in 1947, the Hòa Hảo accepted French aid to re-equip troops as the movement broke up into provincial zones, each controlled by its own military leaders.

Meanwhile, new monasteries were opened for the training of novice monks in the three regions: Trà Vinh in 1946, Cholon and Hanoi in 1949. By 1953, Ấn Quang pagoda had become the southern regional centre, amalgamating with three other southern monasteries in the process. One of the key lay supporters for the establishing of such monasteries was Mai Thọ Truyền who, early in 1951, engineered the formation of the Southern Buddhist Studies Association. In June 1951 it combined with the *Sơn Môn* Sangha formed in Hue in 1947, and the North Vietnamese Sangha formed in Hanoi in 1949, to form the National United Sangha (otherwise translated as the United Buddhist Church). It was to include all Zen, Pure Land and Theravāda groups. The first task was to 'unify the lay associations, reform the *sangha*, codify rituals, disseminate teachings and establish the Buddhist Youth organisation' (Mai Thọ Truyền 1962, 88). Ironically, it was Mai Thọ Truyền who, for unknown reasons, kept the Southern Buddhist Studies Association segregated from the National United Sangha, prompting Nguyễn Lang (1994, 275) to lament about a 'first schism' occuring around 1964.

POST-COLONIAL RESISTANCE

On assuming the role of Head of State of southern Vietnam in 1950, Emperor Bảo Đại signed *Decree No. 10* placing the same political control on religious groups as the French had held previously. The infamous *Decree No. 10* put all religious organizations, except the Catholic and Protestant missions, in the category of public associations. Article 7 of the decree stipulates that 'permission to establish an association can be refused without any explanation given'. Permits could be withdrawn if the authorities decided that 'security reasons' dictated such measures. The anti-Viet Minh objective of this decree was obvious, and caused resentment towards the pro-French Bảo Đại government among traditional Buddhist, *Cao Đài* and *Hòa Hảo* groups. The government tried to dress up its image by lending support to Buddhist groups such as *Thuyền Lữ'* in Central Vietnam and *Cổ Sơn Môn* in the South. However, these groups did not grow greatly in numerical strength because of a lack of competent leadership (Nguyễn Lang 1994, 362–3).

The 1951 National Buddhist convention, held at Từ' Đàm pagoda in Hue, is regarded by many as a milestone in the national consolidation of Buddhist groups. Formation of the National Unified Sangha also brought to public attention the prominent position of the heads of large temples such as Thích Tịnh Khiết, and talented younger monks such as Thích Trí Quang of Central Vietnam and Thích Thiện Hoa of the South, who were to become household names in the tumultuous 1960s. Soon after the National Association joined the World Fellowship of Buddhists, a reception of the Buddha's relics in September 1952 in Saigon attracted 50,000 people. This successful public gathering of dominant urban groups signalled a triumph and galvanization of nationalism and Buddhism. It also justified the urban Buddhists' claim to have inherited a more authentic and homogeneous form of practice. Mai Thọ Truyền (1962, 88) comments that the gathering 'somewhat eclipsed or overshadowed the influence of sundry sectarian groups'. Later in the article, he defines 'the disorderly sundry groups' as those who 'call themselves Buddhist but blithely frequent the Holy Sages (Thánh) temples to make offerings or continue to worship [mainly] ancestors, a chief Confucian practice, [or engage in other] superstitious practices' (Mai Thọ Truyền, 1962, 89). By ignoring the historical pattern of Vietnamese syncretism, the modern élite's dominance could not have been expressed in a more definitive manner.

Following the defeat of French forces and the division of Vietnam at the 17th parallel according to the 1954 Geneva Convention, the collective yearning for a non-violent solution to the armed conflict appeared more urgent, adding impetus to a revival of Buddhism, particularly in the South. On assuming power in 1955, Diem retained *Decree No. 10*, thus taking up the anti-Communist drive left behind by the French and now endorsed by the USA. In 1957, the annual commemoration of the Buddha's birthday (Vesak) was struck off the list of official holidays, dealing a serious blow to what the Buddhists regarded as their rightful religious status. The government did not anticipate the consequence of their politically expedient measure: in defiance of the ban, Vesak that year was celebrated 'ten times as big'.[36] After this the National Buddhist Association lobbied successfully of the government to reinstate the holiday.

However, the southern Buddhists' efforts to construct a national identity were stifled by the state in repressive measures which later grew to a fatal degree. Nevertheless, Nguyễn Lang maintains that the struggle against the Diem regime merely added to the disillusionment and disaffection within the intellectual, business and youth sectors of society. Until then, lack of action had been partly caused by an inability to capitalize on public feelings. It was not until May 1963 that a flashpoint was reached, when Buddhist flags were not allowed to fly on Vesak.

The Cold War increasingly worsened suspicion and antagonism on both sides in Vietnam towards religious groups. However, a few charismatic leaders emerged among the ranks of senior monks. One major example was Thích Trí Quang who, in 1956, expressed his yearning for a Vietnam outside the Cold War conflict. In stating that only in neutral countries, such as India and Burma, could Buddhism breathe easily he was correct in his premonition of the collective agony of the 1960s, a period in which he became a prominent Buddhist leader. Thích Thiện Minh was another important figure, who believed that Buddhism was capable of providing cultural identity and leadership for the Vietnamese in the modern world (Schecter, 1967).

A neutral Vietnam open to an unrestricted development of Buddhism was not possible. Disaffection mounted, culminating in the suicide as a human sacrificial torch of Thích Quảng Đú'c in July 1963. The *Ủy Ban Liên Phái Bảo Vệ Phật Giáo* (Inter-school Committee for the Defense of Buddhism) was formed. For the first time the word 'struggle' (*đấu tranh*) was used in official *sangha* language. Six more self-immolations by fire followed that of Reverend Thích Quảng Đú'c, and at least one self-mutilation occurred before the downfall of Diem's government.

One may wonder, as does Marr (1987), why Diem did not worry about the Buddhists until it was too late, when monks and nuns staged huge anti-government demonstrations and shocked the whole world with public self-immolations. There may be several reasons including Diem's overestimate of communist infiltration of Buddhism,[37] but on the other hand, if we ask why the Buddhists themselves did not seem to know their strength, then perhaps Thích Nhất Hạnh's musings merit consideration. For him, 1963 represented a singularity in the Buddhist struggle of the 1960s. Political opposition, spontaneously cemented in the face of ruthless government oppression, united Buddhists and non-Buddhists alike. Afterwards, although the Buddhists commanded the headlines and enjoyed power second only to that of the military, 'purity' of action was lost as Buddhists began to act like other groups, with plots and ends in mind. This led Thích Nhất Hạnh to remark:

> I certainly don't mean to say that the more we carry the struggle forward, the more we fall spiritually or morally. But I think the motive of the struggle determines almost everything. You see that people are suffering and you are suffering, and you want to change. No desire, no ambition, is involved. So, you come together easily! I have never seen that kind of spirit again, after the 1963 coup. We have done a lot to try to bring it back, but we haven't been able to.
> ... It was so beautiful. (Queen and King 1996, 328)

This comment may sound politically naïve, yet it must be appreciated that the philosophical concept of 'desireless action' underpins Thích Nhất Hạnh's thinking here. It should also be understood against the background of criticisms levelled at Buddhists for their 'failure' to channel the people's massive power into a definite agenda (see Schecter 1967). Whether or not the failure stemmed from an inability to set clearer objectives for the Buddhist political struggle in South Vietnam, it is worthwhile considering the 'Appended Statement' to the 10 May 1963 Declaration sent by the Inter-school Committee for the Defense of Buddhism to the Government:

1. Vietnamese Buddhism does not aim to topple the government.
2. Vietnamese Buddhism has no enemies. Its objective of struggle is not against the Catholic Christians but the unjust government policies towards religions.
3. The Buddhist struggle is based on social justice.
4. The Buddhist struggle is carried out according to the way of non-violence.
5. Vietnamese Buddhists will not, in this struggle, let themselves be used by any person or groups.

As for the *Decree No. 10*, the Appended Statement proposes that the government lift all the restrictions of this decree from all religions, and set up a 'special regime for the religions, including Buddhism and Christianity' (Nguyễn Lang 1994, 400). The fiery self-sacrifice of Thích Quảng Đú'c that followed two months after the Statement brought the entire crisis to a head.

SCHISMS

If the right/left division of the 1930s was underpinned by socialist trends in thinking, the outlook of the 1960s was more concerned with valid forms of peaceful social action. Observing the effectiveness of the welfare model imported by the Catholics, the younger generation of Buddhist students no longer accepted the traditional model of short-term welfare aid supplied by temple-based monks and nuns. Long term efforts towards self-enlightenment or merit making were no more attractive. Chân Không's account in her biography, of her conversation with her Buddhist teacher, the Venerable Thích Thanh Tù', illustrates the gap between the two camps:

> One time I told him [Thay Thanh Tu], 'Even though Catholics are in the minority in our country, they take care of orphans, the elderly, and the poor. The Buddha left his palace to find ways to relieve the suffering of people. Why don't Buddhists do anything for the poor and hungry?' Thay Thanh Tu answered, 'Buddhism changes people's hearts so they can help each other in the deepest, most effective ways, even without charitable institutions.' This sounded good, but I did not feel satisfied.[38]

Such differences were not always resolved amicably by the leaders of the *sangha*. The way in which Thích Nhất Hạnh was ousted from Ấn Quang temple was particularly disruptive and demonstrated a grievous lack of any mechanism for conflict resolution. As Chân Không (1993, 29) again recounts:

> Two years later, I learned that while Thay [Ven. Thich Nhat Hanh] was in Dalat for a teaching tour, someone at An Quang Pagoda, out of jealousy, erased Thay's name from the records of the *livret de famille* of the temple. This was equivalent to expelling him from the temple 'family.' Thay had helped found the An Quang Pagoda in the early 1950s. He had been teaching there since 1954 and was one of the first teachers. All the young monks were fond of him and whole-heartedly supported his efforts to renew the teachings and practice, but the more conservative elders were not supportive of his innovations, and Thay withdrew to Phuong Buoi Monastery until his hurt was transformed.

This, then, was the beginning of a second split within the National Sangha. Whichever way these alliances went, young Buddhist welfare workers were at serious risk. By 1966, anti-war and anti-American demonstrations by Buddhists were publicly supported by a group of military officers of the South Vietnamese forces. The government's resolute suppression of these activities marked a point of non-return. It was soon realized then that it would be impossible to find a middle ground between the National Liberation Front and American-backed Saigon government (Marr, 1987). For Thích Nhất Hạnh particularly, this meant forced exile overseas from 1967.

As a 'Third Force', Buddhism was criticized by Western observers as directionless, lacking the potential for galvanization into a political force to replace South Vietnam's ruling group. In effect, the Buddhists were accused of two opposing defects. They were too passive when they advocated contemplative quietism, but as soon as concerted social action was taken, were easily misled, without direction, and devoid of organizational structure while their leaders were simply too power-drunk to mobilize their followers. In other words, as a political force, they were doomed to disintegration from the outset.

Are these criticisms wholly valid, particularly when we still do not know (a) how and to what extent communist agents infiltrated the National Sangha,[39] and, more importantly, (b) how deep the paradox between pacifist self-perfecting and participation in violent national politics runs in each individual Buddhist? Again, how much of the undoing of the Buddhist peace movement was due to the popular belief that a Buddhist political leadership should never take an active role in the running of the country? It could be that the lack of a long term direction points to the absence of a shared cultural identity among Vietnamese Buddhists. In this light, remarks by outsiders such as Thomas Merton are worth considering:

> While many of his [Thích Nhất Hạnh] countrymen are divided and find themselves, through choice or through compulsion, supporting the Saigon government and the Americans, or formally and explicitly committed to Communism, Nhất Hạnh speaks for the vast majority who know little politics but who seek to preserve something of Vietnam's traditional identity as an Asian and largely Buddhist culture. (Thích Nhất Hạnh, 1967, 5)

In reality a spirited search for peace continued despite the ruthless measures employed by both warring sides to quash any 'third force' or 'neutralist elements'. Among the differing anti-war views of the time the Buddhism peace option was never silent. Alternative Buddhist searches for a non-violent halt to the war also took place outside the urban discourses of the monastic monks, both before and after the dramatic turn of 1966. Buddhist intellectuals such as Ngô Trọng Anh represented a distinct voice in the world peace debate at the time. In insisting that the Vietnamese, especially Buddhists, must eschew dualistic thinking which inevitably leads to factionalism, Ngô Trọng Anh saw that the only way to bring peace to the country was to embark on the non-dualistic, 'non-ismic' (*advaya*) Buddhist path (Ngô Trọng Anh 1973, 281–2).[40]

Closer to the grass-roots level, Nguyễn Thành Nam, known as the 'Coconut Monk', a French-trained engineer turned Daoist, expounded a plan for North–South political reconciliation which resonated with the southern rural-based populace.[41] Leaders of other new groups of spiritual self-cultivators appealed to a variety of personal paths to peace. The *Hồng Môn* [Great Gate] founder, an ex-leader in the Viet Minh's Patriotic Women's Association, who included nationalistic features in her ethico-religious discourse, or healers such as So'n Kim of *Tịnh Độ Cư' Sĩ* and Đỗ Thuần Hậu of the *Non-Doing Mysticism* group, continued to enjoy large if somewhat ephemeral followings (Thanh Quan Phạm Văn Ân, 1967; Hồ Văn Em, 1983). Lone figures in the quest for enlightenment through renunciation, these self-cultivators did not advocate withdrawing into other-worldliness but wished to assist people overcome suffering and misfortune while expounding a variety of modern salvationist discourses.

By the early 1970s, the few intellectuals and students in the Youth School for Social Service created by Thích Nhất Hạnh continued testing new interpretations of the *bodhisattva* mission symbolized by Guanyin (i.e. Avalokiteśvara) and outlined in the *Diamond Sutra*'s doctrine of no-self (Chân Không 1993). For critics such as Trần Văn Giàu, ex-Viet Minh leader and prominent intellectual, the Thích Nhất Hạnh group was ideologically bankrupt and, given the crushing pressure of the American war, their welfare programmes could achieve no more than the South Vietnamese government's policy of strategic hamlets.[42] In the postwar scene of politico-economic change, such ideological pronouncements can be more easily contextualized.

CONCLUSION

Following reunification of the country under the socialist system in 1975, there was evidence of state oppression of Hòa Hảo and Cao Đài groups and some Christians and Buddhists, with deaths of monks and nuns in re-education camps being reported (Boyle and Sheen, 1997, 252). Many urban Buddhists, judging by the continuing arrests and detention of religious adherents, monks and nuns included, may have felt justified in their perception that little had changed in the level of state oppression since the Diem days. Perhaps present state–*saṅgha* relations should be viewed in a historical context which is not confined to the current regime alone, but extends further back – at least to the political arena of the 1940s. The issue is complicated by the choice individual monks and nuns made – to be on one side or the other of the political divide constructed decades ago – and it is also influenced by the manner in which the incumbent government draws the religio-political boundary. In such a context, the reasons the *Tịnh Độ Cu' Sĩ* (Householder Pure Land – Amidist) group has for negotiating to join the current state-sponsored Vietnamese National Buddhist Sangha (*Giáo Hội Phật Giáo Viet Nam*) are not that different from those which some ex-affiliates of the Southern Buddhist Studies Association or the Unified National Sangha have for trying to remain outside.

If it did not change the outcome of the war, Buddhism has become, especially since 1975, more than just a solace to offset the material hardship that arrived with the peace. Harsh changes in economic conditions between 1975 and 1990 have given Buddhism an opportunity to prove itself still capable of revitalization. This revival has brought into relief the continued tension between the socialist regime and the *saṅgha*, not least because of the former's tight control of all institutions (Marr 1987). The resurgence of self-cultivation away from the monastic atmosphere may be the result of such vigorous state institutional control. However, given that this is not new to modern Vietnamese religiosity, such a political climate only reinforces 'household asceticism' as an immanent cultural matrix.

With a national economic renovation (*đổi mới*) policy, launched in 1986, actual relaxation of state control came a few years later, together with the return of popular festivals and traditional patterns of worship. Ritual materials and sermons by learned and eloquent monks and nuns find a wide home-based target audience with the easy circulation of cassette tapes and videos. From the early 1990s, greater mobility has enabled pilgrimages between the southern provinces and Hanoi in organized bus tours. Through this efflorescence of religious activity, the market economy and religion now face each other; a rationale of thrift against a groundswell of extravagance in the 'other' older economy – of boon, ostentation and pomp. In this context, restraints informed by Zen rhetoric and the pervasive non-rational, multiple personality of popular religions continue to manifest in opposite ways, embodying the dialectical tension which motivates the perennial opposition of centralizing orthodoxy and local diversification. That dialectical tension also underpins both state politics and doctrinal competition.

NOTES

1. I do not propose here to define what 'religion' is, but will base my approach on the premise, as outlined by Geoffrey Benjamin (1990), that at the core of religion is an act of direct and articulated communication between the self and a non-empirical

entity addressed in the second person *Thou*. Thus trance, 'animism' and mediumism may be included in the wider category of 'religious practice'. In this way the demarcation between text-and-clergy based and folk/popular Buddhism is dispensed with and terms such as 'popular or folk' may be seen as part of an elite cultural hegemonic discourse. Buddhism, then, refers to a combination of factors, eg. believers' identification with relevant tenets (the 'Triple Gems') or rituals, a body of specialists, icons, or texts, but not necessarily with all of them.

2. Leopold Cadière (1953) an astute observer of Vietnamese customs and culture, held a rigidly purist view that Vietnamese were not Buddhists, being predominantly believers in supernaturalism.

3. See for example, Đào Duy Anh, [1938], *Việt Nam Văn Hóa Sử' Cu'o'ng*, Quan Hải Tùng Thu', repub. TP Ho Chi Minh, 1992, pp. 261–3. It is well known that more women than men attend Buddhist temples. Additionally, Buddhism and Daoism have been relegated to the realm of healing and mortuary rites. The two religions may have enjoyed the royal support of most Nguyễn kings and their wives and mothers, but politically, Confucianism remained dominant throughout this period. See Cooke (1997).

4. Minh Su' is the name of a group originally headed by Chinese masters, with a medicine dispensary or 'hall' attached to each temple, hence its name ending with the word *Đu'ờng* (Hall). It is popularly referred to as the *Phật Đu'ờng* group. The Minh Su adherents also practice spirit writing as one of their routine activities. See Ho Tai (1983).

5. Actually, no recorded dynasty or monarch, all the way down to the Nguyễn, dispensed with Buddhist ritual.

6. See Le-van Hao, (1964, 54–5).

7. Thích Mật Thể was an erudite monk who came from the Thù'a Thiên (Huế) area. He formally joined the Communist government in 1946 after being elected as representative of Thùa Thiên. See Nguyễn Lang (1994, 209–14).

8. Ngô Tòng Châu, one of the senior officials and tutor of Prince Canh, petitioned Gia Long against the Buddhists. He reportedly told the prince: 'It is good that our king has declared war on Buddhism. I am surprised there are people who do not approve of his action and even go against it. I do not personally hate bonzes, but realise that the wrongdoings of Buddhism and Daoism are worse than those of Duong or Mac. That is why I cannot keep silent'. Tong Chau's campaign was possibly entangled with his power struggle against the prince's French mentor and adviser to lord Nguyen Anh, Father Pigneau de Behaine. The Buddhists may have been the secondary target.

9. Keith Taylor has demonstrated how legitimacy and authority were manipulated and bolstered through the cultural politics of spirit cult, by analysing the discourse of the fourteenth century semi-official text of spirit hagiographies *Việt Điện U Linh Tập* [Compilation of the Occult Palace of Viet]. See Taylor, K., in *Southeast Asia from the 9th to the 14th Century*, D.G. Marr and A. Milner (eds), Singapore & Canberra: Institute of Southeast Asian Studies.

10. Ngô Đú'c Thọ *et al.* (1973, 10). These sites are divided into four types: temples (*đền*), shrines (*miếu*), the village communal houses (*đình*) and Buddhist temples (*chùa*). Bearing in mind that there is one or more village communal house and at least one Buddhist temple for each officially recorded village, this selection, as the compilers point out, is not a representative sample of countrywide distribution. Furthermore, a number of entries have been left out owing to paucity of details. The four groups are distributed as follows:

584 shrines (*đền, miếu*)

377 Buddhist temples and ashrams (*chùa, am*)

93 village communal houses (*đình*)

10 Daoist temples (*đạo quán*)

Although the compilers do not specify how they have arrived at only four types of temple from such a diversity of source genres, this typology is, in all likelihood, élite-oriented. Local naming reveals at least a blurring of categories. In the Mekong delta, for instance, some shrines (*miếu*) are called communal houses (*đình*) by villagers, and function accordingly. Elsewhere evidence suggests that a number of Buddhist temples were used as village meeting places, a traditional *đình* function, and as military bases for local rebels when the circumstances so favoured thus (see for example Tạ Chí Đại Tru'ò'ng 1989 170–1). At its best, each entry provides geo-historical details, poetry by literati and commentary on these scenic temple landscapes. The discourse points to consolidation of political power and the bolstering of legitimacy for the ruling élite. It would be no surprise if this discourse was found in places to oppose, or to be at variance with, the local ethos and mythology. Local records are more likely to counterpoint court literature on temples. Therefore the ruling élite's desire to record myths and tales was not merely to serve archival or scholarly interests.

11. A cursory look at the proportion of culturally significant buildings listed tells us that the most numerous of the four types were the shrines (*đền*). This indicates how ruling élites in the past were anxious for the spirits to be on their side. The number of Buddhist temples (*chùa*) in the compilation takes up nearly 36 per cent or more than a third, compared with only 1 per cent of 'purely Daoist' temples. The rest are consecrated to spirits, in a country where the 'three teachings' are said to blend in a system of belief not unlike that of pre-modern China.

12. The élite's Zen fundamentalist bias figures in Buddhist historiography, as Nguyen Cung Tu (1995), for example, observes in his analysis of texts on lineages and related historical documents, where evidence does not bear out the claimed continuity of lineages from Chinese Zen schools.

13. The authors at the Institute of Hán Nôm Research (Ngô Đú'c Thọ *et al.*, 1993), who compiled the above-mentioned list of all temples in Vietnam that have been recorded in 150 extant official as well as semi-official sources, are a case in point. From this literature survey, they have noted evidence of a revitalization of Buddhism in the seventeenth and eighteenth centuries. Judging by the separate treatments of Buddhism in the *Hồng Đú'c* Code of the Lê dynasty in the fifteenth century and the *Gia Long* Code in the nineteenth century, Coulet also concludes that Buddhism flourished in the kingdom from the fifteenth to the nineteenth century (Coulet, 1929, 28). The reason Coulet gives is that, when the Tang and Qing law code was copied, regulations for Buddhist sects found in them were not omitted. Other authors, such as Minh Chi *et al* (1993, 25), argue that since *Hồng Đú'c* Code made no reference to Buddhism as a religion, oppressive measures in the fifteenth century must have been of an administrative rather than and ideological or political nature. These 'administrative measures' resulted, nonetheless, in a forcing of the monks who did not pass public examinations on scriptural knowledge to return to the laity. The same authors establish that from the sixteenth to the eighteenth century, a revival took place during the Mạc dynasty with temples repaired and new ones built. After the Lê were restored Trịnh lords also repaired and built new temples. The Zen schools of *Trúc Lâm, Tào Động* and *Lâm Tế* were revived and unification with Confucianism was also mooted among literati. The nineteenth century was held by these authors to have

been a period of limited decline. They assert that during this period, Buddhism maintained its long-held position in Vietnamese society. Restrictive policies and criticism by the court could lessen its prestige to some extent, but could not stop its continuing development.

14. *Bù'u So'n Kỳ Hu'o'ng* (Strange Fragrance of the Precious Mountain, hereafter BSKH) is a millenarian Buddhist group with a charismatic founder called Phat Thay Tay An (Buddha Master of the Western Peace) who appeared on the southern scene around the mid nineteenth century. See Ho Tai, (1983).

15. Ileto argues for a similar situation in the Philippines and, indeed, with many mass movements in Southeast Asia. See Ileto (1992, 198–9).

16. The hardship was referred to as 'Dharmic perils' (*pháp nạn*).

17. Further on the work of Tịnh Độ Cu Sĩ see Do, M.T., *Charity and Charisma, the Dual Path of the Tinh Dô Cu Si, a Popular Buddhist Group in Southern Vietnam*, Social and Cultural Issues No. 2 (98), ISEAS Working Papers.

18. This blending of Buddhism and Confucianism, as Woodside (1969) notes, was pervasive among Vietnamese élites of the 1800s.

19. Tuệ Giác, a contemporary historian, maintains that modern Vietnamese Buddhist reform was Chinese-inspired. The central figure was Daixu (1889–1947), who wrote volumes on reforming Buddhism in China and founded the Chinese Buddhist Society in 1929. Thiện Chiếu translated some of his books and the periodical *Hai Chao Yin* (Sound of the Tide). See Woodside, (1969, 12), and Ch'en (1964, 455–7).

20. A Confucian scholar, Đỗ Thuần Hậu did not meet his teacher until he was 50, after which his life changed dramatically. He found his healing and other supernatural powers through training in meditation. For a short biography, see Đỗ Thuần Hậu (1994), *Phép Xuất Hồn* [Soul Travel Method]. For the 'Coconut Monk', see *infra*, n. 36.

21. An ex-accountant working for the Bank of Indochina, Nguyễn Kim Muôn changed his life to a full-time pursuit of self-cultivation and in the end established several temples from Gia Định (1933) to Phú Quốc island (1940s). Between 1928 and 1935 he published, over thirty titles of *sūtra* translations, manuals and essays on self-cultivation, each up to 100 pages long.

22. Anonymous, 'Đàn bà trong Phong Trào . . .', *Phụ Nữ' Tân Văn*, no. 248.

23. The author of the article, signed 'H.T' in *Tràng An* newspaper in 1935, has not been identified. Nguyễn Lang, *Việt Nam Phật Giáo . . .*, 1994, v.3, 23.

24. Nguyễn Lang, (1994, 24).

25. Nguyễn Lang, (1994, 27–8).

26. Two rivers refer to the 'Front' (Tiền Giang) and the 'Rear' (Hậu Giang) of the Mekong River in southern Vietnam. The word 'Tế' in 'Kiêm Tế' is believed to refer also to 'Kinh Bang Tế Thế' (economic endeavours).

27. Ven Trí Thiền and his associates were arrested in a police raid where weapons were discovered in the temple headquarters of the association in 1939. Trí Thiền was sent to Côn Lôn prison island and reputedly died there, according to a returnee, in 1945 (Nguyễn Lang, 1994, 73–4).

28. He was known to have produced six volumes, each with over 600 to 900 verses. Around 800,000 copies of each were printed. Nguyễn Văn Hầu (1969, 42–8).

29. See Do, M.T., *Charity and Charisma*.

30. McHale (1993) quoting from Nguyễn An Ninh, 1938, *Phê Bình Phật Giáo* [Critique of Buddhism], My Tho: Đông Phu'o'ng Thu' Xá. 6, 44.

31. Thiện Chiếu joined the Nam Kỳ Kh'ỏi Nghĩa movement in the Hốc Môn, Bà

Điểm area north of Saigon in 1940. He went to live in northern Vietnam after the 1954 Geneva Convention and died in Hanoi in 1976 (Nguyễn Lang 1994, 80–1).

32. Nguyễn Văn Hầu, a, b (1969, 249).
33. The Tinh Đô group's welfare activities helped to forge a primary social bond with the poor, a remarkable achievement which contributes to their survival and growth. See Do, M.T., (1998), *Charity and Charisma.*
34. See Huỳnh Minh, (1965a; 1966a&b; 1968; 1971; 1972).
35. Nguyễn Lang mentions a work which reflects these conflicts and pains experienced by young Buddhists who joined the revolution, *Nhũ'ng Cặp Kính Mầu* (The Coloured Glasses), 1965a, 1965b, was written in 1947, but was not published until 1965.
36. Nguyễn Lang, (1994, 385).
37. Diem's over-estimation and the Saigon-based US authorities' ill-informed perception of Communist inspired activities were probably mutually reinforcing. See for example, Blair, A., (1995), pp. 26–30.
38. Chân Không (1993, 15).
39. See Trần Hồng Liên (1996, 93–4).
40. In arguing for a 'peaceful heart-mind' as a precondition for a peaceful world, he also emphasizes a balance of both affective and cognitive aspects in Buddhist compassion; in other words, joyful openness (*hỷ xả*) must accompany compassion if Buddhist welfare work is to differ from that of other charity associations.
41. Thành Nam actually graduated as *agent technique*, equivalent to 'assistant engineer' in some British systems. Among his notable achievements was the fact that he lived only on fruits and coconut milk from 1943, hence the nickname 'Coconut Monk'. Other achievements were his 14-metre-high pole-like *Bát Quái* (Chinese *pakua*, eight trigrams) tower where he prayed for national independence and peace, and his three-storey *Prajñā* Boat, a Buddhist symbol of salvation through insightful knowledge, which survives now as a tourist curiosity in Bến Tre province. See Huỳnh Minh (1965b).
42. See Trần Hồng Liên (1996, 69).

BIBLIOGRAPHY

Anonymous (1933) 'Phụ Nữ' vó'i Cuộc Vận Động Tôn Giáo ỏ' Nam Kỳ' [Women and the Religious Movement in Cochinchina], *Phụ Nữ' Tân Văn* [Women's News], 225, 28 November.

——(1934) 'Đàn Bà Trong Tôn Giáo' [Women in Religion], *Phụ Nữ' Tân Văn* [Women's News], no. 248, 24 May.

Benjamin, G. (1990) 'Notes on the Deep Sociology of Religion', *Department of Sociology Working Paper* no. 85, revised, National University of Singapore.

Berrigan, D., Thich Nhat Hanh (1975) '*The Raft is not the Shore*, Boston, IL: Beacon Press.

Blair, A. (1995) *Lodge in Vietnam: A Patriot Abroad.* New Haven, CT: Yale University Press.

Boyle, K. and J. Sheen (eds) (1997) *Freedom of Religion and Belief: A World Report.* London and New York: Routledge.

Cadière L. (1953) *Croyances et Pratiques Religieuses des Vietnamiens,* Vol. 1. Saigon: Imprimerie Nouvelle d'Extreme Orient.

Chân Không Cao Ngọc Phu'ọ'ng (1993), *Learning True Love: How I learned and Practiced Social Change in Vietnam.* Berkeley, CA: Parallax Press.

Ch'en, K (1964) *Buddhism in China, a Historical Survey*. New Jersey: Princeton University Press.

Clarke, J.J. (1997) *Oriental Enlightenment, the Encounter between Asian and Western Thought*. London: Routledge.

Cooke, N (1997) 'The Myth of Restoration: Dang-Trong Influences in the Spiritual Life of the Early Nguyen Dynasty (1802–47)', in A. Reid (ed.) *The Last Stand of Asian Autonomies – Responses to Modernity in the Diverse State of Southeast Asian and Korea, 1750–1900*. London: Macmillan Press.

Coulet, G. (1929) *Cultes et Religions de l'Indochine Annamite*. Saigon: Imprimerie Commerciale C. Ardin.

Đoàn Trung Còn, (?1950) *Đạo Lý Nhà Phật* [Buddhist Teachings]. Saigon: Phật Học Tòng Thu' [author's publication].

Đỗ Thuần Hậu (1994) *Phép Xuất Hồn* [The Method of Soul Travel], California: Đại Nam.

Faure, B. (1991) *The Rhetoric of Immediacy: A Cultural Critique of Chan / Zen Buddhism*. Princeton, NJ: Princeton University Press.

Gheddo, P. (1970) *The Cross and the Bo-Tree – Catholics and Buddhists in Vietnam*, trans. C.U. Quinn. New York: Sheed & Ward.

Hà Tân Dân (1974) *Hệ Phái Tú' Ân Hiú Nghĩa* [Four-Indebtedness Sect]. Saigon: Phật Giáo Bửu Sơn Kỳ Hương.

Hamilton, M.B. (1995) *The Sociology of Religion, Theoretical and Comparative Perspectives*. London: Routledge.

Hickey, G.C. (1964) *Village in Vietnam*. New Haven, CT: Yale University Press.

Hiebert, M. (1994) *Vietnam Notebook*, 2nd edn. Hongkong: Review Publishing.

Ho Tai, H.T. (1983) *Millenarianism and Peasant Politics in Vietnam*. Cambridge: Harvard University Press.

Hồ Văn Em (1983) *Tôi Tầm Đạo* [I Seek the Way]. California: Nhà In Vô Vi.

Huỳnh Minh (1965a) *Đia Linh Nho'n Kiệt-Tỉnh Kiến Hòa (Bến Tre)* [Supernatural Land, Outstanding People – Kiến Hòa (Bến Tre) province], pub. by the author, Saigon.

——(1965b) *Đò'i Khổ Hạnh Ông Đạo Dù'a – Tu-sĩ Nguyễn Thành Nam* [The Ascetic Life of the Coconut Monk – Self-Cultivator Nguyễn Thành Nam], pub. by the author, Saigon.

——(1966a) *Bạc Liêu Xu'a và Nay* [Bạc Liêu Past and Present], pub. by the author, Saigon.

——(1966b) *Cần Tho' Xu'a và Nay* [Cần Tho' Past and Present], pub. by the author, Saigon.

——(?1968) *Đinh Tu'ò'ng Xu'a và Nay* [Đinh Tu'ò'ng Past and Present], pub. by the author, Saigon.

——(1971) *Sa Đéc Xu'a và Nay* [Sa Đéc Past and Present], pub. by the author, Saigon.

——(1972) *Tây Ninh Xu'a và Nay* [Tây Ninh Past and Present], pub. by the author, Saigon, repub. Tây Ninh Đồng Hương Hội Úc Châu.

Ileto, R. (1992) 'Religion and Anti-colonial Movements', in Tarling, N. (ed.), *The Cambridge History of Southeast Asia*, Vol. 2, Chapter 4. Cambridge: Cambridge University Press.

Keyes, C.F. (1977) *The Golden Peninsula – Culture and Adaptation in Mainland Southeast Asia*. Honolulu: University of Hawaii Press.

Le-van Hao (1964) 'Introduction a l'Ethnologie du Den et du Chua', *Revue Sud Est Asiatique*, Bruxelles.

McHale, S. (1993) 'Imagining Human Liberation: Vietnamese Marxists Confront

Buddhism', paper prepared for *The Nordic Institute of Asian Studies Conference on Vietnam*, Copenhagen, Denmark, 19–21 August.

——(1995) 'Printing and Power: Vietnamese Debates over Women's Place in Society', in Taylor, K. and Whitmore, J. (eds), *Essays into Vienamese Pasts.* Ithaca, N: Cornell University Southeast Asia Program.

Mai Thọ Truyền (1962) *Le Bouddhisme au Vietnam.* Saigon: Xá Lợi Pagoda.

Marr D.G. (1979) 'Vietnamese Historical Reassessment, 1900–1944', in Reid, A. and Marr, D. (eds) *Perceptions of the Past in Southeast Asia.* Singapore: Heinemann Educational Books (Asia), 313–39.

——(1981) *Vietnamese Tradition on Trial, 1925–1945.* Berkeley, CA: University of California Press.

——(1987) 'Church and State in Vietnam,' *Indochina Issues 74*, April, Center for International Policy, Indochina Project.

——(1995) *Vietnam 1945: The Quest for Power.* Berkeley, CA: University of California Press.

Minh Chi, Ha Van Tan and Nguyen Tai Thu (1993) *Buddhism in Vietnam: From Its Origin to the 19th Century.* Hanoi: The Gioi.

Ngô Đức Thọ *et al.* (1993) *Từ' Điển Di Tích Văn Hóa Việt Nam* [Dictionary of Vietnamese Cultural Monument-Relics]. Hanoi: Khoa Học Xã Hội.

Ngô Trọng Anh *et al.* (1973) *Đu'ờng Trở' Về* [The Way Home]. Saigon: Ca Dao.

Nguyen, Cung Tu (1995) 'Rethinking Vietnamese Buddhist History: Is the *Thiền Uyển Tập Anh* a "Transmission of the Lamp" Text?', in Taylor, K. and Whitmore J. (eds), *Essays into Vietnamese Pasts*, Studies on Southeast Asia No. 19. Ithaca, New York: Cornell University Press.

Nguyễn Kim Muôn (1929) *Thờ' Trờ'i Tu Phật* [Worship Heaven, Cultivate the Buddhist Way]. Saigon: Xừa Nay.

——(1932) *Tại Sao Tôi Tu Phật* [Why I Cultivate Myself in the Buddhist Way]. Saigon: Đú'c Lừu Phửờng.

Nguyễn Lang (1994) *Việt Nam Phật Giáo Sử Luận* [Essays on the History of Vietnamese Buddhism], Vol. 3, repub. Hanoi: Văn Học.

Nguyễn Tài Thừ *et al.* (eds) (1992) *History of Buddhism in Vietnam.* Hanoi: Social Sciences Publishing House.

Nguyễn Văn Hầu (1969) *Nhận Thức Phật Gió Hòa Hảo* [An In-Depth Look at Hoa Hao Buddhism]. Saigon: Hửờng Sen.

Nguyễn Văn Huyên (1944) *La Civilisation Annamite.* Hanoi: Collection de la Direction de l'Instruction Publique de l'Indochine.

Phạm Gia Tuân (1954) *Le Panthéon Bouddhique au Vietnam.* Hanoi: pub. by the author.

Queen, C.S. and King, S.B. (eds) (1996) *Engaged Buddhism–Buddhist Liberation Movements in Asia.* Albany, NJ: State University of New York Press.

Rambo, A.T. (1982) 'Vietnam: Search for Integration', in Caldarola Carlo (ed.), *Religions and Society in Asia and the Middle East.* The Hague: Mouton.

Schecter, J. (1967) *The New Face of Buddha.* Tokyo: John Weatherhill.

Smith, B.L. (ed.) (1973) *Tradition and Change in the Theravada Buddhism: Essays on Ceylon and Thailand in the 19th and 20th centuries*, Contributions to Asian studies Vol. 4. Leiden: E.J. Brill.

Swearer, Donald K. (1970) *Buddhism in Transition.* Philadelphia: The Westminster Press.

Tạ Chí Đại Trửờng (1989) *Thần, Ngu'ờ'i và Đất Việt* [Spirits, People and the Land of Viet]. California: Văn Nghệ.

——(1973) *Lịch Sử' Nội Chiến ở Việt Nam 1771–1802* [A History of Civil War in Vietnam, 1774–1802]. Saigon: Ản Tiêm.

Thanh Quan Phạm Văn Ân (1967) *Lu'ợ'c Sử' Hồng Môn* [Outline History of Hồng Môn], Saigon: Gia Định.

Thích Mật Thể (1960) *Việt Nam Phật Giáo Sử' Lu'ợ'c* [A Summary History of Vietnamese Buddhism], repub. Đà Nẵng: Minh Đức.

Thích Nhất Hạnh (1967) *Vietnam, Lotus in the Sea of Fire.* London: SCM Press.

Trần Hồng Liên (1996) *Phật Giáo Nam Bộ* [Southern Vietnamese Buddhism]. Ho Chi Minh City: Nhà Xuất Bản Thành Phố Hồ Chí Minh.

——(1995) *Đạo Phật trong Cộng Đồng Ngu'ờ'i Việt ở Nam Bộ – Việt Nam từ' Thể Kỳ XVII đến 1975* [Buddhism in Vietnamese Community in Southern Vietnam from the 17th Century to 1975]. Hanoi: Xuât Ban Khoa Hoc Xa Hồi.

Trần Quang Văn (1929) *Kinh Chi' Cách Tu Niệm ở Nhà và Cách Đi Cúng Chùa Chùa của Chùa Du' Khánh (Gocong)* [Sutra of the Way of Householder Self-Cultivation and of Attending Pagodas (Gocong)]. Saigon: Đú'c Lu'u Phu'o'ng.

Trần Trọng Kim (1935) *Phật Giáo trong Ba Bài Diễn Thuyết* [Buddhism in Three Speeches], repub. 1958. Saigon: Tan Viet.

Trần Văn Giáp (1968) *Phật Giáo Việt Nam* [Vietnamese Buddhism], trans. Tuệ Sỹ from *Le Bouddhisme au Vietnam.* Saigon: Ban Tu Thu Vien Dai Hoc Van Hanh.

Welch, H. (1968) *The Revival of Buddhism in China.* Cambridge MA: Harvard University Press.

Woodside, A (1969) 'Vietnamese Buddhism, the Vietnamese Court, and China in the 1800's,' in Wickberg, E. (ed.) *Historical Interaction of China and Vietnam: Institutional and Cultural Themes.* Center for East Asian Studies, University of Kansas, 11–24.

INDEX